PENGU

CHRONICLE

GEOFFREY OF VILLEHARDOUIN was born in around 1150 in the county of Champagne, east of Paris. In 1185 he was appointed to the office of marshal of Champagne, a post that nurtured both his administrative and military expertise. Having taken a crusade vow in 1199 he was subsequently appointed as an envoy and was privy to crucial decisions made by the leaders of the Fourth Crusade, which ended in the conquest of Constantinople from its Greek Christian rulers in April 1204. Villehardouin was appointed as marshal in the Latin empire of Constantinople. It was probably in late 1207 that he began dictating *The Conquest of Constantinople*, his only known written work and perhaps the earliest example of historical writing in French prose. He died between 1212 and 1218, in circumstances that remain obscure.

JOHN OF JOINVILLE was born in 1224 or 1225 into a family prominent in the county of Champagne. In 1233 he inherited the office of seneschal of Champagne that would give him a leading role in the administrative affairs of the county. He joined the first crusade led by King Louis IX of France, and in 1248 set out on a campaign that would take him to Egypt and the Near East over its six-year course. Joinville became a close friend of Louis IX and after their return to France he was a familiar figure at the royal court, but refused to join Louis on his second crusade. He honoured Louis's memory by giving evidence to the enquiry that established his friend's sanctity and by composing *The Life of Saint Louis*, which he completed in 1309. Joinville died eight years later, at the age of at least ninety-two.

CAROLINE SMITH studied History at Trinity Hall, Cambridge, from where she graduated with a Ph.D. in 2004. Her publications include *Crusading in the Age of Joinville* (2006). She lives and works in New York, where she continues to pursue her research on the crusades and thirteenth-century French society, and on the life and writings of John of Joinville.

JOINVILLE *and* VILLEHARDOUIN

Chronicles of the Crusades

Translated with an Introduction and Notes by
CAROLINE SMITH

PENGUIN BOOKS

PENGUIN CLASSICS

Published by the Penguin Group
Penguin Books Ltd, 80 Strand, London WC2R 0RL, England
Penguin Group (USA) Inc., 375 Hudson Street, New York, New York 10014, USA
Penguin Group (Canada), 90 Eglinton Avenue East, Suite 700, Toronto, Ontario, Canada M4P 2Y3
(a division of Pearson Penguin Canada Inc.)
Penguin Ireland, 25 St Stephen's Green, Dublin 2, Ireland (a division of Penguin Books Ltd)
Penguin Group (Australia), 250 Camberwell Road, Camberwell, Victoria 3124, Australia
(a division of Pearson Australia Group Pty Ltd)
Penguin Books India Pvt Ltd, 11 Community Centre, Panchsheel Park, New Delhi – 110 017, India
Penguin Group (NZ), 67 Apollo Drive, Rosedale, North Shore 0632, New Zealand
(a division of Pearson New Zealand Ltd)
Penguin Books (South Africa) (Pty) Ltd, 24 Sturdee Avenue, Rosebank, Johannesburg 2196, South Africa

Penguin Books Ltd, Registered Offices: 80 Strand, London WC2R 0RL, England

www.penguin.com

This edition first published in Penguin Classics 2008

024

Translation and editorial material copyright © Caroline Smith, 2008
All rights reserved

The moral right of the translator and editor has been asserted

Set in 10.25/12.25 pt PostScript Adobe Sabon
Typeset by Rowland Phototypesetting Ltd, Bury St Edmunds, Suffolk
Printed and bound in Great Britain by Clays Ltd, Elcograf S.p.A.

ISBN: 978-0-140-44998-3

www.greenpenguin.co.uk

Contents

Acknowledgements   vii
Chronology   viii
Introduction   xi
Further Reading   xlii
A Note on the Translations   xlvi
Maps   li

GEOFFREY OF VILLEHARDOUIN

  The Conquest of Constantinople   1

JOHN OF JOINVILLE

  The Life of Saint Louis   137

Appendix I: Two 'Crusade Songs'   337
Appendix II: Epitaph for Geoffrey III
  of Joinville   346
Notes   349
Glossary   383
Indexes   391

Acknowledgements

A general vote of thanks is due to those faculty and students at Saint Louis University (St Louis, Missouri) and at Fordham University (New York City), who have shared in and enriched my enthusiasm for Villehardouin and Joinville and their works as I have prepared this translation. They have helped bring this project to fruition, often unwittingly, in many and various ways. Particular thanks are owed to those colleagues who took the time to read and comment on portions of this work as it was in preparation: Paul Cobb, Peter Edbury, Cecilia Gaposchkin, Thomas Madden, Jonathan Riley-Smith and Suzanne Yeager. I am also indebted to Jonathan Berkey, who provided very useful information and guidance concerning the Islam-related passages in *The Life of Saint Louis*. I am grateful to Penguin Classics not only for providing me with the opportunity to produce this translation, but for assigning Lindeth Vasey to work on the typescript with me; her careful and thoughtful attention has improved my work greatly. All of these people have made much appreciated contributions and have helped me avoid numerous errors; those that remain are all of my own making. As ever, Nick Paul has aided and enhanced my work in his roles as historical consultant and reader, but also, and most importantly, through his readiness to share in the minor frustrations and great joys that accompanied this undertaking.

Caroline Smith

Chronology

1095 November: Proclamation of the First Crusade by Pope Urban II

1096–9 The First Crusade

1099 July: Fall of Jerusalem to the First Crusade

1144 December: Edessa falls to the Muslims

1145 December: Proclamation of the Second Crusade

1147–9 The Second Crusade

c. **1150** Birth of Geoffrey of Villehardouin

1171 March: Mass arrest of Venetians in the Byzantine Empire and confiscation of their property

1182 May: Massacre of Italians in Constantinople

1185 Geoffrey of Villehardouin appointed marshal of Champagne

1187 July: The Battle of Hattin

October: Fall of Jerusalem to Saladin; proclamation of the Third Crusade

1189–92 The Third Crusade

1191 July: Surrender of Acre to King Richard I of England and King Philip II of France; Philip departs for France

1192 September: Treaty of Jaffa between King Richard and Saladin ends Third Crusade

1198 August: Pope Innocent III proclaims the Fourth Crusade

1199 November: Geoffrey of Villehardouin among those to take the cross at Ecry-sur-Aisne

1201 February: Treaty of Venice (the leadership of the Fourth Crusade engages a Venetian fleet)

25 May: Death of Count Thibaut III of Champagne

September: Marquis Boniface of Montferrat assumes leadership of the crusade army

1202–4 The Fourth Crusade

1202 Summer: Crusaders gather at Venice

November: Zara falls to Venetian and crusader forces

1203 January: The Treaty of Zara (the leaders of the Fourth
Crusade promise assistance to Prince Alexius)

July: The first siege of Constantinople; Emperor Alexius III
flees the city

1 August: Coronation of Alexius IV as co-emperor with
his father, Isaac II

1204 February: Co-emperors deposed; coronation of Alexius V
(Mourtzouphlus) as emperor of Constantinople

April: The second siege of Constantinople; the crusaders
and Venetians capture and sack the city

May: Election and coronation of Count Baldwin of
Flanders as emperor

1205 April: The Battle of Adrianople; Emperor Baldwin is
captured and subsequently killed

1206 August: Coronation of Henry of Hainaut as emperor

1207 September: Death of Boniface of Montferrat

After September: Earliest point at which Geoffrey of Villehardouin may have begun composition of *The Conquest of
Constantinople* (he dies between 1212 and 1218)

1213 April: Proclamation of the Fifth Crusade

1214 25 April: Birth of the future King Louis IX of France

1217–29 The Fifth Crusade

1219 November: Fall of Damietta to the forces of the Fifth
Crusade

1221 August: Defeat of the forces of the Fifth Crusade at
Mansurah

1224/5 Birth of John of Joinville

1226 29 November: Coronation of Louis IX (Blanche of Castile
is regent until 1234)

1229 February: Emperor Frederick II negotiates return of
Jerusalem to Christians

1233 John of Joinville inherits the office of seneschal of

Champagne (exercised on his behalf by his mother until 1239)

1239–41 The Barons' Crusade

1239 November: Defeat of crusader raiding party led by Counts Henry of Bar and Amaury of Montfort at Gaza

1244 August: Jerusalem captured by the Khwarizmians

    October: The Battle of La Forbie

    December: Louis IX takes the cross

1248 Late summer: Departure of Louis IX's crusade army from France

1249 6 June: Damietta falls to Louis IX

1250 8 February: The Battle of Mansurah

    April: Louis IX and his companions surrender and are taken prisoner by the Egyptians

    May: Assassination of Turanshah, sultan of Egypt, initiates the Mamluk sultanate; Louis IX and the leading crusaders are released and sail to Acre

1251–3 March: Louis IX and his forces arrive at Caesarea, Jaffa (May 1252) and Sidon (June 1253)

1254 April: Louis IX and his companions set sail from Acre and return to France (July)

    December: Louis IX issues his 'great ordinance' for the reform of royal government

1261 July: Recapture of Constantinople by the Byzantines

1263 Mamluks begin a series of conquests of Christian strongholds in Syria

1267 March: Louis IX takes the cross for the second time, Joinville refuses to do so

1270 July: Departure of Louis IX's crusade army from France

    25 August: Louis IX dies outside Tunis

1282 Joinville testifies to the enquiry into Louis IX's sanctity

1291 May: Fall of Acre to the Mamluks

1297 August: Louis IX's sanctity is proclaimed by Pope Boniface VIII

1309 October: Joinville completes the composition of *The Life of Saint Louis*

1317 Death of John of Joinville

Introduction

The two works in this volume, both of which contain eyewitness accounts of thirteenth-century crusade campaigns, constitute a striking testimony to the fascination with crusading felt by the authors and their contemporaries, and they have long been familiar to modern audiences that share the same interest. Neither Geoffrey of Villehardouin nor John of Joinville was a professional writer, and their experiences on crusade were instrumental in prompting them to record their memories for posterity, which was a most unusual thing for a layman to do. The fruits of their labours, *The Conquest of Constantinople* and *The Life of Saint Louis* respectively, are remarkable both for the gripping first-hand accounts of crusade campaigns they present and as two of the earliest examples of historical writing in French prose. *The Conquest of Constantinople* recounts the Fourth Crusade, which was diverted from its intended target, Muslim Egypt, and instead went on to conquer the Christian city of Constantinople in 1204; Villehardouin was a leading figure in this most controversial of crusades. Joinville relates in intimate detail his experiences as a participant in King Louis IX of France's first crusade, which took him to north Africa and the Near East from 1248 to 1254, and gives an account of his friend King Louis's saintly life.

A brief survey of the historical context for the crusades of the thirteenth century and of the society and culture from which Villehardouin and Joinville came may assist the first-time reader. In the decades since Penguin Classics first published a translation of these works,[1] the quantity and range of scholarship on the crusades has increased substantially. The intensity of this scholarly debate is reflected in the variety of opinions as to what a crusade was. A broad definition might be that crusades were campaigns fought by Christians against perceived enemies of their faith in the hope and expectation of a penitential reward (a release from the penalties due for sin). The wars conducted in order to capture or defend the city of Jerusalem and other Christian holy sites in the Near East from Muslim control between the end of the eleventh century and the late thirteenth century readily qualify as crusades in the view of all historians, but campaigns fought in other theatres and against other opponents (including heretics, pagans and fellow Christians) in the Middle Ages and beyond were often described as crusades by contemporaries and are treated as such by many modern scholars.[2] (Readers who wish to deepen their understanding of the many complex and compelling issues associated with the history of the crusades are encouraged to make use of the suggestions in Further Reading.)

Latin Christendom and Its Neighbours at the Turn of the Thirteenth Century

In 1095 Pope Urban II called on fighting men to join a campaign to liberate the Holy Sepulchre and Christian population of the Near East from Muslim rule. A Christian theology of just or holy war was not new, but what was new was, first, the formulation of his appeal, which coupled rousing images of the hardships and insults allegedly inflicted on Christ's homeland and his people with the promise of great penitential reward and, secondly, the impact of this message. Tens of thousands of people, men and women of all ages and backgrounds, were inspired to abandon their everyday lives and join a lengthy and arduous armed pilgrimage to Jerusalem. In July 1099 the forces of the First Crusade captured the city. This was an astounding event that helped convince them and their fellow Latin Christians (members of the western Church over which the pope ruled) of the divine approbation and assistance that backed up their bloody exertions, which had cost many thousands of Muslim, Jewish and Christian lives.

Over the century that followed Latin Christians would be called upon to imitate the actions of those first crusaders in order to defend and extend their control over the Christian holy places (often referred to as 'Outremer' or the land overseas). By 1108 four crusader states had been established – the kingdom of Jerusalem, the counties of Edessa and Tripoli, and the principality of Antioch – but from the outset they were desperately short of manpower. The majority of those who had survived to see Jerusalem's conquest in 1099 returned to the West soon afterwards, a fact that has helped historians overturn the misconception that crusade armies were filled with Europe's land-hungry 'younger sons', eager to establish themselves in the Near East. Although military forces of modest proportions did come from the West to lend support to the fledgling crusader states, the most significant influx was pilgrims. The need to protect them inspired one of the most striking innovations associated with the crusades: the foundation of the first military religious orders, the Order of the Temple and the Order of the Hospital of Saint John of Jerusalem (the Templars and Hospitallers). Their members took vows and followed rules very similar to those of monastic orders, but were committed to fight as well as to pray, and their skills quickly became indispensable in the protection not only of visiting pilgrims but of the crusader states.

In the military orders we have evidence that there were people whose dedication to the cause of Christian control of the holy places was lifelong and absolute. For most people in the West, support for the crusading ideal (which was probably widespread, if not universal) did not translate into any real commitment. Indeed, calls for assistance from the Latin Christians in the East to their co-religionists in the West only prompted an organized, Europe-wide response when disaster struck the crusader states. The Second Crusade was launched after Edessa fell to the Muslims in 1144. Hopes for success were high when the forces of the Second Crusade, which included the armies of the kings of France and Germany, set out in 1147, but the campaign was abandoned two years later, after an attempt to capture the city of Damascus failed.

The shock that triggered the Third Crusade was much more profound. After inflicting a crushing defeat on Jerusalem's army at Hattin in July 1187, Saladin, ruler of Egypt and Syria, went on to seize nearly all the strongholds in the crusader kingdom – only the port of Tyre remained in Christian hands. The loss of Jerusalem itself, three months later, spurred Christians in the West into action. This time the kings of Germany, France and England felt compelled to respond, and three great armies made their way eastwards. Although the Third Crusade recaptured the port city of Acre, it failed to win back Jerusalem. It might have done so had the French king, Philip II, not left the campaign early. His personal and political rivalries with Richard I of England lay behind his decision to do so, demonstrating the ease with which a crusade campaign could be diverted by extraneous concerns. This is a theme encountered again in considering Geoffrey of Villehardouin's account of the Fourth Crusade.

When in 1198 the newly elected Pope Innocent III issued the call that launched the Fourth Crusade, the impending centenary of the First Crusade's capture of Jerusalem and the more recent failure of the Third Crusade to reconquer it would have weighed heavily on his mind and on many Latin Christians'. His announcement was at once an acknowledgement of the grave dangers facing the remaining Christian territories in the Near East and an expression of a hope and belief that, with God's help, the Holy Sepulchre and other holy places might be in Christian hands once more.

Contact and conflict between Latin Christians and Muslims did not begin with the crusades. There had long been a Muslim presence in western Europe; most of Spain had been under Muslim rule since the eighth century and Sicily since the ninth. Muslims from Sicily also became raiders and settlers in the southern Italian peninsula. In these regions Muslims and Latin Christians (as well as people of other religions – Jews in Spain and Greek Christians in Sicily) had lived alongside each other for many generations, in societies characterized by a degree of religious toleration and cultural exchange, as well as tension.

The balance of military and political power in both Spain and
Sicily had shifted to favour Latin Christians before the First
Crusade; the rulers of the Christian kingdoms in northern Spain
began to make inroads against their Muslim neighbours earlier
in the eleventh century, while the Norman conquest of Sicily
and southern Italy was completed just a few years before the
departure of the First Crusade. In both cases the Christian
conquerors received support from the papacy and the ongoing
conflict in Spain would, over the course of the twelfth century,
come to be a species of crusade in its own right. But the confron-
tation between Christians and Muslims in the twelfth-century
Near East was different from the fighting in Europe. It was
not an extension of a long-running territorial dispute, and the
crusaders arrived on the scene in Syria and Palestine quite
unexpectedly, presenting the already unsettled Islamic communities there with new challenges.

The Islamic Near East was bitterly divided at the time; vast
regions to the north and east were controlled by Seljuq Turks
who were adherents of Sunni Islam and had for decades been
at war with the ruling dynasty of Egypt, the Fatimids, who were
Shi'ite Muslims and whom the Seljuqs therefore condemned as
heretics. The lands in which the crusaders settled had been key
battlegrounds in these wars; Jerusalem itself had been taken
from the Seljuqs by the Fatimids in 1097. To complicate matters
further, power within the Seljuq Empire was fragmented, and
events in and around Jerusalem were of peripheral concern
in the empire's capital in Baghdad. While the rival military
commanders and princes who exercised authority in the Near
East were the most threatened by the arrival of the Christians,
for the first fifty years they were primarily concerned with
fighting each other. Sometimes they even made treaties and
alliances with the crusader states in order to fight their fellow
Muslims more effectively.

In religious terms the continuing confessional divide between
Sunni and Shi'a was of greater concern to Islamic powers than
the sudden arrival of the Latin Christians. It was left to lone
voices within the wider Muslim community to express distress
at the sufferings wrought on their co-religionists by the

crusaders, and to urge action against them. One such voice was 'Ali bin Tahir al-Sulami, who wrote (in the early twelfth century) the *Kitab-al-jihad* (*Book of Holy War*) in which he urged his fellow Muslims to work for personal spiritual renewal and to unite to expel the Christian invaders.[3] A fundamental element of Islam quite distinct from Christian holy war in terms of its origins, expressions and aims, *jihad* requires all Muslims to strive constantly for inner purity (this is the internal *jihad*, the first element of the programme al-Sulami promoted), while circumstance might compel the able-bodied to engage in a struggle against people or powers not subject to Islam (the external or physical *jihad*, the second element). Before 1099 the practice of the external *jihad* had waned in the Islamic communities of the Near East, and al-Sulami's work was an early call for a revival of *jihad* spirit and action. Had he lived long enough he would have seen his wish fulfilled, though the revival of enthusiasm for the external *jihad* in the mid twelfth century may have been as much a result of movements for religious reform within the wider Sunni Islamic world as of the arrival of Christian settlers.

Nonetheless, the crusaders were obvious targets once Muslim leaders emerged who possessed the military skill, personal ambition and aura of piety required to effectively propagandize and prosecute the external *jihad*. In the middle decades of the twelfth century the ruler of Damascus and Aleppo, Nur ad-Din, channelled the energies of his fellow Sunni Muslims in Syria against both Fatimid Egypt and the crusader states. Under his rule *jihad* propaganda emphasized the special significance to Muslims of Jerusalem (from where the Prophet Muhammad had ascended into the heavens in the course of his Night Journey). Saladin, his successor, capitalized on Nur ad-Din's efforts, by uniting Egypt and Syria under his control, thus ending the former confessional and political disunity of the Muslim Near East. From this powerful position he was able to crush the Latin Christians in 1187 in the Battle of Hattin and recapture Jerusalem. These feats have earned Saladin, in recent times especially, a reputation as an archetypal *jihad* warrior.

Throughout the period in which *jihad* ideas were being fostered, there were many Muslims inside the crusader states living under Christian rule. The population of Syria and Palestine in 1099 was diverse: as well as Muslims (both Sunni and Shi'i) there were substantial communities of Jews and Eastern Christians (Armenians, Nestorians and Maronites among others). All had reason to be wary of Latin Christian rule, but it was the Muslims and Jews, as non-Christians, who had most cause for concern. Their fears were realized in the course of the First Crusade and in its immediate aftermath; the conquests in Syria and Palestine were accompanied by massacres, most famously at Jerusalem itself, and some non-Christians were driven from their homes. But a policy of violent persecution was unsustainable; the realization soon dawned on the massively outnumbered Latin Christians that the crusader states would only be viable if they found a way to coexist with the local populations. Under a system similar to that which governed the lives of Christians and Jews in Muslim lands, Jews and Muslims in the crusader states were required to pay special taxes and wear distinctive clothing. Their legal status placed them at the bottom of the scale, with Eastern Christians above them and Latin Christians set apart at the top.

But people of all faiths were free to practise their religion, and there were numerous instances in which the shared traditions of Muslims, Jews and Christians brought them into apparently respectful contact. A famous example comes from Usama ibn Munqidh, a Muslim who encountered Christians both on and off the battlefield during the twelfth century and wrote a fascinating memoir in his old age. He was in the habit of going to pray inside a former mosque, close to the al-Aqsa mosque in Jerusalem, that had been converted into a church run by the Templars, whom Usama described as his friends. On one such occasion the peace of his prayer was broken: he was assaulted by a furious Christian man who tried to force him to face east as he prayed. Usama was able to continue his prayers because a group of Templar knights expelled his assailant from the church; they explained apologetically that this man was newly arrived from the West and had never seen a Muslim at prayer before.[4] But neither the friendship between Usama and the

Templars nor the violent reaction of the recently arrived Christian should be taken as being typical. The different faith communities in the crusader states tended to look at each other in terms of stereotyping and prejudice. Usama's friendship with the Templars and with other Christians did not prevent him from writing an account of the Latin Christians that was, in general, scathing of them and contemptuous of their religion. The balance between curiosity and condemnation in Christian–Muslim encounters is a theme I will return to in considering John of Joinville's *Life of Saint Louis*.

Instead of fighting Muslims, Geoffrey of Villehardouin and most of his fellow participants in the Fourth Crusade did battle with Christians. How it was that the Fourth Crusade was diverted from its intended target of Muslim Egypt and ultimately conquered the Greek Orthodox Byzantine empire will be considered in more detail below, but it was merely the most dramatic episode in a long history of Latin Christian involvement with Byzantium in the course of the crusades.

When Urban II launched the First Crusade, two powers claimed the right to leadership of the Christian world. In the West the pope and his followers asserted that, as the heir of Saint Peter, he held ultimate spiritual authority over all Christians, and from the mid eleventh century onwards the papacy was controlled by reformers who pressed these claims forcefully. In the East the emperor at Constantinople (whose lands are known as the Byzantine Empire) believed he was the supreme ruler of Christendom because he was heir to the legacy of Emperor Constantine I, who in the fourth century had become the first of the Roman emperors to adopt Christianity and who had founded their beloved imperial city. As the head of the Byzantine state and the Greek Orthodox Church, the emperor in Constantinople claimed a pre-eminent worldly authority bolstered by his special religious role. Ideological and doctrinal differences between the Roman and Greek Churches had caused tension before 1095, but the lines of communication between them had been maintained in order to pursue the possible unification of the two Churches and because the two

communities – who were, after all, both Christian – were potentially useful allies.

The First Crusade began with the mutual hope that Latin
and Greek Christians might collaborate. The Byzantines had
for some time made use of mercenaries from the West, and
when the emperor called on Urban II in 1095 to encourage
fighting men to make their way eastwards to help him fight the
Seljuq Turks, he probably expected to be joined by a modestly
sized force of professional knights. In the event it was a quite
different kind of army: massive, unruly, hungry and driven by
a fierce religious zeal. The crusaders felt badly let down when
their expectations of Byzantine support for their campaign were
not fulfilled, and the Byzantines in turn felt betrayed when lands
that had formerly been theirs were claimed by the crusaders.

This helped seal a mutual mistrust between Latins and
Greeks. Although over the course of the twelfth century there
would be repeated attempts by the Latins to draw the Byzantines into their crusading projects in a useful way – the material
support that Constantinople might provide was potentially
massive and could not be ignored – the latter's response was
deeply frustrating. For the Byzantine emperors, the need to
work in the interests of the empire (and above all to ensure
Constantinople's safety), while maintaining their claim to
supreme Christian authority, overrode all other concerns. This
meant alternating between courting westerners and rulers of
the crusader states and undermining them, sometimes by
cooperating with Muslim powers. This policy helped fix an
impression in western minds that the Greek Christians were
profoundly untrustworthy.

There was resentment of westerners in Constantinople, too,
that had nothing to do with crusading. Italian merchants –
especially from Venice, Genoa and Pisa – had for decades been
a strong presence in Constantinople, the largest and richest
market in the world, and benefited from trading privileges that
aroused jealous anger among the local population. On two
occasions concerted action was taken against Italians in Constantinople. In the first it was the Byzantine government itself
that acted: in 1171 all the Venetians in the empire were arrested

and their property confiscated, and many remained in prison until 1183. But with hindsight they may have seen this long captivity as a blessing for in 1182 the first of a series of coups in a period of serious political instability in Byzantium was accompanied by a massacre of Constantinople's remaining Italian population. This time it was Constantinople's mob rather than its emperor who lay behind this action, and although it was specifically Italians who were targeted, people throughout western Europe and the Latin East were horrified. The first century of crusading saw relations between Greek and Latin Christians become both more intense and more confused and fragile. The breaking point would come with the Fourth Crusade.

The World of Villehardouin and Joinville: French Knightly Society and Literary Culture

As well as providing accounts of crusades, *The Conquest of Constantinople* and *The Life of Saint Louis* are fascinating reflections of the values and concerns of the society and culture that the authors and their fellow crusaders lived in and were shaped by. Their status as knights, as Christians and as inhabitants of the lands that would come to form the country we know as France were key features of Villehardouin and Joinville's world. The thirteenth century was a vital one in the formation of France and its literary culture, and both writers were important witnesses to and participants in this process.

Although men and women from every walk of life took the cross and joined crusade campaigns, the people whom the papacy most wanted were members of western Europe's arms-bearing elite, which by the thirteenth century had developed into a knightly class with its own distinctive lifestyle, values and tastes. Geoffrey of Villehardouin and John of Joinville shared with their knightly colleagues an awareness that their material and social standing, as well as their highly prized personal honour, were dependent on their ability to secure and defend, often by force, possession of property and rights, whether their own or that of the lord they served as a vassal.

The skills, resources and bravery required by horse-borne combat were essential to performing these tasks effectively, as well as to the knightly self-image.

Alongside their worldly concerns, which required a readiness for violence, most knights felt a profound sense of spiritual obligation. Religious faith and the fate of one's soul were constant preoccupations. In order to counter the sinfulness that was an inevitable consequence of living a normal, active life, knights and women of their social class (like all laymen and -women) engaged in penitential pilgrimages to the shrines where saints' relics were housed and, if they had the means, gave generous gifts to the religious communities that cared for these shrines and would pray for the donors' souls. These dual tendencies in knighthood – towards violence and piety – may appear contradictory to modern eyes and could be troubling to medieval people too. A large part of the appeal of crusading to the military elite lay in the way it reconciled these competing impulses, lending knighthood the qualities of a vocation akin to monasticism.

From the outset the French-speaking world had a special part to play in the crusades. Although people from many regions of Europe – Germany, England, Italy, the Low Countries and Scandinavia among them – responded to the proclamation of the First Crusade, the French-born Urban II had directed his initial appeal specifically at members of the French landed and military elite; and their descendants would continue to play a prominent role in the crusades. It is worth clarifying that the terms 'France' and 'French' did not refer to clearly defined geographical, political or linguistic units in the central Middle Ages. Throughout this period the king of France was a member of a dynasty known as the Capetians. The territories within which the earlier Capetian kings exercised effective authority were limited to a relatively small area around their capital at Paris, but they claimed sovereignty over a much larger area and over more extensive rights. In the thirteenth century the extent, in both geographical and qualitative terms, of the authority wielded by the kings of France would grow substantially as the Capetians used political manoeuvring, military might and judicious marriage alliances to secure meaningful recognition of their supremacy over regions close to their power base in the north as well as territories further south.

Among those regions was the county of Champagne, to the east of Paris, home to both Geoffrey of Villehardouin and John of Joinville. The counts of Champagne were able to exercise power independently throughout most of the twelfth and thirteenth centuries but were nonetheless attached to the kings of France by feudal ties and family connections. In 1284, when the heiress to Champagne, Joan (who was also queen of Navarre), married the future King Philip IV of France, Champagne was finally claimed by the Capetians. Men like Villehardouin and Joinville, high-ranking members of the society and administration of Champagne, had a primary loyalty to the county but also felt an association with the wider France into which Champagne was increasingly bound. Hence both authors refer to themselves and their fellow crusaders as 'French' or 'Franks'.

Their sense of 'Frenchness' would have been enhanced by the thriving literary culture in what is the northern half of modern-day France that shared a common dialect known as Old French (examples of which may be found in Appendix I). Villehardouin's and Joinville's knightly peers would have listened to the stories of war recounted in epic poems known as *chansons de geste*, to the tales of knightly quests for spiritual fulfilment or the affection of their beloved told in romances, or to songs whose lyrics touched on a wide range of the dilemmas or desires shared by men and women of high social standing. While the crusades and themes associated with crusading appear in all these different genres, they feature prominently in the *chansons de geste*, a number of which describe legendary wars supposedly fought by Christians against Muslim enemies. By the late twelfth century one group known as the Old French Crusade Cycle and based (sometimes very loosely) on the history of the First Crusade had been collected and written down for circulation among performers.

Some members of the knightly class participated more actively in French literary culture as patrons or writers, and Champagne seems to have been notable for spawning or

INTRODUCTION

attracting such individuals. Countess Marie, who ruled the
county in the late twelfth century and appointed Geoffrey of
Villehardouin as her marshal, was a patroness of the famous
romance writer, Chrétien of Troyes, for example. A number of
well-known songwriters were associated with Champagne;
John of Joinville's lord, Count Thibaut IV of Champagne, was
only the most famous and high-ranking. When Villehardouin
and Joinville left their homeland to go on crusade, they found
the campaigns could bring poets together, as was most clearly
the case on the Fourth Crusade. Three of the crusaders mentioned by Villehardouin – Conon of Béthune, Guy the castellan
of Coucy and Hugh of Berzé – are known for the lyrics they
composed. A song attributed to Hugh V of Berzé, 'S'onques
nus hom pour dure departie', which blends themes of love and
crusading and was probably written in the early stages of the
Fourth Crusade, is included in Appendix I.

Both Villehardouin and Joinville came from an environment
in which literary achievement was valued, and they are known
to have been in close contact with accomplished poets, which
may make it less surprising that they embarked on their own
writing projects. What is striking, though, is that both of them
broke with established traditions in vernacular literature by
rejecting the verse form used in works written primarily by or
for audiences of laymen and -women. Villehardouin's account
of *The Conquest of Constantinople*, alongside a second work
of the same name produced by Robert of Clari, another participant in the Fourth Crusade, are the earliest surviving examples
of French historical writing in prose.[5] They coupled vernacular
language – French, the language of easy communication with
their knightly peers and of rousing stories – with the prose form
of didactic and functional texts. The latter were 'truth-telling'
and instructional texts such as Scripture, sermons and legal
documents. By choosing prose both Villehardouin and Joinville
emphasized their seriousness of purpose and in doing so Villehardouin also helped set a landmark in the history of French
literature.

Geoffrey of Villehardouin and the Fourth Crusade

Born around 1150, Geoffrey of Villehardouin helped bring his family to prominence in the county of Champagne. In his early career he demonstrated the qualities – loyalty, sound judgement, military ability – the counts of Champagne required of their leading officials. In 1185 he was appointed marshal of Champagne, where he served as one of the counts' closest advisers and administrators, with particular responsibility for military matters. It is likely that he accompanied Count Henry II on the Third Crusade. His loyalty and proven abilities as a military manager and envoy were recognized and rewarded by the leaders of the Fourth Crusade; he was appointed marshal of the Latin empire of Constantinople after the city's fall in 1204. As far as we know, he never returned to Champagne, but the precise date and circumstances of his death are obscure; there is no reference to him in our sources after 1212, and he was certainly no longer alive in 1218, when pious donations were made in his memory.

In *The Conquest of Constantinople*, his only known writing, Villehardouin provided a clear, chronological account of the events of the Fourth Crusade and the early years of the Latin empire of Constantinople. It ends in September 1207, and it is likely that Villehardouin and the scribe to whom he dictated his narrative embarked on the process of composition not long after. Villehardouin gives no indication in his work as to why he wrote, and *The Conquest* does not include a preamble or address to its intended recipient or recipients of the sort often found in medieval works (such as Joinville's *Life of Saint Louis*). Instead Villehardouin launched straight into his narrative, and his work ends with equal abruptness. Attempts to ascribe a motivation to his writing are therefore to some extent speculative, but it is clear that he wanted to inform the French speakers in the West about the remarkable events of his crusade. His work seems to have enjoyed early popularity; it survives in the relatively large number of six manuscripts (compared with only one manuscript for Robert of Clari), all of which were produced in the West, five in the thirteenth or fourteenth centuries.

More complex motives than straightforward reportage have been imputed due to Villehardouin's central role in the events of the Fourth Crusade. The course of the campaign has been well documented,[6] and the summary that follows is intended to highlight the key decisions that made this crusade, and Villehardouin's account of it, controversial to contemporaries and more recent commentators alike.

In 1200 the most high-ranking and powerful men to have taken the cross sent a group of envoys, including Villehardouin, to make arrangements for the transport of the crusaders to north Africa. At Venice the envoys confirmed a treaty with Doge Enrico Dandolo but as the planned departure date of June 1202 approached, it became clear that the crusaders would not be able to raise sufficient men or money to meet the costs of the fleet. In the hope of fulfilling their obligations to Venice and of pursuing their expedition against the Muslims, the leaders of the crusade agreed to help Doge Enrico recapture the Dalmatian port of Zara. There was stiff opposition to this scheme within the army and within the Christian community more widely (including from the pope) because it called on crusaders to be ready to use force against Zara's Latin Christian inhabitants and ruler, the king of Hungary, who had himself taken the cross. The decision by the crusade leadership to go ahead lost them a number of outraged colleagues and earned them temporary excommunication.

While the crusaders' debt to Venice was only deferred, and not fulfilled, by the assistance they had provided in Zara's recapture, another possible solution arose. A young prince named Alexius claimed that his father and he had been unjustly dispossessed of the Byzantine empire, and proposed that if the crusaders helped him, he would reward them so generously that they would be able to pay the Venetians and have ample resources to proceed with their campaign against the Ayyubids, Saladin's heirs in Egypt and the Near East. Alexius also promised them a substantial Byzantine contingent under his leadership, if the Latins so desired. Opinion within the crusade army was once again divided; opponents believed it would lead the crusaders even further away from their initial goal and might see them once more compelled to violence against Christians. But the leadership agreed to this scheme and in July 1203, after a brief assault against Constantinople which prompted the incumbent emperor to flee, Alexius and his father were installed as co-emperors.

Alexius proved unable to keep his extravagant promises. And then he and his father were ousted in a coup, so the crusaders decided they would take what was due to them by force. Having sought and gained assurances from their religious leaders that their actions would be justified and even meritorious, and having made plans for the division of spoils, land and power, the crusaders and Venetians launched their second attack on Constantinople in April 1204. After their second assault succeeded, the city was abandoned to their control, and three days of plunder ensued before the conquerors settled down to elect the first Latin emperor of Constantinople.

Villehardouin continues describing the challenges faced as the Latins sought to bring the rest of the empire under their control in the face of opposition from the native Greek population, from Kalojan, ruler of the Vlacho-Bulgarian state ('King Johanitsa' to Villehardouin), and from Theodore Lascaris, ruler of the Byzantine successor state founded at Nicaea. Although there were success stories (the conquest of Morea, for example, in which Villehardouin's nephew played an important part), the military capabilities of the Latins were severely tested, and they suffered a number of defeats, most notably at Adrianople in April 1205. This period also strained relationships among the Latins, as individuals sought to secure their own share in the conquest of the empire.

The fall of the city in 1204 was clearly not the end of the story of the conquest of Constantinople as far as Villehardouin was concerned, but it is his account of the events leading up to this point that have attracted most attention. The capture of Constantinople was the climax of a crusade that went far astray from its original aims; instead of fighting Muslims and working towards the recapture of Jerusalem, the participants several times used violence against fellow Christians, and they capped their 'achievement' by sacking Constantinople, further injuring the already beleaguered population and fabric of the great city. Some modern commentators think the events of 1202–4 undermine any claim the crusaders might have to a moral or spiritual purpose and instead reveal baser motives: greed and a desire for conquest.

It has even been suggested that the fall and sack of Constantinople in 1204 were the culmination of a plot hatched much earlier, in which the Venetians, members or associates of the crusade leadership, and maybe even the pope may have been involved. Adherents of this theory have looked on *The Conquest of Constantinople* as a work of propagandist deception, and they point to discrepancies between it and the accounts of other participants in and eyewitnesses to the Fourth Crusade as evidence that Villehardouin deliberately misled his readers. For example, his version of the immediate aftermath of the conquest of Constantinople is contradicted by Robert of Clari, a low-ranking knight from Picardy in northern France. Robert was scathing of the crusade leaders whom he felt betrayed the rank and file of the army by wrongfully and greedily withholding the city's spoils.[7] But while his comments can be cited as evidence of the leaders' greed, Villehardouin in turn is just as scathing of the behaviour of the men of Robert's class. (The special value of Robert's work is that it reflects the concerns of the humbler crusaders.) Similarly, the eloquent and impassioned lament for his beloved Constantinople presented by Nicetas Choniates, a prominent member of the Byzantine administration, has moved many readers, as have his assertions that this was a result of a western plot,[8] but these are the product of anger and instinct, rather than sound information. Indeed, although there are reasons why any of the parties accused of plotting Byzantium's downfall might have had an interest in instituting Latin rule in Constantinople, no convincing evidence has been found to prove that anyone embarked on the crusade with this as the goal, and modern scholars have therefore acquitted Villehardouin of complicity in a plot.

This does not mean, however, that Villehardouin's claim never to have lied (§ 120) should be taken at face value. Recent historians, especially those who examine the crusade as primarily a western European phenomenon, have tended to identify the original treaty negotiated between Venice and the crusaders as the root cause of the controversial diversion of the Fourth Crusade. Both sides had a lot invested in this deal (in terms of emotion and reputation, as well as money), and neither the Venetians nor the crusaders could simply back out when the situation became difficult. The need to preserve a unity of purpose between and among the Venetians and the crusaders, and to maintain the forward momentum of their project compelled all the leaders to make a series of decisions that with hindsight might seem calculated to lead to Constantinople's fall, but which in the moment were practical necessities. According to this view chance was the most important factor that led the crusaders to Constantinople.

This theory suggests that, as one of the negotiators of that ill-fated treaty, Villehardouin had reason to present the course of events it set in train in a positive light. Hence, while he may not have set out to misrepresent, he did not always fully disclose relevant information and appears to gloss over aspects that might reflect badly on the crusade leadership. For example, Villehardouin's depiction of Innocent III's dealings with the crusade army suggests that the pope was for the most part straightforwardly supportive of their actions, when the relationship was in fact much more fraught (for example, §§ 31, 107). Similarly, Villehardouin's assertion that the lack of enthusiasm demonstrated by the people of Constantinople when the young Prince Alexius was presented to them was due to fear (rather than disdain) had been proved wrong well before he began work on *The Conquest* (§ 146); this passage reflects the *hope* that accompanied the events it describes rather than the experience that had informed the author since that time.

Some of Villehardouin's testimony should be treated with caution, but in other important respects – knowledge of the crusade's chronology or the terms of treaties or agreements, for example – his chronicle has been shown to be remarkable for its accuracy, so much so that it has been suggested that he might have made use of documents or contemporary notes. The proven accuracy on such points highlights his privileged status as a member of the crusade's inner circle, a trusted envoy of the leadership who was 'present at all the councils' at which key decisions were made (§ 120). For the theorists who emphasize chance, *The Conquest of Constantinople* is a source of unparalleled value because of the access it allows to the internal workings of the Fourth Crusade.

Historians of Byzantium bring a different perspective that places emphasis on events in Constantinople and relations between Byzantium and the West over the long term. As described above, relationships between Latin and Greek Christians could blow hot and cold and in the context of the crusades this helped generate, on the part of the Latins, a sense that their Greek counterparts should be allies but could be dangerous opponents. While the former may have helped bring the forces of the Fourth Crusade to the walls of Constantinople, it was their anger and despair that a Byzantine emperor had once more failed to follow through on his promises to a crusade army that led them to attack it. In this view the fall of Constantinople was the culmination of an interaction between Latin and Greek Christians that was decades – and centuries – old.

Villehardouin's work expresses disappointment and frustration at the Greeks' conduct, and a sense that the values of the Greeks and Latins were fundamentally at odds. He emphasized the Greeks' treachery (for example, §§ 211, 271, 333), and he and his Frankish companions were shocked by the perfidy and violence that were a feature of Byzantine political life. Villehardouin reported his colleagues' reactions to the news that one claimant to the imperial throne had put out the eyes of another: 'it was firmly declared that men who so wickedly betrayed each other had no right to hold lands' (§ 272).

The qualities that Villehardouin failed to see in the Greeks, and which he looked for in his companions, were above all those of loyalty and courage. *The Conquest of Constantinople* may be characterized as a tale of loyalties maintained and abandoned. Villehardouin and his colleagues who remained with the army stayed true to the oaths they had sworn to the Venetians; they stood firm in their sense of justice which informed them it was right to help the dispossessed Prince

Alexius (and to turn against him when he failed to keep his
promises); and they kept faith with each other, not allowing
the break up of their army. And Villehardouin portrays them
as loyal to God, who had set them on the course of the crusade
and who rewarded their steadfastness and courage by granting
them the 'honour and victory' of Constantinople's conquest
(§ 251). He consistently presents the crusade as directed by
divine providence; successes were the gift of God and setbacks
his punishment for sinfulness (for example, §§ 181, 190, 238,
251). The crusaders who failed to join the main body of the
army when it gathered at Venice (for example, §§ 59, 67) or
deserted during the course of the campaign (§§ 101–6, 109–
10) were singled out for their lack of loyalty: they achieved
little through their crusades besides a bad reputation (§§ 49–
50, 103, 229–31).

The Conquest is thus an account of the triumph of virtue
over vice, and of group cohesion over individual ambition. As
such its ethos is akin to that of the *chansons de geste*. The
style of Villehardouin's narrative is for the most part cool
and detached; he wrote in the impersonal third person and
proceeded briskly and straightforwardly, focusing on what happened rather than providing detailed descriptions that might
suggest his own response. There are exceptions: he lingers
briefly to describe the awesome sight of the great city of Constantinople, for example (§§ 127–8), and comments on the
sadness with which the crusaders left home (§ 47) and the
moving grandeur of the scene when the crusade fleet was about
to set sail from Corfu (§§ 119–20). These suggest the influence
of literary models; emotional leave-taking scenes and awe-
inspiring descriptions of departing fleets are among the *topoi*
that recur in vernacular literature. Both were employed in Joinville's *Life of Saint Louis*, while a number of songs, including
Hugh of Berzé's 'S'onques nus hom pour dure departie' used
the 'separation motif' in describing the distress caused by a
lover's departure on crusade. Villehardouin's use of literary set
pieces ties his work into existing French literary traditions, but
it is perhaps most of all in the values expressed that his work
takes on the qualities of a 'courtly' history.

The second half of *The Conquest of Constantinople* suggests the danger of situations in which the values of loyalty and courage were abandoned, and when individual ambitions or fears overturned knightly unity. These subversive forces were at work in the 'grievous misfortune' of his friend Boniface of Montferrat's death, with which Villehardouin's narrative closes; many of the marquis's men panicked and fled, deserting him in battle (§§ 498–500). Villehardouin may have hoped that his work would rouse those who heard it to unite in support of the hard-won empire. As it transpired, the Latin empire never attracted the material or human resources it needed; after several wearying decades for the Latins, Constantinople was returned to Byzantine control in 1261.

John of Joinville and the Crusades of Louis IX

Innocent III was determined to ensure that future crusade projects would not be diverted from their intended purpose. New measures aimed at guaranteeing the efficient gathering of human and financial resources had been set in place when he announced a new crusade to the East in 1213. He did not live to see the Fifth Crusade's initial success in conquering the Egyptian port city of Damietta in 1219 or its subsequent collapse when confronted by the Ayyubid sultan of Egypt's forces and the flood waters of the Nile. Emperor Frederick II of Germany incurred the wrath of the papacy when he failed to join the campaign to Egypt, and thus it was as an excommunicate and on his own initiative that he set out for the East in 1228, and negotiated with the sultan of Egypt for the return of Jerusalem to Christian hands. This episode is characteristic of the response of the Ayyubids to the Latins in the Near East in the first half of the thirteenth century. With Saladin's death in 1193 the political unity of his lands came to an end: the Ayyubid empire was a confederation of effectively independent territorial units ruled over by his heirs, who were more concerned with maintaining their power bases and gaining the upper hand over each other than with ousting their Christian neighbours. So the Latins, by now an established part of the Near East's political landscape, were most useful to the competing Ayyubid powers as allies; anti-Latin *jihad* propaganda subsided. The forces of the so-called Barons' Crusade, which arrived in the Near East in 1239 as the truces agreed by Frederick II expired, saw little military action beyond an engagement in which a crusader raiding party was wiped out in a vainglorious defeat; the territorial gains secured by the crusade leaders came via negotiation.

In 1244 Jerusalem was lost by the Christians for good; the Khwarizmians, Turkish nomads allied to the sultan of Egypt, captured it in August and sealed their success with victory over the Christians and their allies from Damascus at the Battle of La Forbie in October. It was then that King Louis IX of France first took the cross. His preparations were meticulous, and when his crusade set sail from France in the summer of 1248, Christians on both sides of the Mediterranean had high hopes for success. Once again it was decided that the crusade should strike at the heartland of Ayyubid power: Egypt. In June 1249 Damietta fell to the Christians, who met little resistance from its Muslim inhabitants. Five months later the crusaders began to advance towards Cairo, but the River Nile and the sultan of Egypt's forces combined to prevent them going beyond the town of Mansurah. February 1250 brought hope and despair. A breakthrough came when the crusaders were informed how they might cross the Nile, and Louis emerged as victor from the battle that awaited them on the other side, although this nominal success came at a great personal cost, as Louis's brother, Count Robert of Artois, was among the many Christians killed in the Battle of Mansurah. Encamped outside the town, the crusaders were hard-pressed by their Muslim opponents and by hunger and disease. By early April their prospects seemed hopeless, and it was decided to retreat to Damietta, but instead they were forced to surrender. During their month in captivity the Mamluks, members of the sultan's elite bodyguard, revolted against him and Ayyubid rule in Egypt came to an end. It was from the Mamluks that Louis was able to buy his own and his companions' freedom, and he sailed to Christian-held Acre, in Syria. Although many of the prominent men in his army favoured a swift return to France, the king decided to stay in the Near East. He and those he persuaded to remain with him spent four years refortifying key Christian strongholds and securing truces with the neighbouring Muslim powers, the Mamluks to the south in Egypt and the Ayyubid sultans of Damascus and Aleppo to the north.

These are the crusading events recounted in John of Joinville's *Life of Saint Louis*. Born in 1224 or 1225, Joinville, like Geoffrey of Villehardouin, came to hold high-ranking office in Champagne. He was seneschal, acting as the counts' close adviser and involved in the administrative affairs of Champagne. By contrast with Villehardouin, Joinville inherited his office upon his father's death in 1233. Members of the Joinville family had held the title of seneschal of Champagne for several generations, and they also seem to have handed down a tradition of participation in crusades; his ancestors were present on the Second, Third, Fourth and Fifth Crusades, and this may have been a factor that led Joinville to respond positively when Louis IX's first crusade was launched, even though he was young (perhaps just nineteen in 1244) and still establishing himself. His youth and relative inexperience as a knight on crusade may be contrasted with Villehardouin's seasoned maturity. Joinville stayed with Louis throughout his time in Egypt and in Syria, and he nurtured a friendship with the king that led him to become a trusted and familiar figure in the French court. Despite, or perhaps because of, his personal attachment to the king, Joinville refused to join him on a second overseas campaign. The king died outside Tunis in northern Africa in 1270, in the course of his new crusade. Joinville continued to attend the royal court, if less frequently than before; his most notable visit was in 1282, when he gave evidence to the inquiry investigating Louis IX's sanctity. Louis was confirmed as a saint in 1297. Joinville was to live a further twenty years, dying in 1317 at the advanced age of at least ninety-two.

The Life of Saint Louis, produced at the request of Joan of Navarre, countess of Champagne and wife of Louis's grandson, Philip IV of France, was completed in 1309. It is an account of 'the holy words and the good deeds' (§ 2) of Joinville's friend and king. These two aspects of Louis's life and sanctity are dealt with in discrete sections (with some material appearing in both, see §§ 39–41 and 634–7, for example), and in this respect conforms to the conventions of medieval hagiography (the writing of saints' lives). It also does so by including accounts of key events in its subject's life to which the author was not witness (the circumstances of birth and death in particular). But Joinville's work is highly unusual for the extent to which the author and his own concerns feature, particularly in its account of Louis's first crusade, which constitutes the greater part of the text (over 550 of its 769 sections).

Joinville's *Life* also diverges from the conventions of hagiography by including a marked element of social and political critique and instruction. By the time he finished it Joan of Navarre was no longer alive, and he therefore dedicated his work to her son, Louis, count of Champagne and future King Louis X of France. In the preface he announced his didactic intentions: 'I am sending it [*The Life of Saint Louis*] to you so that you and your brothers and others that hear it might heed its good lessons and put those lessons into practice, and thereby make themselves pleasing to God' (§ 18). It is clear that Joinville felt Louis IX's heirs had failed to live up to their saintly ancestor's example; he commented on their extravagance in matters of dress (§ 25) and their tolerance of profane speech (§ 22), and Joinville admonished them to consider how their conduct would be measured against Saint Louis's (§ 761). But although Joinville clearly intended the *Life* to act as an exemplar, he was not (unlike most hagiographers) unerringly positive, for he criticized Louis's apparent coldness to his wife and children (§§ 593–4), and what Joinville viewed as the king's excessive display of emotion on hearing of his mother, Queen Blanche's, death (§§ 603–4). (Blanche was another of the member of the Capetian royal family whom Joinville presented in an unsympathetic light (for example, §§ 606–8).)

Joinville's criticisms of the Capetians provide one possible explanation for the apparently limited circulation of his *Life of Saint Louis* in the early years of its existence; its recipients may not have wanted to encourage the reproduction and distribution of a work they felt reflected badly on them. The text survives in only three manuscripts, one from the 1330s or 1340s, and the other two, which represent a different tradition or version of the text, from the mid sixteenth century. A third tradition (in which Joinville's text was significantly reworked) is attested in a pair of early printed editions of the sixteenth and seventeenth centuries. Joinville's work features in only one extant library catalogue from the later Middle Ages and was not referred to or used by other medieval authors. All this suggests that for several generations the *Life* was looked upon as awkward or unsatisfactory, perhaps because of its judgements on the Capetians, or its strangeness as a work of hagiography, or because its focus on the author and his life meant it was of limited relevance to the wider history of Louis's reign.

The idiosyncrasies of *The Life of Saint Louis* have led scholars to question when and how Joinville produced it. Did he start from scratch when Joan of Navarre asked him, or had he already dictated an account of his time on the crusade and did he use this as the core of his narrative? Adherents of the former theory cite Joinville's references to events or persons contemporary with composition (for example, §§ 35, 108), which suggest he was at work in the early fourteenth century, while those who follow a two-stage composition theory highlight the potential ambiguities in this dating evidence and point to marked qualitative differences between Joinville's crusade narrative and the rest of the *Life*. These include the text's lack of balance in describing Louis's life (his first crusade took up only six years of his fifty-six-year life but occupies more than half of Joinville's narrative) and the focus on the experiences of the author (including details that have nothing at all to do with Louis, see §§ 501–4, for example). It has been suggested that if Joinville did produce an independent account of his time on Louis's first crusade, he may have done so in the early 1270s, at which time several events may have prompted him. Louis's death in 1270 would have been one important spur, as might the marriage of Joinville's son to Mabille of Villehardouin, great-granddaughter of the author. The union of the two families by marriage may have introduced Joinville to Geoffrey's *The Conquest of Constantinople* or reminded him of it, encouraging him to produce a similar work.

Joinville is known to have written more than one work. He composed a *Credo* (an exposition of the Creed through text and illustration, a later version of which has survived) and an epitaph for one of his ancestors that contains an outline genealogy of his family detailing their involvement in crusades (see Appendix II). He has also been proposed as the lyricist for the song, 'Nus ne porroit de mauvese reson', which was written to promote Louis IX's remaining in the Near East in 1250 (see Appendix I). These texts share with the *Life* a connection with the crusades. The *Credo* was first written while Joinville was in Syria and includes anecdotes from the crusade. The epitaph focuses on the crusading achievements of his ancestors, and the lyrics, if they were Joinville's work, responded to and were composed in the context of crusading events. All his writings suggest Joinville's deep interest in crusading but it is *The Life of Saint Louis* that is of particular historical value.

Joinville's work does have flaws as a source for Louis IX's first crusade. Like Villehardouin he was an eyewitness, but he did not have the same close involvement in planning or decisions. Although Joinville came to be a trusted friend of the king and attended meetings to which all the high-ranking men of the army were summoned, he was not part of the royal household nor an official adviser and therefore sometimes had to rely on others for information (for example, §§ 7, 9). His perspective on the conduct of the campaign focused on the personal. Nor did he share Villehardouin's keen understanding of the crusade as a military concern, and his accounts of key engagements such as the landing of the crusade army at Damietta (§§ 150–63) and the Battle of Mansurah (§§ 216–47) centre on his own experiences and do not give a clear sense of how these engagements were conducted as a whole. And, while Villehardouin's account is highly accurate on points of detail, Joinville's has been shown to be faulty in some instances (for example, §§ 146, 495).

Where Joinville's narrative comes into its own is in relating

the attitudes, experiences and concerns of an individual crusader. The reader gains a strong sense of his knightly values,
which in many respects coincide with those expressed in *The
Conquest*; for example, loyalty was clearly of great importance
to him, and could be seen in the admirable conduct of individuals (for example, §§ 308–9) or in the effectiveness of a
military unit whose members were bound to each other by
family or feudal ties (§ 247). Acts of bravery were praised
(§§ 258–60) unless they were recklessly wasteful (§§ 174–6).
Where Joinville's account contrasts most strikingly with that of
Villehardouin is in depicting the fear and horror of battle.
At Mansurah he and his colleagues engaged in close-quarters
combat, and he described the horrific wounds inflicted on his
companions when they were stranded and set upon by the
enemy. In this situation (as in others) Joinville felt his only
recourse was to prayer (§§ 224–5).

Expressions of the author's personal faith are more readily
found in *The Life of Saint Louis* than in *The Conquest of
Constantinople*. Joinville's commitment to the practice of pilgrimage comes through clearly, and like many of his prede-
cessors and contemporaries (including Villehardouin), he used
pilgrimage vocabulary to describe crusading journeys (for
example, §§ 5, 19, 146), but the strength of his association
between crusading and pilgrimage is borne out in his actions.
Before his departure on crusade he received the traditional staff
and purse of a pilgrim and undertook a barefoot pilgrimage to
local religious houses (§ 122), and in the Near East he went on
pilgrimage to the shrine of Our Lady of Tortosa (§ 597). These
and other pilgrimages he mentions demonstrate his commitment to this penitential activity, and his devotion to the relics
preserved at the shrines he visited. His and his contemporaries'
enthusiasm is reflected in his refusal to accept any gift from the
prince of Antioch besides the relics he offered (§ 600). Like
Villehardouin, Joinville looked on successes or reprieves as gifts
from God (§§ 165, 279), but the divine rewards he believed
were available to individual crusaders are more richly
described. For example, *The Life of Saint Louis* provides evidence of a belief that crusading could lead to martyrdom, but

Joinville only referred to a small number of people by this word (Louis IX was among them, see §§ 5, 393, 538) and this special status seems to have been reserved in his mind for those who demonstrated a particular readiness for self-sacrifice and suffering.

As well as providing a window on to the social and religious values of an individual crusader, the *Life* is a rich fount of incidental information concerning life on crusade, for example, practical concerns such as raising money and arranging transportation (for example, §§ 112–13, 136) or organizing a crusading household (§§ 501–4). The great variety of people and groups involved in a crusade is also evident, for in the *Life* we encounter not only those men who took the cross but also the women and children who accompanied them (§§ 275, 397–400); we hear of the military orders and of the residents of the crusader states, and the potential for rivalries or tensions between these groups and the crusaders (§§ 218–19, 380–82); and also come across low-ranking knights, craftsmen and people of humble social status who followed the army (§§ 171, 274, 595).

Participation in the crusade brought Joinville into contact with non-Christians. The Muslims he describes were fearsome and potentially brutal opponents capable of atrocities such as massacres of the sick and wounded (§§ 305, 330, 370) and of prisoners (§ 334). Like Villehardouin's Greeks, Joinville's Muslims could be treacherous; the Ayyubid sultan was disloyal to his emirs by bringing outsiders into the Egyptian administration, and was repaid with betrayal by the Mamluks (§§ 348–50). Collectively, Muslims are usually presented in negative terms, but individuals might be praised for their bravery or prowess (§§ 198–9), for their kindness (§ 325) or for their trustworthiness (§§ 401–2). One man, whom Joinville called 'my Saracen', protected and supported him during his captivity (§§ 321–32). Joinville engaged his Muslim captor in conversation on religious and moral issues on more than one occasion (§§ 326–7, 330–31). Joinville also had the opportunity to talk to a Christian convert to Islam (§§ 394–6). In each of these exchanges his belief in the superiority of his faith is apparent, but he seems to have been interested and open in his interactions with Muslims and was certainly much more so than Louis, who refused outright to have the convert in his presence.

Joinville's wide-ranging curiosity is shown in the stories he recounted about the extravagances and intrigues of oriental rulers (§§ 141–5), and about a number of different communities in the East, including the Bedouins (§§ 249–52), the Cumans (§§ 495–8) and the Mongols (referred to by Joinville as 'Tartars', §§ 471–89). The alien environment of north Africa and the Near East also seems to have fascinated him; he was amazed to see a fossil for the first time (§ 602) and reported in detail what he had learned about the River Nile (§§ 187–90).

These passages of *The Life of Saint Louis* reflect the anecdotal style of the work as a whole; in the account of Louis IX's saintly life, within which he described his own time on crusade, Joinville presented a collection of stories that he found memorable and valuable, supplemented with information concerning the later years of Louis's reign from a historical work (§ 768). As in *The Conquest of Constantinople* Joinville's serious ness of purpose – to inform and instruct – is reflected in his use of prose, but his anecdotal style means that the *Life* often lacks the clear chronology and lucidity that characterize Villehardouin's work. Another contrast between them lies in Joinville's use of the first person, which lends his work a more intimate narrative tone. He too used literary conventions including the description of an impressive departing fleet (§ 146) and the sadness of leaving home (§ 122), but in the latter he added a personal twist to the *topos* by suggesting his affection for his castle and his young children. Joinville's interest in human relationships and emotions comes through in his descriptions of private conversations in which personal thoughts, opinions and guidance are shared. His attention to detail in describing such encounters – such as their setting, how participants were dressed, the physical relationship or contact between them – is evidence of a desire not just to recall but to vivify his account of the events and people (for example, §§ 37–8, 431–3). The intimacy of his style helps bring life to our understanding of the saintly Louis, Joinville himself and their crusading companions.

By the time Joinville completed *The Life of Saint Louis* there was no longer a Christian presence in Palestine and Syria. Following Louis IX's first crusade the Mamluks increased in might and in the 1260s they began destroying the remaining crusader settlements. In 1270 Louis IX embarked on a second crusade, in which Joinville refused to participate and which he viewed as deeply misguided (§§ 730–37); it did nothing to check the Mamluks' progress and brought about the king's death. In 1291 Acre, the last of the crusader states' major cities, fell. Although plans for a new crusade to recover the Christian holy places would be made in the fourteenth century, manpower, resources and will were not raised in adequate measure. Crusading did not end in the thirteenth century – men and women would continue to take the cross and to fight perceived enemies of Latin Christendom for several centuries thereafter – but the events of this period were a watershed for the cause of Christian possession of the holy places in and around Jerusalem. No period saw such intense crusading activity as that witnessed by Geoffrey of Villehardouin and John of Joinville, and there are no better testimonies than theirs to the experiences and beliefs of those who took the cross.

NOTES

1. Joinville and Villehardouin, *Chronicles of the Crusades*, trans. M. R. B. Shaw (Harmondsworth: Penguin, 1963).
2. The debate over the definition of crusading is summarized and assessed in Norman Housley, *Contesting the Crusades* (Oxford and Malden, MA: Blackwell, 2006), chapter 1.
3. Al-Sulami's *Kitab-al-jihad* has not been translated into English; Carole Hillenbrand discusses it in *The Crusades: Islamic Perspectives* (Edinburgh: Edinburgh University Press, 1999), pp. 105–8.
4. Usama ibn Munqidh, *The Book of Contemplation: Islam and the Crusades*, trans. and ed. Paul M. Cobb (London: Penguin, 2008), p. 147.

5. It is possible that some material from the French prose continu-
    ations of the famous history of events in the Near East written
    in Latin in the twelfth century by William, the Archbishop of
    Tyre (*Historia Rerum in Partibus Transmarinis Gestarum*), may
    have been composed before the turn of the thirteenth century, but
    the authorship and dating of this material (which only survives in
    later adaptations) remains obscure.

6. The most complete account of the Fourth Crusade is Donald
    Queller and Thomas Madden, *The Fourth Crusade: The Con-
    quest of Constantinople*, 2nd edn (Philadelphia: University of
    Pennsylvania Press, 1997).

7. Robert of Clari, *The Conquest of Constantinople*, trans. Edgar
    Holmes McNeal (New York: Columbia University Press, 1936,
    reprinted 2005), pp. 100–102; 126.

8. *O City of Byzantium: The Annals of Niketas Choniates*, trans.
    Harry Magoulias (Detroit: Wayne State University Press, 1984);
    for Choniates' conspiracy theory, see pp. 295–6; for his account
    of the sack of Constantinople and his lament for the city, see
    pp. 314–20.

Further Reading

There is now a great quantity and range of scholarship available to readers interested in the crusades, medieval France and French literature, and the works of Geoffrey of Villehardouin and John of Joinville. The titles listed below are recent books in English likely to be of interest or use to general as well as specialist readers. It is the history of the crusades that has seen the largest increase in scholarly attention and debate in recent decades, and a useful survey and discussion of trends in crusade historiography is provided in Norman Housley's book *Contesting the Crusades*.

CONTEMPORARY ACCOUNTS OF THIRTEENTH-CENTURY CRUSADES TO THE EAST

Andrea, Alfred, *Contemporary Sources for the Fourth Crusade*, The Medieval Mediterranean 29 (Leiden and Boston: Brill, 2000)

Arab Historians of the Crusades, trans. Francesco Gabrieli and E. J. Costello (Berkeley: University of California Press, 1969)

Choniates, Nicetas, *O City of Byzantium: The Annals of Niketas Choniates*, trans. Harry Magoulias (Detroit: Wayne State University Press, 1984)

Robert of Clari, *The Conquest of Constantinople*, trans. Edgar

Holmes McNeal (New York: Columbia University Press, 1936; reprinted 2005)

Crusader Syria in the Thirteenth Century: The Rothelin Continuation of the History of William of Tyre with part of the Eracles or Acre Text, trans. Janet Shirley (Aldershot: Ashgate, 1999)

The Seventh Crusade, 1244–1254: Sources and Documents, ed. and trans. Peter Jackson (Aldershot: Ashgate, 2007)

THE CRUSADES: INTRODUCTORY AND GENERAL WORKS

Harris, Jonathan, *Byzantium and the Crusades* (London and New York: Hambledon and London, 2003)

Hillenbrand, Carole, *The Crusades: Islamic Perspectives* (Edinburgh: Edinburgh University Press, 1999)

Housley, Norman, *Contesting the Crusades* (Oxford and Malden, MA: Blackwell, 2006)

—, *The Crusaders* (Stroud, Gloucestershire and Charleston, SC: Tempus, 2002)

Riley-Smith, Jonathan, *The Crusades: A Short History*, 2nd edn (London: Continuum, and New Haven: Yale University Press, 2005)

—, *What were the Crusades?*, 3rd edn (San Francisco: Ignatius Press, 2002)

Tyerman, Christopher, *Fighting for Christendom: Holy War and the Crusades* (Oxford: Oxford University Press, 2004)

—, *God's War: A New History of the Crusades* (London: Allen Lane, and Cambridge, MA: Belknap Press of Harvard University, 2006)

MEDIEVAL FRANCE AND FRENCH LITERATURE

Beer, Jeanette, *Early French Prose: Contexts of Bilingualism and Authority* (Kalamazoo, MI: Medieval Institute Publications, Western Michigan University, 1992)

Bouchard, Constance Brittain, *Strong of Body, Brave and Noble: Chivalry and Society in Medieval France* (Ithaca, NY: Cornell University Press, 1998)

Duby, Georges, *The Chivalrous Society*, trans. C. Postan (Berkeley: University of California Press, 1977)

Hallam, Elizabeth, and Judith Everard, *Capetian France, 987–1328*, 2nd edn (Harlow and New York: Longman, 2001)

Trotter, David, *Medieval French Literature and the Crusades (1100–1300)* (Geneva: Librairie Droz, 1988)

Zink, Michel, *Medieval French Literature: An Introduction*, trans. Jeff Rider (Binghamton, NY: Medieval and Renaissance Texts and Studies, 1995)

GEOFFREY OF VILLEHARDOUIN AND THE FOURTH CRUSADE

Angold, Michael, *The Fourth Crusade: Event and Context* (Harlow and New York: Longman, 2003)

Lock, Peter, *The Franks in the Aegean, 1204–1500* (London and New York: Longman, 1995)

Madden, Thomas, *Enrico Dandolo and the Rise of Venice* (Baltimore: Johns Hopkins University Press, 2003)

Phillips, Jonathan, *The Fourth Crusade and the Sack of Constantinople* (London: Jonathan Cape, 2004)

Queller, Donald, and Thomas Madden, *The Fourth Crusade: The Conquest of Constantinople*, 2nd edn (Philadelphia: University of Pennsylvania Press, 1997)

JOHN OF JOINVILLE AND THE
CRUSADES OF LOUIS IX

Gaposchkin, M. Cecilia, *The Making of Saint Louis: Kingship, Sanctity, and Crusade in the Later Middle Ages* (Ithaca, NY: Cornell University Press, 2008)

Jordan, William Chester, *Louis IX and the Challenge of the Crusade: A Study in Rulership* (Princeton, NJ: Princeton University Press, 1979)

Richard, Jean, *Saint Louis: Crusader King of France*, ed. Simon Lloyd, trans. Jean Birrell (Cambridge: Cambridge University Press, 1992)

Smith, Caroline, *Crusading in the Age of Joinville* (Aldershot: Ashgate, 2006)

A Note on the Translations

The Conquest of Constantinople and *The Life of Saint Louis* first appeared together in English in 1908, when Sir Frank Marzials's translations were published by the Everyman's Library series under the title *Memoirs of the Crusades*.[1] Penguin Classics' publication of M. R. B. Shaw's translations as *Chronicles of the Crusades* in 1963 once again paired these two works in English, but there has been no equivalent publication in French.[2] While for English-reading audiences the crusading content of both works seems to have particular interest, for readers of French Joinville's *Life of Saint Louis* is significant at least as much for its account of Louis IX's sanctity and his career as a whole as for its telling of the king's first crusade. This should serve as a reminder that the pairing of these works as crusading texts is a recent invention.

The translations here have been made from the critical editions of Edmond Faral and Jacques Monfrin: Geoffroy de Ville-hardouin, *La conquête de Constantinople*, ed. Edmond Faral, 2 vols (Paris, Société d'édition 'Les belles lettres': 1938–9; 2nd edn, 1961) and Jean de Joinville, *Vie de Saint Louis*, ed. Jacques Monfrin (Paris: Dunod, 1995).

The full text of *The Conquest of Constantinople* survives in six manuscripts, none of them the original manuscript produced by the scribe to whom Villehardouin dictated his narrative. The extant manuscripts are:

1. Oxford, Bodleian Library, ms Laud Misc. 587 (designated O), of the second half of the fourteenth century

2. Paris, Bibliothèque Nationale, ms français 4972 (designated A), of the second half of the fourteenth century
3. Paris, Bibliothèque Nationale, ms français 2137 (designated B), of the thirteenth century
4. Paris, Bibliothèque Nationale, ms français 12204 (designated C), of the thirteenth century
5. Paris, Bibliothèque Nationale, ms français 12203 (designated D), of the thirteenth century
6. Paris, Bibliothèque Nationale, ms français 24210 (designated E), of the fifteenth century

Faral divided these manuscripts into two groups. The first,
comprising manuscripts O and A, apparently originated in the
same model (a manuscript no longer extant from which O
and A or their antecedents were copied): they share important
characteristics, including decorative elements, division into
paragraphs and most significantly, distinctive readings and
errors. Many of these errors are reproduced in two early printed
editions of The Conquest (those of Blaise de Vigenère (Paris,
1585) and Guillaume Rouille (Lyon, 1601)), which Faral therefore treated as part of the same group as manuscripts O and A
(group I). None of the shared errors of group I appears in
manuscripts B, C, D and E, although this group (group II)
shares other readings and errors that suggest that these four
manuscripts originated in a single, lost model. Among the
manuscripts of group II, Faral identified B as closer to that
model than C, D and E.

Although the manuscripts of group I (O and A) are of later
date than those of group II, Faral concluded that they attest an
older version of The Conquest, closer to the putative original,
since the vocabulary and formulations used in the members of
group I are often more archaic, and because there are instances
in which the manuscripts of group II seem to offer a more
readily understandable reading, but a less authentic and sometimes misleading one (see § 22 and ch. 1 n. 14, for example).
Faral therefore preferred group I to group II, choosing manuscript O as his base. The only instances in which he felt compelled to correct O were when it offered a unique reading that

conflicted with a reading shared by one of the other members of group I and one or all of the manuscripts in group II; only rarely did he choose to reject the reading of O and other members of group I in favour of a reading attested only in group II, and a full list of variants accompanies his edition. Faral did not 'correct' the sometimes erratic orthography of manuscript O, though he did emend errors of noun declension and adjectival agreement that he felt were likely to have been introduced by copyists.

Neither the manuscript transcribed from Joinville's dictation of *The Life of Saint Louis* nor the copy of the work presented by him to the future Louis X of France in 1309 is extant. Three manuscripts do survive:

1. Paris, Bibliothèque Nationale, ms français 13568 (designated *A*), of the 1330s or 1340s
2. Paris, Bibliothèque Nationale, ms nouvelle acquisition français 6273 (designated *B*), produced 1520–40, in an updated French (of the sixteenth rather than the fourteenth century)
3. Paris, Bibliothèque Nationale, ms français 10148 (designated *L*), produced 1520–40, also in an updated French

In addition, there survive two early printed editions, those of Antoine Pierre de Rieux (Poitiers, 1547) designated *P*, and Claude Ménard (Paris, 1617) designated *M*. While it is clear that manuscripts *B* and *L* are closely related to each other, having shared a model, and that the printed editions *P* and *M* likewise shared a model, the relationship of these pairings to manuscript *A*, and of any of these examplars to Joinville's original or to the presentation copy of Louis X, remains uncertain. Monfrin's task in preparing his edition was therefore a delicate one; while he took the oldest manuscript, *A*, as his base, he could not discount the readings of manuscripts *B* and *L*, and of printed editions *P* and *M*, since in many cases *A* exhibits errors and omissions, and the readings offered by later versions of the text are clearly superior in some instances. Monfrin was obliged to use *A* as his base manuscript (it being the only one copied in French of the fourteenth century), but he could not follow a simple rule in deciding when and how to correct it; he had to make careful judgements wherever there were discrepancies, and his edition provides a list of variants.

The aim in this translation has been to provide a readable modern English rendering of the texts that while not literal is both accurate and clear. By contrast with Shaw's earlier translations, it has been deemed essential to preserve distinctive features of the Old French texts, including ones that might seem unusual or awkward to twenty-first-century readers. These include direct addresses to the readership or audience (for example, §§ 104 and 165 of *The Conquest*), which are important reminders of both the way these works were produced (by dictation) and how they were expected to be read (out loud, and to a group). Similarly, the repetition of specific phrases (as in §§ 7, 9, 11, 13 of *The Life*) may seem heavy-handed, but is an element of authorial style too distinct to be omitted. Effort has been made to vary the vocabulary used within the translation, both to prevent it becoming tiresome to readers and to suggest the variety and richness of meanings possible within Old French, but embellishment or fleshing out of the text has been avoided. In places long and unwieldy sentences have been broken up, or the word order changed, so as to convey the sense of the text clearly; this has happened more often with Joinville's work than with Villehardouin's, since *The Life* is in general less straightforward than *The Conquest* both in terms of its organization of content and the author's style. To avoid confusion, people or places have been identified specifically in some passages of the translation when in the original text only pronouns were used.

The division of both texts into numbered sections (§§), a convention established by the nineteenth-century editions of Natalis de Wailly, has been reproduced here for the convenience of those readers who wish to use this translation in conjunction with editions or secondary works that refer to them. The grouping of these sections into paragraphs does not always reflect that of the manuscripts which, in the case of *The Life* in particular, sometimes included either very long paragraphs or very abbreviated ones; the grouping made here is intended to make the text manageable and easy to follow. Similarly, this translation has been divided into titled chapters so that readers may navigate the texts more easily and comfortably; these divisions are not present in the manuscripts.

Where a standard English equivalent of a person's name or title exists (such as Geoffrey for 'Geoffroy', or John for 'Jean') this has been used, except when the non-English version is the one readers are more likely to know, for example the Venetian doge Enrico Dandolo (rather than 'Henry Dandolo'). Place names are similarly presented in an English version where one exists, generally using the medieval rather than modern form, as in the case of Zara (modern-day Zadar). The use of words and phrases no longer in current use and of foreign words has been avoided, except where no acceptable modern English equivalent exists, and these and other specialist terms are included in the glossary.

Notes to the translation are not intended to be exhaustive but to identify key figures and dates, provide clarifications or corrections on points of fact and highlight details likely to be of particular interest. Readers who would like further information are encouraged to consult the more extensive notes provided by Faral and Monfrin.

NOTES

1. Villehardouin and De Joinville, *Memoirs of the Crusades*, trans. Sir Frank Marzials (New York: Dent, 1908).
2. Joinville and Villehardouin, *Chronicles of the Crusades*, trans. M. R. B. Shaw (Harmondsworth: Penguin, 1963). Villehardouin's and Joinville's works have appeared together in French, though as part of a larger collection of medieval primary sources: *Historiens et Chroniqueurs du Moyen Age: Robert de Clari, Villehardouin, Joinville, Commynes*, ed. Albert Pauphilet (Paris: Editions de la Nouvelle Revue Française, 1938).

Maps

1. Europe and the Mediterranean in the age of Villehardouin and Joinville's Crusades
2. Geoffrey of Villehardouin's 'Romania'

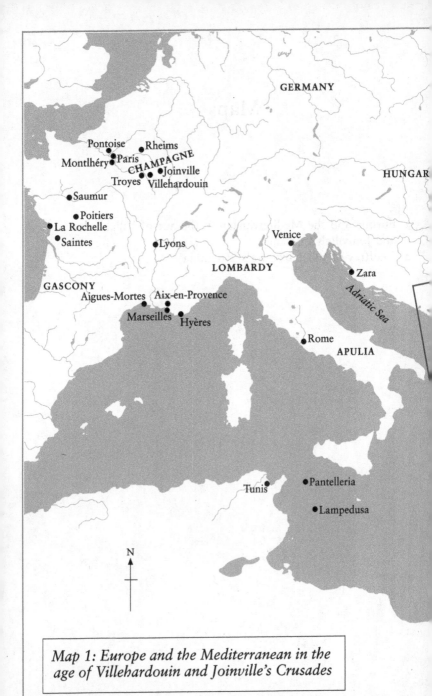

Map 1: *Europe and the Mediterranean in the age of Villehardouin and Joinville's Crusades*

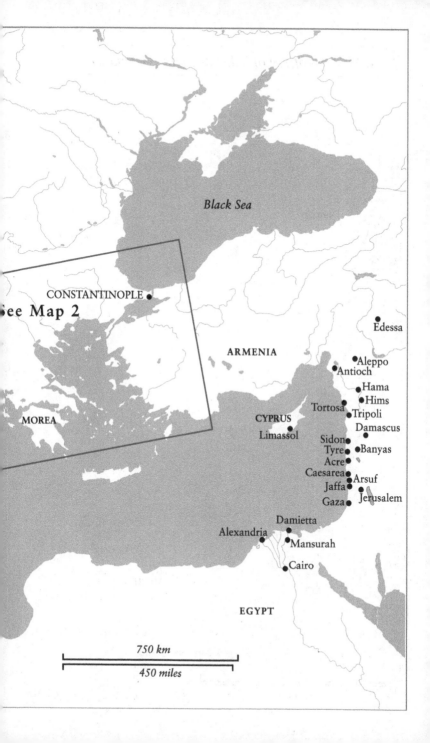

Black Sea

CONSTANTINOPLE •

See Map 2

• Edessa

ARMENIA

•Aleppo
•Antioch

•Hama
•Hims

Tortosa•
•Tripoli

CYPRUS
Limassol•
Damascus

Sidon•
Tyre• •Banyas
Acre•
Caesarea•
Jaffa• •Arsuf
Gaza• •Jerusalem

MOREA

Damietta•
Alexandria•
•Mansurah
Cairo•

EGYPT

750 km

450 miles

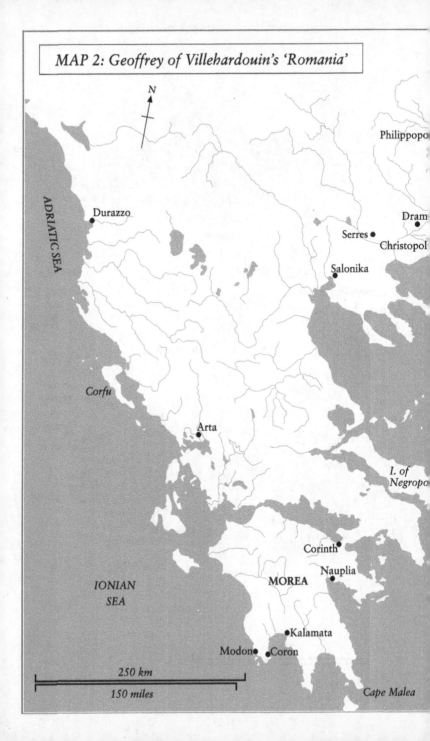

MAP 2: *Geoffrey of Villehardouin's 'Romania'*

N

ADRIATIC SEA

Durazzo

Philippopo

Dram

Serres

Christopol

Salonika

Corfu

Arta

*I. of
Negropo*

Corinth

Nauplia

IONIAN
SEA

MOREA

Kalamata

Modon Coron

250 km

150 miles

Cape Malea

ACHO-BULGARIAN LANDS

BLACK SEA

Thermae • Akilo

Beröe •

Stenimaka •

R. Arda

Adrianople •   Bizöe •

Nikitza •   Arcadiopolis •   Philia •

Bulgarophygon •

Demotika •   Pamphilon •   Tchorlu   Selymbria   CONSTANTINOPLE

Cariopolis •   • Scutari

Rodosto •   Athyra   Chalcedon

Mosynopolis •   Panedon   Heraclea   Charax •

Makri •   Ipsala •   Roussion •   • Nicomedia

Trajanopolis •   Kibotos •

Enos   Apros •   STRAITS OF SAINT GEORGE   • Nicaea

Cyzicus •

Espigal   • Panormos   Leopadeion •

Poemanenos •   • Apollonia

Abydos •

Adramyttion •

AEGEAN SEA

Philadelphia •

I. of Andros

GEOFFREY OF
VILLEHARDOUIN

The Conquest of
Constantinople

Contents

1 Preparations for the Fourth Crusade   5
2 The Crusade Army at Venice   16
3 The Conquest of Zara   22
4 From Zara to Constantinople   30
5 The First Siege of Constantinople   41
6 Alliances Renewed and Abandoned   52
7 The Second Siege of Constantinople   62
8 The Election of an Emperor and its
  Aftermath   69
9 The Latins take Possession of their Lands
  and the Greeks Resist   82
10 Johanitsa's First Campaigns Against the
   Latin Empire   90
11 The Regency of Henry of Hainaut   102
12 War on Two Fronts in Emperor Henry's
   Early Reign   119

CHAPTER I

Preparations for the Fourth Crusade

(1197–1202)

[1] Know that 1197 years after the incarnation of Our Lord Jesus Christ, in the reign of the Roman Pope Innocent, of King Philip of France and of King Richard of England, there was a holy man in France whose name was Fulk of Neuilly.[1] This Neuilly is located between Lagny-sur-Marne and Paris, and he was the parish priest of the town. And this Fulk of whom I speak began to preach God's word in France[2] and in other neighbouring lands, and Our Lord performed many miracles for him. [2] Know that this holy man's renown spread so far that it reached Pope Innocent, who sent word to France and instructed the *preudomme* to preach the cross with papal authority. Later he sent one of his cardinals who had taken the cross, Master Peter Capuano, and through him offered the indulgence I describe here: all those who would take the cross and serve God for a year in the army would be free from all the sins they had committed and confessed. People's hearts were greatly moved because the indulgence was so generous, and many of them took the cross because of this.

[3] In the year following the preaching of the word of God by this *preudomme*, Fulk, a tournament was held in Champagne, at the castle of Ecry. By God's grace it so happened that Thibaut, count of Champagne and Brie, took the cross along with Count Louis of Blois and Chartres.[3] This took place at the start of Advent.[4] Now, you should know that this Count Thibaut was a young man no more than twenty-two years old, and Count Louis no more than twenty-seven. These two counts were nephews and first cousins of the king of France and nephews of the king of England[5] moreover. [4] As well as these

two counts, two of the greatest barons of France took the cross: Simon of Montfort[6] and Renaut of Montmirail. Word spread far and wide through the land when these two eminent men took the cross.

[5] In Count Thibaut of Champagne's lands, Bishop Garnier of Troyes took the cross and so did Count Walter of Brienne, Geoffrey of Joinville (the seneschal of the county) and his brother Robert,[7] Walter of Vignory, Walter of Montbéliard, Eustace of Conflans and his brother Guy of Plessis, Henry of Arzillières, Ogier of Saint-Chéron, Villain of Nully, Geoffrey of Villehardouin (the marshal of Champagne) and his nephew Geoffrey, William of Nully, Walter of Fuligny, Evrard of Montigny, Manassiers of l'Isle, Maccaire of Sainte-Menehould, Milon le Bréban, Guy of Chappes and his nephew Clarembaut, Renaut of Dampierre, John Foisnon, and many other worthy men not mentioned in this book.

[6] Gervase of Châteauneuf and his son Hervé took the cross with Count Louis, as did John of Vierzon, Oliver of Rochefort, Henry of Montreuil, Payen of Orléans, Peter of Bracieux and his brother Hugh, William of Sains, John of Friaize, Walter of Godonville, Hugh of Cormeray and his brother Geoffrey, Hervé of Beauvoir, Robert of Frouville and his brother Peter, Orry of l'Isle, Robert of le Quartier, and many others not mentioned in this book.

[7] In France, Bishop Nivelon of Soissons took the cross and so did Matthew of Montmorency and his nephew Guy the castellan of Coucy,[8] Robert of Ronsoy, Frederick of Yerres and his brother John, Walter of Saint-Denis and his brother Henry, William of Aulnay, Robert Mauvoisin, Dreux of Cressonsacq, Bernard of Moreuil, Enguerrand of Boves and his brother Robert, and many other *preudommes* whom this book will keep quiet about for now.

[8] At the beginning of the following Lent, on Ash Wednesday, Count Baldwin of Flanders and Hainaut[9] took the cross at Bruges along with his wife, Countess Marie, who was Count Thibaut of Champagne's sister. Afterwards the count's brother Henry took the cross and so did his nephew Thierry (the son of the late Count Philip of Flanders), William the advocate of

Béthune and his brother Conon, John of Nesle the castellan of
Bruges, Renier of Trit and his son Renier, Matthew of Walincourt, James of Avesnes, Baldwin of Beauvoir, Hugh of Beaumetz, Gerard of Mauchicourt, Odo of Ham, William of
Gommegnies, Dreux of Beaurain, Roger of Marcke, Eustace
of Salperwick, François of Colemi, Walter of Bousies, Renier
of Mons, Walter of Stombe, Bernard of Somergem, and many
preudommes this book does not speak of.

[9] Afterwards Count Hugh of Saint-Pol took the cross. His
nephew Peter of Amiens took the cross with him, and so did
Eustace of Canteleux, Nicholas of Mailly, Anseau of Cayeux,
Guy of Houdain, Walter of Nesle and his brother Peter, and
many other people we are unsure of. [10] After this Count Geoffrey of Perche took the cross as did his brother Stephen, Rotrou
of Montfort, Yves of la Jaille, Aimery of Villeray, Geoffrey of
Beaumont, and many others whose names I do not know.

[11] Then the barons held a conference at Soissons to discuss
when they should leave and in which direction they should go.
At that time they could not come to any agreement since it
seemed to them that not nearly enough people had taken the
cross so far. Less than two months later in that same year all
the counts and barons who had taken the cross gathered for a
meeting at Compiègne. Many opinions were given and taken,
as a result of which it was determined that they would send
out the best envoys they could find and give them full authority,
equivalent to that of their lords, to attend to all their affairs.

[12] Thibaut, the count of Champagne and Brie, sent two of
these envoys, Baldwin, the count of Flanders and Hainaut, sent
two, and Louis, the count of Blois, sent two. Count Thibaut's
envoys were Geoffrey of Villehardouin, marshal of Champagne, and Milon le Bréban, Count Baldwin's envoys were
Conon of Béthune[10] and Alard Maquereau, and Count Louis's
envoys were John of Friaize and Walter of Godonville. [13] The
counts placed all their business in the hands of these six envoys.
They provided them with the appropriate charters, to which
their seals were attached, declaring that they would be strictly
bound by whatever agreements the six men made in all the
seaports and other towns they visited.

[14] The six envoys set out as you have heard. They conferred together and agreed that they could be confident of finding a greater supply of ships at Venice than at any other port. They rode on, day after day, until they arrived there in the first week of Lent.[11]

[15] The doge of Venice was a most wise and most venerable man whose name was Enrico Dandolo.[12] He and the other people of Venice treated the envoys most honourably and they were very pleased to welcome them. When the envoys presented the letters from their lords, the Venetians were very curious about what business had brought them to their country. In these letters of credence the counts said that their envoys should be trusted as if they were the counts themselves, and that they would be bound by whatever agreements the six men made.

[16] The doge said to them, 'My lords, I have examined your letters. We acknowledge your lords to be the most exalted of men without crowns, and that they instruct us to have faith in what you say to us and to have absolute confidence in the arrangements you make. So, tell us what it is that you would like.'

[17] And the envoys replied, 'Sir, we would like it if you would summon your councillors – tomorrow, if it is convenient for you – and we will tell you what our lords ask of you in their presence.' The doge asked them for a delay of four days; his council would gather then and they could make their request.

[18] They waited until the appointed day and then they went inside the doge's palace, which was very grand and beautiful. They found the doge and his council in a chamber and delivered their message thus: 'Lord doge, we have come to you on behalf of the great barons of France who have been signed with the cross in order to avenge Jesus Christ's dishonour and to conquer Jerusalem, if God so permits. And because they know that no people have such great power as you and your people, they beg you, for the love of God, to have pity on the land overseas and for Jesus Christ's injury, and to consider how they might obtain ships and a fleet.'

[19] 'How would the barons wish to acquire them?' asked

the doge. 'In whatever way that you urge or advise them,' replied the envoys, 'assuming they have the means to do so.' 'This is certainly a substantial request they are making of us,' said the doge, 'and it seems they are planning an ambitious expedition. We will give you our response a week from today. And don't be surprised that this date is a long way off, since it is necessary to give a lot of thought to such a major undertaking.'

[20] At the end of the time set by the doge the envoys returned to the palace. I cannot tell you all the arguments that were put forward and debated there, but this was the doge's final word: 'My lords,' he said, 'we will tell you what we have decided, subject to the approval of our great council and the people of Venice, and you may consider whether you have the will and the means to go ahead.

[21] 'We will build horse transports to carry 4,500 horses and 9,000 squires, with 4,500 knights and 20,000 foot sergeants travelling in ships. And we will agree to provide food for all these horses and people for nine months.[13] This is the minimum we would provide in return for a payment of four marks per horse and two marks per man. [22] All the terms we are offering you would be valid for one year from the day of our departure from the port of Venice to do service to God and Christendom, wherever that might take us. The total cost of what has just been outlined would amount to 94,000 marks.[14] [23] And what's more we will provide, for the love of God, fifty armed galleys, on condition that for as long as our association lasts we will have one half of everything we capture on land or at sea, and you will have the other. Now you should consider whether you have the will and the means to go ahead.'

[24] The envoys left, saying they would confer together and give their response the next day. They consulted and discussed together that night and agreed they should go ahead. The following day they came before the doge and said, 'Sir, we are ready to confirm this arrangement.' And the doge said he would discuss the matter with his people and would let the envoys know what transpired.

[25] The next day, the third after he made his proposal, the doge – who was a most wise and venerable man – summoned

his great council, which was made up of fifty of the wisest men of that land. Using his intelligence and powers of reason – which were both very sound and very sharp – he persuaded them to favour and accept the arrangements. More people were brought into the meeting, first one hundred, then 200 and then 1,000, so that all of them might give their backing and approval. Then at least 10,000 people were gathered together in the church of Saint Mark – the most beautiful church there is – and the doge told them to listen to a Mass of the Holy Spirit and to pray to God for his guidance concerning the request the envoys had made of them. And they did so most willingly. [26] When Mass had been said the doge called for the envoys and instructed them to ask all these people humbly whether it was their will that this agreement be made. The envoys came to the church, where they were observed with great interest by many people who had not seen them before.

[27] With the agreement and approval of the other envoys, Geoffrey of Villehardouin, marshal of Champagne, announced their intentions, and said, 'My lords, the most eminent and powerful barons of France have sent us to you, and they beg you to take pity on Jerusalem, which is enslaved by the Turks, and to be willing, for God's sake, to join them in avenging Jesus Christ's dishonour. They have chosen you for this task since they know that no other people have such a mighty power on the seas as do you and your people. And they have ordered us to prostrate ourselves at your feet and not to get up until you have agreed to take pity on the Holy Land overseas.'

[28] Immediately the six envoys knelt at the feet of the Venetians, weeping heavily. The doge and all the others called out with one voice, their hands reaching to the skies, and said, 'We agree! We agree!' Then there was such a great din and a great uproar that it seemed as if the earth was quaking. [29] When that great din and outpouring of pity had subsided – and no man had ever seen one greater – the good doge of Venice, who was most wise and venerable, climbed up into the pulpit to speak to the people. He said to them, 'My lords, behold the honour God has done you. The finest men in the world have rejected all other people and asked for your partner-

ship in achieving such a noble task as the deliverance of Our Lord.'

[30] I cannot recount to you all the fine and fitting words the doge said, but the matter was settled and charters were prepared the following day, duly drawn up and set in order. When this had been done our intended destination was kept a secret. Cairo had been chosen because it would be easier to destroy the Turks through an attack on Egypt rather than anywhere else, but it was announced simply that we were going overseas. At that time it was Lent, and it was settled that the barons and pilgrims should be at Venice by the feast of Saint John[15] in the following year, 1202 years after the incarnation of Jesus Christ, and that the ships should be ready to receive them.

[31] When the documents had been made and sealed they were brought before the doge at the great palace where the great and small councils were gathered. And when the doge presented them with his charters, he knelt, weeping heavily, and swore on relics to uphold in good faith the terms laid out in them. All his councillors, forty-six in number, did likewise. The envoys responded with their oath to uphold the treaty in good faith, swearing on behalf of their lords and in their own right. Know that many tears of pity were shed there and that both parties immediately sent messengers to Pope Innocent at Rome so that he might confirm their agreement, which he did most willingly.[16]

[32] While at Venice the envoys borrowed 2,000 marks of silver and handed them over to the doge so that work on the fleet might begin. Then they took their leave in order to return to their own country and rode on, day after day, until they arrived at Piacenza in Lombardy. Geoffrey of Villehardouin and Alard Maquereau left the group there to return directly to France, while the others went to Genoa and Pisa to find out what help those cities would offer for the land overseas.

[33] As Geoffrey, marshal of Champagne, crossed the Mont Cenis pass, he met Count Walter of Brienne, who was going to Apulia to conquer lands belonging to his wife, the daughter of King Tancred,[17] whom he had married since taking the cross. Walter of Montbéliard, Eustace of Conflans and Robert of

Joinville were going with him, and a large number of the high-ranking and worthy Champenois men who had taken the cross. [34] When Geoffrey told them the news of their achievements in Venice, they were overjoyed and were very pleased about how things had worked out. They said to him, 'We are already on our way, and when you return to Venice you will find all of us ready there.' But events unfold as God wishes and it so happened that they were unable to join the army later, which was a great pity since they were worthy and brave men. With this they parted ways, each continuing on their own journey.

[35] Marshal Geoffrey rode on, day after day, until he reached Troyes in Champagne, where he found his lord, Count Thibaut, sick and dispirited. But the count was gladdened by Geoffrey's arrival, and when Geoffrey had told him the news of the envoys' achievements, he was so pleased that he said he would go for a ride, which he had not done for a long while. So he got up and set out on his ride, but alas! What a great pity that was! For he never went riding again after that day.

[36] His illness increased and intensified, so much so that he made his will and testament. He divided up the money he had gathered to take on campaign among his vassals and friends, and he had many good ones – no man of his time had more. And he gave an order that each man who received some of this money should swear on relics to commit themselves to the army formed at Venice, as he himself had promised to do. Many of those men did not uphold this oath, and many were rebuked as a result. The count ordered that another portion of his funds be set aside to go with the army, to be spent as and when it would be seen to be of use.

[37] Thus the count died,[18] and of all the men in the world he made the finest end. A large number of his family members and vassals were gathered there. It is not fitting to describe the grief displayed on that occasion, which was greater than that ever shown for any other man. But this was just as it should have been, for no man of his age was loved more by his vassals and by others. He was buried alongside his father[19] in the church of Saint Stephen at Troyes. He was survived by his

wife, the countess; her name was Blanche, and she was most beautiful and most virtuous. She was the daughter of the king of Navarre, and had borne the count a little girl and was pregnant with a son.[20]

[38] When the count had been buried, Matthew of Montmorency, Simon of Montfort, Geoffrey of Joinville (who was seneschal of Champagne) and Marshal Geoffrey went to Duke Odo of Burgundy and said to him, 'Sir, you can see the injury the land overseas has sustained. We wish to urge you, for God's sake, to take the cross and aid the land overseas in place of the count. We would hand over all his funds to you and would swear on relics, and make others swear too, to serve you loyally, just as we would have done him.' [39] He chose to refuse. You should know that he could have chosen much better. Geoffrey of Joinville was charged with taking the same message to Count Thibaut of Bar-le-Duc, who was the cousin of the late count of Champagne. And he too refused.

[40] Count Thibaut of Champagne's death was of grave concern to the pilgrims and to all those who were due to enter God's service. They held a conference at Soissons at the end of the month[21] to determine what they could do. In attendance were Count Baldwin of Flanders and Hainaut, Count Louis of Blois and Chartres, Count Geoffrey of Perche, Count Hugh of Saint-Pol and many other *preudommes*.

[41] Marshal Geoffrey told them what had been said and offered to the duke of Burgundy and the count of Bar-le-Duc, and how these men had refused. 'Pay attention, my lords,' he said. 'I will give you one piece of advice, if you will allow me. Marquis Boniface of Montferrat[22] is a fine *preudomme*, and one of the most highly respected men alive today. If you were to ask him to come here, to take the sign of the cross and put himself in the count of Champagne's place, and if you were to give him the leadership of the army, he would accept straightaway.' [42] Many views were expressed, both for and against, but the conclusion of the debate was one to which everyone gave their assent, both the great men and the lesser. Letters were written and messengers chosen to fetch the marquis. He came on the appointed day, via Champagne and through

France, where he was received with great honour by his cousin, the king of France, among others.

[43] He went to a conference called at Soissons, where there were a great many of the counts and barons and crusaders. When they heard that the marquis was coming they went out to meet him and showed him great honour. The next morning the conference convened in an orchard at the abbey of my lady Saint Mary of Soissons. There they asked the marquis to accept what they had offered him, pleading with him, for God's sake, to take the cross, to take up leadership of the army, to fill Thibaut of Champagne's place and to take charge of his funds and his men. They fell down at his feet, weeping heavily, and he in turn fell at their feet, saying he would do so most willingly.

[44] Thus the marquis responded to their pleas and assumed leadership of the army. Straightaway the bishop of Soissons, my lord Fulk the holy man and two Cistercian abbots whom he had brought with him from his country led him into the church of Our Lady and fastened the cross to his shoulder. And so that conference came to an end; the next day the marquis took his leave to return to his country and set his affairs in order. He said that each man should do likewise, and that he would meet them in Venice.

[45] The marquis left to attend the chapter of the Cistercians held at Cîteaux on the feast of the Holy Cross in September.[23] There he found a very large number of the abbots and barons and other people; my lord Fulk went there to preach the cross. Odo the Champenois of Champlitte and his brother William took the cross there, as did Richard of Dampierre and his brother Odo, Guy of Pesmes and his brother Aimon, Guy of Conflans and many good men from Burgundy whose names are not written down here. Then the bishop of Autun took the cross and so did Count Guy of Forez, Hugh of Berzé (both father and son of that name)[24] and Hugh of Coligny. Further south, in Provence, Peter Bremond also took the cross, along with a good number of others whose names are not known.

[46] Thus the barons and pilgrims were making preparations throughout many lands. But alas! What a great misfortune befell them the following Lent, just before they were due to

I PREPARATIONS FOR THE FOURTH CRUSADE 15

depart! Count Geoffrey of Perche was bedridden by illness. He made his will so that his funds and the leadership of his men within the army would pass to his brother, Stephen. The pilgrims would gladly have avoided this exchange if God had so willed it.[25] In this way the count met his end and died, which was truly a great loss since he was an eminent and honoured baron and a good knight. Great grief was shown throughout his lands.

CHAPTER 2

The Crusade Army at Venice

(April–September 1202)

[47] After Easter, as Pentecost approached,[1] the pilgrims began to set out from their homelands. Know that many tears of sorrow were shed as they left their lands, their people and their friends. They rode through Burgundy and across the Alps, and, having made their way via Mont Cenis and Lombardy, they started to assemble at Venice. They encamped on an island in the harbour which is named after Saint Nicholas.[2]

[48] Around that time a fleet left Flanders by sea, carrying a great number of good men-at-arms. The leaders of that fleet were John of Nesle the castellan of Bruges, Thierry, son of Count Philip of Flanders, and Nicholas of Mailly. They made a promise to Count Baldwin of Flanders, sworn on relics, that they would go through the Straits of Morocco[3] and join the count and the army forming at Venice at whatever location they heard the army had set out for. Because of this the count and his brother Henry sent with the fleet some of their own ships, loaded with clothing and food and other provisions. [49] This fleet was very fine and well supplied. The count of Flanders and the pilgrims set great store by it since the majority of their valued sergeants departed with this fleet. But they did not keep the promise they had made to their lord and all the other pilgrims, because these men (like many others) were afraid of the great danger that the army gathered at Venice had undertaken to face.

[50] The army was let down in this way by the bishop of Autun, Count Guy of Forez, Peter Bremond and plenty of others, who were greatly blamed as a result and achieved little where they did go. Among the French, Bernard of Moreuil let

them down and so did Hugh of Chaumont, Henry of Airaines, John of Villers, Walter of Saint-Denis and his brother Hugh, and many others who refused to travel to Venice on account of the peril awaiting them there. They went instead to Marseilles. They were greatly dishonoured and heavily blamed for this, and they encountered great misfortune afterwards.

[51] Now we will leave these men aside to tell you about the pilgrims, of whom a large number had already arrived at Venice. Count Baldwin of Flanders had already come, along with many others. News reached them there that large numbers of the pilgrims had taken other routes to other ports, and this prompted great concern because they would not be able to keep their side of the treaty or pay the money they owed to the Venetians.

[52] The leaders at Venice decided among themselves that they should send trustworthy envoys to Count Louis of Blois and Chartres and to the other pilgrims who had not yet arrived to reassure them and to implore them to have pity on the land overseas, as well as to warn them that no other route held the prospect of success except that via Venice. [53] Count Hugh of Saint-Pol and Geoffrey, marshal of Champagne, were chosen as envoys. They rode out to Pavia in Lombardy, where they found Count Louis with a great many good knights and good men. Through their words of reassurance and entreaty they steered significant numbers of men towards Venice who had been going to other ports by other routes.

[54] Nonetheless, many good men left at Piacenza to follow alternative routes that took them to Apulia. Among them was Villain of Nully, who was one of the best knights in the world, Henry of Arzillières, Renaut of Dampierre, Henry of Long-champ and Giles of Trazegnies. He was Count Baldwin of Flanders and Hainaut's liegeman, to whom the count had given 500 *livres* of his own money so that he might join him on the expedition. Along with these men went a great many knights and sergeants whose names are not written down here.

[55] This meant that many fewer people went to join the army at Venice which – as you will hear later – met with great misfortune as a result.

[56] Thus Count Louis and the other barons arrived at Venice, where they were received with great celebration and joy, and set up camp on the island of Saint Nicholas with the others. The army was a most impressive one, made up of worthy men; no one has ever seen an army more impressive or with so many combatants. The Venetians opened markets for them that were sufficiently well stocked to meet all the needs of men and horses. The fleet they had prepared was so well equipped and handsome that no Christian man has ever seen another more handsome or better equipped, and in fact there were enough *nefs*, galleys and horse transports for at least three times the number of people in the army.

[57] Oh! What great damage was done when the others who went to different ports did not go to Venice! Christendom would certainly have been exalted and the land of the Turks laid low. The Venetians had fulfilled their side of the agreement very well and done more besides, and now that they were ready to get under way they called on the counts and the barons to uphold their side of the agreement and pay them their money. [58] Fees for passage were sought within the army. There were numerous people who said they could not pay their own way in full, and the barons took whatever they could get from them. In this way people in the army paid the cost of their passage – as far as they could – when the barons requested it. But once these payments had been collected, the barons did not have even half the sum they needed.

[59] The barons conferred among themselves and they said, 'Sirs, the Venetians have upheld our agreement to the letter and have done more besides, but we do not have nearly enough people to pay them what we owe with fees for passage. This is the fault of those who went to other ports. So each of us should, for God's sake, give some of our own money so that we might meet our commitments. It would be better for us to hand over all our money than to default – which would mean that we would forfeit all we have raised and that we would have broken our agreement – for if the army disbands the delivery of the land overseas will be abandoned.' [60] There were strong objections to this from the majority of the barons and of the

other people. They said, 'We have paid for our passage. If the
Venetians are willing to take us, we will gladly go. But if they
are not willing, we will take care of ourselves and make our
way by other means.' They said this because they wanted the
army to disband. Those on the opposing side said, 'We would
rather offer all our money and set out with the army in poverty
than see it broken up and destroyed, for God will certainly
repay us when it pleases him.'

[61] The count of Flanders began to hand over whatever he
had and whatever he could borrow. Count Louis did likewise
and so did Marquis Boniface, Count Hugh of Saint-Pol, and
those who supported their party. You would have seen many
beautiful dishes of gold and silver carried to the doge's lodgings
as payment. When they had paid what they could they still
lacked 34,000 marks of silver from what they owed. This was
very pleasing to those who had held on to their money, not
wishing to offer anything, since they were sure the army would
be abandoned and broken up. But God, who gives hope to the
hopeless, did not wish this to happen.

[62] The doge spoke to his people, saying, 'My lords, these
men cannot pay us anything more. Whatever we have been paid
by them is ours to keep under the terms of an agreement
they cannot now fulfil. But our right to it would not be upheld
by everyone, rather we and our country would be soundly
blamed. So let's make them an offer. [63] The king of Hungary
has captured Zara in Slavonia⁴ from us, which is one of the
strongest cities in the world. We will never recover the city with
our own forces except we have the help of these men. Let's ask
them to help us take Zara, in return for which we will suspend
their debt to us of 34,000 marks of silver until such time as
God allows us and the pilgrims to win sufficient booty together.'
These were the terms on which the offer was made. There was
much opposition from those who wanted the army to disband,
but the agreement was made and confirmed nonetheless.

[64] They gathered one Sunday in the church of Saint Mark
where a great feast was being celebrated⁵ with the Venetians
and most of the barons and pilgrims in attendance. [65] Before
high Mass had begun the doge of Venice, whose name was

Enrico Dandolo, climbed up into the pulpit and spoke to his people, saying, 'My lords, you are joined with the finest men in the world in the most noble endeavour anyone has ever undertaken. I am an old and weak man and am in need of rest – my body is ailing. But I see that no one knows how to lead and command you as I, your lord, can. If you are willing to consent to my taking the sign of the cross in order to protect and guide you, while my son stays here to defend this land in my place, I will go to live or die with you and the pilgrims.'

[66] And when they heard this, everyone cried out with one voice, 'We beg you for God's sake to do so, to go ahead and come with us.' [67] There was a great outpouring of compassion among the Venetians and the pilgrims, and many tears were shed because this *preudomme* had such good reason to stay. He was an old man, and although he had handsome eyes in his head, he could not see at all, having lost his eyesight after sustaining a head wound.[6] But he had plenty of heart. Oh! How unlike him were the people who had gone to other ports, wanting to stay out of harm's way!

[68] He then stepped down from the pulpit and went before the altar. Weeping heavily, he got down on his knees and a cross was sewn on to a large cotton cap for him. This was because he wanted people to be able to see it. The Venetians began to take the cross in great throngs and large numbers; only a very small number of them had taken the cross up to that day. Our pilgrims were overjoyed and greatly moved by the doge's cross-taking, on account of his wisdom and accomplishments.

[69] The doge took the cross as you have heard, and then the *nefs*, galleys and horse transports began to be handed over to the barons for departure. So much time had already passed that September was upon us.

[70] Now you will hear about one of the most amazing and most momentous occurrences of which you have ever been told. At that time there was an emperor at Constantinople whose name was Isaac. He had a brother whose name was Alexius,[7] whom he had ransomed from a Turkish prison. This Alexius seized his brother the emperor, put the eyes out of his head and made himself emperor through the treacherous act of which

you were just told. Alexius kept Isaac in captivity for a long time along with one of his sons, who was also called Alexius. This son later escaped from prison and fled in a boat to a coastal city called Ancona. From there Alexius went to King Philip of Germany, who had married his sister.[8] He came to Verona in Lombardy and stayed for a while in that town, where he encountered numerous pilgrims who were on their way to join the army.

[71] The people who had helped Alexius escape and who remained with him, said to him, 'Sir, take note that there is an army close by at Venice of the finest men and the best knights in the world, who are going overseas. You should appeal to them to take pity on you and your father, who were so unjustly dispossessed. If they are willing to help you, you should do whatever they ask of you. There's a chance they might be moved by your plight.' Alexius said that he would do this very gladly and that their advice was sound.

[72] And so he chose his messengers and sent them to Marquis Boniface of Montferrat,[9] who was the leader of the army, and to the other barons. When the barons gave them an audience, they were greatly taken aback by what they heard and replied, 'We quite understand what you're saying. We will send envoys to King Philip in company with Alexius, who is on his way there now. If Alexius is willing to aid us in the recovery of the land overseas, we will help him conquer his lands, which we understand were usurped unjustly from him and his father.' Thus envoys were sent to Germany, to the young prince from Constantinople and to King Philip of Germany.

[73] Before the events we have just described, news arrived in the host which greatly saddened the barons and the other people; lord Fulk the holy man, the saintly man who had first preached the cross, had met his end and had died.

[74] Following this episode a company of very fine men from the German empire arrived, which was a cause for great joy. The bishop of Halberstadt had come, along with Count Berthold of Katzenellenbogen, Werner of Borlanden, Dietrich of Looz, Henry of Ulm, Dietrich of Diest, Roger of Suitre, Alexander of Villers and Wierich of Daun.

CHAPTER 3

The Conquest of Zara

(October 1202–March 1203)

[75] Then the ships and the horse transports were distributed among the barons. Ah, God! What fine warhorses were put on board! When the ships had been loaded with arms and food, and the knights and sergeants had embarked, their shields were hung round the sides and on the ships' castles alongside their banners, of which there were many splendid ones. [76] Know that they were carrying more than 300 petraries and mangonels in those ships, and many of every kind of machine useful for capturing a city. No finer fleet ever set sail from any port. This took place during the week following the feast of Saint Rémy,[1] 1202 years after the incarnation of Jesus Christ. Thus they left the harbour at Venice, as you have just heard.

[77] On the eve of the feast of Saint Martin,[2] they arrived before Zara in Slavonia and saw the city fortified with lofty walls and tall towers; you would have sought a finer, stronger, more impressive city in vain. And when the pilgrims saw it they were greatly astounded and said to one another, 'How could such a city be taken by force, unless God himself brought it about?'

[78] The first ships to arrive before the city dropped anchor to wait for the others. The following morning the weather was particularly fine and clear, and all the galleys arrived along with the horse transports and other ships behind them. They took the harbour by force, breaking the chain[3] (which was a very strong and well-made one), and then went ashore on the opposite side of the port from the city. You would then have seen many knights and many sergeants come out of the ships, and many fine warhorses unloaded from the horse transports along

with many fine tents and many pavilions. The army thus set up camp and laid siege to Zara on the feast of Saint Martin.

[79] At that point not all the barons had arrived. The marquis of Montferrat had not yet come; he had stayed behind to attend to some business of his own. Stephen of Perche remained unwell and at Venice, and Matthew of Montmorency likewise. When they had recovered, Matthew of Montmorency came to join the army at Zara. But Stephen of Perche did not act so properly, for he abandoned the army and went to spend some time in Apulia. With him went Rotrou of Montfort and Yves of la Jaille, as well as many others who were scorned as a result. They took the March passage to Syria.[4]

[80] The day after the feast of Saint Martin some of Zara's people left the city and came to talk to the doge of Venice, who was in his pavilion. They told him they would surrender the city and all their possessions to his authority if their lives would be spared. And the doge said that he would in no way accept this offer or any other unless it was done on the advice of the counts and barons; he would go and discuss the matter with them.

[81] While he went to speak to the counts and barons, the group of men you have heard about before, who wanted the army to disband, talked to the messengers from Zara, saying, 'Why do you want to surrender your city? The pilgrims won't attack you, you have nothing to fear from them. If you can defend yourselves against the Venetians, you'll be safe.' One of these men, whose name was Robert of Boves, was chosen to go to the walls of the town and spread the same word there. Then the messengers returned to the city, and negotiations were suspended.

[82] When the doge of Venice came to the counts and barons, he said to them, 'My lords, the people inside want to surrender the city to my power if their lives will be spared. I will not accept this offer or any other unless it is on your advice.' And the barons replied to him, 'Sir, we advise you to accept, and moreover we urge you to do so.' He said he would do this. They all returned together to the doge's pavilion to conclude the agreement, only to find that the messengers had already left on the advice of those who wanted the army to break up.

[83] The abbot of Vaux[5] (a Cistercian monastery) then stood up and said to them, 'My lords, on behalf of the Roman Pope I forbid you to lay siege to this city. For it is a Christian city and you are pilgrims.' When the doge heard this he was greatly angered and annoyed. He said to the counts and barons, 'My lords, this city was ready to submit to me and your men have taken it from me. You made an agreement with me to help me capture it, and I now call on you to do so.'

[84] The counts and barons and those who supported their party all began to speak at once, 'Those who sabotaged this agreement have acted outrageously; not a day has passed without them working to break up the army. We will be shamed if we do not help him take the city.' They went to the doge and said to him, 'Sir, we will help you capture the city in spite of those who are against it.'

[85] Thus their decision was made. The next morning they went and made camp in front of the gates of the city, setting up their petraries and mangonels and other engines, of which they had a great number. On the seaward side of the city scaling ladders were mounted on the ships. The petraries began to take shots at the walls and towers of the city. This assault lasted a good five days. Then they set the miners to work on one of the towers where they began to undermine the wall. When those inside saw this they asked for a truce on the same terms they had rejected because of the advice of those who wanted the army to break up.

[86] In this way the town was surrendered to the authority of the Venetian doge and the lives of the inhabitants spared. The doge came to the counts and barons and said to them, 'My lords, we have captured this city through God's grace and your own. Winter has come and we won't be able to set out from here until Easter since we wouldn't find a source of provisions anywhere else. This city is very rich and well stocked with all we might need; let's divide the town in two, one half for us and the other half for you.' [87] This was done as had been agreed. The Venetians had the half of the city towards the port, where the ships were anchored, and the French had the other. Then the lodgings on each side were allocated appropriately,

and the army decamped and came to take up quarters inside the city.

[88] On the third day after they had taken up their lodgings, a great calamity struck the army around the hour of vespers. A fight broke out between some of the Venetians and the French, a very widespread and very fierce one. Men were running to arms throughout the city, and the commotion was so great that there were few streets where there was not intense fighting with swords, lances, crossbows and bolts. Many people were wounded or killed.

[89] But the Venetians could not continue to fight; they began to lose heavily. The *preudommes* of the army, wishing to put an end to this wickedness, came fully armed into the midst of the brawl and began to break it up. Having put a stop to the fight in one place, they had to start the process again in another. This situation lasted well into the night, and it was only with great effort and great suffering that the fighting was broken up everywhere. Know that this was the greatest cause for grief any army ever knew; the whole force could easily have been lost. But God would not permit it.

[90] Great losses were suffered on both sides. A high-ranking Flemish man called Giles of Landas was killed there; he was struck in the eye and died of this wound in the course of the fight along with many others whose deaths were less widely spoken of. The doge of Venice and the barons had to work hard all the following week to keep the peace in the wake of this brawl, but their efforts were sufficient so that peace was maintained, thanks be to God.

[91] Two weeks later Marquis Boniface of Montferrat arrived (he had been absent until then), as did Matthew of Montmorency, Peter of Bracieux and many other *preudommes*. After another two weeks the envoys arrived from Germany who had been sent by King Philip and the young prince of Constantinople. The barons and the doge of Venice gathered at a palace where the doge had taken up residence. The messengers began to speak, saying, 'Sirs, we have been sent to you by King Philip and the son of the emperor of Constantinople, the brother of the king's wife.

[92] ' "My lords," says the king, "I am sending you my wife's brother, and in doing so I place him in the hands of God – may he save the young man from death – and in yours. Since you have left home in the cause of God, right and justice, you should, if you are able, restore their inheritance to those who have been wrongly dispossessed. And Alexius will offer you the most favourable terms ever offered to anyone and give you the greatest possible assistance in conquering the land overseas. [93] First, if God permits you to restore him to his inheritance, he will place the entire empire of Romania in obedience to Rome, from which it has formerly been cut off. Secondly, he understands that you have spent your own money and that you are now poor. Therefore, he will give you 200,000 marks of silver and provisions for the whole army, both the great men and the lesser. He will also go with you in person to the land of Egypt, accompanied by 10,000 men (or he will send them at his expense, if you think that would be better). He will provide you with such service for one year. And throughout his life he will maintain 500 knights in the land overseas, supported with his own money."

[94] 'Sirs,' said the envoys, 'we have been given full authority to conclude these negotiations if you wish to go ahead on your part. You should know that no offer so large has ever been made to anyone; he who refuses it has no great urge for conquest.' The counts and barons told them that they would discuss the matter, and a council was held the following day. When they had all assembled the envoys' offer was laid before them.

[95] Many points of view were expressed. The Cistercian abbot of Vaux spoke along with those who wanted the army to disband. They said they could not agree to this at all, for they would be campaigning against Christians. This was certainly not what they had set out to do; they wanted to go to Syria instead. [96] Those on the other side responded, 'Dear lords, you cannot achieve anything in Syria, as you can well see from the example of those who abandoned us to take themselves off to other ports. You should know that if the land overseas is ever to be recovered, it will be achieved by way of either Egypt or Greece, and that if we reject this treaty we will be forever shamed.'

[97] And so the army was in discord. You should not be surprised that the laymen were in disagreement, since the white monks of the Cistercian order within the army were equally divided. The abbot of Loos,⁶ who was a very holy man and a *preudomme,* and other abbots who sided with him preached sermons and urged people for God's sake to keep the army together and to go along with the treaty, for this was the means by which the land overseas could most easily be recovered. And in turn the abbot of Vaux and those who followed him preached very frequently, saying that all this was wrong and that they would rather go to the land of Syria and do what they could there.

[98] At that point Marquis Boniface of Montferrat asserted his position together with Baldwin, count of Flanders and Hainaut, Count Louis of Blois and Count Hugh of Saint-Pol and their followers. They said they would support the treaty; it would be dishonourable to refuse it. Then they went to the doge's residence, the king of Germany's envoys were summoned and the leaders of the army confirmed the agreement, as it was described to you earlier, with sworn oaths and sealed charters.

[99] This book's report to you is that only twelve oaths were sworn by the French party;⁷ no more could be secured. Among those to swear were the marquis of Montferrat, Count Baldwin of Flanders, Count Louis of Blois and Chartres, Count Hugh of Saint-Pol and eight other men who sided with them. In this way the treaty was concluded, the charters drawn up and the time fixed when the young prince should arrive: two weeks after Easter.

[100] Thus the French army stayed for the whole of that winter at Zara, opposed by the king of Hungary. Know that men's hearts knew no peace, for one group strove to break up the army and the other to keep it together.

[101] Many of the rank and file ran away in merchants' ships. A good 500 made off in one ship; all of them drowned and were lost. Another group ran away over land, thinking to escape through Slavonia, but the peasants of that land attacked them and killed a good number of them. The rest fled back to the army. In this way the army was severely depleted with each

passing day. Around the same time one man of high rank in the army, Werner of Borlanden from Germany, arranged to be taken away in a merchant ship and abandoned the army; he was greatly blamed for this.

[102] It was not long after this that one of the high-ranking French barons, Renaut of Montmirail, who had the support of Count Louis, begged to be sent as a messenger to Syria in one of the fleet's ships. He swore with his right hand on relics (all the knights going with him did the same) that within two weeks of arriving in Syria and having passed on their message they would return to the army. With this agreement he left the army along with his nephew Hervé of Châteauneuf, William the vidame of Chartres, Geoffrey of Beaumont, John of Frouville and his brother Peter and many others. But they did not keep the oaths they swore at all well, for they did not return to the army.

[103] Then some news arrived in the camp which was very gladly received. This was that the Flemish fleet you heard about earlier[8] had arrived at Marseilles. John of Nesle the castellan of Bruges (the leader of that force), Thierry the son of Count Philip of Flanders and Nicholas of Mailly informed the count of Flanders, their lord, that they would spend the winter at Marseilles and that he should let them know his wishes so that they might do as he commanded. Having taken advice from the doge of Venice and from the other barons, he ordered them to set sail at the end of March and to come to meet him at the port of Modon in Romania. But alas! They were untrue to their word and never fulfilled this agreement with the barons. Instead they went to Syria, where they knew they would not achieve anything. [104] Now you may know, my lords, that if God had not loved this army it could certainly not have held together, seeing as so many people wished it ill.

[105] The barons conferred among themselves and decided they would send envoys to the pope at Rome because he harboured ill feeling towards them on account of the capture of Zara. Two knights and two clerics whom the barons knew would be capable of this mission were chosen as the messengers. One of the clerics was Bishop Nivelon of Soissons, and the other

Master John of Noyon, who was Count Baldwin of Flanders's chancellor. Of the knights one was John of Friaize and the other Robert of Boves. They swore faithfully on relics to deliver their message in good faith and to return to the army.

[106] Three of them kept their word well and the fourth badly. This was Robert of Boves, who carried out his mission in the worst possible way, broke his promise and took himself off to Syria after the others. The other three did very well and delivered their message just as the barons had requested, saying to the pope, 'The barons beg you to forgive them for the capture of Zara. They did this as men would who had no better option, and this was because of the defection of those who had gone to other ports and because otherwise they would not have been able to keep the army together. And they call on you, as they would their loving father, to give them your orders, which they are ready to obey.'

[107] The pope told the envoys that he knew well that they were constrained to do this because of others' failings. He had great pity for them on this account and sent his greetings to the barons and pilgrims, telling them that he absolved them as his sons.[9] He instructed them and begged them to keep the army together because he well understood that without that army no service to God could be performed. And he gave full authority to Bishop Nivelon of Soissons and Master John of Noyon to bind and loose the pilgrims until such time as the cardinal joined the army.

CHAPTER 4

From Zara to Constantinople

(April–June 1203)

[108] So much time had passed that Lent had already arrived. The barons prepared their fleet to sail at Easter.[1] When the ships were loaded, on the day after Easter, the pilgrims set up camp outside the town by the port, while the Venetians razed the city to the ground along with its towers and walls.

[109] And then an episode unfolded which was of grave concern to the people in the army. One of the high-ranking barons, whose name was Simon of Montfort, had made a pact with the king of Hungary, who was an enemy of the army, to go over to his side and abandon the army. With him went his brother Guy of Montfort, Simon of Neauphle, Robert Mauvoisin, Dreux of Cressonsacq, the abbot of Vaux (who was a monk of the Cistercian order) and many others. And it was not long after this that another high-ranking man in the army called Enguerrand of Boves left with his brother Hugh. They took with them as many people from their country as they could.

[110] These people left the army as you have heard. This was a great injury to the army and a shame to those who inflicted it. Then the ships and transports began to set sail, and it was decided that they should take port at Corfu, an island that was part of Romania. Those who arrived first would await those who followed until they had all gathered. And so they did.

[111] Before the doge and the marquis set off from the harbour at Zara with the galleys, Alexius, son of Emperor Isaac of Constantinople, arrived there having been sent by King Philip of Germany. He was welcomed with very great joy and very great honour. The doge provided him with such galleys and

vessels as he needed, and thus they set sail from the port of Zara. With a good wind they sailed as far as Durazzo, where the inhabitants surrendered the town to their lord very willingly when they saw him, and swore their loyalty to him.

[112] They set sail from Durazzo and arrived at Corfu where they found the army encamped in front of the town, with tents and pavilions set up and horses taken ashore from the transports to be fed and exercised. And when they heard that the emperor of Constantinople's son had arrived, you would have seen many good knights and good sergeants rush to greet him leading many fine warhorses. Thus Alexius was welcomed with very great joy and very great honour. He pitched his tent in the middle of the camp, and the marquis of Montferrat set his own up next to it; King Philip had entrusted Alexius, whose sister he had married, to the marquis's care.

[113] They remained on that most rich and fertile island for three weeks, but during their stay a hard and onerous misfortune befell them. A large number of those who wanted the army to break up and who had previously worked to undermine it talked among themselves and said that this expedition seemed to them likely to be very long and very dangerous, and so they would stay on the island and let the army leave. With help from the people of Corfu they would, once the army had departed, send word to Count Walter of Brienne, who held Brindisi at that time, that he should send ships to take them there.

[114] I cannot give you the names of all those involved in this affair. But I will tell you the names of some of the main ringleaders. They included Odo the Champenois of Champlitte, James of Avesnes, Peter of Amiens, Guy the castellan of Coucy, Ogier of Saint-Chéron, Guy of Chappes and his nephew Clarembaut, William of Aulnay, Peter Coiseau, Guy of Pesmes and his brother Aimon, Guy of Conflans, Richard of Dampierre and his brother Odo, and many others who assured them privately that they would join their party but who dared not do so openly out of shame. And indeed this book bears witness that more than half the army were in agreement with them.

[115] When the marquis of Montferrat and Count Baldwin of Flanders, Count Louis and the count of Saint-Pol, and the

barons who sided with them heard about this they were greatly
distressed and said, 'Sirs, we are in a wretched situation: if these
men leave us, in addition to those who already have done so at
numerous other points, our army will be doomed and we will
be unable to conquer anything. Let's go to them and beg them
for God's sake to take pity on themselves and on us, to resist
dishonouring themselves and not to impede the delivery of the
land overseas.'

[116] This plan was agreed upon and they all went together
to a valley where the other party was in conference, taking with
them the emperor of Constantinople's son and all the bishops
and abbots in the army. When they arrived in the valley they
got down on foot and the members of the other party, seeing
them arrive, dismounted from their horses and went to meet
them. The barons fell at their feet, weeping heavily, and said
they would not move until the men there had promised not to
leave them.

[117] And when these men saw this they felt great compassion and wept bitterly to see their lords, their relations and
their friends fall at their feet. They said that they would discuss
the matter, and took themselves aside to confer. The conclusion
of their discussion was that they would stay with the barons
until the feast of Saint Michael[2] on condition that the barons
would swear on relics, as was customary, that at whatever
point after that date the others should so request it, the barons
would within two weeks, in good faith and without any trickery, provide them with a fleet that would take them to Syria.
[118] This pact was approved and sealed with sworn oaths.
And there was then great joy throughout the army, and the
people returned to the ships and the horses were put into the
transports.

[119] They left the port of Corfu on the eve of Pentecost[3]
1203 years after the incarnation of Our Lord Jesus Christ. All
the army's *nefs*, all its horse transports and all its galleys were
gathered there, along with a good number of other merchant
ships that set sail with them. The day was fine and clear, the
wind pleasant and gentle. They unfurled their sails to the wind.
[120] Geoffrey, marshal of Champagne – who dictated this

work without ever knowingly telling a lie, and was present at all the councils it records – gives sure witness that such a beautiful sight was never seen. It certainly seemed that this was a fleet destined to conquer lands for, as far as the eye could see, all that could be seen were the sails of ships and other vessels and this filled men's hearts with joy.

[121] Thus they sailed the sea until they reached Cape Malea and the straits in the sea[4] there, where they came across two ships carrying pilgrims, knights and sergeants who were on their way back from Syria. These were some of the people who had sailed from the port of Marseilles. When they saw the fleet, so beautiful and well-equipped, they were so ashamed that they dared not show themselves. Count Baldwin of Flanders and Hainaut sent his ship's boat to find out who these people were, and they identified themselves. [122] One sergeant let himself down over the side of the ship into the boat. He called out to the people on board the ship, 'Whatever belongings of mine are still on board are yours. I'm going with these men, since it looks certain they must conquer lands.' This was a great credit to the sergeant and he was warmly welcomed in the army. And it is because of this that it is said that one can turn back from a thousand wicked ways.

[123] The army sailed on as far as Negroponte,[5] which is a very fine island with a very fine town, also called Negroponte. The barons held a council there, and Marquis Boniface of Montferrat and Count Baldwin of Flanders and Hainaut set out with a large number of the transports and galleys, taking Emperor Isaac's son to an island called Andros. When they came ashore the knights in this party armed themselves and overran the land. The people of the island surrendered themselves to Emperor Isaac's son, and gave him enough of their wealth to make peace with him.

[124] They got back on board their ships and made their way across the sea. A great misfortune then befell them; a high-ranking man called Guy, the castellan of Coucy, died and his body was cast into the sea.

[125] The other ships, those that had not turned off along that course, had entered the mouth of the Abydos channel,

where the Straits of Saint George enter the open sea.[6] They sailed up the straits to the very fine and well-situated city of Abydos, which sits on the side of the Straits of Saint George that lay towards the land of the Turks. They took port there and went ashore, and the people of the city came out to meet them and surrendered the town to them, as if they dared not try to defend it. And the army protected the town very well, so that its inhabitants did not lose even a *denier*'s worth of their property. [126] They stayed there for a week to wait for the *nefs*, galleys and transports that were yet to arrive. During that time they collected grain from the land since it was harvest time. They had great need of it because their supplies were low. In the course of that week all the ships and the barons arrived; God gave them fair weather.

[127] Then they all set sail together from the port of Abydos, and you could have seen the Straits of Saint George to the east abloom with *nefs* and galleys and transports; it was a wondrous thing to behold this beautiful sight. And so they sailed up the Straits of Saint George until they reached the abbey of Saint Stephen, three leagues from Constantinople. There the people on board the *nefs*, galleys and transports had a full view of Constantinople. They took port and anchored their vessels.

[128] Now you may be assured that those who had never seen Constantinople before gazed at it for a long time, barely believing there was such a great city in all the world. They saw its high walls and mighty towers, with which the city was completely encircled, as well as the fine palaces and impressive churches, of which there were so many that none could believe it if he did not see it with his own eyes, and they could be seen the length and breadth of the city, which is the sovereign of all others. Know that there was no man there so bold that his flesh did not tremble, which should come as no surprise for never was such a great project undertaken by as many men[7] since the creation of the world.

[129] The counts and the barons and the doge of Venice then went ashore and held a conference in the church of Saint Stephen. Many opinions were stated and heard there. This book cannot recount to you all the arguments that were made, but

the conclusion of the council came when the doge of Venice rose to his feet and said to them, [130] 'My lords, I know more about the situation in this country than you do, for I have been here before.[8] Yours is the most pressing business and the most perilous enterprise any men have ever undertaken, and because of this it is necessary for us to proceed carefully. You should know that if we were to make our way over land, the territory is vast and open and as our people are poor and short of supplies, they would spread out across the land looking for food. There is a very large population in this country, and we would not be able to keep watch over everyone and not lose some of them, which is the last thing we need since we have so few people for the task we wish to fulfil. [131] There are islands nearby – you can see them from here – which are inhabited and where grain and meat and other useful things are raised. Let's go there to take port, and we will collect the land's grain and produce, and when we have gathered provisions, we will go before Constantinople and do whatever Our Lord has planned for us. For those who are well supplied make war more confidently than those who have no provisions.' The counts and the barons agreed to this advice, and they all returned to their *nefs* and other vessels.

[132] They rested that night and in the morning, on the feast of my lord John the Baptist celebrated in June,[9] their banners and pennons were hoisted on the ships' castles and their shields uncovered and hung from the sides of the ships. Each man examined the weapons he needed to fulfil his duties, knowing that they would be put to use before long. [133] The sailors raised the anchors and unfurled the sails to the wind. God gave them a good wind, such as they needed, and they came before Constantinople, passing so close to the walls and the towers that they could take shots at many of the Greek ships. There were so many people on the walls and on the towers that it seemed as if the whole population of the city was there.

[134] But it was Our Lord God's will that they reverse the decision taken the previous evening to go to the islands – it was as if no one had ever heard mention of it. They made for the mainland as directly as possible and took port in front of one

of Emperor Alexius's palaces, at a place called Chalcedon which was opposite Constantinople on the other side of the straits, towards the land of the Turks. This was one of the most beautiful and charming palaces any eyes might ever have seen, with all the physical comforts a princely residence should have.

[135] The counts and the barons went ashore and set up lodgings in the palace and in the surrounding town, most of them putting up their pavilions. Then the horses were brought out of the transports, and the knights and sergeants disembarked with all their arms, so that the only men left in the ships were the sailors. The region was beautiful and prosperous and abundant in all things; the mounds of freshly harvested grain left in the fields were sufficient for everyone to take as much as they wanted, and these were people who had great need of it.

[136] They stayed at the palace the following day and on their third day at Chalcedon, God granted them a good wind; the sailors weighed their anchors and unfurled their sails to the wind, so that they could sail against the current one league above Constantinople, to another palace of Emperor Alexius's, called Scutari. There they anchored the *nefs* and the transports and all the galleys. The knights who had been lodged in the palace at Chalcedon came overland along the coast.

[137] And so the French army encamped by the Straits of Saint George, at Scutari and further up the coast. When Emperor Alexius saw this he had his own forces come out of Constantinople to install themselves on the other bank, opposite them. He had his tents erected so that his opponents might not come ashore in strength against him. The French army remained thus for nine days and those who had need of provisions – and that was everyone in the camp – sought them out.

[138] During this period a company of very good men went out from the camp in order to keep guard over it so that no one could attack it. They also protected the foragers and reconnoitred the surrounding area. Among that company were Odo the Champenois of Champlitte and his brother William, Ogier of Saint-Chéron, Manassiers of l'Isle and Count Gerard, who came from Lombardy and was one of the marquis of

Montferrat's men. They had with them at least eighty knights, all of whom were very good men.

[139] They spotted tents at the foot of the mountain, a good three leagues away from the camp. This was the emperor of Constantinople's lord admiral,[10] who had at least 500 Greek knights. When our men saw them they formed their forces into four battalions and decided to go and attack the Greeks. When the Greeks saw them they formed their forces into battalions and lined up in front of the tents, waiting. And our men charged at them very vigorously. [140] With the help of Our Lord God this skirmish was over quickly; the Greeks turned their backs, routed at the first clash, and our men chased them for a good long league. They won a great number of warhorses, rouncies, palfreys, he-mules and she-mules, tents and pavilions, and such booty as you would expect in such a situation. And so they went back to the camp, where people were very pleased to see them, and they divided up their winnings as was fitting.

[141] On the following day Emperor Alexius sent a messenger with a letter to the counts and barons. This messenger was called Nicholas Rosso and he had been born in Lombardy. He found the barons in the fine palace at Scutari, where they were in conference, and he greeted them on behalf of Emperor Alexius of Constantinople, delivering his letter to Marquis Boniface of Montferrat. The marquis accepted it and it was read aloud in front of all the barons. This book will not report all the many passages of the letter, but after all its other contents came the notification of credence, so that we might have faith in the man who had brought the letter, whose name was Nicholas Rosso.

[142] 'Dear sir,' said the barons, 'we have examined your letter, which tells us we should credit what you say, and we certainly will do so. Now, speak as you wish.' [143] Standing before the barons the messenger said, 'My lords, Emperor Alexius informs you that he knows well that you are the best of men among those who do not wear crowns, from the best land there is, and he is deeply perplexed as to why or for what purpose you have come to his lands and to his kingdom. You

are Christian, he is Christian and he well understands that you set out to recover the Holy Land overseas, the Holy Cross and the Sepulchre. If you are poor and needy he will gladly give you some provisions and some money, and then you can leave his lands. He does not wish to do you any harm, but he has the power to do so. For, if you had twenty times as many men you would not be able to escape if he wished you ill; you would be killed and destroyed.'

[144] With the agreement and the advice of the other barons and the doge of Venice, Conon of Béthune – who was a fine knight, and wise and eloquent – rose to his feet and replied to the messenger, 'Dear sir, you have told us that your lord is deeply perplexed as to why our lords and our barons have entered his kingdom and his lands. They have not entered his kingdom or his lands at all, since he holds them wrongfully and as a sin against God and against justice. This kingdom and these lands belong to his nephew, son of his brother Isaac, who is seated among us on a throne here. But if he wishes to offer himself to the mercy of his nephew and return to him the crown and the empire, we will urge the young man to pardon him and grant him sufficient means to live richly. And if it is not to deliver such a message, do not be so bold as to come back here again.' Then the messenger left and went back to Constantinople, to Emperor Alexius.

[145] The barons discussed the matter among themselves and announced the next day that they would show Alexius, the son of the emperor of Constantinople, to the people of the city. And so they had all the galleys armed, and the doge of Venice and the marquis of Montferrat boarded one of them taking Alexius, the son of Emperor Isaac, with them. Those knights and barons who wished to go boarded the other galleys.

[146] And so they went right up to the walls of Constantinople and showed the young prince to the Greek people, saying, 'Behold your natural lord, and know that we do not come to do you harm; rather we come to protect you and to defend you if you will do as you ought. For the man you are obeying as your lord rules you wrongfully, and thus sins against God and justice; you well know how disloyally he behaved

towards his own lord, towards his own brother, by blinding him and by unjustly and sinfully depriving him of his empire. Behold here the rightful heir. If you side with him you will be doing your duty, and if you do not do so, we will do our worst to you.' Not a single person of that land or of that country gave any sign that they sided with the young prince, out of fear and dread of Emperor Alexius.[11] And so the galleys turned back to the camp and each man went to his quarters.

[147] The next day, once the barons had heard Mass, they gathered for a conference which was held on horseback in the middle of the fields. You could have seen many handsome warhorses there, and many knights mounted on them. This council was held to discuss how many battalions and of what sort they should have. There was lively debate of one proposal and another, but the conclusion of the conference was that the vanguard was entrusted to Count Baldwin of Flanders, since he had a very large number of good men, archers and cross-bowmen, more than any other man in the army.

[148] Afterwards it was decided that the count's brother Henry should form the second battalion with Matthew of Walincourt, Baldwin of Beauvoir, and many other fine knights who were with them from their lands and from their country. [149] The third battalion was formed by Count Hugh of Saint-Pol, his nephew Peter of Amiens, Eustace of Canteleux, Anseau of Cayeux, and many fine knights from their lands and their country. [150] The fourth battalion was led by Count Louis of Blois and Chartres, and it was very large and powerful and feared since he had a very great number of good knights and good men there. [151] The fifth battalion was formed by Matthew of Montmorency and the Champenois: Marshal Geoffrey of Champagne was a member of this battalion along with Ogier of Saint-Chéron, Manassiers of l'Isle, Milon le Bréban, Macaire of Sainte-Menehould, John Foisnon, Guy of Chappes and his nephew Clarembaut, and Robert of Ronsoy. All of these men made up the fifth battalion, and you should know that there were many fine knights in it. [152] The sixth battalion was formed by the men of Burgundy. Odo the Champenois of Champlitte was in this battalion with his brother William,

Richard of Dampierre and his brother Odo, Guy of Pesmes and his brother Aimon, Othon of la Roche, Guy of Conflans and the men from their lands and their country. [153] The seventh, very large, battalion was led by Marquis Boniface of Montferrat. This one was made up of the Lombards, the Tuscans, the Germans, and all the men from the region between the mountain of Mont Cenis and Lyons, on the Rhône. All of these men were in the marquis's battalion, and it was settled that it should have the rearguard.

[154] They appointed a day on which they would re-embark the *nefs* and other vessels in order to storm the shore, and either live or die. And you should know that this was one of the most hazardous enterprises ever undertaken. The bishops and clergymen spoke to the people, explaining to them that each of them should make his confession and draw up his will, since they did not know when God would summon them to him. And men throughout the army did this most willingly and most piously.

CHAPTER 5

The First Siege of Constantinople

(July–August 1203)

[155] The appointed day arrived and all the knights entered the transports with their warhorses. The knights were fully armed, with their helmets laced, and the horses were caparisoned and saddled. The other people, those who did not play such an important role in battle, all went aboard the large *nefs*, while every galley was armed and made ready.

[156] It was a fine morning, a little after sunrise. Emperor Alexius awaited them with numerous battalions and a vast array of equipment on the other side of the straits. Trumpets were sounded. Each galley was towing a transport ship so that the crossing might be made more easily. Nobody asked which ship should go first, but instead each of them landed as soon as they were able to. The knights came out of the transports, leaping into the sea up to their waists, fully armed, their helmets laced and their lances in their hands. The good archers, the good sergeants and the good crossbowmen did the same, each group going ashore as soon as they reached land.

[157] The Greeks made a great show of being ready to resist, but when the knights came to lower their lances the Greeks turned their backs and fled, abandoning the shore. Know that no one ever made such an audacious landing. Straightaway the sailors began opening the doors of the transports and bringing forward the gangplanks so that the horses could be led out. The knights then began to mount their horses and the battalions to form up in the designated order. [158] Count Baldwin of Flanders and Hainaut rode ahead, leading the vanguard, and the other battalions followed behind, each riding out in their proper order. They went as far as the site where Emperor

Alexius had encamped, from where he had retreated towards Constantinople, leaving his tents and pavilions set up. Our men seized plentiful booty there.

[159] The consensus among our barons was that they should encamp by the port, next to the Tower of Galata. It was here that the chain that came across the harbour from Constantinople was fixed. You should know with certainty that anyone who wanted to enter the port of Constantinople had to get past that chain. Our barons saw clearly that if they did not take this tower and break the chain they would be in a dire, deadly situation. And so they set up camp that night next to the tower in the Jewish quarter, which is called Estanor and is a pleasant and prosperous neighbourhood.

[160] They kept a close watch all that night. The next day, at the hour of terce, the people inside the Tower of Galata attacked them and the inhabitants of Constantinople came in boats to assist them. Our men ran to arms. James of Avesnes and his company joined battle on foot, and you should know that he was charged at fiercely and was struck in the middle of his face with a lance. He was in danger of being killed but one of his knights, whose name was Nicholas of Jenlain, mounted his horse and protected his lord very well, so well that he was highly praised as a result. [161] The alarm was raised in the camp. Our men rushed from all directions and drove their opponents off vigorously so that many of them were captured or killed. A good number of the Greeks did not turn back towards the tower but instead made for the boats by which they had come, and more of them were drowned there, while a few escaped. Those who returned to the tower were so closely followed by the men from the army that they could not close the gate. Intense fighting resumed there at the gate and the tower was taken by force and the people inside captured. A good number were either killed or taken prisoner.

[162] Thus the fortress of Galata was taken and the port of Constantinople won by force. This was a great comfort to those in the army and they gave great thanks to Lord God for it, while the people inside the city were downcast. The following day the *nefs*, galleys, transports and other vessels were brought

inside the port, and the men of the army held a council to determine what they should do, whether to attack the city from the sea or by land. The Venetians were of the firm opinion that the scaling ladders should be raised on the *nefs* and that all assaults should be made from the sea. The French said that they did not know nearly as well as the Venetians how to make themselves useful on the sea, but that they would be of much greater assistance on land when they had their horses and arms. The conclusion of the meeting was that the Venetians would attack from the sea, and the barons and the rest of the army by land.

[163] They remained encamped for four days, and on the fifth[1] the entire force armed itself and the battalions rode out, in their designated order, passing above the port until they were directly opposite the palace of Blachernae. The fleet came through to the far end of the port, until they were level with the army. At the point the army had reached a river flows into the sea and it could not be crossed except by using a stone bridge. The Greeks had torn that bridge down, and the barons set the army to work throughout that day and night to repair it. By morning the bridge was restored and the battalions armed themselves; they rode out one after another, in their designated order, and arrived outside the city. None of its inhabitants came out against them, which was a great surprise since for each man in the army there were 200 in the city.

[164] The barons decided to set up camp between the palace of Blachernae and Bohemond's castle, which was an abbey[2] encircled by walls. The tents and pavilions were erected, revealing an awesome prospect; along the three-league length of the landward walls of Constantinople, the entire army was only able to lay siege to one gate. The Venetians were at sea in the *nefs* and other vessels, setting up the scaling ladders, mangonels and petraries; their assault was very well organized. And the barons, for their part, made similar preparations on land, setting up petraries and mangonels.

[165] Know that the army was never at peace, for there was no hour of day or night at which there was not an armed battalion outside the gate to keep watch over the engines and

defend against sorties. But in spite of this the Greeks still came out of that gate and others to harass them, keeping the army so hard pressed that the whole force was called to arms six or seven times a day. No one could go in search of food more than four crossbow-shots away from the camp, and supplies were very low. They had a little flour and bacon, but no fresh meat except from the horses that were killed. You should know that the food available throughout the camp only amounted to a three-week supply. This was a most perilous situation, since never, in any city, had so many people been besieged by so few.

[166] A very good scheme was settled upon. They surrounded the whole camp with solid timbers, strong barriers and sturdy palisades, and this made their position much stronger and more secure. The Greeks made such frequent sorties against the camp that they allowed our men no rest, although the forces from the camp drove them back very fiercely and the Greeks suffered losses every time they ventured out.

[167] One day the Burgundians were on guard when the Greeks made a sortie against the camp. A strong force of their best men came out of the city and the Burgundians made a counter-attack, repulsing them vigorously but approaching so close to the gate that people inside the city threw large pieces of stone at them. One of the finest of the Greeks from Constantinople, who was called Constantine Lascaris,[3] was captured there by Walter of Neuilly, who took him prisoner while the Greek was still mounted on his horse. In the same incident William of Champlitte had his arm broken by a stone, which was a great pity since he was very brave and very worthy. [168] I cannot begin to recount to you all the blows, wounds and deaths suffered there. But before the fighting had ceased a knight from the retinue of Henry, Count Baldwin of Flanders and Hainaut's brother, joined the fray. He was called Eustace of le Marchais, and his only armour was a gambeson, an iron cap and a shield at his neck. He acquitted himself very well as he drove the enemy off, and received high praise as a result. There were few days on which no sortie was made, but I cannot tell you about all of them. Our men were so hard pressed that no one could sleep or rest or eat without being armed.

[169] Another sortie was made from a gate on higher ground. The Greeks once again suffered substantial losses, but a knight was killed there whose name was William of Gy. Matthew of Walincourt conducted himself very well on that occasion, although he lost his horse when it was killed at the gate's drawbridge, and many of those who took part in this skirmish performed impressively. At the gate below the palace of Blach-ernae, where the Greeks ventured out most frequently, Peter of Bracieux won more praise than anyone else since he was encamped the closest to it and therefore most often arrived on the scene.

[170] These dangers and labours lasted nearly ten days, until one Thursday morning[4] all was ready for the assault, including the scaling ladders. The Venetians too had all in order at sea. It was decided that during the attack three of the seven battalions should stay outside the camp to guard it while the other four would undertake the assault. Marquis Boniface of Montferrat defended the camp from the side towards the fields, along with the Champenois battalion (led by Matthew of Montmorency) and the Burgundians. Count Baldwin of Flanders and Hainaut was going to lead the attack with his men, aided by his brother Henry, Count Louis of Blois and Chartres, Count Hugh of Saint-Pol, and those in their service.

[171] They set two scaling ladders against a barbican near the sea. The walls were heavily defended by English and Danish men,[5] and the assault was good and strong and hard. Two knights and two sergeants, by their own sheer force, climbed the scaling ladders and captured the wall from their opponents. At least fifteen men climbed up on to the wall after them to fight hand-to-hand with battle-axes and swords. The men inside the barbican fought back, driving our forces off fiercely and capturing two of our men. These prisoners were taken before Emperor Alexius, which pleased him greatly. And so the assault by the French came to a halt, with a good number of men wounded and injured; the barons were greatly distressed.

[172] Meanwhile the doge of Venice had not neglected his duty; he had drawn his *nefs* and transports and other vessels into a single line, which extended for a good three crossbow-shots'

length. This line began to approach the shore beneath the walls
and towers. You would have seen mangonels taking shots from
the *nefs* and transports, while crossbow bolts were loosed and
bows fired quickly and repeatedly as those inside the city vigorously defended the walls and towers. The scaling ladders on the
nefs were brought against the walls so forcefully that in several
places there were clashes of swords and spears. The din was so
great that it seemed as if land and sea quaked. And you should
know that the galleys did not dare to land.

[173] Now you will hear of a wondrous and brave feat: the
doge of Venice – who was an old man and could not see a thing
– was in the prow of his galley, fully armed and with the banner
of Saint Mark before him. He called out to his men that they
should put him ashore: if they refused he would punish them
harshly. And so they brought the galley to land and themselves
leapt forth, taking the banner of Saint Mark ashore ahead of
the doge. [174] When the Venetians saw that the banner of
Saint Mark had landed and that their lord's galley had reached
land before them, each of them felt himself ashamed and they
all went ashore. Those in the transports leapt out as and when
each saw his chance and made their way to land. Then you
would have seen an astounding assault. Geoffrey of Villehardouin, the marshal of Champagne, who composed this work,
is your witness that more than forty people told him honestly
that they saw the banner of Saint Mark of Venice on one of the
towers, although no one knew who had carried it there.

[175] And now you will hear of a prodigious miracle; those
inside the walls fled, abandoning them as our men entered the
city as and when each saw his chance. They captured twenty-
five of the towers and set their own men to defend them. The
doge called for a boat to send messengers to the barons of the
army to let them know that the Venetians had taken twenty-five
towers and were sure they could never be recaptured. The
barons were so overjoyed that they could not believe this to be
true. In the meantime the Venetians began to send some of the
warhorses and palfreys they had captured in the city by boat to
the camp.

[176] When Emperor Alexius saw that the Venetians had

thus entered the city, he began to send his own men out against them in great numbers. And when the Venetians saw that they would not be able to hold out against them, they set fires between themselves and the Greeks. The wind was blowing from where our men were positioned, and the fires began to grow to such a size that the Greeks could not see our men, who then retreated to the towers they had taken and captured.

[177] At that point Emperor Alexius of Constantinople, together with his forces, left the city through other gates – ones at least a league away from our camp. So many people were coming out that it seemed as if the whole world was on the move. The emperor organized his battalions out in the countryside and then rode on towards our camp. When our French forces saw them they ran to arms from all directions. On that day Henry, the brother of Count Baldwin of Flanders and Hainaut, was guarding the siege engines along with Matthew of Walincourt, Baldwin of Beauvoir and the men of their retinues. Emperor Alexius had directed a large body of men to come out from the city through three of its gates to face them while he attacked the camp from the other side.

[178] Then the six French battalions left the camp in their designated order and lined up in front of the palisade. Each knight had his sergeants and squires on foot behind his horse's hindquarters, while the archers and crossbowmen were in front of them. One group was formed of knights on foot, of whom there were fully 200; these were men who no longer had any horses. They calmly held this order in front of the palisades, which made very great sense since, were they to have gone out into the countryside to engage with the enemy they would have encountered such a vast number that our whole force would have been engulfed by them.

[179] It appeared as if the entire plain was covered with enemy battalions. They approached slowly, keeping to their formation. This certainly seemed a perilous situation, since our men had only six battalions while the Greeks had a good sixty of them, all of which were larger than any one of ours. But our forces were lined up in such a way that no one could come at them except from the front. Emperor Alexius advanced far

enough that each side could fire at the other, and when the doge of Venice learned of this he had his men retreat from and abandon the towers they had conquered, declaring that he wished to live or die with the pilgrims. And so they made their way by boat to the camp, the doge himself coming ashore first, followed by as many men as he had been able to bring with him.

[180] The pilgrims' and Greeks' battalions were face to face for a long while, since the Greeks did not dare to come and attack their position and the pilgrims refused to move away from the palisade. When Emperor Alexius saw this he began to withdraw his forces, and once they had regrouped he had them retreat. Seeing this, the pilgrim army began to ride out slowly towards them, and the Greek battalions in turn set off in retreat to a palace called the Philopatrion.

[181] Know that God has never delivered any people from such great danger as he did the army that day. Know moreover that there was no man present so brave that he did not feel very glad about this. Thus they left off battle that day; God's will was that nothing more should transpire. Emperor Alexius withdrew into the city while the men of the army returned to their lodgings and removed their armour, feeling very weary and overwrought. They ate and drank little, for their supplies were very low.

[182] Now heed the miracles of Our Lord, all of which are beautiful, wherever he chooses to perform them. That very night Emperor Alexius of Constantinople took what he could carry of his treasure and set off with those of his followers who wished to leave; thus they fled, abandoning the city. The people of the city were left behind in amazement. They made their way to the prison where Emperor Isaac – who had had his eyes put out – was being held. They dressed him in the imperial robes and brought him to the great palace of Blachernae, where they seated him in the high throne and promised him obedience as their lord. Then, with advice from Emperor Isaac, they chose messengers and sent them to the army to inform the emperor's son and the barons that Emperor Alexius had fled and Isaac was restored as emperor. [183] When the young prince heard this he called for Marquis Boniface of Montferrat, who in turn

summoned the barons throughout the camp. Once they had gathered in Emperor Isaac's son's pavilion, he passed this news on to them. It is impossible to describe their joy on hearing this, for never in the world was there any greater. Our Lord received much pious praise from everyone, for he had come to their aid so soon, and had lifted them up from so lowly a position to set them on high. And on this account one can rightly say: 'He whom God wishes to help, no man may harm.'

[184] Soon day began to break, and the army started its preparations. Everyone in the camp armed himself since they did not in the least trust the Greeks. But messengers began to venture out of the city, one by one or in pairs, bringing the same news. The decision made by the barons and counts and by the doge of Venice was that they should send envoys into the city to find out how matters stood there and, if what they had been told was true, to ask the father to confirm the same terms they had agreed with his son. Otherwise they would not let his son enter the city at all. The envoys were chosen. One was Matthew of Montmorency and Geoffrey, marshal of Champagne, was another, along with two Venetians sent on behalf of the doge.

[185] The envoys were accompanied as far as the gate; it was opened for them and they got down from their horses. The Greeks had placed Englishmen and Danes bearing battle-axes along the route from the gate as far the palace of Blachernae. There the envoys found Emperor Isaac, so richly attired that one would seek in vain for a man more lavishly dressed. The empress, his wife, was alongside him – a most beautiful woman who was the sister of the king of Hungary.[6] There were so many other high-ranking men and women present that one could barely turn round, and the ladies were all as richly dressed as could be. And all those who had been opposed to the emperor the previous day were now subject to his will.

[186] The envoys came before Emperor Isaac who, along with everyone else, showed them great honour. He was told by them that they wanted to talk to him privately, on behalf of his son and the barons of the army. The emperor rose to his feet and went into a side chamber, taking with him only the empress,

his chancellor, his translator and the four envoys. With the agreement of the other envoys Geoffrey of Villehardouin, marshal of Champagne, announced their business, saying to Emperor Isaac: [187] 'My lord, you can see what service we have performed for your son and how well we have honoured our agreement with him. But he may not enter this city until he has given us a guarantee that he will keep his promises to us. He asks you, as his son, to confirm the agreement with us on the same terms and in the same manner as he has done.' 'What are the terms of this agreement?' asked the emperor. And the envoy replied, 'I will tell you what they are. [188] He promised in the first instance to place the entire empire of Romania in obedience to Rome, from which it has formerly been cut off. Then, to give 200,000 marks of silver to the army along with a year's supply of provisions for both the higher and lower ranks. To lead 10,000 men in his own ships and to support them at his own expense for one year, and to maintain 500 knights for the defence of the land overseas for the rest of his life. Such is the agreement your son has with us. He has confirmed it with sworn oaths and sealed charters, with the support of King Philip of Germany, your daughter's husband. It is our wish that you should confirm it too.'

[189] 'In truth,' said the emperor, 'this agreement is a most burdensome one, and I do not see quite how it can be fulfilled. However, you have done both my son and myself such service that if you had been granted the whole empire you would have well deserved it.' Many different opinions were stated and restated there. But the outcome was that the father confirmed the terms of the agreement just as the son had done, with sworn oaths and with charters bearing golden seals. One charter was handed to the envoys, who then took their leave of Emperor Isaac and returned to the camp, where they told the barons that they had succeeded in their mission.

[190] The barons then mounted their horses and led the young prince with great joy into the city, to his father. The Greeks opened the gate to him and welcomed him with very great rejoicing and very great celebration. Father and son were both highly delighted, since they had not seen each other for a

long time and because with God's help above all, but also with help from the pilgrims, they had been lifted out of such great poverty and distress to such an exalted position. And so there was great rejoicing inside Constantinople and among the pilgrims in their camp on account of the honour and victory God had granted them.

[191] The next day the emperor and his son asked the counts and barons whether they would, please God, go and set up camp on the other side of the port, near Estanor. This was because there would be the risk of clashes between them and the Greeks if they were to take up residence in the city, and it might even lead to the city's destruction. The barons said they had already served Prince Alexius in so many ways that they would not now refuse what he and his father requested of them. And so they went to set up camp on the other side of the water, where they stayed peacefully and quietly, and were plentifully supplied with good food.

[192] Now you may know that many people from the army went to look at Constantinople,[7] its sumptuous palaces, its many impressive churches and its great riches, of which no other city ever had as many. It is impossible even to begin to describe all the saints' relics since there were as many in the city at that time as there were in the rest of the world put together. The Greeks and the French thus came into close contact in all areas of life, in trade and other concerns.

[193] By common agreement between the Franks and the Greeks it was settled that the new emperor would be crowned on the feast of Saint Peter, at the beginning of August.[8] Thus it was planned, and so it was done. He was crowned most nobly and most honourably, as was customary for Greek emperors. Not long afterwards he began to pay the money he owed to the army, which was shared out among its members to reimburse the fee for his passage each man had paid at Venice.

CHAPTER 6

Alliances Renewed and Abandoned

(September 1203–March 1204)

[194] The new emperor often went to visit the barons in the camp and showed them great honour, as much as he was able to do. And so he should have done, since they had served him very well. One day he came to speak to the barons privately in the lodgings of Count Baldwin of Flanders and Hainaut. The doge of Venice and the most important barons had been summoned there secretly, and the emperor set forth his business, saying, 'My lords, I am emperor by God's grace and by yours, and you have performed for me the highest service any people have ever done for a Christian man. But you should know that many people make a show of kindness towards me who do not care for me at all, and the Greeks have great contempt for the fact that I came into my inheritance through your efforts. [195] The time is drawing near for your departure, and the pact between you and the Venetians only lasts until the feast of Saint Michael.[1] I cannot fulfil my commitments to you in so short a period. You should know then, if you will allow me to say so, that the Greeks hate me on account of you. If you leave I will lose this land and they will put me to death. Alternatively, you could do this one thing I ask of you: stay until March, and in return I will extend the lease of your fleet until the feast of Saint Michael next year, and pay the Venetians for it. I will also meet your material needs until Easter. During this time I will bring my lands to heel and will not be in danger of losing them again. In this way my obligations towards you may be fulfilled, since I will have received the money due to me from all my lands. I will also have prepared a fleet that I might lead alongside you or send with you, as I have pledged to do.

And then you will have all summer, from beginning to end, to make war.'

[196] The barons said they would discuss this proposal in private. They well understood that what he said was true and that his plan represented the best hope for both him and them. They told him that they could do nothing without the agreement of the whole army, and that they would discuss the matter with their colleagues and report back to him with their findings. Emperor Alexius then left them to go back to Constantinople, while the barons stayed in the camp and called a conference for the following day to which all the barons and leaders of the army were summoned, along with the majority of the knights. At this meeting the full proposal was set forth, just as the emperor had presented it to them.

[197] There was very great discord within the army that came, as it had on many occasions, from those who wanted the army to disband; it seemed to them that the expedition was going on too long. The same party that had encouraged dissent at Corfu called on their colleagues to keep their oaths, saying, 'Provide us with ships as you swore to us you would. We want to go to Syria.'

[198] Others called on them, pleading, and said, 'Sirs, for God's sake let us not lose the honour God has given us. If we leave for Syria now we will arrive at the start of winter and it will be impossible for us to fight, with the result that Our Lord's work will remain undone. But if we wait until March we will leave this emperor in a good position and set off rich in money and provisions. Then we can make for Syria and launch our attack on the land of Egypt. Our fleet will stay with us until the feast of Saint Michael, and from then until Easter, since the Venetians won't be able to leave us during winter. In this way the land overseas might be conquered.'

[199] Right and wrong were of no concern to those who wanted to see the army disband, only that the force should break up. But those who wanted to keep the army together made their case so effectively that, with God's help, the matter was brought to the end in such a way that the Venetians swore an oath to continue to provide the fleet for a year from the feast

of Saint Michael. Emperor Alexius paid them enough to go ahead with this agreement. For their part, the pilgrims swore to continue their association with the Venetians on the existing terms until the same date. Thus concord and peace were brought to the army.

[200] A great misfortune then befell it. Matthew of Montmorency, who was one of the best knights from the kingdom of France and one of the most highly valued and deeply loved, died. This was a great sorrow and a great loss, one of the most profound to strike the army through the death of one man. He was buried in a church dedicated to my lord Saint John of the Hospital of Jerusalem.

[201] Afterwards, with the agreement of the Greeks and the French, Emperor Alexius left Constantinople with a very large body of men to secure the empire and subject it to his authority. Most of the barons went with him, the others staying to guard the camp. Marquis Boniface of Montferrat accompanied him, as did Count Hugh of Saint-Pol, Henry the brother of Count Baldwin of Flanders and Hainaut, James of Avesnes, William of Champlitte, Hugh of Coligny, and a good number of other people this book will not mention. Count Baldwin of Flanders and Hainaut stayed in the camp, along with Count Louis of Blois and Chartres and the majority of the pilgrims.

[202] Know that in the course of the emperor's expedition all the Greeks, from both sides of the Straits of Saint George, subjected themselves to him, to his will and to his authority, offering him loyalty and homage as their lord. The only exception was Johanitsa, the king of Vlachia and Bulgaria.[2] This Johanitsa was a Vlach who had rebelled against Emperor Alexius's father and uncle and made war on them for twenty years, conquering so much land from them that he made himself a powerful king. You should know that he had captured nearly half of the empire's territory on the western side of the Straits of Saint George. This man did not subject himself to the emperor's authority or mercy.

[203] While Emperor Alexius was absent on campaign, a great misfortune struck Constantinople. A large brawl broke out between the Greeks and the Latin residents of the city, of

which there were a large number. I do not know which group wickedly set fire to the city, but the blaze was so widespread and intense that no one could put it out or bring it under control. When they saw this the barons of the army, who were encamped on the other side of the port, were deeply saddened and felt great pity as they watched those noble churches and fine palaces crumble and fall, and the broad streets of merchants' shops engulfed by flames. But there was nothing more they could do. [204] Fire seized the area towards the harbour, and spread out from there across the most densely populated part of the city as far as the sea on the other side, level with the church of Saint Sophia. The fire lasted for a week, during which time no one was able to extinguish it and the front along which it burned extended fully half a league. No one could tell you the damage it caused in terms of the money and property lost, nor in terms of the lives of men, women and children, many of whom burned to death.

[205] None of the Latins who had been resident inside Constantinople, no matter where they came from, dared stay in the city any longer. And so they gathered up their wives and children and whatever they had been able to bring out of the fire and they boarded boats and ships to cross the harbour to where the pilgrims were. The numbers were not trifling; there were at least 15,000 people of both higher and lower condition who, in the wake of their crossing, would prove to be of great use to the pilgrims. In this way the Franks and the Greeks parted ways, and were not nearly as friendly as they had been before. No one knew who should be blamed for this, which weighed heavy on the minds of people on both sides.

[206] Around that time something happened that was most distressing to the barons and the people of the army. The abbot of Loos, who was a holy man and a *preudomme*, and wished only good things for the army, died. He had been a monk of the Cistercian order.

[207] Emperor Alexius remained absent on his expedition for a very long time; he returned to Constantinople on the feast of Saint Martin.[3] There was great rejoicing at the arrival of this force; the Greeks and the women from Constantinople rode

out in long cavalcades to meet their friends and the pilgrims
went to greet theirs, which brought them all very great joy. And
so the emperor made his way back inside Constantinople, to
the palace of Blachernae, while the marquis of Montferrat and
the other barons returned to be with the pilgrims.

[208] Having settled his affairs very effectively the emperor
believed he was no longer dependent on the barons and began to
act haughtily towards them and the people who had done him
such good. He no longer came to see them in their camp as he
had done before. The barons sent messengers to him, begging
him to pay them their money as had been agreed. He put them off
with one delay after another. He made meagre, paltry payments
from time to time but in the end they dwindled to nothing.

[209] Marquis Boniface of Montferrat, who had done him
greater service and was on better terms with him than the
other barons, went to visit him frequently. He reproached him
for his unjust treatment of them and reminded him of the great
service they had given him – never had such great service been
performed for any man. But he just put the barons off and
failed to keep any of his promises to them; before long they
realized and understood clearly that all his intentions were
wicked.

[210] The barons of the army and the doge of Venice held a
council. They said they recognized that this man would not
uphold any of their agreements and that he never told them the
truth. They should send trustworthy envoys to him to demand
his fulfilment of their treaty and to reprove him for his treatment
of them. If he was willing to do as he ought, the envoys should
accept his offer; if he was unwilling they should defy him on
behalf of the barons and the doge and assure him that they
would recover what was due to them by whatever means
necessary.

[211] Conon of Béthune, Geoffrey of Villehardouin, the marshal of Champagne, and Milon le Bréban of Provins were
chosen by the barons to deliver this message, and the doge of
Venice sent three high-ranking men from his council. And so
the envoys mounted their horses, their swords set at their sides,
and rode out together to the palace of Blachernae. And you

should know that they were going in great danger and at great risk because of the Greeks' treachery. [212] They dismounted at the gates and entered the palace, where they found Emperor Alexius and his father Emperor Isaac seated in two thrones, side by side. Next to them sat the empress. She was the father's wife and the son's stepmother; she was the king of Hungary's sister and was a beautiful and good woman. There were a large number of high-ranking men and women present, so that this court certainly appeared to be that of a powerful prince.

[213] With the agreement of the other envoys, Conon of Béthune, who was most wise and well-spoken, set forth their business: 'My lord, we have come to you on behalf of the barons of the army and the doge of Venice. Know that you should be mindful of the service they have performed for you, which everyone knows about and which is clear for all to see. You swore, both you and your father, that you would uphold your agreement with them and they have your charters to prove it. But you have not fulfilled the terms nearly as well as you should. [214] They have called on you to do so numerous times, and we call on you on their behalf in the presence of your own barons, to satisfy the terms of the agreement in place between you and them. If you do so they will be very pleased. If you do not do so you should know that from this time forward they will not regard you as their lord or as their friend. Instead they will recover what is owed to them by whatever means necessary. They inform you that they will do no harm to you or to anyone else until they have delivered a statement of defiance; they have never acted deceitfully and it would be against the custom of their country to do so. Now, you have heard our message and will make whatever decision you please.'

[215] The Greeks found this challenge most astounding and most shocking. They said that no one had ever been so bold as to dare defy the emperor of Constantinople in his own hall. Emperor Alexius and the other Greeks looked on the envoys with faces full of ill will, faces that on many earlier occasions had shown such kindness.

[216] There was a great uproar in the hall. The envoys turned on their heels and made for the gate, where they mounted their

horses. They all felt very glad to have passed through the gate, which is not surprising as they had escaped from a very dangerous situation in which they could very easily have all been killed or captured. They returned to the camp and told the barons how they had got on. And so the war began; each side striking the other as and when they could, both on land and at sea. The Franks and Greeks clashed in many places but never – thank God – did they meet in battle without the Greeks suffering heavier losses than the Franks. The war dragged on a long time, into the depths of winter.

[217] And then the Greeks came up with a grand scheme. They took seventeen large ships and filled them all with timbers, tinder, tow, barrels and pitch, and waited until the wind was blowing very hard from their side of the water. And then one night at midnight they set fire to the ships and unfurled their sails to the wind. The flames burned so high that it seemed as if the whole world was on fire. Then the ships were sent in the direction of the pilgrims' fleet. The alarm was raised in the camp and men rushed to arms from all directions. The Venetians ran to their ships, as did everyone else who had vessels there, and began intensive efforts to rescue them.

[218] Geoffrey, the marshal of Champagne, who dictated this work, is your faithful witness that no people ever defended themselves more effectively at sea than did those Venetians. They leapt into galleys and into barges and *nefs*, took hold of the burning vessels using grappling irons and by sheer force dragged them out of their harbour towards the enemy; they released the boats into the current and sent them, ablaze, down the straits. So many Greeks had come to the shoreline that they were endless and innumerable, and their cries were so loud that it seemed as if land and sea were quaking. They boarded barges and lifeboats and took shots at our men who were fighting the fire, some of whom were wounded.

[219] As soon as they heard the alarm the knights in the camp armed themselves and went out into the fields in their battalions one after the other, their order determined by where they were lodged in the camp. They feared the Greeks might come and attack them from the countryside.

[220] They endured this labour and distress until day had fully broken. But with God's help our people lost nothing, except one Pisan ship full of merchandise which was consumed by the fire. They would have faced very grave danger had their fleet burned that night; they would have lost everything and been unable to leave by land or sea. This was the reward Emperor Alexius wished to give for their service to him.

[221] The Greeks, who were thus embroiled with the Franks, saw there was no longer any possibility of peace. Behind closed doors, some of them came to the conclusion they should betray the emperor. One of them was better regarded by Emperor Alexius than any of the others, and had done more to encourage him into conflict with the Franks. This Greek was called Mourtzouphlus.[4]

[222] On the advice and with the agreement of the others, the following plan was put into action. One night at midnight, while Emperor Alexius was sleeping, Mourtzouphlus (who had himself been appointed to guard him) and his companions seized the emperor in his bed and threw him into a prison cell. With the assistance and approval of his fellow Greeks, Mourtzouphlus donned the scarlet boots[5] and made himself emperor; he was later crowned at Saint Sophia. Now listen and hear if ever any betrayal so wicked was carried out by any people.

[223] When Emperor Isaac heard that his son had been captured and Mourtzouphlus crowned, he was very afraid. He was seized by an illness but it did not last very long, and he died. Emperor Mourtzouphlus had the imprisoned son poisoned two or three times, but it was not God's will that he should die. Then Mourtzouphlus murdered him by strangulation, and when this deed had been done he had word spread everywhere that Alexius had died naturally. Mourtzouphlus had him buried with imperial honours and made a great show of grief.

[224] But murder will out; both the Greeks and the French soon knew without doubt that the murder had been committed as you have just heard it described. The barons of the army and the doge of Venice held a conference at which the bishops and the clergy were present. All the clergy, including those with

a mandate from the pope, agreed with the assessment presented to the barons and pilgrims; anyone who committed such a murder had no right to possess lands, and all those who had consented to the crime were complicit in it. And, above and beyond all this, the Greeks had withdrawn from obedience to Rome.

[225] 'We therefore tell you,' said the clergy, 'that this battle is right and just. If you have the right intention of conquering this land and placing it in obedience to Rome, all those of you who die here having made your confession will receive the same indulgence the pope has granted you.'[6] You should know that this was a great comfort to the barons and pilgrims.

[226] The war between the Franks and the Greeks was fierce; there were no lulls in the fighting, instead it steadily grew and intensified. Few were the days without a clash either on land or at sea. Henry, Count Baldwin of Flanders' brother, led one raid in which most of the best men in the army took part. James of Avesnes went with him, as did Baldwin of Beauvoir, Odo the Champenois of Champlitte and his brother William, and the men from their countries. They set out from the camp one evening, around vespers, and rode through the night. Late the next morning they came to a pleasant town called Philia, captured it and seized livestock, prisoners, clothing and food as booty, which they sent in boats down the Straits of Saint George to the camp. (This town is situated on the Russian Sea.)[7]

[227] They stayed in this town for two days, enjoying its plentiful supplies. On the third day they set out with all their livestock and booty and rode back towards the camp. Emperor Mourtzouphlus had received word that this group had left the camp, and he set out from Constantinople by night with a large number of his men. They took up position to ambush the returning raiders, and spotted them making their way with all their livestock and their booty. The Greeks watched the battalions pass, one after another, until the rearguard appeared. This was formed by Henry, Count Baldwin of Flanders' brother, and his men. Emperor Mourtzouphlus charged at them as they entered a wood. They turned to face him and the two sides clashed very fiercely.

[228] With God's help Emperor Mourtzouphlus was defeated and was himself very nearly taken prisoner. He lost his imperial banner and an icon that had been carried before him. He and the other Greeks set great store by this icon, which bore an image of Our Lady. He also lost as many as twenty of the best knights he had. Emperor Mourtzouphlus was routed as you have heard, but intense fighting continued between him and the Franks. Much of winter had already passed; it was now around Candlemas[8] and Lent was approaching.

[229] Now we will leave the men before Constantinople and tell you instead about those men who had gone to other ports than Venice, and those with the Flemish fleet that had spent the winter at Marseilles before all its ships crossed to Syria in the summer. There were so many of them that they far outnumbered those outside Constantinople. Now you will hear what harm was done when these men did not join that force; had they done so Christendom would have been forever exalted. But because of their sins God did not wish this to happen. Some of them died as a result of the sickly climate in Syria and others went back to their own countries. None of them ever achieved anything noteworthy or useful in the lands they visited.

[230] One company of very good men set out to go to Antioch, to join Bohemond, prince of Antioch and count of Tripoli, who was at war with King Leon, the ruler of the Armenians.[9] This company was on its way to fight as mercenaries for the prince. The Turks in that region knew this and laid an ambush along the route they had to take. They charged and did battle with the Franks, routing them so completely that not one of them escaped; they were all killed or captured.

[231] Villain of Nully, one of the best knights in the world, was killed there as were Giles of Trazegnies and many others. Bernard of Moreuil was taken prisoner along with Renaut of Dampierre, John of Villers and the blameless William of Nully. You should know that none of the eighty knights that had been in that company escaped; they were all killed or captured. And this book is your faithful witness that no man abandoned the army at Venice without some hurt or shame befalling him. This is why he is but wise who keeps to the better path.

CHAPTER 7

The Second Siege of Constantinople
(April 1204)

[232] Now we will leave these men behind and speak of those still outside Constantinople, who had most carefully prepared their siege engines and set up their petraries and mangonels on board the *nefs* and transports, along with every other kind of machine useful in capturing a city. Scaling ladders had been attached to the *nefs'* yardarms to reach astonishing heights. [233] Seeing this the Greeks began to strengthen the city's fortifications on the opposite side of the straits. Constantinople was already heavily defended with high walls and tall towers, but there were no towers so tall that they did not decide to raise them further by constructing two or three more levels out of wood; never was a city so well fortified. And so both the Greeks and the Franks were hard at work throughout most of Lent.

[234] The men of the army held a conference to decide how they should proceed. There was lively debate, back and forth, but the conclusion of the meeting was that if God granted them entry into the city by force, all the booty seized should be gathered together and then shared out among the entire force, as was fitting. And if they did take control of the city, six Frenchmen and six Venetians would be chosen who would swear on relics that they would elect as emperor the man they believed would be of greatest benefit to that land. The man made emperor as a result of this election would receive one-quarter of all their conquests both inside and outside the city, and would have the palaces of Bucoleon and Blachernae. The remaining three-quarters of their conquests would be divided equally, half going to the Venetians and half to the people of the army. Twelve of the wisest men from the pilgrim army and

twelve from among the Venetians would be chosen who would then distribute fiefs and possessions among the men, determining what service each of them owed to the emperor.

[235] This arrangement was confirmed and sealed with sworn oaths by both the French and the Venetians. It was agreed that in a year's time, at the end of March, anyone who wished to leave could do so. Those who stayed in that country would be retained in the emperor's service under terms to be determined when the time came. In this way the pact was set out and confirmed. All those who did not uphold it would be excommunicated.

[236] The fleet was very well prepared and armed, and all the pilgrims' provisions were loaded on board. On the Thursday after mid-Lent[1] everyone boarded the ships and the horses were led into the transports. Each battalion had its own vessels which were all ranged side-by-side, *nefs* dispersed among the galleys and transports. This was a great marvel to behold; and this book bears faithful witness that the attacking forces, arranged in this way, extended over fully half a French league.

[237] On Friday morning the *nefs* and galleys and other vessels drew near the city in due order and the assault began, very strong and very hard. In many places men came ashore and went as far as the walls, and in many other places the ladders on board the *nefs* approached so close that the men on the walls and towers and the men on the ladders exchanged spear-blows hand-to-hand. The assault went on in this way, very hard, very strong and very fierce, in more than a hundred places until it was nearly the hour of none. [238] But, because of our sins, the pilgrims were repulsed in this attack. Those who had come ashore from the galleys and transport ships were driven back by force. Know that our army's losses that day were greater than the Greeks', who were heartened as a result. There were some who withdrew from the assault with their ships, and others who stayed at anchor so close to the city that they fired with petraries and mangonels one against the other.[2]

[239] In the evening the men of the army and the doge of Venice held a meeting, and they gathered in a church on the other side of the straits, the side where they had set up camp.

Many opinions were exchanged there, and the men of the army were greatly dismayed because of their misfortune that day. Many of them advised that they should attack from the other side of the city, the side that was not so well fortified. The Venetians, who knew more about the sea, said that if they went to that side the water's current would carry them down the straits and they would not be able to stop their ships. And know that there were some who wished that the current or the wind would take the ships down the straits – they did not care where they were taken, as long as they might leave that land and be on their way. This was no wonder, for they were in great peril.

[240] Much was said, back and forth, but the outcome of the discussion was that they would re-equip themselves the next day, which was Saturday, and all day on Sunday, and then on Monday they would attack. They would bind together, two-by-two, the *nefs* equipped with ladders, and in this way they would attack a single tower with two ships. They had seen that day that if only one ship attacked a tower each ship was overwhelmed, as the men on the tower outnumbered the men on the ladders. For this reason it seemed a sound proposal that two ladders would be more of a threat to a tower than one. This was done as had been agreed, and thus they waited out Saturday and Sunday.

[241] Emperor Mourtzouphlus had come and set up camp with all his forces in an area in front of our point of attack, and had pitched his red tents. Matters continued thus until Monday morning when the men in the *nefs*, transports and galleys were armed. The people of the city feared them less than they had done at first, and they were in such good spirits that all one could see along the walls and towers was people. Then the assault started, fierce and awesome, and each of the vessels attacked straight ahead. The cries from the battle were so great that it seemed that the earth was quaking.

[242] The assault went on in this way for some time, until Our Lord raised a wind known as Boreas,[3] which drove the *nefs* and other vessels further on to the shore than before. Two *nefs* which had been bound together, one of which was called

the *Pilgrim* and the other the *Paradise*, came before a tower, one on one side and the other on the other side – as God and the winds directed them – so that the *Pilgrim*'s ladder landed on the tower. Straightaway a Venetian and a French knight called Andrew Dureboise entered the tower, and others entered after them. Those who had held the tower lost heart and fled.

[243] When the knights in the transports saw this, they came ashore and raised ladders against the face of the wall. They climbed up the wall by force and captured at least four of the towers. Men began to leap from the *nefs* and transports and galleys as and when each saw his chance. They broke through at least three of the gates and entered inside. They began to lead the horses out of the transports, and the knights mounted them and rode straight to Emperor Mourtzouphlus's camp. He had ranged his battalions in front of his tents, but when they saw the mounted knights coming, they lost heart and fled, and the emperor took flight through the streets to the palace of Bucoleon.

[244] Then you might have seen Greeks being struck down, and horses and palfreys seized along with he-mules, she-mules and other booty. There were so many dead and wounded that they were endless and innumerable. Many of the great men of Greece turned and fled towards the gate of Blachernae. The hour of vespers had already passed, and the men of the army were wearied by battle and killing. They began to gather in a great square inside Constantinople. Since they scarcely believed they could bring the city – with its mighty churches and strong palaces and all the people it held – under their control within a month, it was agreed they should camp near to the walls and towers that they had already captured. This was done as had been agreed.

[245] And so they set up camp outside the walls and outside the towers, close to their ships. Count Baldwin of Flanders and Hainaut lodged in Emperor Mourtzouphlus's red tents, which he had abandoned still pitched, and Henry, the count's brother, camped outside the palace of Blachernae. Marquis Boniface of Montferrat and his company camped near the most built-up part of the city. And so the army was encamped as you have

heard, Constantinople having been taken on the Monday before Palm Sunday.[4] Count Louis of Blois and Chartres had suffered from a quartan fever throughout the winter and could not bear arms. You should know that this was a great loss to the men of the army, for he was a very good knight but he was bed-ridden in one of the transports.

[246] Thus the men of the army, who were very tired, rested that night. But Emperor Mourtzouphlus did not rest; instead he gathered all his men, saying he would go and attack the Franks. But he did not do as he said; rather he rode out along other streets, as far away as he could from the men of the army, and came to a gate known as the Golden Gate. Through this he fled and abandoned the city, and those who were able to do so fled after him. The men of the army knew nothing of all this.

[247] During the night, near to Marquis Boniface of Montferrat's camp, certain men – I'm not sure who – set a fire between themselves and the Greeks, fearing that the Greeks might attack them. The city began to catch fire and burned very fiercely. It burned all that night and the next day until vespers. This was the third fire in Constantinople since the Franks arrived in that country, and more houses were burned than there are in the three largest cities in the kingdom of France.

[248] That night passed and day came. It was Tuesday morning. Everyone in the camp, both knights and sergeants, armed himself and each man joined his own battalion. They left their quarters thinking that they would encounter a greater battle than they had yet fought, since they did not know that the emperor had fled that very day. They found no one to oppose them.

[249] The marquis of Montferrat rode out along the shore, straight towards the Bucoleon. When he arrived there the palace was given up to him on the condition that the lives of those inside would be spared. There they found many of the most noble women in the world, who had fled to the palace: the sister of the king of France, the former empress, and the sister of the king of Hungary, another former empress,[5] and many other noble women. It is impossible to describe the treasures

there were in that palace, for there were so many that they were endless and innumerable.

[250] Just as this palace was given up to Marquis Boniface of Montferrat, so the palace of Blachernae was given up to Henry, brother of Count Baldwin of Flanders, on condition that the lives of those inside would be spared. There too were found treasures so very great that there were no fewer than in the Bucoleon. Each man garrisoned the castle that had been given up to him with his own men and had the treasure guarded. The other men had scattered throughout the city and seized much booty, and the spoils were so great that no one could tell you how much it amounted to in gold, silver, tableware, precious stones, samite, silk cloth, garments of vair, grey fur and ermine, and all the fine things that were ever found on Earth. And Geoffrey of Villehardouin, marshal of Champagne, bears faithful witness in accordance with his certain knowledge, that no such spoils were won in any city since the creation of the world.

[251] Each man chose lodgings that pleased him, and there were plenty to go round. And so the army of pilgrims and Venetians established their quarters. There was great rejoicing at the honour and victory that God had granted them, for those who had been in poverty were now in wealth and luxury. Thus they celebrated Palm Sunday and the following Easter Sunday[6] in God-given honour and joy. And they certainly should have praised Our Lord, since they had no more than 20,000 armed men among them, and they had conquered 400,000 men or more in the strongest city in all the world, a great city and the best fortified.

[252] On behalf of Marquis Boniface of Montferrat, who was leader of the army, and on behalf of the barons and the doge of Venice, it was then made known throughout the camp that all valuables should be brought forward for collection, as had been promised with sworn oaths and on pain of excommunication. Three churches were named as the sites for this collection, where the French and Venetians set the most trustworthy men they could find to keep guard. And individuals began to come forward with their booty and it was gathered together.

[253] Some were honest in presenting their spoils, others deceitful. Greed, which is the root of all evil, knew no restraint; from that time forward greedy people started to hoard things for themselves, and Our Lord started to love them less. Oh, God – they had behaved so loyally up to that point! And Lord God had demonstrated that in all their affairs he had honoured and exalted them over all other people. But on many occasions good people suffer because of the wicked.

[254] The money and booty were gathered, but you should know that not nearly all of it was brought forward. A good number of people held on to their spoils, despite the threat of excommunication by the pope. What was brought to the churches was gathered together and shared equally between the Franks and the Venetians, as all parties had sworn to do. And know that once this division had been made the pilgrims paid 50,000 marks of silver to the Venetians, and they then had around 100,000 marks of silver to share among their own men. This was how they distributed it: two foot sergeants received the same as one mounted sergeant, while two mounted sergeants received the same as one knight. And you should know that no one received more than this on account of his higher rank or particular prowess, unless it was decided in advance that he should have it – or unless he stole it. [255] And know that those found guilty of stealing met with severe justice – a good number were hanged. One of the count of Saint-Pol's knights, who had kept booty for himself, was hanged with his shield still at his neck. But there were many, of both higher and lower ranks, who had kept their booty and were not found out. You should be certain that the spoils were large; apart from what was stolen and the Venetians' share, they amounted to around 400,000 marks of silver as well as around 10,000 horses of various kinds. Thus were the spoils of Constantinople distributed, as you have just heard.

CHAPTER 8

The Election of an Emperor and its Aftermath

(April–August 1204)

[256] All the people of the army met in an assembly and stated their wish that an emperor be elected, as had been agreed. Their discussions went on so long that they fixed another day on which they would appoint the twelve men who would make the election. Inevitably, a large number of men yearned for or lusted after a dignity as great as that of emperor of Constantinople. But the principal disagreement on this point concerned Count Baldwin of Flanders and Hainaut and Marquis Boniface of Montferrat; everyone said that one of these two men should be emperor.

[257] When the *preudommes* of the army realized that they all supported either one or other of these two men, they talked among themselves and said, 'Sirs, if we elect one of these two eminent men, the other will be so jealous that he will leave with all his men, and the land might be lost as a result. The land of Jerusalem was nearly lost in a similar situation, when Godfrey of Bouillon was chosen as ruler in the wake of its conquest. The count of Saint-Gilles was so jealous that he persuaded some of the other barons and as many other people as he could to leave the army; a good number of them did as he wished and so few remained in Jerusalem that they would have lost that land[1] had God not come to their aid. We must be mindful of this, and take care that the same thing doesn't happen to us. [258] Let's think about how we might keep both of them here, and how the other may be satisfied regardless of which one of them is, by God's will, elected as emperor. Whoever is elected emperor should give the other man all the land on the other side of the Straits of Saint George, towards the land of the Turks, along

with the island of Greece,[2] and he will be the emperor's vassal for these lands. In this way both men might be induced to stay.' This was done as had been agreed; the two candidates consented to the arrangement most graciously. The day of the meeting came and everyone assembled. Twelve men were chosen, six from one side and six from the other, who swore on relics that they would in good faith elect the man who would be most effective and the best governor of the empire.

[259] Thus were the twelve chosen, and a day was appointed for the election. When that day arrived they gathered at an elegant palace – one of the most beautiful in the world – where the doge of Venice had taken up residence. There was so great a number of people assembled that it was truly amazing; everyone wanted to see who would be elected. The twelve men whose duty was to make the election were called forward and were sent to a most magnificent chapel inside the palace. Its door was locked from the outside and they were all alone; the barons and knights waited inside a great palace, away from the chapel.

[260] The conference lasted until they reached agreement. One of the electors, Bishop Nivelon of Soissons, was appointed with the approval of all his colleagues to speak on their behalf. They all left the chapel and went to where the barons and the doge of Venice were. Now, you may be assured that they were being watched by a throng of men who wanted to discern the results of the election. The bishop made the announcement, saying, 'My lords, we have agreed – thank God! – to appoint an emperor, and you have all sworn to support whichever man we choose and to come to his aid should anyone oppose him. We name him at the hour of God's birth:[3] Count Baldwin of Flanders and Hainaut.'

[261] A cry of joy rose up from the palace, and the count was taken from there to the church. Marquis Boniface of Montferrat was foremost among those at his side to escort him, and he showed the count all possible honour. Thus was Count Baldwin of Flanders and Hainaut elected as emperor, and the date of his coronation was set for three weeks after Easter.[4] And you may be assured that the most sumptuous robes were made for this coronation, as was only fitting.

[262] Before the day of the coronation Marquis Boniface of Montferrat married the empress (Emperor Isaac's widow, who was the king of Hungary's sister). During the same period one of the most high-ranking barons in the army died, whose name was Odo the Champenois of Champlitte; his brother and his friends wept and mourned him deeply. He was buried with great honour in the church of the Apostles.

[263] Coronation day arrived, and Emperor Baldwin was crowned with great honour and great joy in the church of Saint Sophia, in the year of Jesus Christ's incarnation 1204. It is impossible to describe the celebration and feasting; suffice to say the barons and the knights were as generous as they could be. Marquis Boniface of Montferrat and Count Louis showed the new emperor the honour due to him as their lord. After the great joy of the coronation he was led with much festivity and in a large procession to the sumptuous palace of Bucoleon, which was as splendid as any palace ever seen. And once the feasting was over the emperor settled down to business.

[264] Marquis Boniface of Montferrat called on the emperor to fulfil their agreement by giving him, as he had committed to do, the land beyond the straits towards the land of the Turks, and the island of Greece. The emperor understood clearly that he was bound to do this, and said that he was very willing to do so. Seeing that the emperor was ready to keep his promise so graciously, the marquis of Montferrat asked him whether he would, in exchange for those lands, give him the kingdom of Salonika,[5] which lay towards the lands of the king of Hungary, whose sister was his wife.

[265] The matter was discussed and many views expressed, but in the end the emperor gave his consent, and the marquis did homage to him for Salonika. There was great rejoicing throughout the army because the marquis was one of the most highly prized knights in the world and was deeply loved by his fellow knights; no one was more generous to them. Thus, as you have heard, was the marquis of Montferrat persuaded to stay in that land.

[266] Emperor Mourtzouphlus had withdrawn less than four days' journey from Constantinople, having left with the

empress who was the wife of Emperor Alexius (who had previously fled the city)[6] and her daughter. This Emperor Alexius
and all his men were at that time in the city of Mosynopolis,
from where he still controlled a large portion of the empire.
The most high-ranking of the Greeks went their separate ways,
many of them crossing over the straits to the side towards the
land of the Turks, where they each seized as much land as they
could for themselves. Other men did the same in other parts of
the empire, each seizing lands in his own region.

[267] As soon as he could, Emperor Mourtzouphlus took a
city called Tchorlu that had surrendered to my lord Emperor
Baldwin. He captured it, ransacked it and seized all that he
found there. When news of this reached Emperor Baldwin, he
held council with the barons and with the doge of Venice; they
all agreed in advising him to set out in full force in order to
conquer his lands. Constantinople should be left with a garrison
to ensure its security, since it was newly captured and inhabited
by Greeks.

[268] The decision was taken; the army was summoned and
it was determined who would remain in Constantinople. Count
Louis of Blois and Chartres, who had been sick and still had
not recovered, would stay along with the doge of Venice. Conon
of Béthune would take charge of the palaces of Blachernae and
Bucoleon in order to defend the city, with Geoffrey the marshal
of Champagne, Milon le Bréban, Manassiers of l'Isle and all
their men. The others prepared themselves to go with the
emperor's army.

[269] Before leaving Constantinople Emperor Baldwin
ordered his brother Henry to set out ahead of him, accompanied
by around a hundred very good knights. They rode from town
to town, and in each place the people swore their loyalty to the
emperor. Thus they went as far as Adrianople, which was a
very fine and wealthy city, where the people welcomed them
very warmly and swore their loyalty to the emperor. Henry and
his men then found lodgings in the city and stayed there until
Emperor Baldwin's arrival.

[270] When Emperor Mourtzouphlus learned that Emperor
Baldwin's forces were on their way, he did not dare stay where

he was. He fled, always keeping two or three days ahead of the
new emperor's men. He went in the direction of Mosynopolis,
where Emperor Alexius was, and sent messengers informing
Alexius that he would assist him and do whatever he commanded. Emperor Alexius replied that he would welcome
Mourtzouphlus as if he were his son; indeed he hoped Mourtzouphlus would marry his daughter and in fact become his son.
And so Emperor Mourtzouphlus encamped outside Mosynopolis, pitching his tents and his pavilions there while Alexius
was lodged inside the city. They then held discussions which
settled that Alexius would give Mourtzouphlus his daughter
and that they would form an alliance; they said they would act
as one.

[271] I am not certain how many days they stayed there, one
in the camp and the other inside the city. But after a while
Emperor Alexius called for Emperor Mourtzouphlus to come
and eat with him, saying they would go to the baths together.
Thus it was planned, and so it was done. As he had been
instructed, Emperor Mourtzouphlus came in secret, accompanied by just a few men. When he had entered the house,
Emperor Alexius called him into a chamber, where he threw
him on the floor and put the eyes out of his head. Such – as you
have just heard it described – was his treachery. Now consider
whether such people as this, who commit such atrocities against
each other, should keep their lands or lose them. When the men
in Emperor Mourtzouphlus's army heard what had happened,
they lost heart and fled, some in one direction and some in
another. Some of them went over to Emperor Alexius and
obeyed him as their lord, joining his following.

[272] Emperor Baldwin had set out from Constantinople
with his entire force. They rode until they came to Adrianople,
where they found his brother Henry and the other people with
him. Along their route, everyone came to surrender to Baldwin
and subject themselves to his will. News reached them that
Emperor Alexius had put out Emperor Mourtzouphlus's eyes,
which prompted intense debate; it was firmly declared that men
who so wickedly betrayed each other had no right to hold
lands.

[273] Emperor Baldwin decided he would ride straight to Mosynopolis, where Emperor Alexius was staying. The Greeks of Adrianople asked Baldwin, as their lord, to leave their town with a garrison to defend them against Johanitsa, king of Vlachia and Bulgaria, who launched frequent attacks against them. Emperor Baldwin left Eustace of Salperwick, a most worthy and most valiant knight from Flanders, with forty very good knights and a hundred mounted sergeants.

[274] And so Emperor Baldwin set out from Adrianople, and rode towards Mosynopolis, where he expected to find Emperor Alexius. All the lands through which he passed came under his command and were subjected to his authority. Seeing this, Emperor Alexius abandoned Mosynopolis and fled. Emperor Baldwin rode on until he arrived before that city, the inhabitants of which came out to meet him and surrender it to his control.

[275] Emperor Baldwin announced that he would stay there and wait for Boniface, the marquis of Montferrat, who had not yet joined the army; he had not been able to travel as quickly as the emperor since he was bringing his wife, the empress, with him. Boniface rode on until he came to the river near Mosynopolis. He set up camp there, pitching his tents and his pavilions, and the following day he went to see and to talk to Emperor Baldwin, and to ask him to fulfil his promise.

[276] 'My lord,' said the marquis, 'news has reached me from Salonika. The people of that country have informed me that they will very gladly receive me as their lord. I have done homage to you for that land, I hold it from you and so I beg you to permit me to go there. When I have secured my lands and my city, I will come back to you bringing provisions and ready to do as you command. Do not ruin my lands for me. Let's go instead, if you are willing, and attack Johanitsa, the king of Vlachia and Bulgaria, who unjustly holds a large part of the empire's land.'

[277] I do not know on whose advice the emperor replied that, regardless of the marquis's views, he intended to go to Salonika as well as taking care of his other concerns in the empire. 'My lord,' said Marquis Boniface, 'I plead with you not to go there, since I can take possession of my lands without

you. If you do go there you will not be doing so for my benefit, or so it seems to me. And you should know for certain that I will under no circumstances go with you; I will rather take my leave of you.' Emperor Baldwin responded that, despite what had been said, he was not in the least deterred from going.

[278] Alas! How ill-advised both men were, and what a great sin was committed by those who encouraged this conflict! For, had God not taken pity on them, they would have lost all the conquests they had made, and Christendom would have been in danger of ruin! Emperor Baldwin of Constantinople and Marquis Boniface of Montferrat parted on bad terms, and on bad advice.

[279] As he had undertaken to do, Emperor Baldwin rode out towards Salonika with all his men and all his might. Marquis Boniface of Montferrat turned back, taking a large body of good men with him. James of Avesnes returned with him, as did William of Champlitte, Hugh of Coligny, Count Berthold of Katzenellenbogen, and the majority of the men from the German empire, who were followers of the marquis. He rode back as far as a castle called Demotika, which was very handsome, very strong and very wealthy. One of the Greek inhabitants of the town surrendered it to him, and once they were inside they put defensive forces in place. As a result of their friendly relations with the empress, the Greeks of the town began to come over to the marquis's side, and after that all the Greeks in the area within one or two days' journey from there came under his authority.

[280] Emperor Baldwin immediately rode straight towards Salonika, coming to a castle called Christopolis, which was one of the strongest in the world. It was surrendered to him and the people of the town swore loyalty to him. Afterwards he came to another castle, called La Blanche, which was very strong and very wealthy. It was likewise surrendered to him, and the people swore loyalty to him. From there he rode to Serres, a strong and wealthy city that was subjected to his authority and to his will; its people swore their loyalty to him. From that place he rode on towards the city of Salonika. He set up camp outside the city, and stayed there for three days. The people surrendered

the city to him – which was one of the finest and most prosperous in Christendom at that time – on the condition that he would maintain the usages and customs upheld by the Greek emperors.

[281] While Emperor Baldwin was in Salonika, subjecting the land to his will and authority, Marquis Boniface of Montferrat took all his men and a large number of his Greek followers and went to Adrianople. He laid siege to the city, pitching his tents and pavilions around it. Eustace of Salperwick was inside with the men the emperor had left there; they climbed up on to the walls and into the towers, preparing to defend themselves. [282] Then Eustace of Salperwick summoned two messengers and sent them to Constantinople. They travelled day and night, until they came to the doge of Venice, Count Louis, and those who had stayed in the city on Emperor Baldwin's behalf. The messengers told them that Eustace of Salperwick sent word that the emperor and the marquis had fallen out with each other, and that the marquis had seized Demotika – one of the strongest castles in Romania as well as one of the richest – and that he had laid siege to Adrianople. The men at Constantinople were very upset to hear this, for they were sure that all the conquests they had made would be lost.

[283] The doge of Venice, Count Louis of Blois and Chartres and the other barons in Constantinople gathered at the palace of Blachernae. They were deeply distressed and vexed, and railed bitterly against those who had caused the quarrel between the emperor and the marquis. At the request of the doge of Venice and of Count Louis, Geoffrey of Villehardouin, marshal of Champagne, was asked to go to the siege of Adrianople and put an end to this conflict if he could; he was highly thought of by the marquis and it was believed he would have more influence in this instance than any other man. Acknowledging their pleas and the perilous situation, the marshal said that he would very gladly go. He took with him Manassiers of l'Isle, who was one of the best knights in the army and one of the most highly respected.

[284] And so they set out from Constantinople and rode on day after day to reach Adrianople, where the siege was taking

place. When the marquis saw them he came out of the camp and went to meet them. With him went James of Avesnes, William of Champlitte, Hugh of Coligny and Othon of la Roche, the most high-ranking members of the marquis's council. When they saw these messengers they showed them great honour and made them very welcome.

[285] Marshal Geoffrey, who was very highly thought of by Marquis Boniface, rebuked him sternly for the way in which he had seized the emperor's lands and laid siege to the people inside Adrianople before informing the men in Constantinople, who would certainly have set matters straight if the emperor had done him any wrong. The marquis vehemently defended his actions, saying that it was the emperor's unjust treatment that had made him act as he had done.

[286] Geoffrey, marshal of Champagne, with help from God and from the barons who advised the marquis, who all had great affection for him, applied himself so assiduously that the marquis agreed to place the matter in the hands of the doge of Venice, Count Louis of Blois and Chartres, Conon of Béthune and Marshal Geoffrey of Villehardouin, all of whom were well informed about the agreement that had been made between the marquis and the emperor. Thus a truce was secured between the people of the besieging army and those inside the city.

[287] And know that the people of the army and those inside the city thanked Marshal Geoffrey and Manassiers of l'Isle very warmly as they set out again; both sides were eager for peace. But while the Franks were happy the Greeks were dismayed, for they would have gladly welcomed war and confusion. Thus the siege of Adrianople was lifted, and the marquis turned back with all his men to Demotika, where his wife was waiting.

[288] The envoys returned to Constantinople and reported the outcome of their efforts; the doge of Venice, Count Louis and all the others rejoiced that the marquis had charged them with establishing peace. Then they employed trustworthy messengers, wrote a letter and sent it to Emperor Baldwin to inform him that the marquis had referred his grievance to them and had given them assurance of his good faith. He, the emperor, should show himself even more willing to submit the case to

them. The arbitrators urged him to do so – since war was utterly
intolerable to them – and to give them an assurance, in the
same way the marquis had done, that he would adhere to their
judgement.

[289] Meanwhile, Emperor Baldwin had attended to his
affairs in the region of Salonika; he set out from there leaving
a defensive force made up of his own men led by Renier of
Mons, a most worthy and valiant man. News reached the
emperor that the marquis had captured Demotika and taken up
residence in the city, that he had seized much of the surrounding
lands and that he had laid siege to the emperor's people inside
Adrianople. Emperor Baldwin was enraged when this news
came, and he made haste to go to break the siege, intending to
damage the marquis as severely as he could. Oh God! What
harm might have been done by this conflict! If God had not
imposed his will, Christendom would have been destroyed.

[290] Emperor Baldwin travelled day after day on his return
journey. While he was outside Salonika, a great misfortune
had befallen his forces; many of them were bed-ridden by sickness. A good number of them then withdrew to castles that the
emperor passed along the way, unable to go further, while
many others were carried on litters and continued in great
distress. Master John of Noyon, Emperor Baldwin's chancellor,
died at Serres. He had been a very good and wise clerk, and had
given great comfort to the army through his fluent preaching of
the word of God. You should know that his death prompted
great sadness among the *preudommes* of the army.

[291] Not long after this another great misfortune struck
them with the death of Peter of Amiens, who was a very rich
and high-ranking man and a good and worthy knight. Count
Hugh of Saint-Pol, his first cousin, grieved very deeply for him,
and his death weighed heavily on everyone in the army. Then
Gerard of Mauchicourt died, and he too was a great loss to the
army, having been one of its most highly valued knights. Giles
of Aunoi also died, and many other good men. Forty knights
died in the course of this journey, leaving the army much the
weaker.

[292] Emperor Baldwin kept riding, day after day, until he

met the messengers who had been sent from Constantinople to find him. One of the messengers was a knight from Count Louis of Blois's lands – he was the count's liegeman – whose name was Bègues of Fransures. He was an able and articulate man, and he delivered the message from his lord and the other barons very spiritedly, saying, [293] 'My lord, the doge of Venice, my lord Count Louis and the other barons at Constantinople send you their greetings as their lord. They also cry out to God and to you against those who stirred up this conflict between you and the marquis of Montferrat, for they have come close to bringing about Christendom's ruin; you acted most unwisely in heeding them. The doge and the barons want you to know that the marquis has placed himself in their hands as concerns your dispute, and they urge you as their lord to do likewise, and to promise to honour their decision. And they would have you know that they will under no circumstances tolerate a war.'

[294] Emperor Baldwin left to call his council, telling the messengers that he would give them his response. Many members of the emperor's council had been among those who helped create this quarrel, and they regarded the message sent by the men at Constantinople as highly insolent. 'Sir,' they said to the emperor, 'you have heard their message to you – that they will not tolerate your taking revenge on your enemy. It appears that if you do not do as they ask that they will turn against you.'

[295] Many proud opinions were put forward, but when it came to making a decision, the emperor was not willing to cut himself off from the doge of Venice or Count Louis or the others who were at Constantinople. And so he replied to the messenger, 'I will not promise to submit my case to their judgement, but I will return to Constantinople without taking any action against the marquis.' Thus Emperor Baldwin arrived at Constantinople, and the barons and the other people went out to meet him and welcomed him with great honour as their lord.

[296] Before four days had passed the emperor came to see clearly that he had been ill-advised to enter into a dispute with the marquis. The doge of Venice and Count Louis then spoke to him, saying, 'Sir, we wish to urge you to submit yourself to

our judgement, just as the marquis has done.' And the emperor
said that he would do so most willingly. Envoys were chosen
who would go to the marquis and bring him back; one of them
was Gervase of Châteauneuf, Renier of Trit was another and
the third was Geoffrey, marshal of Champagne. The doge of
Venice sent two of his own men.

[297] The envoys rode on day after day until they arrived at
Demotika, where they found the marquis and his wife, the
empress, with a host of worthy people. They announced that
they had come to fetch him, and Marshal Geoffrey asked him
to keep his promise, to come to Constantinople and give his
consent to the peace negotiated by the arbitrators. The envoys
would conduct the marquis safely to Constantinople, as well as
all those who might accompany him.

[298] The marquis took advice from his men, some of whom
agreed that he should go while others urged him to do no such
thing. But the outcome of the meeting was that he went with
the envoys to Constantinople, taking fully a hundred knights
with him. They rode out, day after day, until they came to the
city, where they were very warmly welcomed. Count Louis of
Blois and Chartres and the doge of Venice went out to meet
them, along with many other worthy people from the army,
who loved them very much.

[299] They all gathered for a conference, at which the former
agreement between Emperor Baldwin and Marquis Boniface
was renewed. Salonika and its lands were returned to the marquis on condition that he placed Demotika, which he had seized
for himself, into the hands of Geoffrey, marshal of Champagne.
The marshal would promise to keep Demotika until he had
received an official messenger or a sealed letter informing him
that the marquis had taken possession of Salonika. At that
point the marshal would return Demotika to the emperor and
imperial authority. Thus, as you have heard, was peace made
between the emperor and the marquis. This prompted great joy
throughout the army, for their conflict might have caused great
harm.

[300] Then the marquis took his leave, setting out for Salonika together with his men and his wife. Envoys from the

emperor went with him, and as they went from castle to castle, each was surrendered to the marquis on the emperor's behalf, along with all its associated rights. They reached Salonika, and its defenders surrendered it on the emperor's behalf. The leader of the garrison, who was a notable *preudomme* called Renier of Mons, had died, and his death was a bitter loss.

[301] The people of the land and the country then began to subject themselves to the marquis, and a great number of them came under his authority. There was one exception: a high-ranking Greek man called Sgouros,[7] who did not want to accept his authority at all; he had seized Corinth and Nauplia, two cities on the coast which were among the strongest under Heaven. Sgouros had no intention of surrendering to the marquis; instead he embarked on a war with him, and many people were drawn to his cause. Another Greek, called Michael,[8] had come with the marquis from Constantinople and was highly thought of by him. But he broke off from the marquis without saying a word, and made for a city called Arta. He married the daughter of a powerful Greek man who had held lands from the Greek emperor, and, after taking control of that land himself, Michael set out to make war on the marquis.

CHAPTER 9

The Latins Take Possession of their Lands and the Greeks Resist

(September 1204–March 1205)

[302] The region from Constantinople to Salonika enjoyed such perfect peace that the roads were safe enough for all to come and go as they pleased between the cities, which was a distance of at least twelve full days' journey. So much time had passed that it was the end of September. Emperor Baldwin was at Constantinople and his lands were at peace and securely under his control. During this period two very good knights died at Constantinople, Eustace of Canteleux and Aimery of Villeray, and this was a great loss for their friends.

[303] Lands within the empire began to be shared out at this time. The Venetians received their share and the pilgrim army the rest. Once each man had been assigned his lands, worldly greed – which has been the cause of so much wickedness – allowed them no peace. They all began to exploit their lands unjustly – some more, others less – and the Greeks began to despise them, and bear ill will towards them in their hearts.

[304] Emperor Baldwin gave Count Louis the duchy of Nicaea, which was one of the highest dignities in Romania. Nicaea lay on the other side of the straits, towards the land of the Turks, where none of the land had yet come under the emperor's authority; indeed, it was holding out against him. Later, he gave the Duchy of Philippopolis to Renier of Trit. [305] Count Louis sent fully 120 knights from among his men to conquer his lands. The leaders of this force were Peter of Bracieux and Payen of Orléans. They set out from Constantinople on the feast of All Saints,[1] crossing the straits to Abydos and going on to Espigal, a coastal city inhabited by Latins. From there they embarked on a war against the Greeks.

[306] It so happened that during this same period the blinded Emperor Mourtzouphlus, who had murdered his lord, Emperor Alexius (who was the son of Emperor Isaac and had been brought to this land by the pilgrims), fled unnoticed across the straits with just a few men. Dietrich of Looz discovered this when Mourtzouphlus's hiding place was betrayed to him, and captured him and took him to Emperor Baldwin in Constantinople. Emperor Baldwin was delighted at this, and took advice from his men as to what he should do with a man who had committed such a treachery against his own lord. [307] The council agreed on the following punishment. There was a column in the centre of the city of Constantinople,[2] one of the highest and most intricately sculpted marble columns anyone has ever laid eyes on. They would have him taken to the top, and then make him jump from it in front of all the people, since it was right that everyone should see high justice being done. And so Emperor Mourtzouphlus was led to the column and taken to the top; all the people of the city flocked to see such a remarkable sight. He was pushed off, and he fell from such a height that when he hit the ground his body shattered completely.

[308] Now hear of a great and wondrous thing: on that column from which Mourtzouphlus had been cast down, there were figures of many different kinds depicted in the marble. Among these was one sculpted in the form of an emperor who was falling down. It had for a long time been prophesied that there would be an emperor in Constantinople who would be thrown down from this same column. And thus were this scene and this prophecy realized.

[309] At about the same time it so happened that, in a similar turn of events, Marquis Boniface of Montferrat, who was near Salonika, captured Emperor Alexius (the man who had blinded Emperor Isaac) along with his wife. He sent Alexius's scarlet boots and imperial robes[3] to his lord in Constantinople, Emperor Baldwin, who was very grateful for them. He later sent Emperor Alexius to prison in Montferrat.[4]

[310] On the following feast of Saint Martin[5], Henry, Emperor Baldwin's brother, left Constantinople and went

down the straits as far as the Abydos Channel, taking 120 very good knights with him. He crossed the straits to the city called Abydos, which he found to be very well stocked with all good things, with grain and with food and with everything his men might need. He seized the city for himself and found lodgings inside it before starting to make war on the Greeks in the surrounding territory. The Armenians in that region, of whom there were a great number, began to come over to his side; they deeply loathed the Greeks.

[311] It was around this time that Renier of Trit left Constantinople to go to Philippopolis, which had been granted to him by Emperor Baldwin. He took with him at least 120 very good knights and rode out, day after day, beyond Adrianople to Philippopolis. The people of that land welcomed and recognized him as their lord, and were very pleased to see him. They had real need of protection because Johanitsa, the king of Vlachia, had oppressed them with war. Renier was a great help to them; he secured possession of a large part of that land, and most of the people who had supported Johanitsa came over to his side. This region saw bitter fighting flare up between them.

[312] The emperor had sent fully a hundred knights across the Straits of Saint George to the region opposite Constantinople, under the leadership of Macaire of Sainte-Menehould. He was accompanied by Matthew of Walincourt and Robert of Ronsoy. They rode out to a city called Nicomedia, which sits on a bay by the sea a good two days' journey from Constantinople. When the Greeks heard they were coming, they abandoned the city and fled. Macaire of Sainte-Menehould and his men lodged themselves in the city, putting a garrison in place and repairing its defences. And they began to make war in the territory round about. [313] The land on that side of the straits was controlled by a Greek lord named Theodore Lascaris,[6] who claimed it by right of his wife. She was a daughter of the emperor who had put out his brother's eyes, and whom the Franks had driven from Constantinople. Theodore Lascaris made war on the Franks wherever they went beyond the straits.

[314] Emperor Baldwin and Count Louis stayed at Constantinople with just a few men. Count Hugh of Saint-Pol was there

too, suffering from a severe attack of gout which afflicted his knees and feet. [315] Not long afterwards a great number of people from the land of Syria arrived by sea in the city, along with some of those who had split off from the army and travelled by other routes. Stephen of Perche and Renaut of Montmirail came in this group; they were cousins of Count Louis, who showed them great honour and was delighted by their arrival. Emperor Baldwin and the other people were very glad to see them too, for they were very high-ranking men, and very wealthy; they brought a large number of good men with them. [316] Hugh of Tiberias came from Syria with his brother Ralph, Thierry of Termonde, and a great many other people from that country, knights, turcopoles and sergeants. Not long afterwards Emperor Baldwin gave the Duchy of Philadelphia to Stephen of Perche.

[317] Among other reports to arrive in Constantinople was one piece of news that deeply saddened Emperor Baldwin. Before becoming emperor he had left his wife, Countess Marie, in Flanders, because she was pregnant and unable to travel. She gave birth to a daughter and later, once she had recovered, set out to go overseas in the wake of her lord. She sailed from the port of Marseilles and had only barely reached Acre when news arrived from Constantinople, delivered by her lord's own messenger, that the city had fallen and that her lord had been made emperor – a cause for rejoicing among all Christian people. [318] Hearing this news, the lady planned to go to join her husband. But she was struck down by illness, and so met her end and died. All Christian people mourned her deeply, for she was a most virtuous woman and had been greatly respected. The people who arrived from Syria by sea brought this news to Constantinople; it was the cause of great grief to Emperor Baldwin and all the barons in that land, who had very much wanted her to be their lady.

[319] During this period, the men who had gone to the city of Espigal under the leadership of Peter of Bracieux and Payen of Orléans refortified a castle called Panormos and garrisoned it with a body of their own men before riding out further, to conquer the land. Theodore Lascaris had obtained as many

men as he could, and on the day of the feast of our lord Saint Nicholas[7] which falls before the Nativity the two forces met on the plain outside a castle called Poemanenos. They did battle with our men, who were at a great disadvantage; Theodore Lascaris had a staggering number of men, while ours had no more than 140 knights alongside a number of mounted sergeants.

[320] But Our Lord grants fortune as he pleases. Through his grace and his good will the Franks overcame the Greeks, defeating and inflicting heavy losses on them. Within a week the Greeks had surrendered a large part of that territory to them; our men took Poemanenos, which was a very strong castle, and Leopadeion, which was one of the finest towns in that land, as well as Apollonia, which was situated on a fresh-water lake and had one of the strongest and best castles one could ever hope to find. And know that with God's help things turned out very well for them and they were able to impose their will in that land.

[321] Not long after these events and on the advice of the Armenians, Henry, Emperor Baldwin's brother, left a number of his men to defend the city of Abydos and set out to ride to a city called Adramyttion, which was two days' journey away from Abydos, on the coast. The city was surrendered to him and he lodged his forces inside it. Most of the people of the surrounding land then surrendered to him, for they knew that the city was very well supplied with grain and food and other useful things. And so Henry and his men made war on the Greeks in this region.

[322] Having been defeated at Poemanenos Theodore Lascaris gathered as many men as he could to form a very substantial army. He appointed his brother, Constantine, one of the most capable Greeks in Romania, as commander of this force. Constantine led his men straight to Adramyttion. Henry, Emperor Baldwin's brother, received word from the Armenians that a great army was on its way to attack him, and so he attended to his affairs and organized his battalions. He had many fine men with him, including Baldwin of Beauvoir, Nicholas of Mailly, Anseau of Cayeux, Dietrich of Looz and Thierry of Termonde.

[323] It so happened that Constantine Lascaris arrived before Adramyttion with his great army on the Saturday before mid-Lent.[8] When Henry learned of their coming he took advice and announced that he would not let himself be surrounded inside the city, instead he would go out to face his opponents. Lascaris approached with his entire army ranged in large battalions of mounted men and foot soldiers, and Henry ventured out of the city to give them battle. The combat was fierce and the fighting intense, but with God's help the Franks overcame and defeated the Greeks. They inflicted many deaths and took many prisoners, as well as much booty. Afterwards the Franks were very comfortable and very rich, because the people of that country gave them their support and began to bring them produce from their lands.

[324] Now we will leave those who were in the vicinity of Constantinople and return to Marquis Boniface of Montferrat, who was at Salonika. He was at war with Sgouros, who held Nauplia and Corinth, two of the strongest cities in the world, and the marquis had laid siege to both places at once. James of Avesnes was outside Corinth with a good number of fine men, while the remainder of Marquis Boniface's forces had gone before Nauplia, to lay siege to that city.

[325] There was an interesting development in that region at about this time. Geoffrey of Villehardouin, who was the nephew of Geoffrey the marshal of Romania and Champagne (he was the son of the marshal's brother), had left Syria with the group that had recently arrived at Constantinople and the winds and chance had carried him to the port of Modon. His ship arrived damaged at the port, and necessity required him to spend the winter in those parts. A Greek man who was a powerful lord in that region heard of this and came to him, showing him much honour and saying, 'My dear lord, the Franks have conquered Constantinople and appointed an emperor. If you are willing to join me I will give you my absolute loyalty, so that we might conquer a good part of this land.' They swore allegiance to each other, and did go on to conquer a large part of the land; Geoffrey of Villehardouin found this Greek man's loyalty to be sincere indeed.

[326] But fortunes change according to God's will, and so this Greek man fell ill, met his end and died. His son rebelled against Geoffrey of Villehardouin and betrayed him, turning the castles the allies had garrisoned against him. Geoffrey heard that the marquis was laying siege to Nauplia and set out to join him with as many men as he could muster. In great danger he rode across the country for six days until he arrived at the besieging army's camp, where he was very warmly welcomed and shown great honour by the marquis himself and by the other people there. They were right to do so, for Geoffrey of Villehardouin was very worthy, very valiant, and an able knight.

[327] The marquis wished to give him sufficient land and money to keep him in his service. But Geoffrey did not want to take anything from the marquis, and instead he spoke to his good friend, William of Champlitte, and said to him, 'My lord, I have just come from a very rich land, called Morea. Gather as many men as you can and let's leave this army and go there, and, by God's will, we may make conquests. Whatever land you might wish to give me from those conquests I will hold from you as your liegeman.' William, who had great love for Geoffrey and great faith in him, went to the marquis and told him what had been suggested. The marquis gave them leave to go.

[328] And so William of Champlitte and Geoffrey of Villehardouin left the army, taking with them about a hundred knights as well as good number of mounted sergeants. They entered Morea and rode as far as the city of Modon. Michael[9], hearing that they had arrived in the region with so small a force, gathered a much larger one for himself, made up of a staggering number of men, and rode out after them with the arrogance of a man who believes he has as much as captured his enemies, and has them in his hands.

[329] When our men heard that Michael was coming they restored the fortifications at Modon, which had been pulled down a long time earlier, and left their equipment and their non-combatant followers inside the town. They rode out for one day and organized their force, such as it was, into bat-

talions; they were at a great disadvantage, having no more than 500 mounted men while their opponent had more than 5,000. But Our Lord grants fortune as he pleases, and so our men fought the Greeks and overcame and defeated them, inflicting heavy losses. They also won a great abundance of horses, arms and other valuables. And then they returned, in great joy and great happiness, to the city of Modon.

[330] After this they rode out to a town on the sea called Coron, and they laid siege to it. They had not been doing so for very long before the town was surrendered to them. William gave it to Geoffrey of Villehardouin, who became his vassal for it and garrisoned it with his men. Then they went to a castle called Kalamata, which was very handsome and strong, and besieged that place too. This castle caused them intense and prolonged trouble, but they persisted with their siege until it was surrendered. Once this had happened many of the Greeks in Morea submitted themselves to them – more than had done so at any earlier time.

[331] Marquis Boniface continued his siege of Nauplia but could not make any headway there because the city was too strong. His men were worn out. James of Avesnes kept up the siege of Corinth as the marquis had left him to do. The shrewd and wily Sgouros, who was inside Corinth, noticed that James did not have very many men and that his guard was not very secure. And so one morning, at daybreak, he led a vigorous sortie against them and came as far as the besiegers' pavilions. A good number of our men were killed before they had a chance to arm themselves. [332] Among the dead was Dreux of Etroeungt, a most worthy and valiant man; his death was greatly mourned. The commander of that force, James of Avesnes, was badly wounded in the leg. People who were present at this event have given faithful witness that it was through his good conduct that they were rescued. And you may know with certainty that they were very nearly all lost, but with God's help they drove the enemy back to the castle by force.

CHAPTER 10

Johanitsa's First Campaigns Against the Latin Empire

(March–April 1205)

[333] The Greeks, who were so deceitful, had not rid their hearts of treachery. By this time they could see that the French had gone their separate ways throughout the land, and that each had his own affairs to attend to, so the Greeks thought that now they would be able to betray them. In secret, Greek envoys were appointed in each and every city in the land and sent to Johanitsa, king of Vlachia and Bulgaria, a man who had made war on them in the past and was doing so even then. These envoys told the king that they would make him emperor and surrender to him, and that they would kill all the Franks. They swore to him that they would obey him as their lord, while he swore to them that he would govern them as he did his own subjects. Thus were their oaths sworn.

[334] Around this time a great misfortune struck in Constantinople. Count Hugh of Saint-Pol, who had been bed-ridden for a long while with gout, met his end and died. This was the cause of very great grief and was a very serious blow; his vassals and friends wept bitterly for him. He was buried with great honour in the church of my lord Saint George of Mangana. [335] Before his death Count Hugh had held a castle called Demotika, which was a very strong and wealthy place, and a number of his knights and sergeants were stationed there. The Greeks, who had sworn oaths to the king of Vlachia that they would betray and kill the Franks, turned against the men in that castle, killing and capturing most of them. Few men escaped but those who did get away fled to a city called Adrianople, which was held by the Venetians at that time.

[336] Not long afterwards the people of Adrianople rebelled,

and the men who were garrisoned inside ventured out, in great peril, and abandoned the city. News of this reached Emperor Baldwin of Constantinople and Count Louis of Blois, who were very short of men. They were much concerned by what they heard, and deeply distressed. They began to receive similar bad news day after day: the Greeks were rising up everywhere and killing those Franks whom they found in possession of the land.

[337] The men who had fled from Adrianople – the Venetians and the others who were with them – made their way to a city called Tchorlu, which belonged to Emperor Baldwin. There they found William of Blanvel, who was defending the city on the emperor's behalf. With help from William, who went along with as many men as he could muster, they turned back to a city called Arcadiopolis, which was around twelve leagues from Tchorlu and belonged to the Venetians. They found it empty, and so they entered and garrisoned it.

[338] Within three days the Greeks in that region had gathered, coming from the lands within a day's journey of Arcadiopolis, to begin a fierce and spectacular attack on the city from all sides. Our men defended themselves very well; they opened the gates and made an assault in full strength. As God so willed it, they overwhelmed the Greeks and began to defeat and kill them. They chased them for a league, killing many of them and winning a good number of horses and lots of valuables. [339] They returned, rejoicing, to the city of Arcadiopolis, and then informed Emperor Baldwin at Constantinople of this victory. He was very pleased as a result. In spite of this they did not dare stay to hold the city of Arcadiopolis and instead left the next day, abandoning it. They made their way back to the city of Tchorlu, where they continued to be in great fear. They were equally frightened of the people inside the city and of the Greeks outside, knowing they had all sworn oaths to the king of Vlachia that bound them to betray the Franks. Many of our men would not risk staying there, and instead came back to Constantinople.

[340] Emperor Baldwin, the doge of Venice and Count Louis then held discussions, for they could see that they were going to lose all their land. They agreed that the emperor should recall

his brother, Henry, who was at Adramyttion; he would have to abandon whatever conquests he had made there in order to come and defend the empire. [341] Count Louis recalled Payen of Orléans and Peter of Bracieux and all the men who were with them at Leopadeion. They were to abandon all their conquests, with one exception: Espigal, a town on the coast, was to be garrisoned with as few men as possible while the others came to the emperor's aid. [342] The emperor instructed Macaire of Sainte-Menehould, Matthew of Walincourt and Robert of Ronsoy, who had at least a hundred knights with them at Nicomedia, to abandon the city and come to his assistance.

[343] On the orders of Emperor Baldwin, Geoffrey of Ville-hardouin, marshal of Romania and Champagne, left Constan-tinople with Manassiers of l'Isle and as many men as they could muster; the number was very small considering that the whole empire might be lost. They rode out as far as the city of Tchorlu, which was three days' journey from Constantinople. There they found William of Blanvel and the men who were with him, deeply afraid, and were able to give them great reassurance. Marshal Geoffrey and his men stayed there for four days, when such men as Emperor Baldwin had been able to spare arrived as reinforcements from Constantinople. This meant that there were eighty knights at Tchorlu on that fourth day.

[344] Marshal Geoffrey and Manassiers of l'Isle and their men then set out and rode on to the city of Arcadiopolis, where they lodged for a day before moving off again. They went to another city, Bulgarophygon; the Greeks had left that place empty and so our men found quarters inside. The following day they rode to a city called Nikitza, which was very fine and strong, and well provided with all things. They discovered that the Greeks had abandoned it and had all gone to Adrianople. This city was just nine French leagues away from Adrianople, where a great number of Greeks were now gathered. And so our men agreed that they should wait there for Emperor Baldwin.

[345] Now this book will tell you of an astonishing occur-rence. Renier of Trit, who was at Philippopolis (at least nine days away from Constantinople) with a good 120 knights, was

deserted by his son, Renier, his brother Giles, his nephew James of Bondues and his son-in-law Achard of Verly. Thinking they would go to Constantinople, they stole away with thirty of Renier's knights, leaving him, as you will see, in great danger. The deserters encountered rebels in those parts; they were attacked and defeated, and taken captive by the Greeks, who handed them over to the king of Vlachia. He had their heads cut off. And you should know that these men were little mourned by our people, since they had acted so shamefully towards a man who should have had their loyalty.

[346] When Renier of Trit's other knights, men who were not as close to him as those who had first deserted, learned what had happened they too abandoned him, fearing the shame of leaving less than the danger of staying. Eighty knights deserted altogether, making off by a different route. Renier of Trit was left among the Greeks with very few men; no more than fifteen knights at Philippopolis and Stenimaka, which was a very strong castle he held and where he was later besieged for a long time.

[347] Now we will leave Renier of Trit and return to Emperor Baldwin, who was at Constantinople with a very small number of men, deeply vexed and much distressed. He was waiting for Henry, his brother, and for all the other men who had crossed over the straits. The first to return to him from beyond the straits were the men from Nicomedia: Macaire of Sainte-Menehould, Matthew of Walincourt and Robert of Ronsoy, who brought around a hundred knights in their company. [348] The emperor was very happy to see them. He talked to Louis, who was Count of Blois and Chartres, and they decided to announce that they would venture forth with such men as they had and follow Geoffrey, marshal of Champagne, who had set out before them. Alas! What a pity they did not wait for all the others to arrive from beyond the straits! For they had few men for such dangerous territory as they would pass through.

[349] And so they left Constantinople with around 140 knights, riding onwards, day after day, until they reached the castle of Nikitza, where Marshal Geoffrey was quartered. That

night they held a meeting together; the conclusion of their discussions was that the next morning they would go before Adrianople and lay siege to the city. They determined their battle order and organized it very well, considering they had so few men. [350] When morning came and day had fully dawned, they rode out as had been planned. They arrived before Adrianople and found the city very well garrisoned; they saw the banners of Johanitsa, king of Vlachia and Bulgaria, above the walls and towers. The city was very strong, very rich and very full of people. The Franks laid siege to it, positioning their very small number of men in front of two of the gates. It was the Tuesday before Palm Sunday.[1] They remained thus outside the city for three days, feeling very ill-at-ease and with very few men.

[351] Enrico Dandolo, the doge of Venice, despite being an old man and completely blind, then arrived bringing as many men as he could – about the same number as Emperor Baldwin and Count Louis had with them. The Venetians encamped in front of one of the gates. The next day they were joined by a company of mounted sergeants, and these men should have been of much more use than they in fact proved to be. Provisions were very low; merchants could not come to them, and they could not go foraging because there were so many Greeks in those parts that it was impossible for them to go anywhere.

[352] Johanitsa, king of Vlachia, was coming with a very large force to lend his support to the people of Adrianople. He was bringing Vlachs, Bulgars and around 14,000 Cumans, who had never received baptism. On account of their lack of food, Count Louis of Blois and Chartres went out foraging on Palm Sunday[2], accompanied by Stephen of Perche, who was the count of Perche's brother, Renaut of Montmirail, who was Count Hervé of Nevers's brother, Gervase of Châteauneuf, and more than half the entire army. [353] They went to a castle called Peutaces, which they found to be very well garrisoned with Greeks and they attacked it with a very intense and very strong assault. But they had no success and so turned back without having captured anything. They spent the week before Easter constructing engines from whatever manner of wood they could

find, and set their miners to work underground in order to bring down the walls. And in this way they observed Easter[3] outside Adrianople, with few men and little food.

[354] Then the news came that Johanitsa, king of Vlachia, was coming towards them to relieve the city. And so our men made their preparations; it was decided that Marshal Geoffrey and Manassiers of l'Isle would guard the camp while Emperor Baldwin and all the others would venture forth if Johanitsa should offer battle.

[355] They waited until Wednesday of Easter week, by which time Johanitsa was already so close that he had set up camp around five leagues away from them. He sent his Cumans to make a pass in front of our camp, at which the alarm was raised throughout the army, and the men rushed out, but not in good order. They chased the Cumans, most unwisely, for at least a full league, and when they decided to turn back, the Cumans fired at them relentlessly, inflicting many wounds on their horses.

[356] They returned to camp and the barons were summoned to Emperor Baldwin's quarters. They discussed what had happened, and it was agreed that it had been a very great folly to have chased these people so far when the Cumans were so lightly armed. The decision made at the end of the meeting was that if Johanitsa were to approach, our men would go out and line up in front of the camp and wait for him there without moving. It would be made known throughout the army that no one should be so bold as to ignore this command, regardless of any cries or clamour he heard. It was decided that Marshal Geoffrey and Manassiers of l'Isle would keep guard on the side of the camp facing the city.

[357] Thus they passed that night, until morning on the Thursday of Easter week arrived. They heard Mass and ate their midday meal. The Cumans came charging right up to their pavilions, at which the alarm was raised and everyone ran to arms, leaving the camp in their designated battalions, as had been decided beforehand. [358] Count Louis was first to venture out with his battalion, and he began to chase the Cumans, urging Emperor Baldwin to follow him. Alas! How poorly they

executed the plan they had made the previous evening! They ended up chasing the Cumans closely for a distance of two leagues, harassing them as they went, when after the lengthy pursuit the Cumans turned back and charged at them, letting loose both arrows and cries.

[359] There were men in our battalions who were not knights and were not skilled in arms; they began to take fright and lose heart. Count Louis, who had been the first to give battle to the Cumans, was severely wounded in two places. The Cumans and the Vlachs began to press down upon them, and the count was unseated from his horse. One of his knights, whose name was John of Friaize, dismounted and set the count on his horse. A good many of Count Louis's men told him, 'Sir, you should move away, for you are very badly injured in two places.' To which he replied, 'It would not be pleasing to our Lord God if ever I should be reproved for having fled the field and deserted the emperor.'

[360] The emperor, who was also being very hard pressed, called his men to him. He told them he would never flee and that they should never abandon him. People who were present that day have given faithful witness that no knight ever defended himself better than he did. The battle lasted a long time; some men bore themselves well, while others took flight. In the end – since God does permit misfortunes to occur – our men were defeated. Emperor Baldwin, never willing to flee, remained on the field with Count Louis. The emperor was captured still alive, while Count Louis was killed.

[361] Among those lost there were Bishop Peter of Bethlehem, Stephen of Perche, who was Count Geoffrey's brother, Renaut of Montmirail, who was the count of Nevers's brother, Matthew of Walincourt, Robert of Ronsoy, John of Friaize, Walter of Neuilly, Frederick of Yerres and his brother John, Eustace of Heumont and his brother John, Baldwin of Neuville, and many others this book will not mention here. Others who were able to escape fled back to the camp.

[362] When Geoffrey, marshal of Champagne, who was keeping guard in front of one of the gates of Adrianople, saw what had happened he set out as soon as he could with as many

men as he could muster. He instructed Manassiers of l'Isle, who was keeping guard at the other gate, to follow him without delay. He rode out with his entire battalion at great speed to meet the men fleeing the battle. All these men rallied around Marshal Geoffrey, and Manassiers of l'Isle, who came as quickly as he could with his own men, joined them. This meant they had a large battalion, to which they added all those fleeing from the battle whom they could stop.

[363] The rout was halted between none and vespers. Many of our men were so afraid that they had fled past the marshal and his force as far as the pavilions and lodgings. Thus did their retreat come to an end. The Cumans, Vlachs and Greeks who were chasing them stopped and harassed our battalion with bows and arrows, while the men of the battalion stood motionless, facing towards them. This was how matters stood until it began to get dark, when the Cumans and Vlachs started to retreat.

[364] Then Geoffrey of Villehardouin, marshal of Champagne and Romania, sent word to the doge of Venice in the camp. The doge was an old man and completely blind, but he was also very wise and worthy and full of vigour. The marshal instructed the doge to come to where the marshal was positioned with his battalion, out in the fields. And the doge did as he was asked. When the marshal saw him, he drew him aside for a private consultation, saying, 'My lord, you can see what a disaster has struck us. We have lost Emperor Baldwin and Count Louis, along with the greater part of our men and the best ones. We should think of how to ensure the safety of those that remain, for if God does not take pity on us we will be lost.' [365] They decided that the doge of Venice would return to the camp to reassure the people there. He would command everyone to arm and equip themselves and remain quietly in their tent or pavilion. Marshal Geoffrey would stay outside the camp with his battalion in full battle order until night came, so that the enemy might not see them move off. Once it was completely dark they would all depart from outside Adrianople. The doge of Venice would leave first and Marshal Geoffrey with those in his company would provide the rearguard.

[366] And so they waited for night, and once it was completely dark the doge of Venice left the camp as planned, with Marshal Geoffrey bringing up the rear. They moved off slowly, taking all their people, those on foot as well as those on horseback, the wounded as well as those who remained unharmed – no one at all was left behind. They travelled towards a city on the coast called Rodosto, which was a good three days' journey away, having set out in the way described to you. And this episode took place in the year of Jesus Christ's incarnation 1205.

[367] On the night of the army's departure from Adrianople it so happened that one group broke off in order to go more quickly and directly to Constantinople; they were heavily blamed for this. Among this company were a count from Lombardy whose name was Count Gerard, who came from the marquis's lands, as well as Odo of Ham, who was the lord of a castle called Ham in the Vermandois region, and a good number of others – as many as twenty-five knights – that this book will not name. [368] They made off in this way immediately after our defeat, which took place on Thursday evening, and they arrived at Constantinople on Saturday evening despite the fact that this journey would normally take five full days. They reported their news to Cardinal Peter Capuano, Pope Innocent's legate, and to Conon of Béthune, who was defending Constantinople with Milon le Bréban and the other good men there. And know that the men who had fled were mightily afraid and were convinced that the rest of the army they had left outside Adrianople would all be lost, for they had had no news of them.

[369] Let us now leave the people at Constantinople in their great sadness and return to the doge of Venice and Marshal Geoffrey, who journeyed all through the night of their departure from Adrianople until daybreak; they reached a town called Pamphilon. Now hear how events unfold according to God's will; Peter of Bracieux, Payen of Orléans, and many of Count Louis's men[4] had spent the night in that town; their company included around a hundred very good knights and 140 mounted sergeants, who were coming from beyond the straits and were on their way to join the army at Adrianople.

[370] When they saw forces approaching they ran to arms in great haste, thinking these were Greeks. They armed themselves and sent scouts to find out what people these were. The scouts discovered that these were men returning from the rout, and so they returned to Pamphilon and told Peter of Bracieux and his companions that Emperor Baldwin was lost, and their lord Louis too, whose lands and country they hailed from, and in whose retinue they had served. [371] No sadder news could have been given them. You would have seen many tears shed and many hands wrung in sorrow and compassion. They went out to meet the others just as they were, fully armed, and rode on until they reached Geoffrey, marshal of Champagne, who was bringing up the rear. He was feeling very ill-at-ease because Johanitsa, king of Vlachia and Bulgaria, had arrived at Adrianople at daybreak with his entire army to find our men gone. He had ridden along the same route, and it was a great relief he had not caught up with them, for they would have been irretrievably lost had he done so.

[372] 'Sir,' they asked Marshal Geoffrey, 'what do you want us to do? We will do whatever you think best.' And the marshal replied to them, 'You can see the condition we're in. But you and your horses are fresh, so you should take over the rearguard while I go ahead to give encouragement to our people, who are very frightened and in great need of reassurance.' They did just as he instructed, and most willingly provided a very sound and fine rearguard. And they did this as men who knew their business ought to, for they were good and honourable knights.

[373] Marshal Geoffrey of Champagne rode ahead to lead his men, and they travelled as far as a town called Cariopolis. He could see that their horses were tired after having ridden all night, and he entered the town and found quarters for them around midday. The men gave their horses something to eat and themselves ate whatever they could find, although this was not much.

[374] They passed all that day in the town, until nightfall. Johanitsa, king of Vlachia, had been following them throughout the day along the same route, and he set up camp about two leagues away from them. Once it was dark all those inside

the town armed themselves and ventured out with Marshal Geoffrey in the vanguard, and the men who had brought up the rear earlier that day did so once more. They journeyed onwards in this way all night and all the next day, in great fear and with great exertion, until they reached the city of Rodosto. This city was inhabited by Greeks and was very wealthy and very strong, but these Greeks did not dare defend themselves, and so our men went inside, found lodgings and were then secure.

[375] The people in the army at Adrianople escaped in this way, as you have heard. They then held a council in the city of Rodosto, and it was agreed that they feared more for Constantinople than they did for themselves. And so they sent reliable messengers by sea, who travelled day and night in order to tell those in the capital not to despair, and that the doge, Marshal Geoffrey and their men had escaped and would return to Constantinople as soon as they could.

[376] At the moment of the messengers' arrival in Constantinople, there were five large and fine Venetian ships in the harbour full of pilgrims and knights and sergeants who were about to leave that land to go home to their own countries. In those five ships there were around 70,000 men at arms, including William the advocate of Béthune, Baldwin of Aubigny and John of Vierzon, who came from Count Louis's lands and was his liegeman, as well as around a hundred other knights whom this book will not name.

[377] Master Peter Capuano, who was cardinal-legate of the Roman Pope Innocent, Conon of Béthune, who was defending Constantinople, Milon le Bréban, and a great number of other good people went to the five ships, and pleading and tearfully begged those about to leave to have mercy and compassion for Christendom and for their liege lords who had been lost in the battle of Adrianople and, for God's sake, to stay. But those people did not want to hear any of this, and so they set sail from the port, unfurled their sails and made their way according to God's will, which was that a wind should take them to the port of Rodosto. They arrived there the day after those who had come to Rodosto following the defeat at Adrianople reached the city.[5]

[378] Marshal Geoffrey and his companions pleaded with them in the same way that the people in Constantinople had done, with tears and sighs, calling on them to have mercy and compassion for that land and to stay there, for they would never be able to help a land in more urgent need. Those on board the ships replied that they would discuss the situation and give them their decision the following day. Now hear what adventures took place in the city of Rodosto that night. [379] There was a knight from Count Louis's lands whose name was Peter of Frouville, who was highly respected and had an honourable reputation. He ran away that night, leaving all his equipment, and boarded John of Vierzon's ship (Vierzon was also in Count Louis of Blois and Chartres's lands). The people on board the five ships, who were due to give their response to Marshal Geoffrey and the doge of Venice in the morning, spread their sails as soon as they saw daylight and left without talking to anyone. They were roundly blamed for this in the lands to which they went as well is in those they had left – Peter of Frouville even more than the others. It is because of this that they say that a man behaves most wickedly who through fear of death does something for which he is ever after reproved.

CHAPTER II

The Regency of Henry of Hainaut

(April 1205–July 1206)

[380] We will not tell you any more about those people now; instead we will tell you about Henry, Emperor Baldwin of Constantinople's brother, who had left Adramyttion and made for Adrianople in order to give support to his brother the emperor. With him had come the Armenians who had helped him against the Greeks – around 20,000 people, including their wives and all their children, who dared not stay on the other side of the straits.

[381] Henry then received the news from Greeks fleeing the scene of the battle that his brother, Emperor Baldwin, had been defeated and was lost, along with Count Louis and the other barons. Afterwards, further news came from those at Rodosto who had escaped from Adrianople; they instructed him to hurry to come to them as soon he could. Because he wished to get there as quickly as possible he left the Armenians behind. These people were travelling on foot and they had their carts and their wives and children with them, which meant they could not move speedily. Since Henry was confident that they would be able to make their own way in safety and had no reason to be fearful, he went ahead and set up camp at a village called Cortacopolis.

[382] On that same day Marshal Geoffrey's nephew, Anseau of Courcelles, joined him. The marshal had sent for him to come from the region of Makri, Trajanopolis and the abbey of Bera,[1] where he had been assigned lands. He came together with the men who had deserted Renier of Trit at Philippopolis. There were around a hundred very good knights in that group and about 500 mounted sergeants, all of whom were

going to Adrianople to give reinforcement to Emperor Baldwin.

[383] Just as the news had reached others, it reached them that the emperor and his force had been defeated, and they too turned to go to Rodosto. They came to find a place to stay at Cortacopolis, the village where Emperor Baldwin's brother Henry was encamped. When Henry saw them approaching he and his men ran to arms, thinking they were Greeks, while Anseau and his company thought the same of them. Once they came close enough each side recognized the other, and they were very happy to see one another; they felt more secure and set up camp to spend the night in the village, staying there until the next morning. [384] The next day they set out and rode straight to Rodosto, arriving in the city that evening. There they found the doge of Venice, Marshal Geoffrey, and the others who had escaped from the rout at Adrianople, and who were very pleased to see them. Many tears were shed out of compassion for their lost friends. Oh God! What a shame it was that the forces gathered at Rodosto had not been with the others at Adrianople when Emperor Baldwin was there; then they would not have suffered any loss. But this was not God's will.

[385] And so they stayed at Rodosto the following day and the one after that, setting their affairs in order. Henry, Emperor Baldwin's brother, was accepted as lord so that he might act as regent of the empire on his brother's behalf. At that time the Armenians who had been coming after Henry suffered a great misfortune. The people of the region assembled and overwhelmed them, all of whom were lost, either captured or killed.

[386] Johanitsa, king of Vlachia and Bulgaria, had his army with him and was in full control of the land; he held the countryside, the cities and the castles. His Cumans had advanced as far as Constantinople. Henry, the regent of the empire, the doge of Venice and Marshal Geoffrey, who remained at Rodosto, three days away from Constantinople, decided how they should proceed. The doge of Venice garrisoned Rodosto with Venetians, since the city was one of theirs. And the next day the rest of the forces were organized into battalions and then rode day after day towards Constantinople.

[387] When they reached Selymbria, a town two days away from Constantinople, which belonged to Emperor Baldwin, his brother Henry garrisoned it with some of his men before riding on with the remainder to Constantinople. He was warmly welcomed there, for the people in those parts were deeply afraid. This should come as no surprise, since so much land had been lost that besides Constantinople the only places the Franks and the Venetians held were Rodosto and Selymbria. All the rest of the empire's lands were under the control of Johanitsa, king of Vlachia and Bulgaria. The Franks and Venetians' only possession beyond the Straits of Saint George was the castle of Espigal; all the rest of that land was held by Theodore Lascaris.

[388] The barons decided they should send word to the Roman Pope Innocent and to France and Flanders and other lands in order to secure assistance: Nivelon of Soissons was sent to fulfil this mission along with Nicholas of Mailly and John Bliaut. The others stayed at Constantinople in profound unease, as people in fear of losing their land would be. This was how matters stood until Pentecost.[2] And during the intervening period a great misfortune befell the people of the army; Enrico Dandolo fell sick, met his end and died. He was buried with great honour in the church of Saint Sophia.

[389] By Pentecost, Johanitsa, King of Vlachia and Bulgaria, had firmly imposed his will on the lands of the empire. He was not able to keep the Cumans in those parts because they were incapable of fighting in the summer heat, and so they returned to their own lands. Johanitsa, with his army of Bulgars and Greeks, marched against the marquis in Salonika. And the marquis, who had heard of Emperor Baldwin's defeat, abandoned the siege of Nauplia and hurried with as many men as he could muster to Salonika, to garrison the city.

[390] Henry, Emperor Baldwin of Constantinople's brother, took as many men as he could muster and rode out against the Greeks at a place called Tchorlu, which is three days away from Constantinople. The town surrendered to him and the Greek inhabitants swore fealty to him, although such oaths counted for little in those days. Henry rode on to the city of Arcadiopolis, which he found abandoned since the Greeks had not

dared to await his arrival. From there he rode on to the town of Bizöe, which was very strong and very well defended by the Greeks; it was surrendered to him. And from there he rode on to the town of Apros, which was likewise heavily garrisoned with Greeks.

[391] As our men were preparing their assault the people of the town offered to surrender. But while negotiations were being conducted on one side of the town, some members of our army broke into it on the other side. Henry, the regent of the empire, and those who were discussing the surrender did not know anything about it, and they were deeply angered. The Franks began to kill the Greeks and to seize goods in the town, taking anything they could. Many people were killed or captured; this was the manner of Apros's conquest. The army stayed there for three days. And the Greeks were so horrified by what had happened at Apros that they abandoned every town and castle in that region, and fled inside Adrianople and Demotika, both of which were strong and fine cities.

[392] At about this time Johanitsa, king of Vlachia and Bulgaria, rode out with his entire force against the marquis and arrived at a city called Serres. The marquis had garrisoned this place very strongly with his men; Hugh of Coligny, who was a very good knight and a man of high rank, was inside the city with the marquis's marshal, William of Arles, and a goodly number of his best men. King Johanitsa of Vlachia laid siege to them, and had barely begun to do so when he broke into the city by force. The fall of Serres caused great harm to our people, for Hugh of Coligny was killed there, struck by a blow to the eye. [393] Once Hugh of Coligny had died, who had been the best man of them all, his companions lost heart and retreated into the castle at Serres, which was very strong. Johanitsa laid siege to the castle, setting up his petraries. He had not main-tained the siege for long when the men inside the castle asked to make terms; their conduct met with great disapproval and they were reproached for it. The terms of their agreement were that they would surrender the castle to Johanitsa, while he had twenty-five of his most high-ranking men swear to grant them safe conduct, with their horses and arms, as far as Salonika

or Constantinople or Hungary – whichever of the three they preferred.

[394] In this way Serres was surrendered. Johanitsa had our men leave and set up camp out in the fields. He made a show of great friendliness to them, sending them gifts. He kept them there for three days before going back on all the promises he had made to them; he had them captured and then stripped them of all their possessions before having them taken to Vlachia naked, unshod and on foot. The poor and low-ranking people who were of little value were taken to Hungary, while those who were of more worth had their heads cut off. Such was the mortal treachery committed by the king of Vlachia, as you have heard, and it was here that our army suffered one of its most wretched defeats. Johanitsa had the castle and city of Serres torn down, and then went after the marquis once more.

[395] Henry, the regent of the empire, rode out towards Adrianople with all his men and, in great danger, laid siege to the city. The number of opponents they faced both inside the city and outside was large, and the enemy pressed so close upon our men that they could not buy provisions or forage for food, except on the smallest of scales. Because of this they set up defensive railings and barricades around the outside of the camp, and it was decided that one group of their men would keep watch over these defences while the others would launch the attack against the city.

[396] They constructed engines of various kinds, set up scaling ladders and many other machines. They put great effort into capturing the city. But this was impossible since the city was very strong and very well defended, and so the siege went badly; many of their men were injured and one of their best knights, whose name was Peter of Bracieux, was struck on the forehead by a rock thrown by a mangonel. He was very nearly killed but, by God's will, he came round and was carried away in a litter.

[397] Seeing that they would not be able to achieve anything at Adrianople, Henry, the regent of the empire, withdrew with the French army. They were harassed by the local people and

by the Greek forces as they went. They kept riding day after day, until they reached a city called Pamphilon, inside which they quartered themselves and remained for two months. They went on expeditions in the direction of Demotika and to many places where they could seize livestock and other valuables. The army stayed in those parts until the start of winter, receiving supplies from Rodosto and from the coast.

[398] Let us now leave Henry, the regent of the empire, at Pamphilon. We will tell you instead about Johanitsa, king of Vlachia and Bulgaria. As you heard described earlier, Serres had been surrendered to him and he had treacherously killed those who had handed the city over to him before riding on towards Salonika. He spent some time in that region, laying waste much of its land. Meanwhile Marquis Boniface of Montferrat was at Salonika, greatly vexed and much distressed by the loss of his lord, Emperor Baldwin, and of the other barons, and by the loss of his castle at Serres and of his own men.

[399] When Johanitsa saw that he would not be able to make further gains, he turned back towards his own country, with his men. The people of Philippopolis, a city that had been given to Renier of Trit by Emperor Baldwin, heard that the emperor had been lost along with many of his barons, and that the marquis had lost Serres. They also saw that Renier of Trit's relatives, his son and his nephew among them, had deserted him and that he had only a few men left. They believed the Franks would never get the upper hand. Some of the inhabitants of Philippopolis (who were Paulician heretics)[3] went to Johanitsa and surrendered themselves to him, saying, 'Sir, ride on to Philippopolis, or send your army there. We will surrender the entire city to you.'

[400] When Renier of Trit, who was still inside Philippopolis, learned of this, he feared that the city would indeed be surrendered to Johanitsa. And so he set out one morning with such men as he had and went to that part of the city where the Paulicians who had given themselves up to Johanitsa lived. He set fire to the neighbourhood and a large part of it burned down. Renier then went on to the castle of Stenimaka, three leagues away, which was garrisoned by his men. He went inside

and was holed up there for a long time, a good thirteen months, in deep uncertainty and great want; their hardship was such that they ate their horses. Stenimaka was nine days' journey away from Constantinople, and the people in either place could get no news of one another.

[401] Johanitsa then sent his army before Philippopolis, and he had not been there long when the inhabitants of the city surrendered to him. After having guaranteed the people their safety, he first of all killed the city's archbishop, and then had some of the high-ranking men of the city flayed alive while others had their heads cut off. The rest of the people were led away in chains. He had the whole city torn down, both the towers and the walls, while the great palaces and fine houses burned and collapsed. Thus was the noble city of Philippopolis destroyed, which had been one of the three finest in the empire of Constantinople.

[402] Let us now leave Philippopolis and Renier of Trit, shut up inside the castle of Stenimaka, and return to Henry, Emperor Baldwin's brother, who had stayed at Pamphilon until the beginning of winter. He then took advice from his vassals and from his barons, and they decided that he should garrison a city called Roussion, which was located in a particularly fertile region at the heart of the empire. The leaders of this garrison were Dietrich of Looz, the seneschal, and Thierry of Termonde, the constable. They were given command of around 140 knights and a large number of mounted sergeants by Henry, the regent of the empire, who ordered them to make war against the Greeks and defend the frontier in that region.

[403] Henry went with the remainder of his forces to the town of Bizöe, and installed a garrison there under the leadership of Anseau of Cayeux, whom he left in charge of around 120 knights and a good number of mounted sergeants. Another city, called Arcadiopolis, was garrisoned by the Venetians. He returned the city of Apros to Theodore Branas, a Greek man who had married the king of France's sister,[4] and who was loyal to the Franks (he was the only Greek who was). The men stationed in these cities made war against the Greeks and undertook many raids, and many were made against them in

return. Meanwhile Henry withdrew to Constantinople with the remainder of his men.

[404] But Johanitsa, king of Vlachia and Bulgaria, who was very powerful and wealthy, had not sat idly by; he had gathered a large force of Cumans and Vlachs, whom he sent into Romania three weeks after Christmas to lend assistance to the people of Adrianople and Demotika. With this reinforcement, the inhabitants of these cities grew bolder and undertook raids against the Franks with greater confidence.

[405] Constable Thierry of Termonde, who was the commander of the French forces at Roussion, made a raid on the fourth day before the feast of Saint Mary at Candlemas.[5] He rode all night with around 120 knights, having left Roussion defended by just a few men. By dawn they had reached a village where some of the Cumans and Vlachs were encamped. The French took them by surprise, without any of the village's inhabitants realizing they had come. Our men killed a good number of the enemy and seized around forty of their horses. And having inflicted this hurt they turned back to Roussion.

[406] That same night a company of Cumans and Vlachs had ridden out to do us what harm they could; there were around 7,000 of them. At daybreak they arrived outside Roussion, and stayed there for a long while. Since the town was garrisoned with just a few men, they closed the gates and climbed up on to the walls. The Cumans and Vlachs turned back, but had not gone more than a league and a half from the town when they came across the French raiding party led by Thierry of Termonde. When the French saw them they formed up into four battalions; they decided to try and retreat into Roussion very slowly and stealthily. If God allowed them to reach the town, they would be safe.

[407] The Cumans, the Vlachs and the local Greeks, who had a great many men, came riding towards them, and when they reached the French rearguard they began to harass them unremittingly. The rearguard was formed by the men of Dietrich of Looz's retinue. Dietrich, who was the seneschal, had returned to Constantinople, and his men were being commanded by his brother, Villain. The Cumans, Vlachs and

Greeks placed them under heavy pressure and wounded many of their horses. The cries and the onslaught were intense, and through sheer force the enemy overwhelmed Villain's men so that they were thrown back on to Andrew Dureboise and John of Choisy's battalion. And so our men had to keep up their resistance for a long while, as they made their retreat. [408] The enemy then renewed their efforts, forcing our men back on to the battalion of Constable Thierry of Termonde and then, not long afterwards, on to the battalion of Charles of Fraisne. While maintaining their resistance our men had moved far enough to come within sight of Roussion, which was less than half a league away. The enemy immediately pressed them even harder and intensified their assault; many of our men and their horses were wounded. And, since God permits bad things to happen, our men could not hold out and were overcome because they had been heavily armed, while their opponents' equipment was light. These enemies now started to massacre them.

[409] Alas! What a wretched day for Christendom! Of all our 120 knights no more than ten escaped; all the others were captured or killed. Those who did get away came fleeing back to Roussion and found shelter with their companions inside the town. Thierry of Termonde died in that battle, as did Orry of l'Isle, who was a most fine and esteemed knight, along with John of Pomponne, Andrew Dureboise, John of Choisy, Guy of Conflans, Charles of Fraisne and Villain, the brother of Seneschal Dietrich. It is not possible for this book to tell you the names of all those who were killed or captured in that battle. One of the greatest sorrows and one of the greatest injuries was inflicted on the Christians in the lands of Romania that day, and it was one of the greatest tragedies ever to strike them too.

[410] The Cumans, Vlachs and Greeks turned back, having imposed their will on that land and having won fine horses and sturdy hauberks. This disaster occurred on the day before the eve of the feast of Our Lady Saint Mary at Candlemas. Those who had escaped this rout and those who had stayed inside Roussion abandoned the town as soon as darkness fell, and fled through the night to reach the city of Rodosto the next morning.

[411] The sad news of this disaster reached Henry, the regent of the empire, as he was taking part in the procession to Our Lady of Blachernae on the feast of Our Lady Saint Mary at Candlemas. Know that this distressed the people in Constantinople very much; they were convinced the empire was lost. Henry decided he would place a garrison at Selymbria, which is two days away from Constantinople, and he sent Macaire of Sainte-Menehould there with fifty knights in order to defend the town.

[412] When Johanitsa, king of Vlachia, got word of what had befallen his men, he was overjoyed; they had killed or captured a great number of the best men among the French. He then summoned as many men as he could raise from throughout his lands and gathered a large army of Cumans and Greeks and Vlachs before entering Romania. Most of the cities there declared their loyalty to him, and all of the castles. The force he had raised was so massive that it was nothing less than a marvel.

[413] Once they heard that their enemy was on his way, the Venetians abandoned Arcadiopolis. Johanitsa rode on until he reached the town of Apros, which was held by Theodore Branas, whose wife was the king of France's sister. He had garrisoned the city with Greeks and Latins; the latter were under the command of Bègues of Fransures, a knight from the region of Beauvais. King Johanitsa made an assault against the town and captured it by storm. [414] The great scale of the mortality and the numbers of people killed at Apros were simply astounding. Bègues of Fransures was brought before Johanitsa, who had him executed immediately. All the other people, those among the Greeks and Latins who were not of great value, the low-ranking men, the women and children, were taken away to Vlachia as prisoners. Johanitsa then had the town, which had been a very fine, very prosperous and very favourably situated place, razed to the ground. Thus, as you have heard, was the town of Apros destroyed.

[415] Twelve leagues away from Apros, on the coast, lay the city of Rodosto. It was very wealthy, strong and large, and it was well defended by a Venetian force. In addition a company

of mounted sergeants, around 2,000 of them, had come to reinforce this garrison. When they heard that Apros had been taken by force and its inhabitants killed, this put such great fear into them that they brought about their own defeat. Because God allows bad things to happen to people, the Venetians rushed aboard their ships, every man for himself – the disorder was such that they could easily have drowned one another. The mounted sergeants, who came from France and Flanders and from other regions, fled overland.

[416] Hear, now, what a catastrophe this was, which need never have happened! The city of Rodosto was so strong and so well enclosed by sturdy walls and good towers that no one would have dared lay siege to it and Johanitsa would not have turned in that direction. But when he heard that the garrison in the city had fled and were a good half-day's journey away, Johanitsa rode on towards Rodosto. The Greeks who had stayed inside the city surrendered to him, and were taken prisoner straightaway, both the high- and low-ranking people (except for a few who managed to escape). Johanitsa had them led away to Vlachia, and then he had the city torn down. Oh! What a great shame this was! For Rodosto was one of the finest cities in Romania, and one of the most favourably situated.

[417] Another town nearby, called Panedon, surrendered to Johanitsa and he had it torn down and destroyed, and its people were led away to Vlachia like those from Rodosto. After that he rode on to the town of Heraclea, which lay beside a good seaport and belonged to the Venetians. They had left only a small garrison there, and so Johanitsa attacked the town and took it by force. Here too many people were killed and the survivors taken away to Vlachia, while Johanitsa had this town razed to the ground as he had the others.

[418] From Heraclea he moved on to the town of Daonum, which was very fine and strong. The inhabitants dared not try to hold out against Johanitsa and so they surrendered to him. He had the town reduced to ruins. Afterwards he rode to the city of Tchorlu, which was surrendered to him and which he then razed to the ground, while its people were led away as captives. In each instance when a certain castle or city was

surrendered after having received assurances from him, he had it destroyed and took its men and women prisoner; he did not keep any of the promises he made.

[419] And then the Cumans and the Vlachs passed before the gates of Constantinople, where Henry, the regent of the empire, remained with such forces as he could raise. He was deeply vexed and worried, since he could not raise as many men as he would need to defend his lands. The Cumans seized the cattle in the region roundabout the city, along with the men, women and children. They tore down towns and fortresses and caused such great devastation that no man has ever heard of destruction on this scale.

[420] Johanitsa's forces then came to a city twelve leagues away from Constantinople that was called Athyra, and which had been granted by Henry, the emperor's brother, to Payen of Orléans. There was a great throng of people in that city because all the people in the surrounding countryside had fled there. Our enemies attacked the city and took it by force. There was a great slaughter once again, greater than in any other town taken by Johanitsa's army. And you should know that at each castle and every city which surrendered and whose inhabitants had received assurances from Johanitsa, everything was torn down and destroyed and the people were taken away to Vlachia in the way you have heard described.

[421] Know, then, that nowhere within five days' journey of Constantinople escaped this devastation; the only exceptions were the towns of Bizöe and Selymbria, both of which had been garrisoned by the French. Anseau of Cayeux was at Bizöe with around 120 knights, while Macaire of Sainte-Menehould was at Selymbria with fifty. Henry, Emperor Baldwin's brother, stayed at Constantinople with the remaining knights. And you should know that they were in dire straits, for besides Constantinople they only held these two towns.

[422] Seeing this, the Greeks in Johanitsa's army – who had surrendered to him after having rebelled against the Franks, and whose castles and cities he had torn down without him ever keeping any of the promises he made to them – deemed themselves betrayed and as good as dead. They discussed their

situation among themselves and came to the conclusion that Johanitsa would treat Adrianople and Demotika in the same way when he came to those places, and if these two cities were destroyed Romania would be lost for good. They secretly appointed messengers and sent them to Theodore Branas, who was at Constantinople. [423] They begged him to plead with Henry, Emperor Baldwin's brother, and with the Venetians, asking them to have compassion for the Greeks and to make peace with them; in return the Greeks would give them Adrianople and Demotika and would all go over to their side. Thus the Greeks and the Franks might form an alliance. A conference was held in Constantinople to discuss this proposal and many opinions were expressed, but the outcome was that Adrianople and Demotika, and all the lands associated with them, would be granted to Theodore Branas and his wife, the empress (who was King Philip of France's sister), and that they would render service to the emperor and the empire for these possessions. Thus was an agreement drawn up and concluded, and peace was made between the Greeks and the Franks.

[424] Johanitsa, king of Vlachia and Bulgaria, who had spent a long time in Romania and who had devastated that land throughout Lent and for a good while after Easter too, then withdrew towards Adrianople and Demotika, thinking that he would treat these cities in the same way he had other places. When the Greeks who were among his forces saw that he was moving towards Adrianople, they began to desert him; sometimes they would flee during the day, sometimes at night; sometimes twenty of them, or thirty, or forty, or a hundred.

[425] When Johanitsa arrived at Adrianople he asked its Greek inhabitants to grant him entry as the people inside other towns and cities had done. But the Greeks told him they would do no such thing, and they said, 'Sir, when we gave ourselves up to you and rebelled against the Franks, you swore in good faith that you would protect us and keep us safe. But you have not done so; instead you have devastated Romania. And we are quite sure that you will do to us what you have done to the Greeks in other places.' Having heard this, Johanitsa went off and laid siege to Demotika, setting up sixteen large petraries

round the city. He also started construction of various kinds of
engines and began to ravage all the surrounding lands.

[426] The people of Adrianople and Demotika chose messengers and sent them to Henry, the regent of the empire, and to
Theodore Branas, both of whom were at Constantinople. The
messengers asked them, for God's sake, to come and relieve
Demotika, which was now under siege. When the people at
Constantinople heard this news, they gathered to discuss
whether they should go to Demotika's aid. There were many
people who were not brave enough to lend their support to an
expedition beyond Constantinople, risking the lives of the few
Christians who remained there. The final decision, however,
was that they should venture forth and go as far as Selymbria.

[427] The cardinal who was the Roman pope's legate[6]
preached a sermon and granted an indulgence to all those who
were going on this campaign and died in battle. Henry then left
Constantinople with such men as he could raise and rode as far
as Selymbria, where he encamped outside the town for about a
week. He received messages daily from Adrianople; they called
on him to have mercy on the people of that city and to come to
their aid, for if he did not help them they would be lost forever.

[428] Henry then took advice from his barons, and the consensus was that he should go to Bizöe, which was a very strong
and fine town. This was done as had been proposed, and they
arrived at Bizöe and set up camp outside the town on the eve
of the feast of Saint John the Baptist in June.[7] Messengers
arrived from Adrianople on the same day that they put up their
tents at Bizoë. They said to Henry, 'Sir, you should know that
without your assistance the city of Demotika will not be able
to hold out for more than a week; Johanitsa's petraries have
broken down the wall in four places and his men have managed
to get up on to the walls twice.'

[429] Henry sought advice as to what he should do. There
was much discussion, back and forth, but in the end he said to
his men, 'My lords, we have come far enough that if we do not
go and relieve Demotika we will be shamed. May each man
therefore make his confession and receive communion, and
then we'll decide how to organize our forces.' They reckoned

that they had around 400 knights, and certainly no more than
that number. Then they summoned the messengers who had
come from Adrianople and asked them to give an assessment
of how many men Johanitsa had. The messengers responded
that he had around 40,000 men-at-arms, not including foot
soldiers, and they were not sure how many of those he had. Oh
God! What a perilous situation this was – for so few men to
take on so many!

[430] On the morning of the feast of our lord Saint John the
Baptist, our men made confession and received communion,
and they moved off from Bizöe the following day. The vanguard
was under the command of Geoffrey, marshal of Romania and
Champagne, who was accompanied by Macaire of Sainte-
Menehould. The second battalion was led by Conon of Béthune
and Milon le Bréban, the third by Payen of Orléans and Peter
of Bracieux, the fourth by Anseau of Cayeux, the fifth by
Baldwin of Beauvoir, the sixth by Hugh of Beaumetz, the
seventh by Henry, Emperor Baldwin's brother, and the eighth
by Walter of Escornais, who had charge of the Flemish forces.
Dietrich of Looz, the seneschal, commanded the rearguard.
[431] They rode on in good order for three days, but no force
has ever gone in search of battle under more perilous conditions.
Two dangers confronted them: their lack of men compared
with the much greater numbers of the opponents they were
going to fight, and their uncertainty as to whether the Greeks
with whom they had made peace would assist them faithfully.
They were afraid that when the critical moment came the
Greeks would go over to Johanitsa, who was, as you have
already heard, very close to capturing Demotika.

[432] When Johanitsa learned that the Franks were coming,
he dared not wait for them and instead burned his engines
and decamped from before Demotika. And you should know
that everyone viewed this as a great miracle. On the fourth
day after his departure from Bizöe, Henry, the regent of the
empire, arrived before Adrianople and set up camp in the most
beautiful meadows in the world, along the riverbank there.
When the people of Adrianople saw they had arrived, they
came out of the city in procession, carrying their crosses and

displaying greater joy than has ever been seen before. And they had good reason for doing so since they had been in a perilous situation.

[433] News then arrived in the Franks' camp that Johanitsa had installed himself at a castle called Rodestuic[8] and so, the following morning, the Frankish army set out in that direction to seek battle. But Johanitsa then decamped and rode on, retreating towards his own lands. Our forces followed him for five days, with Johanitsa always keeping ahead of them. On the fifth day our army encamped in a pleasant spot by a castle called Fraïm, where they stayed for three days.

[434] It was then that a company made up of some of the best men in the army left because of a disagreement they had with Henry, Emperor Baldwin's brother. The leader of this group was Baldwin of Beauvoir and he was joined by Hugh of Beaumetz, William of Gommegnies and Dreux of Beaurain. Around fifty knights altogether left with this company, thinking that the remainder of the army would not dare stay in those parts to face their enemies.

[435] Henry, the regent of the empire, held a meeting with those barons he had with him, and they decided that they should keep riding onwards. And so they moved on for another two days and then set up camp in a most beautiful valley, near a castle called Moniac. This castle was surrendered to them, and they spent about five days there before it was suggested they should go and relieve Renier of Trit, who was besieged inside Stenimaka, where he had been shut inside the town for a good thirteen months. While Henry stayed at the camp near Moniac with most of his men, the rest went to rescue Renier of Trit at Stenimaka.

[436] And know that those who went on this expedition did so in great peril. Few rescue missions so dangerous have ever been undertaken; they had to ride across enemy territory for three days. Among those to take part were Conon of Béthune and Geoffrey of Villehardouin, marshal of Romania and of Champagne, Macaire of Sainte-Menehould, Milon le Bréban, Peter of Bracieux, Payen of Orléans, Anseau of Cayeux, Dietrich of Looz, William of Perchay, and a battalion of

Venetians led by Andrew Valera. And so they rode on towards the castle of Stenimaka, until they came within sight of that place.

[437] Renier of Trit was at the barricade outside the walls of Stenimaka when he caught sight of the vanguard being led by Marshal Geoffrey, and then of the other battalions that were following behind it in good order. But he was not sure what people these were, and it was no wonder that this sight frightened him, as it had been a long time since he had received any news of his compatriots and he thought that these were the Greeks coming to lay siege to him.

[438] Geoffrey, marshal of Romania and Champagne, sent turcopoles and mounted crossbowmen ahead to ascertain the situation at the castle; they were not sure whether Renier of Trit and his men were dead or alive, as it was such a long time since they had heard news of them. Renier of Trit and his retinue recognized these men as soon as they arrived outside the castle, and you can easily understand that they were overjoyed to see them. They then came out of the castle and hurried to meet their friends, to their great and mutual delight.

[439] The barons found quarters in the very pleasant town below the castle, from where the fortress had formerly been besieged. When they talked to Renier of Trit the barons said they had often heard rumours that Emperor Baldwin had died in one of Johanitsa's prisons, but that they didn't trust these reports at all. Renier of Trit said that it was indeed true that Emperor Baldwin was dead, and this convinced the barons. Many of them were deeply upset – if only they could have done something to make matters different! [440] And so they spent the night in the town before leaving the next morning and abandoning Stenimaka. They kept riding for two days, and on the third they came to the camp where Henry, the emperor's brother, was waiting for them; they had set up their quarters beneath the castle of Moniac, which was located on the River Arda. The people of the army were overjoyed that Renier of Trit had been freed from confinement, and it was a great credit to those who had gone to liberate him since they had done so in the face of great danger.

CHAPTER 12

War on Two Fronts in Emperor Henry's Early Reign

(August 1206–September 1207)

[441] The barons decided they should go to Constantinople and have Emperor Baldwin's brother, Henry, crowned. They left Theodore Branas at Adrianople with all the Greeks of that region and with forty knights placed in his charge by Henry, the regent of the empire. And so Henry and the other barons went to Constantinople, riding day after day until they reached that city, where they were very warmly welcomed. On the Sunday after the feast of Our Lady Saint Mary in August[1] they crowned Henry, with great rejoicing and with great dignity, in the church of Saint Sophia. This took place in the year of the incarnation of Our Lord Jesus Christ 1206.

[442] The emperor had been crowned at Constantinople, as you have just heard, and Theodore Branas had been left in the region of Adrianople and Demotika; when Johanitsa, king of Vlachia and Bulgaria, heard of this, he gathered as large a force as he could. Branas had not rebuilt any of Demotika's fortifications, which had been damaged by Johanitsa's petraries and mangonels, and he had installed only a small garrison there. And so when Johanitsa advanced on Demotika, he was able to take it, and tore the walls down right to the ground. He overran the surrounding country, seizing men, women and children, and livestock too; there was utter devastation. The people of Adrianople, seeing how Demotika had been lost, called on Emperor Henry to come to their aid.

[443] And so Emperor Henry summoned as many men as he could and ventured forth from Constantinople, riding day after day towards Adrianople in full battle order. When Johanitsa, king of Vlachia and Bulgaria, who was in those parts, heard

that the emperor was coming, he turned back towards his own lands. Emperor Henry kept riding until he arrived at Adrianople, where he set up camp in the fields outside the city.

[444] The Greeks of that region came to him and told him that Johanitsa had carried off men, women and livestock, that he had ruined Demotika and ravaged all the surrounding lands, and that he was still within a day's journey of Adrianople. The emperor resolved to go and do battle with Johanitsa, if the king allowed him to catch up, in order to rescue the men and women who were being led away captive. And so Henry rode out after Johanitsa, though he always managed to stay ahead of the emperor, who maintained his pursuit for four days before arriving at a town called Beröe.

[445] When the people inside the city saw the emperor's army approaching, they fled into the mountains and abandoned the town. The emperor had come with his entire force, and they set up camp outside the town, which he found well stocked with grain and food and other useful things. And so they stayed there for two days, and the emperor had his men overran all the surrounding countryside, where they seized a good quantity of livestock, including oxen, cows and buffalo in large numbers. They then set out from Beröe with all this booty and rode to another town, a day's journey away, that was called Blisme. Just as the inhabitants at Beröe had deserted their town, so did those of Blisme and, once again, Henry found this town to be stocked with all sorts of provisions, and he set up camp outside it.

[446] They were then informed that the captives (both men and women) who had been carried off by Johanitsa, along with their animals and their carts, were in a valley three leagues away from their camp. Emperor Henry then arranged that the Greek men of Adrianople and Demotika would go and find them, assigning them two battalions of knights in order to do so. Thus it was planned, and so it was done on the following day. The commander of one of the battalions was Eustace, Emperor Henry of Constantinople's brother,[2] while Macaire of Sainte-Menehould led the other. [447] These men and the Greek contingent rode to the valley they had been told about, and there they found the captives, just as they had been informed.

Johanitsa's men attacked those of Emperor Henry; men, women and horses on both sides were wounded, but with strength from God it was the Franks who had the upper hand. They gathered up the captives and brought them back at the head of their convoy.

[448] You should know that this rescue mission was no small undertaking, for there were a good 20,000 captives – men, women and children – along with 3,000 carts loaded with their clothes and possessions, not to mention the livestock they had, of which there was a great deal. Their journey back to the camp was around two leagues long. They arrived there that night, which brought great joy to Emperor Henry and all the other barons. The captives were given their own quarters, apart from the army, so that they would not lose a *denier*'s-worth of their belongings. The emperor stayed there the following day for the sake of those who had just been rescued, but on the day after that he moved off from those parts and rode day after day until he reached Adrianople.

[449] He then parted ways with the men and women he had rescued; each of them went wherever he or she wished, to their native towns or villages, or to other parts. The livestock – of which there was a great abundance – was divided among the people in the army in line with customary practice. Emperor Henry stayed at Adrianople for five days before riding to Demotika in order to find out how badly damaged the defences there were, and to establish whether the city could be refortified. They set up camp in front of the city, and he and his barons could see that the condition of the defences made it pointless to try to rebuild them.

[450] One of Marquis Boniface's barons, whose name was Othon of la Roche, then arrived in the camp as an envoy. He was there to discuss the marriage that had already been proposed between Marquis Boniface of Montferrat's daughter and Emperor Henry, and he brought news that the lady had arrived from Lombardy, from where her father had sent for her, and that she was at Salonika. Both sides confirmed their agreement to the marriage, following which the envoy Othon of la Roche returned to Salonika.

[451] The emperor gathered his forces once more; they had been busy storing the booty they had won at Beröe safely in the camp. Day after day they rode out beyond Adrianople, going far enough to enter the lands of Johanitsa, king of Vlachia and Bulgaria. They came to a city called Thermae which they captured and entered, seizing a great quantity of spoil. They stayed there for three days and overran all the surrounding country, where they won lots of booty and destroyed a town called Akilo.

[452] On the fourth day they left Thermae, which was a beautiful and pleasantly situated town where the world's loveliest hot springs flow. The emperor destroyed the city, burning it and carrying off a very large quantity of booty, both livestock and other goods. They then rode day after day to reach Adrianople. They stayed in those parts until the feast of All Saints[3], by which time they could no longer make war because winter was setting in. And so Emperor Henry then turned back and went to Constantinople with all his barons, who were greatly wearied by fighting. Henry left one of his men among the Greeks at Adrianople; his name was Peter of Radinghem and he was accompanied by twenty knights.

[453] At that time a truce was in place between Emperor Henry and Theodore Lascaris, who controlled the land on the other side of the Straits of Saint George. But Lascaris did not uphold the terms of the truce; instead he abused and broke them. And so the emperor decided to send Peter of Bracieux beyond the straits to the city of Espigal, where he had been assigned lands. He was accompanied by Payen of Orléans, Anseau of Cayeux and Emperor Henry's own brother Eustace and by a good number of the emperor's best men, amounting to 140 knights. They made war on Theodore Lascaris with great vigour and ferociousness, doing great damage in his lands.

[454] They rode to a place called Cyzicus, which was almost completely surrounded by the sea: only one side was not on the water. The entrance through which one reached the town had formerly been fortified with walls, towers and trenches, but these were virtual ruins. The French force entered the town and Peter of Bracieux, to whom this place had been granted, started

work to refortify it. He built castles at each of two points of entry into the town. He and his companions used Cyzicus as a base from which to overrun the land controlled by Lascaris, seizing plentiful booty and large quantities of livestock, which they brought back to the town. Theodore Lascaris made frequent raids on Cyzicus, and his men and Peter's did battle on a number of occasions, and losses were inflicted on both sides. The fighting in those parts was vicious and intense.

[455] Let us now leave the men at Cyzicus, and turn our attention to Dietrich of Looz, the seneschal of the empire and the rightful lord of Nicomedia. That town is one day away from Nicaea, the chief city in Theodore Lascaris's lands. Dietrich returned to the region with a good number of Emperor Henry's men to discover that the castle at Nicomedia had been torn down. And so he set up defences and fortifications around the beautiful and vast church of Saint Sophia, from where he conducted his war in that region.

[456] At about this time Marquis Boniface of Montferrat left Salonika and went to Serres, a town that had been ruined by Johanitsa. The marquis restored its fortifications, and then did the same at a castle called Drama, which is in the Philippi valley. All the people in the surrounding region surrendered to him and obeyed him as their lord. He spent the winter in those parts.

[457] Enough time passed for Christmas to come and go. A messenger from the marquis then came to the emperor in Constantinople, informing him that the marquis had sent his daughter by galley to the town of Enos. Emperor Henry sent Geoffrey, marshal of Romania and Champagne, and Milon le Bréban to fetch the lady. And so they rode, day after day, until they arrived at the town of Enos. [458] There they found the lady, who was both very virtuous and very beautiful. They greeted her on their lord's behalf and brought her back to Constantinople with great honour. Emperor Henry married her in the church of Saint Sophia on the Sunday following the feast of Our Lady Saint Mary at Candlemas.[4] The marriage was celebrated with great joy and great pomp; both bride and groom were wearing crowns, and the wedding feast at the Bucoleon

palace was a splendid occasion, with everyone in attendance. And so the emperor was married to the daughter of Marquis Boniface; her name was Empress Agnes.

[459] Theodore Lascaris, who was at war with Emperor Henry, appointed messengers and sent them to Johanitsa, king of Vlachia and Bulgaria. Through these messengers he informed the king that all Emperor Henry's men were on the side of the Straits of Saint George towards the land of the Turks, fighting against him, and that the emperor was at Constantinople with only a few men. Now would be a good time to take vengeance on him. Lascaris said that he would be fighting the emperor on one side, and that the king should move against him from the other; the emperor had so few men that he would not be able to defend himself against them both. Johanitsa had gathered a large army of Cumans about him, and he also prepared as large a force of Vlachs and Bulgars as he could. By this point enough time had passed for Lent to have arrived.[5]

[460] Macaire of Sainte-Menehould had started work on refortifying a castle at Charax, which was situated in a bay by the sea, six leagues away from Nicomedia in the direction of Constantinople. William of Sains began to rebuild the defences of another castle, at Kibotos, which is on the opposite side of the bay of Nicomedia from Charax, in the direction of Nicaea. And you should know that Emperor Henry and the barons in the region around Constantinople had many concerns to attend to in those parts. Geoffrey of Villehardouin, marshal of Romania and Champagne, is your faithful witness that at no time have any people ever been so burdened with war, for they were scattered among so many different places.

[461] Johanitsa then set out from Vlachia with all his army and with the large force of Cumans who had entered his service, and he invaded Romania. The Cumans advanced right up to the gates of Constantinople while Johanitsa laid siege to Adrianople. He set up thirty-three large petraries, which launched missiles at the walls and towers. The only people inside Adrianople besides the Greeks were Peter of Radinghem and ten knights, who had been stationed there by the emperor. The Greeks and Latins together sent word to Emperor Henry

that Johanitsa had besieged them in this way, and they called on him to come to their aid.

[462] The emperor was very perturbed when he heard this news, since his forces had split up to go to a number of places on the other side of the straits, while he remained in Constantinople with only a few men. He decided to venture forth from the city with such forces as he could muster two weeks after Easter, and he ordered the large body of his men at Cyzicus to come and join him. This party, including Emperor Henry's brother Eustace, Anseau of Cayeux, and most of the men who had been with them, set out from Cyzicus by sea, leaving Peter of Bracieux there with a meagre force.

[463] On hearing the news that Adrianople had been besieged and that Emperor Henry had been compelled to recall his forces, uncertain as to whether he should rush to one place or another, since he was oppressed by war on all sides, Theodore Lascaris used all his efforts to gather the largest force he could. He set up his tents and pavilions in front of the gates of Cyzicus, where he clashed with the Frankish forces on numerous occasions, sometimes winning and sometimes losing. When Lascaris discovered there were only a few men inside the town, he set apart a large portion of his army and such ships as he had at sea and sent them to the castle of Kibotos, where William of Sains had been rebuilding the defences. They launched an assault against the castle, by land and by sea, on the Saturday of mid-Lent.[6]

[464] There were forty very good knights inside Kibotos, led by Macaire of Sainte-Menehould. Their castle still lacked proper fortifications, which meant that Lascaris's men could come at them with swords and lances. The Greek forces attacked our men with great ferociousness both by land and by sea, in an assault that lasted throughout that Saturday. The men inside the castle defended themselves very well, and this book is your faithful witness that no forty knights ever had to protect themselves against so many men and in such perilous circumstances. This could be seen clearly because not even five of the knights there escaped without being wounded. Only one of them died; he was a nephew of Milon le Bréban, whose name was Giles.

[465] Before this assault had got under way on Saturday morning, a messenger had sped to Constantinople, where he found Emperor Henry sitting down to eat in the Bucoleon palace. The messenger told him, 'My lord, you should know that the people of Kibotos are under attack by land and by sea. If you do not hurry to their aid, they will all be captured or killed.' [466] The emperor had with him Conon of Béthune, Marshal Geoffrey of Champagne, Milon le Bréban, and just a few other men. They made their decision swiftly; the emperor should go to the shore and board a small ship, and the others would find whatever vessels they could. It was then made known throughout the city that people should follow the emperor, who urgently needed to bring help to his men who would otherwise be lost. You might then have seen the city of Constantinople swarming with Venetians and Pisans and other expert seafarers; they ran to the ships, each man going aboard as and when he got his chance. With them went the knights with all their arms and armour, and each ship set sail from the harbour as soon as it could, following after the emperor.

[467] And so they made their way, powered by their oars, all that evening and through the night, until dawn broke on the following day. Emperor Henry had pressed on with such energy that he came within sight of Kibotos shortly after sunrise, and could see the forces surrounding the castle both on land and at sea. The people inside the town had not slept at all that night; despite their injuries and ailments they had spent the hours of darkness barricading themselves inside, as people would who expected nothing other than death.

[468] When the emperor saw that Lascaris's forces were moving in to renew their assault on Kibotos, he was as yet accompanied by just a few of his own men. Marshal Geoffrey was alongside him in another ship, as were Milon le Bréban, some of the Pisans, and a few other knights; in all the emperor had seventeen ships, both large and small, while the opposing side had a good sixty. He could see that if he were to wait for the rest of his men to arrive, it would allow the Greeks to attack the people inside Kibotos again, and those people would all be

killed or captured. And so he and his companions decided to do battle with their enemies at sea.

[469] They rowed onward abreast; everyone on board was armed and had their helmets laced. When their enemies who were ready to attack the castle saw them coming, they were quite sure that this was a rescue mission and so they pulled their own vessels back from the castle and turned to engage the newcomers. The entire opposing army, which was made up of a large number of men both on foot and on horseback, took up position on the shoreline. And when the people on board the Greek ships saw that the emperor and his men kept coming at them despite this, they drew back to where their colleagues were on the shore so that the army might lend them support by firing arrows and launching missiles.

[470] The emperor kept the opposing forces under siege with his seventeen ships until shouts could be heard of those coming from the direction of Constantinople. Before darkness fell so many of these ships had arrived that they dominated the sea in all directions. Our men, already armed, spent the night in their anchored ships. They had decided that as soon as they saw daylight they would go and attack their enemies on the shore and seize their ships. But around midnight the Greeks dragged all their ships up on to land, set fires inside them and burned every one of them before they decamped and fled.

[471] Emperor Henry and his men were overjoyed that God had granted them this victory and that they had rescued their men. When morning came the emperor and all the others went to the castle of Kibotos, where they found that most of the people were very unwell and badly injured. The emperor and his forces kept guard at the castle, which they realized was so poorly fortified that it was not worth trying to hold. And so they withdrew with all their people into the ships leaving the castle abandoned.

[472] Johanitsa, king of Vlachia, who had laid siege to Adrianople, gave the city no rest; his petraries – of which he had a considerable number – hurled missiles at the walls and at the towers, damaging them badly. He also set miners to work on the walls and launched numerous assaults. The Greeks and

Latins inside the city fought back as best they could but sent frequent messages for help to Emperor Henry, letting him know that if he did not come to their aid they would be completely lost. The emperor was deeply vexed because when he wished to go and lend support to his people in one place, Theodore Lascaris put such pressure on his forces elsewhere that he was compelled to turn back.

[473] Johanitsa spent the whole month of April outside Adrianople, and he came so close to capturing the city that he had razed the walls and towers down to the ground in two places, enabling his men to fight hand to hand with swords and lances against those inside. He was able to launch vicious assaults, but the city's defenders kept up their stern resistance; many people were killed and injured on one side and the other.

[474] Since events transpire according to God's will, the Cumans whom Johanitsa had sent out to ravage the land had seized plentiful booty, which they brought back to the camp at Adrianople. But they said they no longer wished to serve Johanitsa and wanted to return to their own lands instead. The Cumans thus deserted Johanitsa and he did not dare remain at Adrianople without them. And so he withdrew from the city, abandoning the siege. [475] Know that this was deemed a great miracle, that a city so close to being captured as this one was should be abandoned by a man as powerful as Johanitsa. But events unfold as God wants them to. The people of Adrianople did not hesitate in repeating their call for the emperor to come quickly, for God's sake, since they knew for certain that if Johanitsa returned they would all be killed or captured.

[476] The emperor was preparing to go to Adrianople with such a force as he could raise when some deeply troubling news reached him. Stirione, who was the admiral of Theodore Lascaris's fleet,[7] had entered the Channel of Abydos at the entrance to the Straits of Saint George with seventeen galleys and had made his way to Cyzicus, where Peter of Bracieux remained with Payen of Orléans. Stirione had laid siege to the town from the sea, while Lascaris did the same from the land. The people from the region around Cyzicus and from Marmara rebelled against Peter of Bracieux, their rightful lord, and

inflicted great harm on him, killing a good number of his men.

[477] When news of this reached Constantinople the people there were greatly alarmed. Emperor Henry consulted his vassals and barons, and the Venetians too. It was their opinion that if they did not go to the aid of Peter of Bracieux and Payen of Orléans, they would be killed and their lands would be lost. And so they equipped fourteen galleys with all possible speed, and the best men among the Venetians and all the emperor's barons went aboard.

[478] Conon of Béthune went aboard one of the galleys with his men, while Marshal Geoffrey of Villehardouin went aboard another with his forces. The third was taken by Macaire of Sainte-Menehould and his company, and Milon le Bréban had the fourth. In the fifth was Anseau of Cayeux, and in the sixth Dietrich of Looz who was seneschal of the empire. William of Perchay boarded the seventh, and the emperor's brother Eustace the eighth. In this way Emperor Henry's best men were distributed among all the galleys. When they set sail from the harbour at Constantinople it was rightly said by everyone who witnessed the event that no galleys had ever been so well armed or had borne better men. And so the expedition to Adrianople was postponed once more.

[479] The men in the galleys sailed down the straits, directly to Cyzicus. I do not know how Stirione, Theodore Lascaris's admiral, knew they were coming, but he withdrew from Cyzicus and fled down the straits. Our ships pursued him for two days and two nights, until they were around forty miles beyond the Channel of Abydos. Once they realized they would not be able to catch him, they turned back and went to Cyzicus, where they found Peter of Bracieux and Payen of Orléans. Theodore Lascaris had decamped from outside the town and had retreated to his own lands. Thus was Cyzicus rescued, as you have heard. Those in the galleys turned back to Constantinople and resumed their preparations for the expedition to Adrianople.

[480] Theodore Lascaris sent the greater part of his army, in full force, to the region of Nicomedia. Dietrich of Looz's men, who had fortified the church of Saint Sophia in the city, and those who were taking shelter inside it, sent word to their lord

the emperor begging him to come and help them because if they did not receive any assistance they would not be able to hold out. Above all else they needed food; their supplies were completely exhausted. Because of their great need Emperor Henry was compelled to abandon the expedition to Adrianople and cross over to the side of the Straits of Saint George towards the land of the Turks with as many men as he could muster, in order to relieve Nicomedia.

[481] When Theodore Lascaris's men learned that the emperor was on his way, they left those parts and retreated towards Nicaea. On hearing of this the emperor decided that Dietrich of Looz, seneschal of Romania, should stay at Nicomedia with all his knights and his sergeants in order to guard the town and the territory round about, while Macaire of Sainte-Menehould was to stay at Charax and William of Perchay at Cyzicus in order to defend the land in those regions.

[482] Emperor Henry then returned to Constantinople with the remainder of his men, and once more made ready to set out on an expedition to Adrianople. While he undertook preparations for this journey, Seneschal Dietrich of Looz (who was at Nicomedia), William of Perchay and their men went on a foraging trip one day. Theodore Lascaris's forces found out about this and ambushed them. Our men were very few in number while their enemies were many. Thus the fighting and brawling got under way but it did not last very long, since the few could not hold out against the many. [483] Dietrich of Looz and his men bore themselves very well. He was brought to the ground twice and his companions had to struggle to help him get back on his horse. William of Perchay was also unhorsed; he was put back in the saddle before being rescued. The Franks, unable to bear the onslaught, were defeated. Dietrich of Looz was captured there, having been wounded in his face so badly that he was in danger of dying. A number of his men were taken prisoner with him, and only a few managed to get away. William of Perchay, whose hand was wounded, escaped on a rouncy. He and the others who managed to flee this rout retreated to the church of Saint Sophia in Nicomedia.

[484] The composer of this history is not sure whether this

is true or false, but he heard one knight blamed for this debacle. His name was Anseau of Remy and although he was a liegeman of Seneschal Dietrich of Looz and a commander of his forces, he had deserted his lord during the battle.

[485] The men who had managed to get back to the church of Saint Sophia at Nicomedia, William of Perchay and Anseau of Remy among them, chose a messenger and sent him in all possible haste to Emperor Henry at Constantinople. The messenger informed him what had happened: that the seneschal and his men had been captured, and that the others were besieged inside the church of Saint Sophia at Nicomedia, with food to last them no more than five days. He was sure that if no one came to their aid they would all be killed or taken prisoner. In response to this distress call the emperor and his forces crossed over the Straits of Saint George as and when they could, in order to relieve the men at Nicomedia. And so, yet again, the expedition to Adrianople was delayed.

[486] Once the emperor was on the other side of the Straits of Saint George, he organized his battalions and then rode, day after day, until he reached Nicomedia. When Theodore Lascaris's forces, which were under the command of his brothers, heard that the emperor was coming, they retreated over the mountain, towards Nicaea. Emperor Henry installed himself, and had his tents and pavilions erected, outside Nicomedia, in a most attractive riverside meadow at the foot of the mountain. He sent his men to ride out across the surrounding territory, for the people in those parts had taken the opportunity to rebel when they heard that Seneschal Dietrich of Looz had been captured. The emperor's forces seized a good quantity of livestock and took numerous captives.

[487] Emperor Henry spent five days in that meadow, and during his stay Theodore Lascaris appointed and sent messengers to him, proposing a two-year truce if the emperor would agree to have the fortifications at Cyzicus and around the church of Saint Sophia in Nicomedia torn down. In return Lascaris would release all the prisoners who had been captured in the rout outside Nicomedia and elsewhere, of whom there were a considerable number in his lands.

[488] The emperor took advice from his men, and they told him that he would not be able to sustain two wars at once, and that it would be better to accept this blow than to endure the loss of Adrianople or the rest of his lands. The proposed truce would also break the alliance between his enemies, King Johanitsa of Vlachia and Bulgaria and Theodore Lascaris, who were on friendly terms and had been working together in their wars. [489] Thus was the matter settled and approved. Emperor Henry summoned Peter of Bracieux, and on his arrival the emperor worked hard to persuade him to hand over Cyzicus. The town was then surrendered to Theodore Lascaris, who reduced it to rubble and did the same to the fortified church in Nicomedia. Thus the truce was confirmed and those fortresses were torn down. Dietrich of Looz was freed, along with all the other prisoners.

[490] Emperor Henry then made his way back to Constantinople and readied himself to go to Adrianople with such men as he could muster. He gathered his army at Selymbria, but so much time had already passed that the feast of Saint John in June[8] was over. They rode out until they reached Adrianople, where they set up camp in the fields outside the city. The people of Adrianople, who had longed for this day, came out of the city in procession and gave the army a very warm welcome. All the Greeks in that region had come for the occasion.

[491] Emperor Henry only stayed outside Adrianople for one day, but this was enough for him to observe the damage Johanitsa had done to the walls and towers with his miners and petraries, much weakening the city's defences. The next day he moved off in the direction of Johanitsa's lands. He rode on for four days and on the fifth came to the foot of the Vlachian mountains, to a town called Eului, which the king had just had resettled. When the local inhabitants saw the army approaching they abandoned the town and fled into the mountains.

[492] The emperor set up camp before the town, and his foragers overran the region, seizing oxen and cows and buffalo in large numbers, along with other animals. Some of the people from Adrianople, who were poverty-stricken and in need of provisions, had brought carts with them, which they loaded

with wheat and other kinds of grain. They also found a plentiful supply of other foodstuffs, which they piled high in the remaining carts. The army stayed there for three days, each of which the foragers spent collecting the spoils of the land. But that region was so mountainous and had so many deep gorges that a number of the pillagers were lost who did not take care where they were going.

[493] In the end Emperor Henry sent Anseau of Cayeux to watch over the foragers. He was accompanied by Henry's brother Eustace, his nephew Thierry of Flanders, Walter of Escornais and John Bliaut. Their four battalions went to protect the pillagers, and in doing so they were taken up into treacherous mountain territory. When the people they were guarding had finished scouring the land and were ready to return, they discovered that the gorges were heavily defended. The local Vlachs had assembled a force that attacked them and inflicted heavy losses of men and horses. They were very nearly defeated; the knights were compelled to get down from their horses and fight on foot. With God's help they were able to get back to camp nevertheless, but they had suffered heavy losses.

[494] The following day Emperor Henry and the French army left that place and rode back, day after day, to reach the city of Adrianople. Here they stored the supplies of grain and other food they were bringing, and the emperor stayed in the fields outside the city for around two weeks.

[495] At about this time Marquis Boniface of Montferrat, who was at Serres, a town he had refortified, undertook a series of expeditions in the direction of Mosynopolis, where the people of the region surrendered to his authority. The marquis appointed messengers and sent them to Emperor Henry, with a request that the emperor come to the river that flows beneath Ipsala in order to talk with him. They had not been able to hold a meeting since they had conquered the empire; the territory between the marquis's and the emperor's lands held so many enemies that neither of them could go to visit the other. When the emperor and his council heard that the marquis was at Mosynopolis, he was overjoyed, and he sent messengers in

return to say that he would go to hold a conference with him on the appointed day.

[496] And so the emperor set out in that direction, leaving Conon of Béthune with a hundred knights to guard Adrianople and its lands. Both men arrived at the place chosen for the meeting, which was in a most beautiful meadow, near to the town of Ipsala. The emperor arrived from one direction and the marquis from another, and they were overjoyed to be reunited. And this should come as no surprise, for they had not seen each other in a long while. The marquis asked for news of his daughter, Empress Agnes, and he was extremely pleased and happy to be told she was heavy with child. The marquis then swore homage to Emperor Henry as his vassal, acknowledging that he held his lands from him as he had done from Emperor Baldwin, Henry's brother. Marquis Boniface then granted to Geoffrey of Villehardouin, marshal of Romania and of Champagne, either the city of Mosynopolis and all the rights associated with it, or the city of Serres, whichever he preferred. Marshal Geoffrey would become the marquis's liegeman for these lands, although the primary loyalty Geoffrey owed to the emperor of Constantinople would be preserved.

[497] They spent two very joyful days in that meadow, and they said that since God had allowed them to come together, they might be able to do further harm to their enemies. They discussed a plan to meet at the end of the month of October with all their forces in the fields outside the city of Adrianople, from where they would go and wage war against the king of Vlachia. They parted ways feeling very happy and pleased; the marquis went to Mosynopolis, while Emperor Henry went to Constantinople.

[498] It was no more than five days after the marquis's arrival at Mosynopolis, when, on the advice of the Greeks from those parts, he set out on a raid to the mountain of Mosynopolis, more than a full day's journey away. Having spent some time there he was ready to leave, but the Bulgars in those parts had assembled a force and could see that the marquis had only a few men with him. They came from all directions and attacked his rearguard. When he heard the call go up the marquis leapt

on to a horse; he was wearing no armour at all but carried a
lance in his hand. As he reached the place where his rearguard
was under assault, he charged at the Bulgars and chased them
off for a good distance.

[499] But Marquis Boniface of Montferrat was mortally
wounded there, struck in the thickest part of his arm, just below
the shoulder, so that he began to lose blood. When his men saw
what had happened, they began to lose heart and despair, and
their sense of proper conduct started to falter. Those alongside
the marquis supported him, but he was bleeding heavily and
began to lose consciousness. Once they realized the marquis
could offer no further assistance, his men began to panic and
to flee. This unfortunate incident led to their defeat. Those men
who had stayed with the marquis – and there were only a few
of them – were killed, while the marquis himself was decapi-
tated. The local inhabitants sent his head to Johanitsa, and this
was one of the greatest joys he ever knew.

[500] Alas! What a grievous misfortune it was for Emperor
Henry and all the Latins in the land of Romania, to lose such
a man as this as a result of such bad luck. He had been one of
the best and most generous barons, and one of the finest knights
there was in all the world. This most unhappy accident occurred
in the year of the incarnation of Jesus Christ 1207.

JOHN OF JOINVILLE

The Life of Saint Louis

Contents

Prologue   141

Part I Louis's Sanctity in Word

1 King Louis's Holy Words and Pious
  Teachings   147

Part II Louis's Sanctity in Deed

 2 King Louis Confronts Rebellious Barons   163
 3 King Louis's Crusade Vow and the
   Voyage to Cyprus   173
 4 The Fall and Occupation of Damietta   182
 5 The Crusaders Venture Along the
   River Nile   191
 6 The Battle of Mansurah   199
 7 From Victory to Captivity   208
 8 The Crusaders in Captivity   225
 9 The Crusaders at Acre   246
10 The Crusaders at Caesarea (Reports
   Concerning the Tartars)   262
11 The Crusaders at Jaffa   274
12 The Crusaders at Sidon   286
13 The Journey Home   300
14 King Louis's Personal and Governmental
   Reforms   312
15 King Louis's Second Crusade, Death and
   Canonization   328

Prologue

[1] To his good lord Louis, son of the king of France, by the grace of God king of Navarre and count palatine of Champagne and Brie,[1] John, lord of Joinville, his seneschal of Champagne sends greetings and love and honour, and his ready service.

[2] Dear lord, I would have you know that my lady the queen, your mother, who loved me very much – may God have tender mercy on her – begged me as fervently as she could to make her a book of the holy words and the good deeds of our king Saint Louis. I promised to do so and with God's help the book has been completed in two parts. The first part describes how he conducted himself throughout his life in accordance with God and the Church and to the benefit of his kingdom. The second part of the book then speaks of his distinguished knightly deeds and impressive feats of arms.

[3] My lord, since it is written, 'Attend first to that which pertains to God, and he will set all other affairs in order for you',[2] I started by having written down that which relates to the three things already mentioned, by which I mean: that which pertains to the well-being of souls and of bodies, and that which pertains to the government of the people. [4] I have had other things written down to do further honour to this true saint, since through them it can be seen quite clearly that no layman of our time ever showed such holiness in life as he did, from the beginning of his reign until the end of his days. I was not there when he died, but Count Peter of Alençon, his son, who loved me very much, was there, and he reported to me the fitting end the king made, as you will find written at the end of this book.

[5] And it seems to me that he was not adequately recognized when they failed to set him among the number of the martyrs,[3] considering the great suffering he endured on the pilgrimage of the cross over the course of the six years I was in his company, and especially because he followed Our Lord as far as the cross; for if God died on the cross so did he, for he was signed with the cross when he died at Tunis.

[6] The second part of the book will tell you of his distinguished knightly deeds and his great acts of bravery. These were such that on four occasions I saw him put his own life in mortal peril in order to save his people from harm, as you will hear hereafter.

[7] The first instance in which he put his life in mortal peril was as we arrived before Damietta. All his councillors urged him, so I have heard, to stay in his ship until he could see how his knights fared as they reached the shore. [8] Their reason for advising this was that if he should land with the knights, and his forces be wiped out with him among them, their project would be a complete loss, whereas if he stayed on his ship he might himself launch another attempt to conquer the land of Egypt. But he did not want to listen to any of them. Instead he leapt into the sea fully armed, with his shield at his neck and his lance in his hand, and was among the first to reach land.

[9] The second occasion in which he put his life in mortal peril was this: as he left Mansurah to go to Damietta he was advised by his council, so I have been given to understand, that he should go to Damietta in a galley. He was given this advice, so it is said, on the grounds that if things went badly for his people he might himself be able to secure their release from prison. [10] This advice was given to him especially on account of his physical frailty, brought on by his several sicknesses; he had a double tertian fever, severe diarrhoea and the sickness that had struck the camp[4] was afflicting his mouth and legs. Nonetheless, he did not want to listen to anyone. Rather he said that he would never abandon his people, and would meet whatever end they met. It so happened that the diarrhoea he was suffering from made it necessary to cut out the seat of his

breeches that night, and the intensity of the camp sickness meant he fainted several times, as you will hear later on.

[11] The third occasion in which he put his life in mortal peril was when he remained in the Holy Land for four years after his brothers',[5] departure. We were in great danger of death at that time because for each man-at-arms the king had in his force during his stay at Acre, the people of that city would have thirty when it was lost.[6] [12] I know of no other reason why the Turks did not come and take us at Acre other than God's love for the king, which struck fear into the hearts of our enemies so that they did not dare come and attack us. Because of which it is written, 'If you fear God, so all those that look on you will fear you.' The king chose to stay against all advice, as you will hear later. He placed his life at risk to save the people of that land, who would have been lost from that moment if he had not remained.

[13] The fourth instance in which he put his life in mortal peril was as we were returning from overseas and were off the island of Cyprus, where our ship struck bottom so violently that the sandbank we had hit tore away eighteen feet of the keel on which our ship was built. [14] After this happened the king summoned fourteen master mariners, from the damaged ship and from others in his fleet, to consult them as to what he should do. As you will hear later on they all urged him to go aboard another ship, for they did not see how this vessel could withstand the pounding of the waves, when the bolts that held the ship's planks together had all been dislodged. They explained the danger facing the ship to the king using an example: during our outward sea voyage a ship in a similar situation had perished. I myself saw, in the count of Joigny's lodgings, the woman and child who were the sole survivors from that ship.

[15] The king responded, 'My lords, I can see that if I leave this ship she will be abandoned. It is my view that since each of the 800 and more people aboard loves their life just as much as I do mine, no one would dare stay on this ship, but would stay on Cyprus instead. I would not on this account – please God – put so many people as there are here in mortal danger, and therefore, I will stay aboard to save my people.' [16] And

so he stayed. And God, in whom he placed his trust, saved us from the perils of the sea for ten weeks, bringing us into safe harbour as you will hear later on. Now, it so happened that Oliver of Termes, who had conducted himself well and vigorously overseas, left the king and stayed on Cyprus; we did not see him for a year and a half. It should be apparent from this that the king prevented any harm to the 800 people on his ship.

[17] In the last part of the book we will speak of his end, and the saintly manner of his death.

[18] Now I must tell you, my lord king of Navarre, that I made a promise to my lady the queen, your mother – may God have tender mercy on her – that I would make this book. I have done so in order to fulfil that promise, and since I see no one who should more properly have it than you, her heir, I am sending it to you so that you and your brothers and others that hear it might heed its good lessons and put those lessons into practice, and thereby make themselves pleasing to God.

PART I

LOUIS'S SANCTITY
IN WORD

CHAPTER I

King Louis's Holy Words and Pious Teachings

[19] In the name of God Almighty, I, John of Joinville, seneschal of Champagne, am dictating the life of our saintly King Louis: what I saw and heard during the six years I was in his company on pilgrimage overseas, and after our return. Before I tell you of his great deeds and his knightly conduct, I will tell you what I saw and heard of his holy words and pious teachings, so that they may be found one after another for the improvement of those who hear them.

[20] This holy man loved God with all his heart and emulated his deeds; this was evident because just as God died on account of his love for his people, so did the king put his own life at risk on several occasions because of his love for his people. He could easily have avoided doing so if he had wished to, as you will hear later on.

[21] His love for his people was apparent in what he said to my lord Louis, his oldest son, when a serious illness struck the king at Fontainebleau: 'Dear son,' he said, 'I beg you to make yourself beloved by your kingdom's people. For in truth I would rather a Scottish man came from Scotland to govern the people of this kingdom honestly and well than that you should govern it unjustly.' The saintly king so loved honesty that he would not even lie to the Saracens regarding an agreement[1] he had made with them, as you will hear later on.

[22] In his eating habits he was so restrained that never in my life did I hear him order a dish, as many wealthy men do. Instead he graciously ate whatever the cook prepared and set in front of him. And in his speech he was equally temperate, for never in my life did I hear him speak ill of anyone or mention

the Devil. The Devil's name is uttered widely in the kingdom now, which I believe cannot be in the least pleasing to God.

[23] He added water to his wine in accordance with what he saw that wine could stand. While we were in Cyprus he asked me why I did not put any water in my wine, and I told him that I was under orders from my doctors, who had told me that I had a large head and a cold stomach, so that I was incapable of becoming inebriated. And he told me that they were misleading me, for if I did not learn to mix my wine with water in my youth but started to do so in my old age, I would be so afflicted by stomach pains and illness that I would never feel well. If, on the other hand, I were to drink my wine without water in my old age, I would be drunk every night, and drunkenness was most unseemly in a distinguished man.

[24] He asked me if I wished to be honoured in this world and to obtain Paradise after death. I said yes, and he told me, 'Then keep yourself from knowingly doing or saying anything that, if the whole world were to come to hear of it, you would not willingly acknowledge by saying: "I did that", or "I said that."' He told me I should take care not to challenge or contradict anything said in my presence – unless I would be led into sin or suffer harm as a result – for harsh words begin the brawls which have brought a thousand men to their deaths.

[25] He said that a man should dress and arm himself in such a way that the *preudommes* of this world might not say that he was making too much of himself, while young men might not say that he was making too little. I reminded the father of the current king[2] of this advice because of the *surcotes* embroidered with coats of arms that are made today. I told him that never during the course of our journey overseas did I see embroidered *surcotes* worn by the king or anyone else. He told me that he had some items of clothing embroidered with his arms that had cost him 800 Parisian *livres*, and I told him that he would have put this money to better use if he had given it to do God's work and had his clothes made from good quality *cendal* with his arms sewn on to them, as his father would have done.

[26] One time King Louis called for me and said, 'I am not so bold as to speak to you, a man of subtle intelligence, of

matters concerning God. Therefore, I have summoned these friars here, since I wish to ask you a question.' The question was this: 'Seneschal, what kind of a thing is God?' And I said to him, 'My lord, God is something so good that there can be no better.' 'Truly,' he said, 'that's a very good response, for the reply you gave is written in this book I have in my hand. [27] Now I would like you to tell me,' he said, 'which you would like better, to be a leper or to have committed a mortal sin?' And I, who never lied to him, replied that I would rather have committed thirty mortal sins than be a leper. When the friars had left, he called me over to him on my own, had me sit at his feet and asked me, 'How could you say that to me yesterday?' And I told him that I would say it again. He said, 'You spoke like a rash fool; you should know that there is no leprosy as foul as being in a state of mortal sin, for a soul taken up by mortal sin is akin to the Devil, and no leprosy could be as repulsive as that. [28] Truly, when a man dies he is cured of the leprosy of his body, but when a man dies having committed mortal sin, he can have no knowledge or certainty that he repented sufficiently in his lifetime for God to have pardoned him; he should fear greatly that his affliction will last as long as God is in Heaven. And therefore I beg you as earnestly as possible,' said the king, 'for the love of God and of me, to keep in your heart a preference that any sickness should strike your body – whether leprosy or any other illness – rather than mortal sin enter your soul.'

[29] He asked me whether I washed the feet of the poor on Maundy Thursday. 'My lord,' I said, 'I would never on any account wash the feet of those wretches!' 'Indeed,' he said, 'that was the wrong thing to say. For you should not hold in disdain that which God did for our instruction. And so I beg you, for the love of God above all but also for love of me, to become accustomed to washing their feet.'

[30] He so valued people who trusted in and loved God, regardless of their background, that he made my lord Giles le Brun constable of France even though he was not from the kingdom of France. This was because he was widely renowned for his faith in and love for God, and indeed I believe he deserved his reputation.

[31] He had Master Robert of Sorbon[3] eat at his table on account of his great reputation as a *preudomme*. One day it so happened that Master Robert sat beside me for the meal, and we were talking quietly to each other. The king reprimanded us, saying, 'Speak up, for your companions think you are talking ill of them. If you are talking at table of matters that we should find pleasing, then speak out loud, and if not then say nothing.'

[32] Once, when he was in a playful mood, the king asked me, 'Seneschal, tell me the reasons why a *preudomme* is more worthy than a *béguin*.' This prompted an argument between me and Master Robert. When we had debated for a long while, the king delivered his judgement and said, 'Master Robert, I would like very much to be called a *preudomme* – provided I was such a man – and I would leave the rest to you. For a *preudomme* is so distinguished and virtuous a being that simply to pronounce the word is satisfying to one's mouth.' [33] On the other hand, he said it was a wicked thing to take what belonged to someone else, since restoring things is so hard that even to say the word 'restore' grates one's throat because of its 'r'-sounds.[4] These 'r'-sounds signify the Devil's rakes, always being dragged behind him to keep hold of those who want to restore another's property. The Devil is so wily in doing so that he induces notorious thieves and usurers to make gifts to God of what they should restore to their victims.

[34] He asked me to take a message to King Thibaut[5] for him, advising him to be on his guard not to let the great sums he was spending on the construction of a house for the Dominicans at Provins become a burden on his soul. 'For while he lives a wise man should use his resources as the executor of an estate would. By which I mean that good executors first make amends for the wrongs of the dead man and restore any property to its rightful owner, and then use what is left of the dead man's estate in charity.'

[35] One Pentecost the holy king was at Corbeil, where he was attended by at least 300 knights. After his meal the king went down into the garden below the chapel and was standing in the doorway talking to the count of Brittany, the father of the current duke – may God preserve him. Master Robert

of Sorbon came to find me there. He took me by the hem of my mantle and led me to the king, with all the other knights following behind us. I asked Master Robert, 'What do you want from me?' And he said, 'I want to ask you whether, if the king were to sit down in this garden and you went to sit higher up on his bench than him, would we be right to reprove you firmly for it?' I told him yes. [36] 'Then you are surely in the wrong,' he said, 'to be more nobly dressed than the king. You are wearing green cloth with vair, and the king is not.' I told him: 'I beg your pardon, Master Robert, but I am not at all in the wrong in wearing green cloth and vair; I inherited my style of dress from my father and mother. It is you who are in the wrong, for you are the son of commoners but have abandoned your father and mother's style of dress and are wearing better quality *camelin* than the king is.' I took the edge of his *surcote*, and of the king's *surcote*, and said to him, 'See whether what I say is true.' And then the king intervened to speak in vigorous defence of Master Robert.

[37] Afterwards, my lord the king called for my lord Philip, his son (father of the current king) and for King Thibaut. He was sitting at the entrance to his oratory and placed his hand on the ground and said to them, 'Sit yourselves down here, right next to me, so that no one can overhear us.' 'Oh! My lord,' they said, 'we would not dare sit so close to you.' And he said to me, 'Seneschal, you come and sit here.' And so I sat, so close to him that my clothes were touching his. He had the young men sit next to me and said to them, 'You have behaved very badly, for although you are my sons you did not do as I asked straightaway. Take care that this doesn't happen again.' And they told him it would not. [38] He then told me that he had called for us so that he could admit to me that he had been wrong to defend Master Robert against me. 'But,' he said, 'I saw that he was so taken aback by what you said that he really needed my help. In any case you should not heed too closely what I said in Master Robert's defence for, just as the seneschal said, you should dress neatly and well, so that your wives will love you the better for it and your people value you more highly. For the wise man says: "You should provide yourself

with clothes and arms in such a way that the *preudommes* of this world might not say that you are making too much of yourself, while young men might not say that you are making too little." '

[39] Now you will hear a lesson he taught me while we were at sea during our return journey from overseas. It happened that a wind known as *garbino*,[6] which is not even one of the four great winds, drove our ship aground off the island of Cyprus. The sailors were so distressed by the blow the ship had taken that they tore at their clothes and their beards. The king leapt from his bed, barefoot and wearing just a *cote* since it was night-time, and went to lie down with his arms stretched out in the shape of a cross before the body of Our Lord,[7] like a man who expected only death. The day after this happened the king summoned me on my own and said to me, [40] 'Seneschal, God has just shown us a fraction of his great power. For one of the lesser winds, which is so minor that we barely recognize its name, might have drowned the king of France, his wife and children, and his people. Now Saint Anselm[8] tells us that such incidents are Our Lord's warnings to us, as if God wanted to say, "I might well have killed you if I had so wished." Saint Anselm said, "Lord God, why are you warning us? These warnings you issue against us do not bring you profit or benefit, for if you had caused us all to be lost you would not have been any worse off because of it, and if you saved us all you would not have been any richer as a result. So the warning you issued to us was not for your own good, but it can benefit us if we know how to take advantage of it." [41] This is how we should make use of this God-given warning: if we think there is anything in our hearts or in our conduct that might be displeasing to God we should rid ourselves of it without delay, while we should immediately take up whatever we believe pleasing to him. If we act in this way, Our Lord will give us greater blessings in this world and the other than we can imagine, while if we do not do so, he will treat us as a good lord treats a bad servant. For if a bad servant does not wish to mend his ways once a warning has been given, his lord will strike him down with death or with other, greater afflictions, worse even than death.' [42] The

current king should beware of this, for he has escaped dangers as great as those we faced, if not greater; let him correct his faults so that God does not strike out cruelly against him or his concerns.

[43] The king strove with all his ability to teach me to believe firmly in the Christian law given to us by God, as you will now hear. He said we should believe the articles of faith so firmly that neither death nor any ill that might befall our bodies should induce us to go against them in either word or deed. And he said that the Devil is so wily that when a man is dying he works as hard as he can to make him die with a doubt on any of the points of the faith. He knows he cannot rob the man of his good works, and that the man will be lost to him if he dies in true faith. [44] Because of this we must be prepared to defend ourselves against this ruse by saying to the Enemy when he sends us such temptations, 'Away with you! You will never tempt me to give up my firm belief in all the articles of the faith. Even if you were to have all my limbs cut off, I would still want to live and die in this belief.' The man who does so vanquishes the Devil with the same staff and sword with which the enemy wished to kill him.

[45] The king said that faith and belief were things we should be fully confident about, even if our only assurance lay in what we had been told. To illustrate this point he asked me a question: what was my father's name? I told him he was called Simon, and he asked me how I knew. I told him I believed myself to be certain and was very confident on this point because my mother had told me so. And then he said to me, 'Then you should believe firmly all the articles of the faith of which the apostles inform us, as you hear when the Credo⁹ is sung each Sunday.'

[46] He told me that Bishop William of Paris had reported to him that a prominent master of theology had come to him saying that he wanted to speak with him. The bishop said, 'Say whatever you wish, master.' But as he was about to speak to the bishop, the master began to weep heavily. The bishop said, 'Speak, master, and don't be upset, for no one can sin so badly that God cannot forgive them.' 'I tell you, my lord,' said the

master, 'I cannot help but cry, for I think I have lost my faith: I cannot induce my heart to believe in the sacrament of the altar as the Holy Church teaches. I am sure I am being tempted by the Devil.' [47] 'Tell me, master,' said the bishop, 'when the enemy sends you this temptation, is it pleasurable?' And the master said, 'No, my lord, on the contrary it distresses me as much as anything could.' 'Now I ask you,' said the bishop, 'would you take gold or silver in return for saying anything with your own mouth that denied the sacrament of the altar or the other holy sacraments of the Church?' 'I would have you know, my lord,' said the master, 'that there is nothing in the world I would accept. I would rather all my limbs were torn from my body than to say such a thing.' [48] 'Now I will talk to you about something else,' said the bishop. 'You know that the king of France is at war with the king of England, and that the castle that is right on their frontier is at La Rochelle in Poitou?[10] Now I want to ask you a question: if the king had entrusted you with the defence of La Rochelle, on the frontier, and he had entrusted me with the defence of Montlhéry, in the heart of France's peaceful lands, to whom should the king feel more grateful at the war's end? To you for defending La Rochelle without loss, or to me for defending Montlhéry without loss?' 'In God's name,' said the master, 'to me, who successfully defended La Rochelle.' [49] 'Master,' said the bishop, 'I say to you that my heart is like the castle of Montlhéry, for I suffer no temptation or doubt concerning the sacrament of the altar. Because of this I can tell you that for every bit of gratitude God feels to me because I have a sound and untroubled faith, he has four times as much for you, since you are defending your heart for him in a miserable conflict, and are so willing to serve him that you would not surrender it for any earthly possession or through fear of physical harm. You should therefore rest easy, for in this case your condition is more pleasing to Our Lord than mine is.' When the master heard this he knelt before the bishop feeling greatly reassured.

[50] The saintly king told me that a number of people from the region of Albi came to the count of Montfort – who was at that time defending the Albigensian lands[11] for the king – and

said that he should come and see the body of Our Lord, which had become flesh and blood in the priest's hands. And he said to them, 'You go ahead and see it, those of you who don't believe it. But I believe it absolutely – this is how the Holy Church explains the sacrament of the altar to us. And do you know what my reward will be,' said the count, 'for having faith during my mortal life in what the Holy Church teaches us? For this I will deserve a crown in Heaven even more than the angels; they see God face to face and therefore cannot but believe in him.'

[51] He told me that there was once a great debate between clerics and Jews at the monastery of Cluny. There was an old knight present whom the abbot provided with bread from the monastery for the love of God, and he asked the abbot to let him open the debate. Reluctantly, the abbot said yes. The knight got up, leaning on his crutch, and said that the most eminent of the clerics and the most eminent of the Jewish masters present should approach him, and they did so. He asked the Jew one question, which was this: 'Master, do you believe that the Virgin Mary, who bore God in her womb and in her arms, was a virgin when she gave birth, and is the Mother of God?' [52] The Jew replied that he did not believe any of this. And the knight said to him he had acted most foolishly when, neither believing in nor loving the Virgin, he had come inside her monastery and her house. 'And,' said the knight, 'you will certainly pay for it.' Then he raised his crutch and struck the Jew with it across his ear, bringing him to the ground. The Jews all turned and fled, carrying off their wounded master. Thus ended the disputation. [53] The abbot went to the knight and told him he had done a very foolish thing. But the knight replied that the abbot had committed a greater folly by organizing such a debate, for there were a great number of good Christians in attendance who before the disputation ended would have left shaken in their faith, having completely misunderstood what the Jews said. 'And I would have you know,' said the king, 'that no man, unless he is a skilled theologian, should debate with Jews. Instead, when a layman hears the Christian law slandered, he should defend it only with his sword, which he should thrust right into the offender's guts as far as it will go.'

[54] King Louis organized his life so that each day he heard his hours sung and a requiem Mass spoken, as well as a sung Mass for the appropriate feast or saint. Every day after dinner he rested in bed, and once he had slept and was refreshed, he and one of his chaplains said the office of the dead privately in his chamber before hearing vespers. Later in the evening he heard compline.

[55] At the castle of Hyères, where we ended our sea voyage, a Franciscan friar[12] came to him. In his sermon he gave the king guidance, saying that he had read the Bible and books that describe infidel princes, and that among neither the faithful nor the infidel had he come across a single kingdom that had been lost or had seen a change of ruler other than as a result of a lack of justice. 'So the king should make sure,' he said, 'now that he is returning to France, to render sound and swift justice to his people, in order that Our Lord might allow him to hold his country in peace throughout his life.' [56] It is said that the *preudomme* who gave the king this guidance lies at Marseilles, where Our Lord performs many beautiful miracles for him. He did not wish to stay with the king more than one day, no matter how the king begged him.

[57] The king never forgot this advice, and thus he governed his lands well and honestly and in accordance with God, as you will now hear. He arranged his affairs so that those of us in his entourage – including my lord of Nesle and the good count of Soissons – would go after hearing Mass to listen to the pleas made at the gate of the city, now known as the 'requests'. [58] When he had returned from church the king summoned us and, sitting at the foot of his bed, had all of us sit around him. He asked us whether there was anyone who required a judgement that could not be made without him. We named them and he had these people summoned so that he could ask them, 'Why aren't you willing to accept what my men are offering you?' They would say: 'My lord, because they are offering us too little.' And he addressed them thus, 'You should accept what has been offered to you.' In this way the saintly man made every effort he could to bring them to a just and reasonable settlement.

[59] During the summer he often went and sat in the woods at Vincennes after Mass. He would lean against an oak tree and have us sit down around him. All those who had matters to be dealt with came and talked to him, without the interference of the ushers or anyone else. He himself would ask, 'Is there anyone here with a case to settle?' Those who did have a case stood up and he said to them, 'Everyone be quiet, and you will be given judgement one after another.' Then he called for my lord Peter of Fontaine and my lord Geoffrey of Villette and would say to one of them, 'Give judgement for me on this case.' [60] Whenever he thought something said by those who spoke on his behalf or on another's behalf needed correction, he said himself how it should be amended. On some summer days I saw him go to the gardens in Paris to render justice to the people. He wore a *cote* made of camlet, a sleeveless *surcote* made of tiretaine and a black mantle made of *cendal* around his shoulders, had his hair neatly combed without a coif, and wore a hat decorated with white peacock feathers on his head. He had carpets laid out so that we could sit round him. Everyone who had a case to bring before him would gather around him at first, and then the king had judgement delivered in the same way as I said took place in the wood at Vincennes.

[61] I saw him on another occasion, again at Paris. All the prelates of France had told him they wanted to talk to him there, and the king went to the palace to hear them. Bishop Guy of Auxerre, the son of my lord William of Mello, was there and spoke to the king on behalf of all the prelates. He said, 'My lord, these lords here present, archbishops and bishops, have asked me to let you know that the Christian community that you should protect is falling into ruin in your hands.' The king signed himself with the cross when he heard these words and said, 'Now tell me how this is so.' [62] 'My lord,' said the bishop, 'it is because excommunication isn't taken seriously these days. People are willing to die without seeking absolution; they don't want to set their affairs with the Church in order. And so we ask you, my lord, for God's sake and in order to fulfil your duty, to order your *prévots* and *baillis* that those who have allowed themselves to remain excommunicate for a

year and a day be compelled to seek absolution, by seizing their property.'

[63] The king's reply to this was that he would happily give such an order in every case in which he was given proof that the excommunicate was in the wrong. And the bishop said that on no account would they give such evidence, for the king was barred from making judgements on such cases. The king said that without this he would not issue any orders, for he would be acting against God and against reason if he forced his people to obtain absolution when churchmen were treating them unjustly. [64] 'To illustrate this,' said the king, 'I give you the example of the count of Brittany. He spent seven years as an excommunicate while he made his case against the prelates of Brittany, and was so assiduous in doing so that in the end the pope condemned all the archbishops and bishops. If I had compelled the count of Brittany to obtain absolution after a year, I would have wronged both God and him.' Then the prelates relented, and never again, from what I have heard, were any demands made on this point.

[65] The peace agreement he sealed with the king of England[13] was made against the wishes of his councillors, who said to him, 'Sir, it seems to us that you will simply be abandoning the land you are giving to the king of England since he has no right to it; his father was judged to have lost it.' To this the king replied that he knew the king of England had no right to it, but there was good reason for handing it over to him, 'For we are married to two sisters[14] and our children are first cousins; it is therefore essential that there be peace between us. And the peace I have made with the king of England does me great honour since he is now my vassal, which was not the case before.'

[66] The king's fairness can be seen from the case of my lord Renaut of Trie,[15] who came to the saint with a document that said the king had given the county of Dammartin-en-Goële to the heirs of the countess of Boulogne, who had recently died. The seal on the document had been broken so that all that was left was the half which showed the lower part of the king's image: his legs and the stool on which his feet rested. He showed

it to all of us who were in his council so that we could help him make a decision. [67] We all told him, without any dissent, that he was in no way obliged to honour that document. He then asked John Sarrasin, his chamberlain, to hand him another document he had asked him to bring. As he held it he said to us, 'My lords, look here at the seal I was using at the time I went overseas. It is quite clear from this that the imprint of the broken seal matches this intact seal. Because of this I could not in good conscience withhold the county in question.' And then he called my lord Renaut of Trie and said to him, 'I restore the county to you.'

PART II

LOUIS'S SANCTITY IN DEED

CHAPTER 2

King Louis Confronts Rebellious Barons

(1226–42)

[68] In the name of God Almighty, we have up to this point recorded some of the pious words and good teachings of our saintly King Louis, so that those who hear them might find them written one after another. This should be of greater profit to those who hear them than if they were recorded among his deeds. Now we will begin the report of his deeds, in the name of God and Saint Louis.

[69] I heard the king say he was born on the feast of Saint Mark the Evangelist[1] that follows Easter. On that day people in many places process carrying crosses, which in France are known as 'black crosses'. This was a form of prophecy of the great number of people who died in the course of his two crusades, both the first in Egypt and the second, during which he himself died at Carthage. There was great mourning in this world and great joy in Paradise for those who died as true crusaders in the course of these two pilgrimages.

[70] He was crowned on the first Sunday of Advent.[2] The introit of that Sunday's Mass is 'Ad te levavi animam meam',[3] etc. It says, 'Dear lord God, I will lift up my soul to you, and I will place my trust in you.' He had great faith in God from his childhood until his death, for at the moment of his death his last words called on God and his saints, especially my lord Saint James and my lady Saint Genevieve.[4]

[71] God, in whom he placed his trust, protected him every day from infancy to the end, and especially during his childhood when his protection was much needed, as you will hear shortly. God likewise safeguarded his soul through the pious teachings of his mother,[5] who taught him to believe in and to love God,

and surrounded him with many men and women of religion.
From his very early childhood she had him listen to all the
hours, and to sermons on feast days. He recalled that his mother
had sometimes told him that she would rather he were dead
than that he commit a mortal sin.

[72] He certainly had need of God's help in his youth, since
his mother, who had come from Spain, had no relatives or
friends anywhere in the kingdom of France. The French barons,
seeing the king was a child and the queen a foreigner, made the
count of Boulogne, his uncle,[6] their leader and acknowledged
him as their lord. Following the king's coronation some of the
barons requested that the queen give them extensive lands, and
when she refused to do so all the barons gathered at Corbeil.
[73] The saintly king told me that neither he nor his mother,
who were at Montlhéry, dared return to Paris until the people
of the city came out, armed, to meet them. He recalled to me
that the road from Montlhéry to Paris was full of people, with
and without arms, all of them calling out to Our Lord to grant
him a good and long life, and to protect him from his enemies.
And God did just that, as you will now hear.

[74] At the assembly of barons at Corbeil, or so it is said,
those present agreed that Count Peter of Brittany,[7] the good
knight, should rebel against the king. It was decided in addition
that they would respond to the king's call to arms against the
count with just two knights each. They would do this to see
whether the count could get the better of the queen who, as
you have heard, was a foreigner. Many people said that the
count would indeed have outdone the queen and the king if
God – who never let him down – had not helped them in these
straits. [75] God's help came in this way: Count Thibaut of
Champagne, who later became king of Navarre,[8] arrived to
serve the king with 300 knights, and as a result of the support
he provided, the count of Brittany was forced to throw himself on the king's mercy. In order to make peace, so it is said,
he had to hand over the counties of Anjou and Perche to the
king.

[76] I need to digress a little from this topic in order to make
sure you have certain things fresh in your mind about which

you will hear more hereafter. So, let me inform you that the good Count Henry the Liberal had two sons by Countess Marie, who was sister of the king of France and of King Richard of England.[9] The elder of these sons was called Henry and the other Thibaut. Henry, the elder of the two, took the cross and went on pilgrimage to the Holy Land when King Philip and King Richard laid siege to and captured Acre.[10] [77] As soon as Acre fell King Philip left to return to France, as a result of which he met with great disapproval. King Richard stayed in the Holy Land and performed so many impressive deeds that the Saracens greatly feared him. So much so that, as is written in 'The Book of the Holy Land',[11] when Saracen children cried the women would shout at them and, in order to silence them, say, 'Be quiet, here comes King Richard!' And when the Saracens' or Bedouins' horses took fright at a bush, they would say to them, 'Do you think it's King Richard?'

[78] King Richard went to considerable lengths to obtain the queen of Jerusalem, the legitimate heir to the kingdom, as a wife for Henry of Champagne,[12] who had stayed in the Holy Land with him. Count Henry had two daughters by this queen, the first of whom became queen of Cyprus,[13] while the other married my lord Erart of Brienne and established a famous lineage, notable in France and Champagne. I will not say any more about Erart of Brienne's wife at the moment, rather I will tell you about the queen of Cyprus, who has a bearing on my current topic. And I will say this: [79] after the king had overcome Count Peter of Brittany, the French barons were all so hostile to Count Thibaut of Champagne that they decided to send for the queen of Cyprus, in the hope that she, the daughter of Henry the Liberal's elder son, might dispossess Count Thibaut, whose father was Count Henry's younger son.

[80] But some among the barons undertook to make peace between Count Peter and Count Thibaut, and the affair was settled with a promise that Count Thibaut would marry Count Peter's daughter. The day of the wedding between the count of Champagne and this young woman was set, and she was due to be brought for the ceremony to a Premonstratensian abbey near to Château Thierry called, so I believe, Val Secret. The

French barons, nearly all of whom were related to Count Peter, made sure she was taken to Val Secret for the marriage, and summoned the count of Champagne, who was then at Château Thierry. [81] As the count of Champagne was on his way to the wedding my lord Geoffrey of La Chapelle came with a letter of credence, as a messenger from the king. He said, 'My lord count of Champagne, the king understands that you have made an agreement with Count Peter of Brittany to take his daughter in marriage. The king warns you not to do so unless you wish to lose all your possessions in the kingdom of France, for you know that the count of Brittany has harmed the king more than any man alive.' On the advice of the councillors he had with him the count of Champagne turned back to Château Thierry.

[82] When Count Peter and the French barons who were waiting for Count Thibaut at Val Secret heard of this, they were almost mad with rage at the humiliation he had caused them and immediately sent for the queen of Cyprus. As soon as she had arrived they took a joint decision to summon what men-at-arms they could in order to invade Brie and Champagne from the direction of the Ile-de-France. Meanwhile the duke of Burgundy, who had married the daughter of Count Robert of Dreux, would invade the county of Champagne from the direction of his lands. They agreed a day on which they would assemble outside the city of Troyes, in order to capture it if they could. [83] The duke summoned as many men as he could and the barons did likewise. The barons came from one direction, burning and tearing down everything in their path, while the duke of Burgundy came from another. The king of France came from still another direction in order to meet them in battle. The count of Champagne's despair was such that he himself had his towns set alight before the barons arrived, so that they might not find them well provisioned. Among others, the count of Champagne burned the towns of Epernay, Vertus and Sézanne.

[84] When the townspeople of Troyes saw they could no longer rely on the protection of their lord, they asked Simon, lord of Joinville (the father of the current lord of Joinville) to come and defend them. Having called all his men to arms, he

set out from Joinville as soon as news from Troyes reached him. Night was falling as he left, and he arrived at Troyes before daybreak. It was as a result of this that the barons failed in their ambition to take that city; Simon's presence meant the barons did no more than pass outside Troyes. They set up camp in the fields at l'Isle-Aumont, where the duke of Burgundy was waiting.

[85] The king of France, who knew where they were, set straight off in that direction in order to fight them. The barons sent messengers to him and asked him to keep back from the battle himself; they would do battle with the count of Champagne and the duke of Lorraine and the rest of the king's army, although they had 300 fewer men than the count and the duke. The king informed them he would never send his men into battle without going with them in person. The barons returned word to him that, if he so desired, they would willingly bring the queen of Cyprus to make peace. To which the king replied that he had no intention of making peace and would not permit the count of Champagne to do so until the barons had left his county. [86] They did leave the county, going from their base at l'Isle-Aumont to set up camp outside the town of Jully. The king installed himself at l'Isle-Aumont, in the place from which he had driven them. When the barons found out that the king had done this, they went to Chaource and, not daring to let the king catch up with them, went on from there to Laignes, which was in the lands of the count of Nevers, a member of their party. In this way the king brought the count of Champagne and the queen of Cyprus into agreement. Under the terms of the peace the count of Champagne gave the queen of Cyprus land with a yearly income of about 2,000 *livres*, while the king paid 40,000 *livres* on the count of Champagne's behalf. [87] In return for these 40,000 *livres* the count of Champagne sold the following fiefs to the king: the county of Blois, the county of Chartres, the county of Sancerre and the viscounty of Châteaudun. Certain people said that the king only held these fiefs in pledge,[14] but I asked our saintly King Louis about it while we were overseas and it is not true at all.

[88] The land given by Count Thibaut to the queen of Cyprus is now held by the count of Brienne and the count of Joigny, because her daughter married the great Count Walter of Brienne,[15] and was the grandmother of the current count.

[89] In order that you will understand the origins of the fiefs sold by the lord of Champagne to the king, I will tell you that Count Thibaut the Great,[16] who is buried at Lagny, had three sons. The first was called Henry, the second was called Thibaut and the third was called Stephen. Henry became count of Champagne and Brie and was known as Henry the Liberal; he was certainly deserving of this name because he was generous towards God and his fellow men. His generosity to God is shown in the church of Saint Stephen at Troyes and in the other churches he founded in Champagne. His generosity to his fellow men is clear from the case of Artaud of Nogent and in many other examples that I would willingly relate to you, if I was not afraid it would encumber my work. [90] Artaud of Nogent was the *bourgeois* the count trusted more than any other in the world, and he was so rich that he built the castle of Nogent l'Artaud with his own money. It so happened that once, at Pentecost, Count Henry was leaving his palace in Troyes to go to hear Mass at Saint Stephen's. At the foot of the steps knelt a poor knight, who said, 'My lord, I beg you for God's sake to give me something from your possessions with which I might be able to marry my two daughters, whom you see here.' [91] Artaud, who was following the count, said to the poor knight, 'Lord knight, it is not polite to make such a request of my lord, for he has given so much that he has no more to offer.' The generous count turned to Artaud and said to him, 'Lord commoner, you are quite wrong to say that I have nothing left to give, since I still possess *you*. Take him, lord knight, for I am giving him to you, and I will guarantee the gift for you.' The knight was not in the least flustered; he took hold of Artaud by his cloak and told him he would not let him go until he had been paid. And before he was released Artaud paid a fee of 500 *livres*.

[92] Count Henry's younger brother was called Thibaut and he became the count of Blois. The youngest brother was called

Stephen and he became the count of Sancerre. These two brothers held all they inherited, their two counties and the possessions associated with them, from Count Henry, and later they held them from Count Henry's heirs to Champagne, until the time when King Thibaut sold them to the king of France, as was described earlier.

[93] Now we will return to our main subject, and say that after he had dealt with the barons, the king held a large court at Saumur in Anjou. I was there and bear witness that it was the most elegantly appointed court I have ever seen. At table the king ate alongside the count of Poitiers, whom he had knighted earlier on the feast of Saint John.[17] Next to the count of Poitiers was Count John of Dreux, whom the king had also just knighted. Beyond the count of Dreux was the count of La Marche and after him the good Count Peter of Brittany. In front of the king's table, opposite the count of Dreux, sat my lord the king of Navarre, wearing a *cote* and mantle of samite handsomely adorned with a belt, a brooch and a golden cap. I stood before him to carve his meat. [94] The king's brother, the count of Artois, stood in front of him to serve his food, while the good Count John of Soissons carved his meat with a knife. Standing guard at the king's table were my lord Humbert of Beaujeu, later constable of France, my lord Enguerrand of Coucy and my lord Archambaut of Bourbon. Behind these three barons, protecting them, there were a good thirty of their knights wearing silk *cotes*, and beyond them there was a large number of sergeants wearing the arms of the count of Poitiers embroidered on silk. The king had dressed in a *cote* of deep blue samite, with a *surcote* and mantle of red samite trimmed with ermine and a cotton cap on his head. The cap did not suit him at all well because he was still a young man at that time.

[95] The king held this feast in the great halls at Saumur, which it was said the great King Henry of England[18] had built in order to hold important celebrations. These halls were laid out like a Cistercian monks' cloister, although I don't think any such cloister was ever so big. And I will tell you why I think this. It is because along the side of the cloister where the king was eating – and he was surrounded by knights and sergeants

who took up a lot of room – there was a table at which twenty bishops and archbishops were eating. And in addition to the bishops and archbishops, at the other end of the cloister from where the king was eating, sat his mother, Queen Blanche.

[96] The queen was served by the count of Boulogne (who later became king of Portugal), and by the good Count Hugh of Saint-Pol and an eighteen-year-old German boy who was said to be the son of Saint Elizabeth of Thuringia.[19] It was said that because of this Queen Blanche kissed him on his forehead as an act of devotion, for she believed his mother must have kissed that place many times.

[97] At the end of the opposite side of the cloister were the kitchens, the cellars, the bakeries and the stores. It was from here that meat, wine and bread were served to the king and queen. Along the other aisles of the cloister and in the central courtyard so many knights were eating that I could not tell you the number. Many people said they had never seen as many *surcotes* or other garments made from cloth of gold and silk at such a feast as were there, and it was said that there were at least 3,000 knights present.

[98] After this celebration the king took his newly knighted brother to Poitiers to take possession of his fiefs. When the king arrived there he would certainly rather have been back in Paris, for he discovered that the count of La Marche, who had eaten at his table on the feast of Saint John, had assembled as many men-at-arms as he could raise at Lusignan, near to Poitiers. The king spent nearly two weeks at Poitiers, since he dared not leave until he came to an agreement with the count of La Marche. I do not know what the terms of this agreement were. [99] I did see the count of La Marche on several occasions, when he came from Lusignan to talk to the king at Poitiers. He always brought with him his wife, the queen of England,[20] who was the mother of the king of England. Many people said that the peace they made with the count of La Marche was unfavourable to the king and the count of Poitiers.

[100] It was not long after the king's return from Poitiers that the king of England arrived in Gascony to make war on the king of France.[21] Our saintly king rode out to meet him in

battle with as many men as he could muster. The king of England and the count of La Marche advanced to give him battle opposite a castle called Taillebourg, which sits on a grim little river called the Charente at a point where the water can be crossed only by a very narrow stone bridge. [101] As soon as the king had reached Taillebourg and the armies were in sight of each other, our men, who were on the same side of the river as the castle, strove to cross the water despite the tricky circumstances, using boats and pontoon bridges. They attacked the English and the fight got underway, fierce and strong. Seeing this, the king faced the danger alongside the others; for each man he had when he crossed the river to where the English were, his enemy had a thousand. But according to God's will, as soon as the English saw the king cross the river, they lost heart and made off into the town of Saintes. A number of our men who were caught up among the fleeing English ended up inside the city and were captured.

[102] Those of our men who were captured at Saintes reported hearing a big argument erupt between the king of England and the count of La Marche. The king said that when the count had summoned him he had been told he would find substantial support in France. That same evening the king of England set off from Saintes and went to Gascony.

[103] The count of La Marche, who could see no prospect of improvement in his situation, gave himself up as a prisoner to King Louis, along with his wife and children. By making peace with him the king obtained a large part of the count's lands. I do not know how much because I was not present on that occasion – I had not yet put on a hauberk[22] – but I heard it said that as well as receiving these lands the count of La Marche gave up a payment of 10,000 Parisian *livres* due to him from the Crown, and a similar sum he was to have been paid each subsequent year.

[104] While we were at Poitiers I saw a knight named my lord Geoffrey of Rancogne. It was said that because of some great outrage inflicted on him by the count of La Marche, Geoffrey of Rancogne had sworn on relics that he would never again cut his hair in the style of a knight, until he had seen

himself avenged on the count either in person or through
another's actions. Instead, he wore his long hair parted like a
woman's. When my lord Geoffrey saw the count of La Marche
kneeling before the king and pleading for mercy, along with his
wife and his children, he had someone fetch a stool, unmade
his parting and had his hair cut in front of the king, the count
of La Marche, and all those present.

[105] I heard from those who took part in them that the king
gave substantial rewards in the course of his campaigns against
the king of England and against the barons. But neither the
gifts he gave nor his expenditure on campaigns, on this side of
the sea or the other, led the king to ask for or to take any
contributions from his own barons, knights and men, or from
his good towns, in a way that gave them cause for complaint.
And this is no wonder, for he acted in accordance with the
advice of the virtuous mother who was by his side, and of the
preudommes who had remained in the king's entourage since
the time of his father and his grandfather.

CHAPTER 3

King Louis's Crusade Vow and the Voyage to Cyprus

(1244–8)

[106] Following the events just described it so happened that God's will was that the king should be taken seriously ill at Paris.[1] It was said that he was so unwell that one of the women attending him wanted to draw the sheet over his face, saying he was dead. But another woman, on the other side of the bed, would not allow her to do this. She said that his soul was still in his body. [107] As the king listened to these two women argue, Our Lord worked in him and restored him immediately to health, for he had been struck dumb and unable to speak. He asked for someone to give him the cross, and they did. When the queen, his mother, was told that he had regained the power of speech she displayed the greatest possible joy, but when she was told by the king himself that he had taken the cross, she demonstrated grief as profound as if she had seen him dead.

[108] After he had taken the cross, so did the king's three brothers: Robert, count of Artois, Alphonse, count of Poitiers and Charles, count of Anjou, who later became the king of Sicily. Hugh, duke of Burgundy, took the cross and so did William, count of Flanders (the brother of Count Guy of Flanders who died recently), the good Hugh, count of Saint-Pol, and his nephew my lord Walter, who conducted himself very well overseas and would have been a most worthy man had he lived. [109] Along with them were the count of La Marche and his son my lord Hugh le Brun, and the count of Sarrebrück and his brother my lord Gobert of Apremont. It was in the count of Sarrebrück's company that I, John, lord of Joinville, crossed the sea in a ship we had hired together because we were cousins.

We were twenty knights in all on that crossing, nine of them
with him, and nine with me.

[110] At Easter in the year of grace 1248 I summoned my
men and my vassals to Joinville. On the eve of Easter,[2] when
all the people I had summoned had arrived, my son John, lord
of Ancerville, was born of my first wife, who was the count of
Grandpré's sister. All that week we feasted and danced, for my
brother, the lord of Vaucouleurs, and the other rich men present
took it in turns to provide a meal on the Monday, Tuesday, Wednesday and Thursday. [111] On Friday I said to them, 'My lords,
I am going away overseas and I do not know if I will return. So if
I have done you any wrong, come forward, and I will right it for
each of you in turn, as I would usually do for anyone who has a
claim to make against me or my people.' I settled these claims on
the advice of all the men of my lands, and, so that I might not
exert any undue influence, I withdrew from the meeting and
followed all their recommendations unquestioningly.

[112] As I did not wish to take any money with me that was
not rightfully mine, I went to Metz, in the Lorraine, to leave a
large portion of my lands in pledge. You should know that on
the day I left our country to go to the Holy Land, I had not
1,000 *livres*-worth of lands, for my lady my mother was still
alive.[3] And so I left with nine other knights; three of us were
bannerets. I mention these things to you because if God, who
has never let me down, had not helped me, I would scarcely
have been able to support myself for so long a time as the six
years I spent in the Holy Land.

[113] As I was preparing to leave, John, lord of Apremont,
count of Sarrebrück[4] by right of his wife, sent word to me
informing me that he had made preparations to go overseas at
the head of a group of ten knights. He said that, if I wished, he
and I might share the hire of a ship. I agreed, and his people
and mine hired a ship at Marseilles.

[114] The king summoned all his barons to Paris and had
them swear an oath that they would offer faith and loyalty
to his children should anything happen to him during the
expedition. He asked this of me, but I was unwilling to swear
an oath because I was not his man.[5]

[115] As I was on my way to Paris, I came across three dead men on a cart whom a clerk had killed, and I was told that they were being taken to the king. When I heard this, I sent one of my squires after them to find out what had happened. The squire told me that the king, when he came out of his chapel, stood on the steps to look at the dead men and asked of the *prévôt* of Paris what had happened.

[116] The *prévôt* told him that the dead men were three of his sergeants from the *Châtelet*,[6] and that they had gone into the backstreets in order to rob people. He said to the king, 'They came across this clerk you see here and stripped him of all his clothes. The clerk, wearing only his chemise, went to his lodgings and took up his crossbow. He had a boy fetch his falchion. When he saw the robbers he shouted to them and said that they would die on that spot. The clerk drew his crossbow, fired and struck one of them in the heart. The other two took flight, while the clerk took up the falchion the boy had been carrying and chased them by the light of the moon, which was bright and clear. [117] One of the robbers decided he would cut through a hedge and into a garden, but the clerk struck him with the sword,' said the *prévôt*, 'and cut right through his leg so that only the boot is holding it on, as you see. The clerk resumed his chase of the other robber, who had decided to enter a stranger's house where people were still awake. The clerk struck him in the head with the falchion, splitting it down to the teeth, as you can see,' said the *prévôt* to the king. 'My lord,' he said, 'the clerk showed what he had done to the householders in the street and then he went to give himself up to your custody. And so, my lord, I am bringing him to you so that you might do as you will with him. Here he is.'

[118] 'My lord clerk,' said the king, 'your bravery has lost you the chance of priesthood, but because of it I will retain you in my pay and you will come with me overseas. I would have you know that this is because I strongly desire my people to see that I will not uphold them in any of their wrongdoings.' When the people who were gathered there heard this, they cried out to Our Lord and prayed that God might give the king a good and long life, and bring him back in joy and health.

[119] I returned to our own country[7] after these events. The lord of Sarrebrück and I made preparations to send our equipment to Auxonne in carts, where it would be put on the River Saône and taken as far as Arles, via the Saône and the Rhône.

[120] On the day I left Joinville I sent for the abbot of Cheminon, who was said to be the greatest *preudomme* of the white order.[8] I heard one account of him while I was at Clair-vaux on the feast of Our Lady (the king was also there), from a monk who pointed the abbot out to me and asked me if I knew him. I said to him, 'Why do you ask?' He replied, 'Because I believe that he is the greatest *preudomme* there is in all the white order. [121] And you should also know,' he said, 'that I have heard a story from a *preudomme* who once lay in the same dormitory where the abbot of Cheminon was sleeping. The abbot had uncovered his chest because of the heat, and the man lying in the dormitory saw the Mother of God go to the abbot's bed and draw his gown across his chest so that the draught might not do him any harm.'

[122] This same abbot of Cheminon gave me my staff and purse.[9] And then I left Joinville, not to enter my castle again until my return. I was on foot, bare-legged and wearing a hairshirt. I went thus on pilgrimage to Blécourt, Saint-Urbain and other shrines thereabouts. As I made my way to Blécourt and Saint-Urbain, I did not want to cast my eyes back towards Joinville at all, fearful that my heart would melt for the fine castle and two children I was leaving behind.

[123] I and my companions ate at Fontaine l'Archevêque, near Donjeux, and there Abbot Adam of Saint-Urbain – may God absolve him – gave a great quantity of fine jewels to me and my knights. From there we went to Auxonne, and from there to Lyons. All our equipment had been loaded on to boats and was taken down the River Saône. The large warhorses were led along beside the boats. [124] At Lyons we entered the river Rhône to go to Arles-le-Blanc. On the Rhône we came across a castle called La Roche-de-Glun, which the king had had torn down because Roger, its lord, was accused of robbing pilgrims and merchants.

[125] In the month of August we embarked on our ships at the Rock of Marseilles. On the day we embarked, the door of the ship was opened, and all the horses we had to take overseas were placed inside before the door was closed again and well caulked – as you would seal a barrel – because when the ship is on the high seas the whole door is underwater.

[126] When the horses were inside, our master mariner called to his sailors who were in the prow of the ship, and said to them, 'Are you ready?' They replied, 'Yes sir, you can let the clerks and priests come forward.' As soon as they had come, the master mariner called to them, 'In God's name, sing!' And they all chanted with one voice *Veni creator spiritus*.[10] The master mariner called to his sailors, 'In God's name, set sail!', and so they did. [127] Before long the wind had filled the sails and taken us out of sight of land, so that we could see only sky and water. Each day the wind took us further away from the lands where we were born. I am describing these events to you to show how foolhardy is he who dares place himself in such peril, when he is in possession of another person's property or is in a state of mortal sin, because seafarers go to sleep in the evening not knowing whether they will find themselves at the bottom of the sea the next morning.

[128] While at sea we experienced a great marvel when we sighted a perfectly round mountain off the Barbary coast.[11] We sighted it around the hour of vespers and sailed all night, believing we must have covered more than fifty leagues. But the next day we found ourselves beneath this same mountain, and this happened to us two or three times. When the sailors saw this all of them were afraid; they told us that our ship was in great danger because we lay off the lands of the Barbary Saracens. [129] Then a *preudomme* priest, known as the dean of Maurupt, told us that there had never been any instance of suffering in his parish, whether as a result of drought or excessive rains or any other affliction, that God and his Mother had not delivered them from as soon as they had made three processions on three successive Saturdays. It happened to be Saturday, and we performed the first procession around the ship's two masts. I myself had to be held up by my arms because

I was seriously ill. We never saw the mountain again after that, and we arrived at Cyprus on the third Saturday.

[130] When we arrived at Cyprus the king was already there. We found a great abundance of the king's provisions: cellars, grain stores and money. The king's supply of wine was such that in the middle of the fields along the shore his people had laid out large stacks of wine barrels that had been bought two years before his arrival. They had been placed one on top of another so that when they were seen from in front they had the appearance of barns. [131] The wheat and barley had been heaped in piles in the fields. When you saw them they looked like hills, because the rain that had fallen on the grain over a long period had made the outermost layer sprout, so that all that could be seen was green grass. And so, when they wanted to take these supplies to Egypt, they broke the outer crust of green grass to find the wheat and barley inside were as fresh as if they had just been threshed.

[132] The king would very willingly have gone on to Egypt without stopping, as I heard him say while we were in Syria, if it had not been for his barons, who urged him to wait for his people who had not yet all arrived.

[133] While the king was staying on Cyprus, the great king of the Tartars[12] sent envoys to him, bringing many amiable and courteous messages. Among these, he sent word that he was ready to help him conquer the Holy Land and deliver Jerusalem from the hands of the Saracens. [134] The king received these envoys most graciously, and sent his own in return. They were away for two years before returning to him. Along with these envoys the king sent the king of the Tartars a tent made in the form of a chapel, which was very costly because it was made entirely from fine scarlet. In order to see whether he might be able to draw the Tartars to our faith, the king had the chapel decorated with images of the Annunciation of Our Lady and all the other points of the faith. These things were sent by the king in the care of two Dominican friars who knew the Saracen language,[13] in order to show and teach the Tartars what they should believe.

[135] The two friars returned to the king at the same time

as his brothers returned to France. They found the king at Caesarea, where he had gone to from Acre after taking leave of his brothers there. He was refortifying the city, since he had neither peace nor truce with the Saracens. I will tell you later how the king of France's envoys were received, just as they themselves recounted it to the king. You will hear many interesting stories from their report to the king, but I do not want to relate them now as this would require me to break off from the subject I have begun, which is as follows. [136] I, who had not 1,000 *livres*-worth of lands, had taken responsibility when I left to go overseas for ten knights, myself included, two of whom were bannerets. It thus transpired that when I arrived in Cyprus, after having paid for my ship, I had only 240 *livres* left, and some of my knights informed me that if I did not secure funds for myself they would leave me. God, who has never failed me, provided for me in this way: the king, who was at Nicosia, sent for me and retained me in his service and put 800 *livres* into my coffers. Then I had more money than I needed.

[137] While we were staying in Cyprus the empress of Constantinople[14] sent word to me that she had come to Paphos (a town on Cyprus), and that Erart of Brienne and I should go and fetch her. When we arrived there, we found that a strong wind had torn the cables of her ship's anchors, and driven the ship towards Acre. The only belongings she had were the mantle she was wearing and a *surcote* for meals. We brought her to Limassol, where the king and queen and all the barons received her most honourably. [138] The next day, I sent her cloth to make a dress and with it a piece of vair. I also sent some tiretaine and *cendal* to line the dress. My lord Philip of Nanteuil, the good knight, who was in the king's entourage, came across my squire as he was going to the empress. When the *preudomme* saw the garments, he went to the king and told him that I had deeply shamed him and the other barons by sending the empress this when they had not been aware of her need.

[139] The empress had come to ask for aid from the king for her husband, who had stayed in Constantinople, and she was so intent on this that she took away a hundred or more duplicate letters from me and her other friends who were there.

These letters bound us on oath to go to Constantinople should the king or the legate[15] wish to send 300 knights there once the king departed from overseas. [140] In order to fulfil my oath, at the time of our departure I told the king in the presence of the count of Eu (whose letter to this effect I have) that if he wished to send 300 knights, I would honour my oath and go. The king replied that he did not have the means; his treasury was not so vast that it was not already drained to the dregs. After our arrival in Egypt the empress went to France and took with her my lord John of Acre, her brother, whom she married to the countess of Montfort.

[141] At the time of our arrival on Cyprus the sultan of Iconium[16] was the richest king in all the infidel world. He had done something astounding, for he had melted down a large quantity of his gold and poured it into earthen pots of the sort used overseas to hold wine, and each of these pots held at least three or four measures of wine. He had the pots broken, and the ingots of gold were placed on display inside one of his castles, so that each person who entered could see and touch them. There were at least six or seven of them. [142] His great wealth was apparent from a large tent that the king of Armenia[17] sent to the king of France, which was worth at least 500 *livres*. The king of Armenia told the king of France that this had been given to him by a *ferrais* of the sultan of Iconium. A *ferrais* is the servant who takes care of the sultan's tents and cleans his houses.

[143] The king of Armenia, who wanted to liberate himself from servitude to the sultan of Iconium, went to the king of the Tartars[18] and placed himself in their service so that he might receive their help. He came away with such a large number of men-at-arms that he would be able to do battle with the sultan of Iconium. The battle lasted a long time, and the Tartars killed so many of the sultan's men that nothing more was heard of him. The reports of this coming battle were widespread in Cyprus, and on this account a number of our sergeants crossed over to Armenia in the hope of profit and in order to join the fight. Not one of them ever returned.

[144] The sultan of Egypt, who was awaiting King Louis's

arrival in his lands in the spring, decided he would go and attack the sultan of Hama,[19] who was his mortal enemy, and went and besieged him inside the city of Hama. The sultan of Hama did not know how to rid himself of the sultan of Egypt, and could see clearly that the sultan of Egypt would certainly overthrow him if he should live long enough. He made a bargain with the *ferrais* of the sultan of Egypt to have him kill his master. [145] This is how he was poisoned: the *ferrais* noticed that the sultan would come and play chess on the mats at the end of his bed each afternoon, and so he placed poison on the mat on which he knew the sultan sat. It so happened that the sultan, who was bare-legged, shifted his weight on to an open sore on his leg, and straightaway the poison entered his exposed flesh and took all power of movement from the side of his body into which it had entered. Each time the venom surged to his heart the sultan was unable to eat, drink or speak for two days. So they left the sultan of Hama in peace, and the sultan of Egypt's people brought him back to his own lands.

CHAPTER 4

The Fall and Occupation of Damietta

(March–November 1249)

[146] At the beginning of March, by the king's command, the king, the barons and the other pilgrims ordered that the ships be reloaded with wine and food in order to leave when the king so instructed. So it was that when all had been put in good order the king and queen boarded their ship on the Friday before Pentecost.[1] The king said to his barons that they should follow him in their ships and sail straight to Egypt. On Saturday the king set sail, and all the other ships too. This was a most beautiful sight for it seemed as if the entire sea, as far as the eye could see, was covered with the canvas of ships' sails. These vessels were numbered at 1,800, both large and small.

[147] The king dropped anchor below a small hill which is called the Point of Limassol, with all the other ships around his. He went ashore on the day of Pentecost. When we had heard Mass, a violent and strong wind coming from the direction of Egypt rose to such effect that of the 2,800 knights the king was taking to Egypt only 700 remained; the rest were torn from the king's company and driven to Acre and other distant lands. They did not return to the king for a long while.

[148] On the day after Pentecost the wind had fallen. The king and those of us who were still with him, as God so desired, set sail once again. We were joined by the prince of Morea[2] and the duke of Burgundy, who had been staying in Morea. On the Thursday after Pentecost the king arrived off Damietta. We found the sultan's entire force on the seashore, and these were very fine men to look at, since the sultan's coat of arms were golden, and they glistened where the sun fell on them. The

noise they made with their kettledrums and Saracen horns was terrifying to hear.

[149] The king summoned his barons to get their advice as to how he should proceed. Many advised him to wait until his people had returned, since only one-third of his men remained with him. He did not want to heed them at all. The reason he gave was that this would give heart to his enemies. Moreover, there is no harbour in the sea off Damietta where he could wait for his people; a strong wind might take the ships and drive them off to other lands, as had happened to the others on Pentecost.

[150] It was agreed that the king would go ashore on the Friday before Trinity Sunday[3] and would go into battle with the Saracens unless they refused to fight. The king ordered my lord John of Beaumont to provide a galley for my lord Erart of Brienne and me in order that we and our knights could land, since the large ships were not able to reach the shore. [151] As God willed it, when I returned to my ship I came across a small boat that was given to me by my lady of Beirut (who was a first cousin of the count of Montbéliard and of mine)[4] in which were eight of my horses. When Friday came, I and my lord Erart of Brienne, fully armed, went to the king to ask for the galley, to which my lord John of Beaumont replied that we were not going to have one.

[152] When our men found out that we were not going to have a galley, they let themselves drop, as and when each saw his chance, from the large *nef* into the ship's boat, so that the boat began to sink. When the sailors saw that the boat was sinking little by little, they fled back on to the *nef*, leaving my knights in the boat. I asked the master mariner how many more people there were in the ship's boat than it could carry and he told me 'twenty men-at-arms'. I asked him if he would take our men safely to the shore if I unloaded that number, and he replied, 'Yes.' I unloaded that many men and in three trips they were all taken to the boat where my horses were.

[153] While I was directing these men a knight named Plonquet, who was one of my lord Erart of Brienne's men, decided

to get down from the large *nef* into the ship's boat, but the boat moved off and he fell into the sea and was drowned.

[154] When I returned to my *nef* I put a squire whom I had knighted, whose name was my lord Hugh of Vaucouleurs, into my little boat along with two most valiant young men whose names were my lord Villain of Versy and my lord William of Dammartin, between whom there was grievous ill-will. No one had been able to make peace between them since they had seized each other by the hair while in Morea. I made them forgive each other's anger and kiss, for I swore to them on relics that we would not take their ill-will ashore with us.

[155] Then we moved off to go ashore and came alongside the boat from the king's great *nef*, in which the king himself was. His people started to shout to us because we were going more quickly than him; they said I should land alongside the standard of Saint-Denis,[5] which was going ashore in another boat, ahead of the king. But I paid no attention to them and instead had us arrive before a large battalion of Turks,[6] in which there were at least 6,000 men on horseback. [156] As soon as they saw we had landed, they came spurring towards us. When we saw them coming we set the points of our shields and drove the shafts of our lances into the sand, with the sharp ends towards the enemy. As soon as they saw the lances set so as to run through their stomachs, they turned tail and fled.

[157] My lord Baldwin of Rheims, a *preudomme* who had come ashore, sent a squire to ask me to wait for him. I told him that I would do so most willingly, for it was fitting to wait for a *preudomme* like him in such a dangerous situation. He was grateful to me for this all his life. He came to us with 1,000 knights, which should prove to you that although when I landed I had no squire, knight or soldier whom I had brought with me from my country, God did not fail to aid me.

[158] To our left landed the count of Jaffa, who was a first cousin of the count of Montbéliard and a member of the Joinville lineage.[7] He made the most magnificent landing, since the galley of his that came ashore was painted all over – both the parts under the sea and those above – with shields bearing his arms, which are *or* with a cross *patée gules*.[8] He had at least

300 rowers in his galley, and for each of them there was a shield bearing his arms, and alongside each shield was a pennon bearing his arms worked in gold. [159] As it came ashore the rowers drove the galley onwards with their oars, so that it seemed as if it was flying. It also gave the impression that thunderbolts were falling from the heavens, because of the sound made by the pennons and because of the kettledrums, drums and Saracen horns that were in the count's galley. As soon as the galley reached the sand, coming up as far on to the shore as it could, the count and his knights leapt down from the galley, very well armed and very well equipped, and came and took up position alongside us.

[160] I forgot to tell you that when the count of Jaffa landed he immediately had his tents and pavilions pitched. As soon as the Saracens saw the tents set up, they all came and assembled in front of us and spurred on again, as if to charge us. But when they saw we would not flee they retreated rapidly.

[161] To our right, a good crossbow-shot's length away, the galley carrying the standard of Saint-Denis landed. When they had come ashore one Saracen charged into their midst, either because he could not hold his horse or because he thought the rest of his companions would follow him, but he was cut all to pieces. [162] When the king got word that the standard of Saint-Denis had landed, he strode quickly across the deck of his boat, and, undeterred by the objections of his companion the legate, he leapt into the sea, where the water came up to his armpits. He went, with his shield at his neck, his helmet on his head and his lance in his hand, to join his men who were on the shore. When he came to land and saw the Saracens, he asked what people these were and was told that they were Saracens. He set his lance under his arm and his shield in front of him, and would have charged at the Saracens if the *preudommes* who were with him had allowed it.

[163] Three times the Saracens sent carrier pigeons to the sultan to let him know that the king had arrived, but they received no message in return because the sultan was in the grip of his sickness. Because of this they thought the sultan was dead and they abandoned Damietta. The king sent a knight into the

city as an envoy to confirm this news, and he returned to the king and said that he had been into the sultan's residences and that it was true. Then the king sent for the legate and all the prelates of the army, who sang *Te Deum Laudamus*[9] at the top of their voices. Then the king and all the rest of us mounted our horses and went to set up camp outside Damietta.

[164] The Turks were unwise to leave the city without cutting the bridge made of boats, because this would have caused us great difficulty. But they did do us great harm as they left by setting fire to the bazaar, where all the merchandise and goods sold by weight were stored. The outcome of this was the same as if someone were tomorrow to set fire – God forbid – to the Petit Pont in Paris.[10]

[165] We should acknowledge that God Almighty granted us great grace when he protected us from death and danger in the course of our landing, since we arrived on foot to attack our mounted enemies. And Our Lord granted us great grace in delivering Damietta to us, which city we might not otherwise have been able take except by starvation. And we can see this quite clearly since it was by starvation that King John took it in our fathers' time.[11]

[166] Our Lord can speak of us as he did of the children of Israel when he said *Et pro nihilo habuerant terram desiderabilem*.[12] And what does he say after that? He says that they forgot God, who had saved them. And I will tell you later on how we forgot him.

[167] First I will tell you about the king, who summoned his barons, both clerics and laymen, and asked them to help him determine how the spoils of the city should be divided. The patriarch[13] was the first to speak. He said, 'My lord, it seems to me that it would be appropriate for you to keep the wheat, barley, rice, and all the food in order to supply the city, and to let it be known throughout the army that all other movable goods should be brought to the legate's lodgings on pain of excommunication.' All the other barons agreed with this advice. But it so happened that the value of all the movable goods brought to the legate's lodgings amounted to only 6,000 *livres*.

[168] When this had been done, the king and his barons

summoned my lord John of Vallery, the *preudomme*, and the king said to him, 'My lord of Vallery, we have agreed that the legate will hand over to you the 6,000 *livres* to be divided up as you think best.' 'My lord,' said the *preudomme*, 'you do me a great honour, for which I thank you. But I cannot accept this honour and this proposition that you offer me – please God – as this would be contrary to the good customs of the Holy Land. According to these customs, when an enemy city is taken, the king should have one-third of the spoils found inside, and the pilgrims two-thirds. [169] King John held firmly to this custom when he took Damietta, and, so our elders say, the kings of Jerusalem before John also held firmly to it. If you were willing to give me two-thirds of the wheat, barley, rice and other food, I would gladly undertake to distribute them among the pilgrims.' The king was not inclined to do this and this was how the matter was left. Because of this many people were aggrieved that the king had broken with the good old customs.

[170] The king's men, who should have treated the people of Damietta considerately, let out stalls to those who wished to sell their goods at the highest rents possible, or so it was said. Word of this spread far afield, which meant that many merchants decided not to come to the camp. The barons, who should have preserved their resources in order to make good use of them at a fitting time and place, took to serving splendid meals and lavish dishes. [171] The rank and file consorted with women of loose morals, and this led the king to dismiss a great many of his men later when we had returned from captivity. I asked him why he had done this, and he told me that he had established beyond any doubt that the people he had sent away had run their brothels within a small stone's throw of his tent, and had done so at the time of the army's greatest troubles.

[172] Now let us return to our main subject, and say that shortly after we had taken Damietta, all the sultan's mounted forces arrived outside the camp and laid siege to it from the inland side. The king and all the knights armed themselves. Fully armed, I went to talk to the king and I found him sitting, also fully armed, on a bench. With him were a number of the

preudomme knights of his battalion, all fully armed. I asked him if I and my men might be allowed to venture just outside the camp to prevent the Saracens attacking our tents. When my lord John of Beaumont heard my request, he shouted at me very loudly and ordered me on the king's behalf not to leave my tent until the king commanded me to do so.

[173] I have already mentioned these *preudomme* knights who were with the king to you; there were eight of them, all good knights who had won prizes for their feats of arms on this side of the sea and the other, and such knights were usually called 'good knights'. The names of the knights in the king's entourage were as follows: my lord Geoffrey of Sergines, my lord Matthew of Marly, my lord Philip of Nanteuil and my lord Humbert of Beaujeu, constable of France. Humbert of Beaujeu was not present because he was outside the camp; he and the master of the crossbowmen, along with most of the king's sergeants-at-arms, were guarding our camp so that the Turks might not do any damage.

[174] Now, it so happened that my lord Walter of Autrèches had armed himself at all points in his pavilion. When he had mounted his horse, a shield at his neck and a helmet on his head, he had the pavilion flaps lifted and spurred on to charge at the Turks. As he left his pavilion, all alone, all the members of his household cried '*Châtillon!*' at the top of their voices. But it so happened that he fell before reaching the Turks and his horse galloped over his body. The horse, decked out with lord Walter's arms, then took off towards the enemy; it was attracted to the Saracens because most of them were mounted on mares. [175] Those who saw this told us that four Turks came at lord Walter, who was lying on the ground. And as they passed by they aimed great blows from their maces at him there where he lay. The constable of France, along with several of the king's sergeants, came to his rescue, and they carried him back to his pavilion in their arms. When he arrived there he could not speak. A number of the army's surgeons and physicians went to him, and since it seemed to them that he was in no danger of dying, they bled him in both arms. [176] Very late that evening my lord Aubert of Narcy said to me that we should

go to see lord Walter, because we had not yet done so and because he was a man of great renown and great valour. We entered his pavilion and his chamberlain came to meet us, asking that we walk softly so as not wake up his master. We found him lying on a rug of fine vair and approached very quietly to discover he was dead. When the king was told of this he said that he would not wish to have a thousand such men, since they would not want to follow his orders, just like this man.

[177] Saracen foot soldiers entered the camp every night and killed people where they found them sleeping. They killed the lord of Courtenay's sentry among others, and left him lying on the table, having cut off his head and carried it away. They did this because the sultan gave a gold bezant for every Christian head. [178] We could be targeted in this way because each battalion took it in turns to carry out night-time patrols of the camp on horseback. When the Saracens wanted to enter the camp they would wait until the commotion made by the battalion and their horses had died down, and then break into the camp in their wake, leaving again before daybreak. Because of this the king ordered that the battalions that normally carried out patrols on horseback should patrol on foot instead. Thus the whole camp could be protected by the men on guard, who were stationed so that each man was within an arm's length of the next.

[179] After this had been done the king decided that he would not leave Damietta until his brother, the count of Poitiers, had arrived, bringing with him French reinforcements. In order that the Saracens might not break into our camp on horseback, the king had it completely surrounded by large trenches, and every night crossbowmen and sergeants would mount guard over these trenches and also over the entrances to the camp.

[180] When the feast of Saint Rémy[14] had passed and no news had been heard of the count of Poitiers, the king and all those in the army were very ill at ease, for they feared he had met with an accident of some sort. I related to the legate how, while we were at sea, the dean of Maurupt had made us perform three processions on three Saturdays, and how, before the third

Saturday, we had arrived at Cyprus. The legate took note of
what I told him and issued a call throughout the camp for
three processions to be held on three Saturdays. [181] The first
procession started from the legate's lodgings, and went to the
church of Our Lady in the city, which had formerly been used
as a mosque by the Saracens but had now been dedicated to
the Mother of God by the legate. He preached a sermon on two
Saturdays, attended by the king and the great men of the army,
to whom he granted a plenary indulgence.

[182] The count of Poitiers arrived before the third Saturday.
It was just as well that he had not arrived sooner, because
during the intervening fortnight there was such a storm in the
sea off Damietta that at least 240 ships, both large and small,
were broken up and destroyed, and all the people in them
drowned and lost. And so if the count of Poitiers had come
earlier, he and his people would all have perished.

[183] Once the count of Poitiers had arrived, the king summoned all the barons in the army in order to determine
which route he should take, whether to Alexandria or Cairo. It
transpired that the good Count Peter of Brittany and most
of the barons in the army agreed that the king should go and
lay siege to Alexandria, because that city had a good harbour
where ships might arrive to bring supplies to the army. The
count of Artois opposed this plan and said that he would only
agree to a march against Cairo, since this was the capital of the
whole kingdom of Egypt, and he said that he who wishes to
kill the serpent must first crush the head. The king set aside all
the other advice from his barons and followed his brother's
recommendation.

CHAPTER 5

The Crusaders Venture Along the River Nile

(November 1249–February 1250)

[184] At the beginning of Advent[1] the king and the army set out in the direction of Cairo, as the count of Artois had advised. Quite close to Damietta we came across a stream that branches off from the great river, and it was decided that the army should halt there for a day and dam the stream so that we could cross. This was achieved quite easily, since we blocked the stream very close to where it left the great river, and this meant that its waters turned back into those of the river without difficulty. The sultan sent 500 of the most finely mounted knights he could find among all his forces to this crossing point on the stream, in order to harass the king's army and delay our progress.

[185] On Saint Nicholas's Day[2] the king gave the command to prepare to move off, and warned that no one should be so bold as to charge at the Saracens who had appeared. It so happened that when the army set off on its march the Turks saw that no one would attack them and heard from their spies that the king had forbidden it. This emboldened the Turks and they attacked the Templars, who formed the first battalion. One of the Turks brought a Templar knight to the ground right at the hooves of the horse of Brother Renaut of Vichiers, who was at that time the marshal of the Temple. [186] When he saw this Renaut of Vichiers cried to his brothers, 'At them, for God's sake! I can't bear this any longer.' He spurred on, and all those in the army did likewise. Our men's horses were fresh, while those of the Turks were already tired. I have heard it said that as a result not one of the enemy escaped and that they were all killed, a good number of them having fled into the river and been drowned.

[187] Before going any further I must tell you about the river that flows into Egypt from the earthly paradise. I am relating these things to you so that you might understand certain things relevant to my story. This river is different from all others because the further that other rivers flow down their course, the more small rivers and small streams flow into them. But no such river or stream flows into this great river. What happens instead is that it arrives in Egypt by just one channel, and then it divides into seven branches that spread out across Egypt. [188] After the feast of Saint Rémy[3] has passed, the seven rivers flood across the land and cover the plains. And when the waters recede the peasants come and work their land, using a plough without wheels to sow the land with wheat, barley, cumin and rice. And these crops grow so well that no one would know how to do it better. No one knows from where this flood comes, unless it comes from the will of God. And if it were not for the flood no good thing would be produced by this land, because since it never rains in this country, the sun's great heat would burn everything. The river is always muddy and because of this the local people who want to drink it take the water in the evening and crush four almonds or four beans into it, and by the morning it is so good to drink that it could not be faulted. [189] Before the great river enters Egypt, people who are used to doing so cast their fishing nets wide across the river each evening. When morning comes they find in the nets such goods as are sold by weight when imported into this country,[4] by which I mean ginger, rhubarb, aloe-wood and cinnamon. It is said that these things come from the earthly paradise, that the wind brings them down from the trees in paradise just as in this country the wind brings down the dry wood in the forests. Such dry wood as falls into this river is sold to us by merchants in this country. The river's water is of such a nature that when we put it in the white earthenware pots they make in Egypt, and hung it from the ropes of our tents the water became, in the heat of the day, as cool as water from a spring. [190] In that land it was said that the sultan of Egypt had tried many times to discover the source of the river. He sent out people who carried with them a sort of bread called 'biscuit' (since it

is baked twice), and they lived on this bread until their return to the sultan. They reported that they had explored the river and come to a vast expanse of sheer rocks that no one was able to climb, and that the river flowed out of these rocks. It seemed to them that there was a great profusion of trees high up on the mountain, and they said that they had found marvellous varieties of wild beasts of different kinds: lions, snakes and elephants that came to look at them from the banks of the river as they made their way upstream.

[191] Now let us return to our initial subject. When the river reaches Egypt it divides into branches, just as I mentioned before. One of its branches went to Damietta, another to Alexandria, the third to Tanis, the fourth to Rexi. It was to this Rexi branch[5] that the king of France came with his entire army. He set up camp between the Damietta and Rexi branches. The sultan's full army encamped along the banks of the Rexi branch opposite our camp in order to prevent us from crossing. This was easy for them since no one could cross that body of water to reach them except by swimming.

[192] The king decided to build a causeway across the river in order to cross over to the Saracens' side. To protect the people who were working on the causeway the king had two towers constructed. These were called cat-castles because there were two towers in front of the cats and two houses behind the towers to shield the people on guard from the shots fired by the Saracens' engines. There were sixteen of these engines directly opposite. [193] When we arrived there, the king had eighteen engines made, of which Jocelin of Cornant was master engineer. Our engines fired at the Saracens' and theirs at ours, but I never heard it said that ours had much impact. The king's brothers guarded the cats during the daytime, and the rest of us knights guarded them at night. And so the week before Christmas arrived.

[194] Only once the cats had been built did we start work on the causeway; the king did not want the Saracens, who took aim and fired at us from the other side of the river, to be able to harm the people who were carrying the earth. In building this causeway the king and the other barons in the army were

very shortsighted. This was because, having blocked one of the river's branches (as I told you earlier), which they did easily since they blocked it right as it left the great river, they believed they could block the Rexi branch at least half a league downstream from where it left the main river. [195] In order to hinder the king's building of the causeway, the Saracens dug holes in the ground on the bank by their camp. When the river reached these trenches the water flowed into them, increasing the width of the channel. So it was that everything we had achieved in three weeks was undone by them in one day, for by whatever extent we dammed up the river from our side, they widened the channel from theirs by digging these holes.

[196] In place of the sultan, who died of the illness he had contracted outside the city of Hama, our enemies had appointed as their commander a Saracen named Scecedin, the son of the sheikh. It was said that Emperor Frederick had knighted him.[6] He ordered a group of his men to come and lay siege to our camp from the direction of Damietta. They did so, crossing over the Rexi river at a town on its banks which is called Sharamsah. On Christmas day I and my knights were dining with my lord Peter of Avallon, and while we were eating the Saracens came spurring right up to our camp and killed several poor people who had gone out into the fields on foot. We went to arm ourselves, but [197] we did not manage to return quickly enough, for we found that our host, my lord Peter, had already left the camp and gone in pursuit of the Saracens. We set spur to follow and rescued him from the Saracens, who had thrown him to the ground. We brought him and his brother, the lord of Val, back to the camp. The Templars, who had responded to the alarm, brought up the rear well and bravely, but the Turks came and harassed us as far as our camp. Because of this the king ordered that the camp should be enclosed by trenches on the Damietta side, from the Damietta to the Rexi branches of the river.

[198] Scecedin, the commander of the Turks I mentioned to you before, was the most esteemed among all the infidels. He bore on his banners the arms of the emperor who had knighted him. His banners had three bands: on one of the bands were

the arms of the emperor, on another were the arms of the sultan of Aleppo and on the third were those of the sultan of Egypt. [199] His name was Scecedin, the son of the sheikh, which means 'the old man, son of the old man'. His name was deemed a very fine one in the infidels' lands, for these are the people in the world who most honour the elderly, whom God has protected from shameful reproach until their old age. This brave Turk Scecedin, so the king's spies reported, bragged that he would eat in the king's pavilions on the feast of Saint Sebastian.[7]

[200] The king, knowing this, organized his forces. The count of Artois, his brother, would guard the cats and the engines, the king and the count of Anjou, who later became the king of Sicily, were stationed to guard the side of the camp towards Cairo, while the count of Poitiers and those of us from Champagne would guard the side of the camp towards Damietta. It so happened that the aforementioned commander of the Turks had his men cross over to the island which lies between the Damietta and Rexi branches of the river, where our army was encamped, and ranged his battalions from one of these branches to the other. [201] The king of Sicily attacked these forces and overcame them. Many of them were drowned in one river or the other, but there remained a large number whom we dared not attack at all because the Saracens' engines were firing at our people in the area between the two rivers. In the course of the king of Sicily's attack on the Turks, Count Guy of Forez broke through the Turkish ranks on horseback. He and his knights attacked a battalion of Saracen sergeants, who brought him to the ground. His leg was broken, and two of his knights carried him back in their arms. It was with great difficulty that the king of Sicily was saved from the perilous situation in which he found himself, but he won high praise that day. [202] The Turks came against the count of Poitiers and against us, and we charged at them and pursued them for a long time. A number of their people were killed, but we returned without loss.

[203] One evening when we were mounting the night-time guard over the cat-castles, it so happened that the Saracens brought forward an engine called a petrary, which they had not

used before, and loaded Greek fire into the engine's sling. When the good knight my lord Walter of Curel, who was with me, saw this, he said, [204] 'My lords, we are in the greatest danger we have yet faced, for if they set fire to our towers and we are inside them, we will be burned and killed, and if we leave the defences we have been charged with guarding, we will be shamed. No one can protect us in this peril except God. So I advise and urge you, each time they launch the fire at us, to get down on your knees and elbows, and pray to Our Lord that he might protect us from this danger.' [205] As soon as they launched the first strike, we got down on our knees and elbows, just as he had instructed us. The fire came between the two cat-castles and fell in front of us, on the spot where the army had been working to dam the river. Our firemen were ready to put out the blaze, and since the Saracens could not fire directly at them because of the wings of the two structures the king had had built there, the Saracens instead fired right up into the clouds so that their arrows fell straight down on to our men.

[206] These were the characteristics of Greek fire: the part that came foremost had the bulk of a vinegar barrel, while the flaming tail that shot from it extended as far as a long lance. It made such a noise as it came that it was as if the heavens thundered; it seemed as if a dragon was flying through the air. The great mass of the fire cast such a great light that one could see as clearly across the camp as if it were day. They launched Greek fire at us three times that night, and fired it at us four times with the frame-mounted crossbow.

[207] Each time our saintly king heard that they had launched Greek fire at us, he sat up in his bed, reached out his hands to Our Lord and said as he wept, 'Sweet Lord God, protect my people for me!' And I truly believe that his prayers served us well in our time of need. Every time that the fire came down that night he sent one of his chamberlains to ascertain how we were faring, and if the flames had done us any harm.

[208] Once when they fired at us the Greek fire fell alongside the cat-castle that my lord of Courtenay's men were guarding, and landed on the bank of the river. A knight known as the Albigensian appeared and he said to me, 'My lord, if you do

not help us we will all be burned, because the Saracens have fired so many missiles at us that it is as if a great hedge of flame were coming towards our cat-castle.' We rushed out and reached the spot to find that what he said was true. We put out the fire, but before we managed to do so the Saracens struck every one of us with arrows fired across the river.

[209] The king's brothers guarded the cat-castles by day, climbing up into the towers in order to fire at the Saracens using crossbows; the bolts could reach the enemy camp. The king had ordered that when the king of Sicily guarded the cat-castles by day, we would have to do so by night. Our hearts were very ill at ease on the day the king of Sicily was on guard, when we were due to take over that night. This was because the Saracens had completely shattered our cat-castles, using the petrary to throw Greek fire at them in broad daylight. They had previously only done so at night. [210] Their engines had been placed so close to the causeway that our army was building to dam the river that no one dared go into the cat-castles. The engines threw large missiles that fell on the causeway and, as a result, our two cat-castles were burned. When this happened the king of Sicily went out of his mind, so much so that he wanted to rush into the fire to put it out. But if he was enraged by this, I and my knights praised God for it because if we had been on guard that evening we would have all been burned.

[211] When the king saw this he sent for all the barons of the army and pleaded that each of them should give some timber from their ships in order to make a cat to dam the river. He explained that it should be clear to them that there was no wood with which to do this other than the timber of the ships that had brought our gear upstream. Each man gave as much as he was willing to, and when the cat was built its timber was valued at over 10,000 *livres*.

[212] The king decided that the cat would not be pushed forward over the causeway until the day came when the king of Sicily was due to keep guard, in order to make amends for the misfortune of the other cat-castles having been burned on his watch. This was done as had been planned; as soon as the king of Sicily took over the guard, they pushed the cat forward

to the spot where the two other cat-castles had been burned. [213] When the Saracens saw this, they readied all sixteen of their engines to fire at the causeway where the cat had been placed. And, seeing that our people were afraid to go into the cat because of the stones thrown by the engines onto the causeway, they brought forward the petrary, launched Greek fire at the cat and burned it right down. God did this very kind deed for me and my knights, since we would have been in great peril as we took guard that evening, just as we would have been in danger on the other watch I mentioned to you.

[214] Seeing what had happened, the king summoned all his barons to receive their advice. They all agreed that they would not be able to build a causeway to cross over to the Saracens, since our people could not dam up one side of the river as quickly as they could widen the other. [215] Then the constable, my lord Humbert of Beaujeu, told the king that a Bedouin had come and told him that he would reveal the location of a good ford in the river on the condition that he was given 500 bezants. The king said he would agree to give the payment to the man as long as he kept his promise. The constable talked to the Bedouin, who said that he would not disclose the ford unless he was given the money in advance. It was agreed that we would pay the money to him, and so it was handed over.

CHAPTER 6

The Battle of Mansurah

(8 February 1250)

[216] The king decided that the duke of Burgundy and the great men of Outremer who were with the army should guard the camp so that no harm might come to it, while the king and his three brothers would cross by the ford that the Bedouin was due to show them. This operation was scheduled to take place on Shrove Tuesday,[1] on which day we came to the Bedouin's ford. As day was breaking we armed ourselves at all points. When we were ready we entered the river and our horses were obliged to swim. Once we reached the middle of the river we found ground on which our horses could set their hooves. On the bank of the river there were at least 300 Saracens, all on horseback. [217] I said to my men, 'My lords, keep watching out to your left! Since everyone is going in this direction, the bank is very muddy and their horses are falling on top of them and drowning them.' And it was most true that some were drowned in the crossing, among others my lord John of Orléans, who had carried a banner *vivré*.[2] We agreed to turn upstream and found a dry path; crossing in this way meant – thanks be to God – that not one of us fell. As soon as we reached the other side the Turks fled.

[218] It had been settled that the Templars would form the vanguard and that the count of Artois would have the second battalion, following the Templars. But it so happened that as soon as the count of Artois had crossed the river, he and all his men threw themselves on the Turks, who fled before them. The Templars let him know that he had done them a great dishonour by going on ahead, when he should have gone after them. They asked him to let them go ahead, as the king had decided they

should. But, as it happened, the count of Artois did not dare reply. This was because of my lord Fourcaut of Merle, who was holding his horse's bridle. This Fourcaut of Merle, who was a very good knight, did not hear what the Templars were saying to the count because he was deaf. Instead he kept shouting, 'At them! At them!' [219] When the Templars saw what was happening, they believed they would be dishonoured if they were to allow the count of Artois to stay ahead of them. And so they all set spur, as and when each saw his chance, and gave chase to the Turks who were fleeing before them, right through the town of Mansurah and into the fields in the direction of Cairo. When they decided to turn back, the Turks flung beams and pieces of timber on them as they went through the narrow streets of Mansurah. The count of Artois died there, with Ralph, lord of Coucy, and so many other knights that the number was estimated at 300. The Temple, so the master told me later, lost 280 armed men, all of them mounted.

[220] I and my knights agreed that we would go and attack a number of Turks who were loading their equipment in their camp over to our left. And so we attacked them. While we were pursuing them through the camp, I saw a Saracen mounting his horse as one of his knights held the bridle. [221] As he had his two hands on his saddle, ready to mount, I struck him with my lance under his armpits and threw him down dead. When his knight saw this he left his lord and the horse, and as I made another pass he thrust his lance between my two shoulders, pinning me down on my horse's neck so hard that I could not draw the sword I had at my belt. I had to draw the sword strapped to my horse, and when the knight saw that I had drawn this sword, he released his lance and left me.

[222] When I and my knights came out of the Saracens' camp, we found a good 6,000 Turks, by our judgement, who had left their tents and retreated into the fields. When they saw us they charged at us and killed my lord Hugh of Til-Châtel, lord of Coublanc, who was with me and carried a banner. I and my knights spurred on and went to the rescue of my lord Ralph of Vanault, who was with me and who had been brought to the ground by the Turks. [223] As I returned, the Turks bore

down on me with their lances. My horse was brought to its knees by the weight, and I went forward over its ears. I got up again as soon as I could, with my shield at my neck and my sword in my hand. My lord Erart of Sivry – may God absolve him – who was nearby me, came to me and told us that we should move towards a ruined house and wait there for the king, who was on his way. As we went there, on foot and on horse, a great horde of Turks rushed at us. They brought me to the ground, rode over me and sent the shield flying from my neck.

[224] When the Turks had passed, my lord Erart of Sivry came back to me and led me as far as the walls of the ruined house, where we were reunited with my lord Hugh of Ecot, my lord Frederick of Louppy and my lord Renaut of Menoncourt. There the Turks attacked us from every side; a number of them got into the ruined house and stabbed us from above with their lances. My knights asked me to hold their bridles for them, and I did so, in order that the horses might not run away. The knights defended themselves against the Turks so vigorously that they received the praises of all the *preudommes* in the army and from those who were witness to the deed and those who heard tell of it. [225] There my lord Hugh of Ecot was wounded by three lance blows in the face, as was my lord Ralph, and my lord Frederick of Louppy by a lance between the shoulders; the wound was so large that blood came from his body as from the bunghole of a barrel. My lord Erart of Sivry received a sword blow full in the face, so that his nose was hanging down over his lip. Then I remembered my lord Saint James, 'Dear lord Saint James, on whom I call, help me and save me in this need!'

[226] As soon as I had made my prayer, my lord Erart of Sivry said to me, 'My lord, if you thought that neither I nor my heirs would be reproved for it, I would go and seek help for you from the count of Anjou, whom I see over there in the fields.' And I said to him, 'My lord Erart, it seems to me that you would do yourself great honour if you were to go and seek help to save our lives, for your own is certainly in danger.' (And indeed I spoke truthfully, for he died of that wound.) He asked the opinion of all our knights who were there, and all advised

him as I had done. When he heard this he asked me to let go of his horse, which I was holding by the bridle with the others, and I did so. [227] He went to the count of Anjou and begged him to come and rescue me and my knights. A great man who was with him advised against this, but the count of Anjou told him that he would do as my knight requested. He turned rein to come to our aid, and several of his sergeants spurred on. When the Saracens saw them, they left us. Ahead of these sergeants came my lord Peter of Auberive, sword in hand, and when he saw that the Saracens had left us, he attacked a large body of them who were holding my lord Ralph of Vanault and rescued him, severely wounded.

[228] As I was there on foot with my knights, who were wounded as I have already described, the king arrived with his entire battalion, accompanied by a great din and great noise of trumpets and kettledrums, and halted on a raised path. I never saw a man so finely armed; he could be seen from the shoulders up, set above the rest of his men, with a gilded helmet on his head and a German sword in his hand. [229] When the king stopped there, the good knights that he had in his battalion, whom I have named for you already, threw themselves among the Turks, along with other valiant knights from the king's battalion. And know that this was a very fine feat of arms, for no one fired either a bow or a crossbow, but rather there were blows of maces and swords from the Turks and our men, who were all ensnarled with each other. One of my squires, who had fled with my banner but had returned to me, brought to me one of my Flemish horses on which I mounted and rode to the king, so that we were side by side.

[230] While we were thus together, my lord John of Vallery, the *preudomme*, came to the king and said to him that he advised that the king should move off to the right, towards the river, in order to have the support of the duke of Burgundy and the others who had been left guarding our camp, and so that the sergeants could have something to drink, since the heat was already very intense. [231] The king ordered his sergeants to go and look for his good knights whom he kept about him as his council, and mentioned each of them by name. The sergeants

went to look for them amid the battle, where there was a great tumult of our men and the Turks. The knights came to the king and he asked them their opinion; they said that my lord John of Vallery had advised him very well. Then the king ordered that the standard of Saint-Denis and his own banners should move off to the right, towards the river. As the king's forces began to move there was again a great din of trumpets, kettle-drums and Saracen horns.

[232] The king had hardly gone any distance when he received several messengers from his brother the count of Poitiers, the count of Flanders and several other great men whose battalions were there. They all begged the king not to move, for they were being so hard pressed by the Turks that they could not follow him. The king recalled all the *preudomme* knights of his council, all of whom advised him to wait. Shortly after, my lord John of Vallery returned, and reproached the king and his council for their delay. After this all his council advised the king that he should move off towards the river as the lord of Vallery had advised. [233] At that moment the constable, my lord Humbert of Beaujeu, came to the king and told him that his brother, the count of Artois, was defending himself in a house in Mansurah and asked that he go to the count's rescue. The king said, 'Constable, go on ahead and I will follow you.' I said to the constable that I would be his knight, and he thanked me very much for this. We set off to go to Mansurah. [234] A sergeant with a mace came to the constable, greatly troubled, and told him that the king had stopped and that the Turks had come between him and us. We turned round and saw that there was a good thousand and more of them between the king and us, and we were only six. I said to the constable, 'My lord, we will not be able to reach the king through these men. Let us instead go upstream and put this ditch that you see in front of you between the Turks and us, and in this way we might return to the king.' The constable did as I advised. And know that if the Turks had taken notice of us they would have killed us all, but they were paying attention to the king and the other great battalions, and assumed that we were some of their own men.

[235] As we came back downstream along the river, between the brook and the river, we saw that the king had reached the water. The Turks were driving back the king's other battalions, striking and hitting them with maces and swords, so forcing all the battalions back to the river with those of the king. The rout there was so great that several of our men attempted to swim across towards where the duke of Burgundy was, but they could not manage this because their horses were tired and the day had become hot. And so, as we came downstream we saw that the river was covered with lances and shields, and with horses and men who were drowning and perishing. [236] We arrived at a small bridge over the brook, and I said to the constable that we should stay to guard this little bridge, 'For if we leave it they will attack the king from this side, and if our people are attacked from two sides, they could well be defeated.' And so we did this. People say that we would all have been lost that day had it not been for the presence of the king himself. The lord of Courtenay and my lord John of Seignelay recounted to me how six Turks came and took the king by the bridle and were leading him away captive when he single-handedly freed himself with the great sword blows he gave them. When his men saw that the king was defending himself, they took heart and abandoned their attempts to cross the river in order to go to his aid.

[237] Straight towards those of us guarding the little bridge came Count Peter of Brittany, from the direction of Mansurah. He had a sword wound across his face from which blood ran down into his mouth. Mounted on a small, sturdy horse, he had thrown his reins over his saddle-bow and held on to it with both hands, so that his men, who were pressing close upon him at the rear, would not force him to quicken his pace. It certainly seemed as if he did not think very much of these men, for when he spat the blood from his mouth, he often said, 'By God's own head, look at them – have you seen such a rabble?' Following his battalion came the count of Soissons and my lord Peter of Noville, who was known as 'Caier', who had suffered blows enough that day. [238] When they had passed and the Turks saw that we were guarding the little bridge and had turned to

face them, the Turks let our men go. I went up to the count of Soissons, whose cousin I had married, and said to him, 'My lord, I believe you would do well if you would stay to guard this little bridge, because if we leave it these Turks that you see in front of you will rush across it, which would mean that the king would be assailed from the rear and from the front.' He asked whether, if he were to stay, would I do so also. And I replied, 'Yes, most willingly.' When the constable heard this, he told me that I should not leave before he returned, and he left in search of help for us.

[239] As I remained there on my horse, the count of Soissons stayed on my right and my lord Peter of Noville on my left. A Turk appeared, coming from the direction of the king's battalion, which was to our rear, and he struck my lord Peter of Noville from behind with a mace, pinning him down on his horse's neck with this blow. He then dashed to the other side of the bridge and rushed among his people. When the Turks saw that we would not abandon the little bridge, they crossed the brook and placed themselves between it and the river, as we had done when we came downstream. And we moved forward against them in such a way that we would all be ready to charge them if they tried to go towards the king or to cross the little bridge.

[240] In front of us were two of the king's sergeants, one of whom was called William of Boon and the other John of Gamaches. The Turks who had positioned themselves between the river and the brook brought forward a whole body of peasants on foot who threw clods of earth at these two men, but they never managed to force them back on us. In the end they brought forward a peasant who three times launched Greek fire at the sergeants. In one of these instances, William of Boon caught the vessel of Greek fire on his round shield; if any of it had landed on him he would have been burned from head to toe. [241] We were all covered with arrows that had missed the sergeants. I happened to come across a gambeson, stuffed with wadding, that had belonged to a Saracen. I turned the open side towards me and used it as a shield, which served me very well, since I was only wounded by their arrows in five

places and my horse in fifteen. It happened too that one of my
bourgeois from Joinville brought me a banner bearing my arms
with an iron lance-head. Each time we saw that the Saracens
were pressing down on the sergeants, we charged at them and
they fled.

[242] While we were there the good count of Soissons joked
with me and said, 'Seneschal, let this pack of hounds howl! For,
by God's coif' – this was the oath he most often swore – 'we'll
talk of this day again, you and I, in the ladies' chamber.'

[243] In the evening, as the sun was setting, the constable
brought the king's unmounted crossbowmen, and they lined up
in front of us. When the Saracens saw our men set foot in the
stirrups of the crossbows, they left us and fled. Then the constable said to me, 'Seneschal, that was well done. You go and
join the king, and don't leave him until he has dismounted and
is in his pavilion.' As soon as I had reached the king, my lord
John of Vallery came to him and told him, 'Sir, my lord of
Châtillon asks that you grant him the rearguard.' The king did
so most willingly, and then moved off. As we made our way, I
had him take off his helmet and gave him my iron cap so that he
might get some air. [244] And then Brother Henry of Ronnay,
provost of the Hospital, who had crossed the river, came to the
king and kissed his mailed hand. The king asked him if he had
any news of his brother, the count of Artois, and he replied
that he had good news of him, for it was certain that the count
of Artois was in Paradise. 'Oh, my lord,' said the provost, 'you
should be greatly comforted for no king of France has ever had
such a great honour as has come to you. In order to attack your
enemies you swam across a river, you defeated them and ran
them from the field, and captured their engines and their tents,
in which you will now sleep tonight.' The king replied that God
should be praised for what he had given him, and great tears
then fell from his eyes.

[245] When we reached the camp we found that some of the
Saracen foot soldiers had taken down a tent and were pulling
on the ropes from one side, while some of our rank and file
were pulling from the other. We charged at them, the master of
the Temple and I, and they fled; the tent was left for our people.

[246] In this battle there were many supposedly worthy men who shamefully fled across the bridge that I was telling you about before. They took flight in panic, and we could not get any of them to stay with us. I could name several of them, but I will refrain from doing so because they are dead.

[247] But I will not hold back when it comes to my lord Guy Mauvoisin, for he came out of Mansurah honourably. He followed the route downstream that the constable and I took upstream. And just as the Turks had forced back the count of Brittany and his battalion, so too did they force back my lord Guy Mauvoisin and his battalion. Both he and his men won great praise that day. And it was no wonder that he and his men acquitted themselves well that day, for I was told by someone who knew his affairs well that his entire battalion, with hardly an exception, were knights of his lineage or knights who were his liegemen.

CHAPTER 7

From Victory to Captivity

(February–April 1250)

[248] When we had defeated the Turks and chased them from their tents, and once all our men had left the Saracen camp, the Bedouins rushed into it in great numbers. They left not one thing in that camp, carrying off everything that the Saracens had left behind. I never heard it said that the Bedouins, who were subject to the Saracens, were thought less of because they would take or steal things; taking advantage of the weak was their custom and their way of life.

[249] Since it relates to my subject, I will tell you what sort of people the Bedouins are. The Bedouins do not believe in Muhammad. Instead they follow the law of Ali, who was Muhammad's uncle.[1] The Old Man of the Mountain, the patron of the Assassins, also follows this law. They believe that when a man dies for his lord, or for any good cause, his soul enters a better and happier body than before.[2] It is because of this that the Assassins are not worried about being killed when carrying out the commands of the Old Man of the Mountain. I will say no more about the Old Man of the Mountain for the time being though, and talk about the Bedouins instead.

[250] The Bedouins do not live in villages or towns or castles; instead they always stay out in the fields. They set up tents each evening – or during the day if the weather is bad – where their servants, wives and children may spend the night. They make their tents using barrel hoops tied to poles – the same way ladies' carriages are made – and over the hoops they throw sheepskins cured with alum, which are called Damascus skins. The Bedouins have long cloaks made from these skins that cover their whole body, legs and feet. [251] When it rains in

the evening, or the weather is bad at night, they wrap themselves up in their cloaks, and unbridle their horses and let them graze nearby. When the next day comes they lay their cloaks out in the sun and beat them and tend to them so that they show no sign of having been wet overnight. They believe no man can die before the day appointed for him. As a result they refuse to wear armour and when they scold their children, they say to them, 'Be accursed like the Frank who wears armour for fear of death.' In battle they carry nothing but sword and spear. [252] Nearly all of them wear tunics like the surplices that priests wear. Their heads are swathed in cloths which come down underneath the chin and make them hideous and repulsive to look at, also because the hair on their heads and of their beards is very black. They live on milk from their livestock, purchasing pasturage for their animals on the plains owned by rich men. No one can say how many Bedouins there are, for they can be found in the kingdom of Egypt, in the kingdom of Jerusalem, and in all the other lands of the Saracens and unbelievers, to whom they make large tribute payments each year.

[253] Since I returned from overseas I have come across certain false Christians in this country who adhere to the law of the Bedouins and say that no man can die before the day appointed for him. This belief is so wicked that it is equivalent to saying that God has no power to help us, for those of us who serve God would be fools if we did not believe that he had the ability to lengthen our lives and to protect us from evil and misfortune. We must believe in him, for he has the power to do all things.

[254] Now I will tell you that the king and the rest of us returned at nightfall from the perilous battle just described, and encamped in the place from which we had driven our enemies. Those of my people who had stayed in the camp from which we had set out brought a tent provided for me by the Templars, and they pitched it in front of the engines we had captured from the Saracens. The king had sergeants stationed to guard the engines.

[255] I was in great need of rest on account of the wounds

I had received earlier in the day, but it turned out that this was not to be, for, as I was lying in bed before day had fully dawned, someone raised the call in our camp, 'To arms! To arms!' I woke my chamberlain, who was sleeping at the foot of my bed, and told him to go and see what was happening. He was very agitated when he came back, and he said to me, 'My lord, get up! Get up! Look – Saracens have arrived on foot and on horse. They have routed the king's sergeants who were guarding the engines and have driven them back on to the ropes of our tents.' [256] I got up and threw a gambeson over my back and an iron cap on to my head and called to my sergeants, 'By Saint Nicholas, they'll not stay here!' My knights came to join me, wounded as they were, and drove the Saracen sergeants from among the engines, as far as a large battalion of mounted Turks that was right next to the engines we had captured. I sent word to the king that he should help us, since I and my knights were unable to put on our hauberks because of the injuries we had sustained. The king sent us my lord Walter of Châtillon, who set himself in front of us, between us and the Turks. [257] When the lord of Châtillon had repulsed the Saracen foot sergeants, they retreated as far as the large battalion of mounted Turks that had taken up position in front of our camp to prevent us from surprising the Saracen army, which was encamped behind them. Eight of the captains of this mounted battalion, who were very well armed, had got down on foot and erected a barricade of stone blocks so that our crossbowmen could not hurt them. These eight Saracens fired volleys of arrows into our camp and wounded several of our people and our horses.

[258] I and my knights assembled and agreed that once night had fallen we would carry off the stones with which they were barricading themselves. One of my priests, who was called my lord John of Voisey, had his own ideas and did not wait for this to happen. He left our camp, all alone, and advanced towards the Saracens wearing his gambeson, with his iron cap on his head and his spear trailing; the tip was tucked under his armpit so that the Saracens would not notice it. [259] When he came close to the Saracens, who paid him no attention because they

could see he was all alone, he withdrew his spear from under
his armpit and rushed at them. Not one of the eight men put up
a defence; instead they all turned and fled. When the mounted
Saracens saw that their captains had taken flight, they spurred
on to rescue them, while a good fifty sergeants sped out of our
camp. The mounted Saracens came spurring on but they dared
not engage with our foot soldiers; instead they swerved aside
when they reached them. [260] When they had done this two
or three times, one of our sergeants grasped the middle of his
spear and hurled it at one of the mounted Turks, striking him
between the ribs. This man trailed the spear off with him, the
iron tip between his ribs. When the Turks saw this they dared
not move one way or the other, and our sergeants carried off
the stone blocks. From that time onwards my priest was well
known in the camp, and people pointed him out to one another
and said, 'Look! There's my lord of Joinville's priest, who
routed eight Saracens.'

[261] These events took place on the first day of Lent.[3] On the
same day, a valiant Saracen whom our enemies had made their
commander in place of Scecedin,[4] son of the sheikh (whom they
had lost in the battle on Shrove Tuesday), took the *cote* of the
count of Artois (who had died in the same battle), showed it to
all the Saracen people and told them that this was the king's
coat of arms and that he was dead. [262] 'I am showing this to
you because a body without a head is nothing to fear, and
neither is a people without a king. Because of this we will attack
them on Friday, if you so wish. In my view you really should
agree to do so, since we cannot fail to take them all now that
they have lost their leader.' And they all agreed that they would
come and attack us on Friday.[5]

[263] The king's spies in the Saracen camp came to tell him
this news. And then the king ordered all the battalion leaders
to have their men armed from midnight onwards and to come
out of their tents as far as the palisade. (This palisade, which
was intended to prevent the Saracens from launching themselves
into the camp, was made of long wooden stakes set into the
ground in such a way that one could pass between the stakes
on foot.) And this was done as the king commanded.

[264] At the moment the sun came up the aforementioned Saracen, who had been appointed their commander, brought up at least 4,000 mounted Turks and had them take up position all around our camp, with himself in their midst. They were ranged from the river that comes from Cairo to the branch which breaks off at our camp and goes to the town called Rexi. When they had done this they brought up before us such a great number of Saracen foot soldiers that they could encircle our entire camp again, just as the men on horseback had. Behind these two battalions I have described to you were ranged all the forces of the sultan of Egypt, to help them if they needed it. [265] When they had done this their commander came forward on a small rouncy to observe the disposition of our forces. And, having seen that our battalions were stronger in one place than in another, he went back and summoned some of his men to bolster his battalions against ours. After this he had the Bedouins, who numbered at least 3,000, move in the direction of the camp guarded by the duke of Burgundy, which was between the two rivers. He did this because he thought the king would send some of his men to the duke in order to assist him against the Bedouins, thus weakening the king's forces.

[266] It took him until midday to make these arrangements. Then he had his kettledrums (called *nacaires*) sounded, and they rushed at us both on foot and on horse. I will tell you first about the king of Sicily, who at that time was the count of Anjou, since he was the first in the line on the Cairo side of the camp. They advanced on him in the same way one does in a game of chess, for they launched their assault with foot soldiers who threw Greek fire at him. The mounted Saracens and the foot soldiers bore down with such force that they overcame the king of Sicily, who was on foot among his knights. [267] Someone came and told the king of his brother's perilous situation. Hearing this, the king spurred into the midst of his brother's battalions, sword in hand, and rushed so far in among the enemy that they set light to his horse's crupper with Greek fire. By making this charge the king rescued the king of Sicily and his men, and drove the Turks from their camp.

[268] Alongside the king of Sicily's battalion was the bat-

talion of the barons of Outremer of which my lord Guy of
Ibelin and my lord Baldwin, his brother, were the commanders.
After their battalion was the battalion of my lord Walter of
Châtillon, full of *preudommes* and fine knights. These two
battalions defended themselves so vigorously that the Turks
were never able to break through or repulse them.

[269] After the battalion of my lord Walter came Brother
William of Sonnac, master of the Temple, with the few brothers
left to him after Tuesday's battle. He had used the engines we
had captured from the Saracens to have a barricade built in
front of his position. When the Saracens came to attack him
they threw Greek fire at the barricade, which was set alight
easily because the Templars had used a large quantity of pine
planks. And know that the Turks did not wait for the fire to
burn out, rather they charged at the Templars through the
blaze. [270] William, master of the Temple, lost one of his eyes
in this battle. He had lost the other on Shrove Tuesday and the
said lord William – may God absolve him – died of his injury.
And know that behind the Templars there was an area of land
of about the size that one man could work in a day. It was so
densely covered with arrows that had been fired at the Templars
by the Saracens that no ground was visible beneath them.

[271] After the Templars' battalion came that of my lord
Guy Mauvoisin, which the Turks were never able to overcome.
The Turks did, however, so inundate my lord Guy with Greek
fire that it was only with great difficulty that his men were able
to put it out.

[272] The barricade that surrounded our camp ran from the
position of my lord of Mauvoisin's battalion towards the river,
coming within the distance of a good stone's throw of it. From
there the barricade continued in front of Count William of
Flanders' forces and reached as far as the river that flowed out
to sea. Our battalion was next to the barricade that came
from my lord Guy Mauvoisin's emplacement. Because Count
William of Flanders' battalion was facing them the Saracens
dared not approach us, and in this God did us a great kindness
since neither I nor my knights had put on our hauberks, as we
were all wounded following Shrove Tuesday's battle.

[273] The Saracens charged at the count of Flanders and his battalion very viciously and vigorously, both on foot and on horse. When I saw this I ordered our crossbowmen to fire at the Saracens on horseback, and when they saw that they were being struck from our direction, the horsemen took flight. Seeing this, the count's men left the camp, threw themselves over the barricade and attacked the Saracens on foot and over-whelmed them. A number of them died and a number of their shields were captured. Walter of la Horgne, who carried my lord of Apremont's banner, gave proof of his vigour in this clash.

[274] After the count of Flanders's battalion was that of the count of Poitiers, the king's brother. The count of Poitiers's battalion was on foot, with only the count himself on horse-back. The Turks routed the count's battalion utterly, and were leading the count away captive. When the butchers and the other men in the camp saw this, along with the women who sold provisions, they raised the alarm in the camp, and with God's help they rescued the count and drove the Turks out of the camp.

[275] After the battalion of the count of Poitiers was that of my lord Josserand of Brancion, who had come with the count to Egypt and was one of the best knights in the army. His men were arranged so that all his knights were on foot, while he was on horseback along with his son, my lord Henry, and the son of my lord Josserand of Nanton. They stayed on horseback because they were children. The Turks overwhelmed his men several times, but each time he saw his men overcome, Josserand of Brancion spurred on and took the Turks from the rear so that, on several occasions, the Turks left his men in order to charge at him. [276] Even so, this would have been of no use in preventing the Turks from killing them all on the field of battle had it not been for my lord Henry of Cône, who was in the duke of Burgundy's force. He was a wise knight, brave and thoughtful, and every time he saw the Turks were coming to attack my lord of Brancion, he had the king's crossbowmen fire at the Turks from across the river. Thus the lord of Brancion came through that day's misfortunes, although he lost twelve

of the twenty knights who were in his company, not counting his other men-at-arms. But he himself was in such a sorry state that he never got to his feet again, and died from his injury in the service of God.

[277] I will tell you about the lord of Brancion. When he died he had been in thirty-six battles and combats from which he had carried off the prize for feats of arms. I once saw him in a company led by the count of Chalon, his cousin. It was Good Friday, and he came to me and my brother and said to us, 'My nephews, you and your men must come and help me, for the Germans are ransacking the church.' We went with him and attacked the Germans, swords drawn, and with great difficulty and a great struggle drove them from the church. [278] When this was done the *preudomme* knelt before the altar and called aloud to Our Lord and said, 'Lord, I beg you to take pity on me, and remove me from these wars among Christians in which I have spent so much of my life, and grant that I may die in your service, so that I may enter your kingdom in Paradise.' I have related this to you because I believe that God granted his wish, as you can tell from what you have just heard.

[279] After this battle on the first Friday of Lent, the king summoned all his barons before him and said to them, 'We owe great thanks to Our Lord since he has done us two honours this week: on Shrove Tuesday we drove our enemies from their camp, in which we are now lodged, and on the following Friday we defended ourselves from them, while we were on foot and they were on horseback.' And he said many other fine words to give them reassurance.

[280] Since it is useful in our pursuit of the matter at hand, I will include some additional information to clarify how the sultans kept their forces well ordered and well organized. The truth is that most of their knights were foreigners, brought by merchants for sale from other lands. The sultans were very eager to buy them, and paid high prices. The people who were brought to Egypt were captured in the East. When one of the kings in the East defeated another, he took the poor people he had conquered and sold them to the merchants, who then brought them back to be sold in Egypt.

[281] The arrangement was that the sultan raised the boys in his household until such time as their beards began to grow. He had bows made that were appropriate for each of them; as soon as they grew stronger they would send these weaker bows to the sultan's arsenal, and the master of the artillery would provide them with the most powerful bow they could draw. [282] These young men, who were called *bahariz*, wore the same arms as the sultan, which were of gold. As soon as their beards began to grow, the sultan knighted them. They wore the sultan's arms, but each was distinctive: by this I mean that some of them added red insignia to the golden coat of arms: roses, bands, birds or other emblems that appealed to them. [283] The men about whom I am telling you were known as the *halqa*, because the *bahariz* slept in the sultan's tents. When the sultan was in the camp, the men of the *halqa* were installed around the sultan's lodgings and constituted his personal body-guard. The sultan's doorkeepers and musicians were installed in a little tent at the entrance to the sultan's lodgings. These musicians had Saracen horns, drums and kettledrums, and made such a din at daybreak and at nightfall that while they could be heard clearly throughout the camp, those close by to them could not hear one another speak. [284] The musicians would never be so bold as to sound their instruments during the day other than on the orders of the commander of the *halqa*. Accordingly, when the sultan wished to issue an order, he summoned the commander of the *halqa* and let him know his orders. Then the commander had the sultan's instruments sounded and all the army would come to hear the sultan's command; the commander of the *halqa* would announce it and the entire army would carry it out.

[285] When the sultan went to war those knights of the *halqa* who performed well in battle would be made emirs, and the sultan would place 200 or 300 knights under their command. The better their performance the more knights the sultan would give them. [286] The reward they receive for their achieve-ments as knights is as follows: once they have attained such valour and such wealth that no one can challenge them, the sultan fears they might kill him or oust him from his lands. He

therefore has them captured and killed in his prison, while he
dispossesses their wives and children. This is what the sultan
did to the men who captured the count of Montfort and the
count of Bar. Baybars did the same to the men who defeated
the king of Armenia.[6] Following this success and believing they
might receive some reward, they went to greet Baybars while
he was hunting wild animals, and they got down from their
horses to do so. His reply to them was, 'I will not greet you',
since they had interrupted his hunting. And he had their heads
cut off.

[287] Now, let me return to my subject, and say that the
sultan who had died had a son[7] aged twenty-five years who was
shrewd, sharp and wily. Because the late sultan suspected that
his son would overthrow him, he had given him one of his
kingdoms in the East. Now that the sultan had died the emirs
sent for his son. As soon as he arrived in Egypt he seized the
golden rods of office from his father's seneschal, his constable
and his marshal, and gave them to those who had come with
him from the East. [288] Seeing this, these emirs and all the
others who had been in his father's council were greatly outraged by the contempt the new sultan had shown them. Fearing
that he would do to them what his father had done to the men
who had captured the count of Bar and the count of Montfort
(as was mentioned before), they strove to secure a promise from
the men of the *halqa* (the men mentioned earlier, who formed
the sultan's bodyguard) that they would, at the emirs' request,
kill the sultan.

[289] After the two battles already recounted, grave troubles
began to afflict our camp. After nine days the bodies of our
people who had been killed at Mansurah came to the surface
of the water. People said that this was because the bile had
decayed. They floated as far as the bridge between our two
camps and could not pass under it because the bridge was low
over the water. There was such a great number that the entire
river was full of corpses from one bank to the other and for at
least as far as a small stone might be thrown. [290] The king
had hired a hundred manual labourers who spent a full week
there. They threw the corpses of the Saracens, which were

circumcised, over the other side of the bridge and let them be carried off downstream. They laid the Christians in large trenches, one with another. I saw the count of Artois's chamberlains and many other people there, searching for their friends among the dead. But I did not hear that anyone was found.

[291] Throughout Lent we ate no fish in the camp besides burbots, and the burbots, which are fish that will eat anything, fed off the dead people. Because of this unfortunate situation and because of the noxiousness of that country, in which no drop of water ever rains, the camp sickness[8] came upon us. The flesh on our legs dried up and the skin on them was spotted black and earthy-brown, like an old boot. Those of us who contracted this illness had the flesh of their gums decay first. No one survived it; they were sure to die. When the nose bled this was the sign that death was certain.

[292] A fortnight later, and to the amazement of many people, the Turks set about starving us out. They moved several of their galleys from upstream of our camp, dragged them overland and put them in the river which came from Damietta, at least a league downstream of our camp. These galleys inflicted famine on us, since because of them no one dared come upstream from Damietta to bring us supplies. We knew nothing about this until we were told of it by the crew of a small ship that belonged to the count of Flanders and which got past the Saracen galleys because of the strength of the current. They also said that the sultan's galleys had captured at least eighty galleys of ours that had come from Damietta, and that the people on board had been killed. [293] Prices in the camp became so high because of this that by the time Easter[9] came an ox was worth eighty *livres*, a sheep thirty *livres*, a pig thirty *livres*, an egg twelve *deniers* and a measure of wine ten *livres*.

[294] Seeing this, the king and the barons agreed that the king should have his army cross over from the camp closer to Cairo into the duke of Burgundy's camp, which was on the river that went to Damietta. In order to take his people across with more safety the king had a barbican built in front of the bridge between our two camps. It was constructed in such way that one could enter the barbican on horseback from either

side. [295] Once the barbican was in place the king's entire force armed themselves. There was an intense assault by the Turks on the king's camp, but despite this neither the fighting men nor any of the other people moved until all the equipment had been carried over to the other side. Then the king crossed, his battalion after him, and all the other barons after them except my lord Walter of Châtillon, who brought up the rearguard. As they entered the barbican my lord Erart of Vallery rescued his brother, my lord John, whom the Turks were leading away captive.

[296] Once the rest of the army had passed through it, those who remained in the barbican were in a perilous position. Since the barbican was not very tall the mounted Turks aimed shots at them, and the Saracen foot soldiers hurled clods of earth in their faces. They would all have been lost were it not for the count of Anjou, later king of Sicily, who went to rescue them and brought them away safely. Among those who were in the barbican that day the prize was won by my lord Geoffrey of Meysembourg.

[297] On the eve of Shrove Tuesday I witnessed something remarkable that I wish to relate to you. On that day my lord Hugh of Landricourt, who had been with me and carried a banner, was buried. As he lay there on a bier in my chapel, six of my knights were leaning against a number of sacks full of barley. Because they were talking loudly in my chapel and were disturbing the priest, I went to tell them to be quiet, and said it was a disgraceful thing for knights and gentlemen to talk while Mass was being sung. [298] And they began to mock me and said, laughing, that they were arranging a new marriage for Hugh of Landricourt's wife. I scolded them and told them that such words were neither right nor seemly, and that they had forgotten their companion too hastily. And God's vengeance on them was such that the following day was the battle of Shrove Tuesday, in which they were all either killed or mortally wounded. Thus the wives of all six needed to remarry.

[299] As a result of the wounds I received on Shrove Tuesday, I was struck by the camp sickness in the mouth and legs, and by a double tertian fever and a head cold so bad that mucus

streamed from my head through my nostrils. Because of these afflictions I took to my sick bed in the middle of Lent, which meant that my priest would sing Mass for me in my tent, at the foot of my bed. He had the same sickness I had. [300] Now, it so happened that on one occasion he passed out during the consecration. When I saw that he was about to fall I leapt from my bed, barefoot and wearing my *cote*, took him in my arms and told him that he should go on with the consecration softly and slowly, and that I would not let go of him until he had finished. He came round and performed his consecration and sang the entire Mass through to the end, though he was never to sing again.

[301] After this the king's council and the sultan's council fixed a date to reach an agreement. The terms of the agreement were these: Damietta would be returned to the sultan, while the sultan would return the kingdom of Jerusalem to the king. The sultan was also bound to protect the sick people who were in Damietta, along with the salted meats (since they did not eat any pork) and the king's siege engines, until such time as the king could send for all these things. [302] The Saracens asked the king's council what guarantee he would give that Damietta would be returned to them. The king's council offered one of the king's brothers, either the count of Anjou or the count of Poitiers, as a hostage until Damietta was returned. The Saracens said they would do nothing unless the king's own person was left as surety. And to this my lord Geoffrey of Sergines, the good knight, said that he would rather the Saracens captured and killed them all than that they should be reproached for having left the king as surety.

[303] The sickness in the camp began to worsen; people had so much dead flesh on their gums that the barbers had to remove it before they could chew their food and swallow it down. It was most pitiful to hear people throughout the camp howling as their dead flesh was cut away because they howled like women in childbirth.

[304] When the king saw that he could not remain there without the certainty of death for him and his people, he commanded them to make ready to set out to return to Damietta

at nightfall on the Tuesday evening after the octave of Easter.[10] He informed the sailors who were in charge of the galleys that they should collect all the sick people and take them to Damietta. The king ordered Jocelin of Cornant, with his brothers and the other engineers, to cut the ropes that held the bridges between us and the Saracens, but they failed to do so.

[305] I and the two knights who remained with me, along with the rest of my household, boarded my boat following the afternoon meal on Tuesday. When night began to fall, I told my sailors to lift the anchor so that we could go downstream. They said that they dared not do so, because the people on board the sultan's galleys, which lay between us and Damietta, would kill us. The sailors had lit great fires to help them in bringing the sick people on to their galleys, and the sick had approached the riverbank. The Saracens came into the camp while I was pleading with the sailors to leave, and I saw by the light of the fires that they were killing the sick people on the bank. [306] While my sailors raised their anchors, those who had been charged with taking the sick people cut the cables of their anchors and the galley moorings and sped down upon our little boats and surrounded us, one on one side and another on the other, nearly forcing us under the water. Once we had escaped this peril and were going down the river, the king, who had the camp sickness and severe diarrhoea, would have been assured of safety in the galleys if he wanted it. But he said that, please God, he would never abandon his people. He fainted several times that evening and because of his severe diarrhoea, he went down to the latrines so often that it was necessary to cut the seat from his breeches.

[307] People called out to those of us sailing downstream that we should wait for the king. Since we were unwilling to do so they fired crossbow bolts at us, which meant that we had to stop until we were given permission to sail.

[308] I will break off here and tell you how the king was captured, just as he himself recounted it to me. He told me that he had left his own battalion and had joined, along with my lord Geoffrey of Sergines, the battalion of my lord Walter of Châtillon, who had the rearguard. [309] And the king told me

that he was mounted on a little rouncy covered with a silk cloth, and that behind him there remained not one of all his knights and all his sergeants besides my lord Geoffrey of Sergines, who led the king to the little village where he would be captured. He did so in such a way, so the king told me, that my lord Geoffrey of Sergines protected him from the Saracens just as a good servant protects his lord's cup from flies. Every time the Saracens came near to him, he took up his short lance which he had placed between the bow of his saddle and himself, couched it under his armpit and charged at them, driving them away from the king. [310] In this way he led the king as far as the little village. There the king was carried into a house and laid, as if he were quite dead, in the lap of a *bourgeoise* from Paris. They thought he would not see the evening. My lord Philip of Montfort arrived there and told the king that he had come from the emir with whom he had negotiated the truce, and that if the king so desired he would go back to him to have the truce remade, in the way the Saracens wanted. The king begged him to go and said that he wanted this very much. Philip of Montfort went to the Saracens, and the emir removed the turban from his head and the ring from his finger as an assurance that he would keep the truce. [311] Meanwhile, a great misfortune struck our people: a treacherous sergeant named Marcel began to call out to our men, 'Lord knights! Surrender yourselves – the king commands you to do so. Do not let the king be killed!' Everyone believed that this order came from the king, and they surrendered their swords to the Saracens. The emir saw that the Saracens were leading our people away prisoner, and he told my lord Philip that there was no need for him to make a truce with our people, since he could see clearly that they had already been captured. [312] As it happened, although all our people had been captured my lord Philip was not taken prisoner since he was an envoy. There is a bad custom in the infidel lands according to which when the king sends envoys to the sultan, or the sultan to the king, and the king or sultan happens to die before the envoys' return, those envoys are taken as prisoners and slaves no matter what side they are from, whether Christian or Saracen.

[313] While the misfortune of being captured befell our people who were on land, so too were those of us on the water captured, as you will hear shortly. The wind was coming at us from the direction of Damietta and this deprived us of the benefit of the current. The knights whom the king had set in his small boats to protect the sick had fled. Our sailors lost their course on the river and ended up in a backwater, which meant we had to turn back towards the Saracens. [314] A little before the crack of dawn those of us who were going by water arrived at the stretch of the river where lay the sultan's galleys that had prevented the arrival of provisions coming from Damietta. There was a great commotion there because they were firing such a great number of bolts charged with Greek fire at us and at our people who were riding along the riverbank that it seemed as if the stars were falling from the sky. [315] When our sailors brought us back out of the backwater into which we had strayed, we encountered the king's small boats, the ones he had assigned to protect our sick people, which were fleeing towards Damietta. A wind then rose up from the direction of Damietta, so strong that it deprived us of the benefit of the current.

[316] On one bank of the river and on the other there were a very great number of our people's vessels that were unable to go downstream. The Saracens had stopped them and captured them. They were killing the people on board and throwing them into the water, and they were carrying off all the chests and baggage from the ships they had seized from our people. The mounted Saracens on the bank were firing bolts at us because we refused to go over to them. My people had dressed me in a jousting hauberk that I wore to avoid being wounded by the bolts falling on our vessel.

[317] At that moment those of my people who were down in the prow of the ship shouted to me, 'Sir! Sir! Your sailors want to take you to land because the Saracens are threatening them!' Feeble as I was, I had myself lifted up by the arms and drew the naked blade of my sword on them; I told them I would kill them if they took me to land. And they replied that I should make my choice; either they would take me to land or they

would anchor me in the middle of the river until the wind fell. I told them I would prefer it if they would anchor me in the middle of the river rather than take me ashore, where I saw our people being slaughtered. And so they anchored for me.

[318] Not long afterwards we saw the sultan's four galleys coming, in which there were at least one thousand men. I then called my knights and my people and asked them what they wanted us to do, whether to surrender ourselves to the sultan's galleys or surrender ourselves to the Saracens on land. We all agreed that we would prefer to surrender ourselves to the sultan's galleys, where they would hold all of us together, rather than surrender ourselves to the Saracens on land since they would split us up and sell us to the Bedouins. [319] Then my cellarer, who was born at Doulevant, said, 'My lord, I don't agree with this decision.' I asked him what he would agree to, and he told me, 'In my opinion we should all allow ourselves to be killed; that way we will all go to Paradise.' But we didn't pay any attention to him.

CHAPTER 8

The Crusaders in Captivity

(April–May 1250)

[320] When I saw that we could not avoid being taken captive, I took my casket and my jewels and threw them into the river, along with my relics. Then one of my sailors said to me, 'My lord, unless you allow me to tell the Saracens you are the king's cousin, they'll kill you all, and us sailors with you.' And I said I was quite willing for him to say what he wanted. When the people on board the first galley, which was coming towards us to ram our vessel from the side, heard what he said, they dropped anchor alongside our vessel.

[321] Then God sent me a Saracen, who came from the emperor's lands.[1] He wore breeches of rough linen, and came swimming across the river to our vessel. He held me around the waist and said to me, 'My lord, you'll be lost if you don't act decisively. It's vital that you jump down from your vessel on to the beak at the end of this galley's keel. They won't even notice you if you jump, since their minds are on the booty on your vessel.' They threw me a rope from the galley and, as God so willed it, I jumped on to the prow. And know that I was shaking so much that if the Saracen had not leapt after me to hold me up I would have fallen into the water.

[322] He took me into the galley, where there were at least eighty of their men, holding me in his arms all the while. The others threw me down and flung themselves on my body to cut my throat, thinking that whoever killed me would be honoured for it. The Saracen still held me in his arms and cried, 'He's the king's cousin!' They threw me down twice in this way, bringing me to my knees once, and then I felt the knife at my throat. God saved me from this ordeal through the Saracen's help. He

brought me to where the Saracen knights were, in the ship's castle. [323] When I had arrived in their midst they took off my hauberk and, taking pity on me, they threw over me my blanket that was made of scarlet and lined with fine vair. It had been given to me by my lady my mother. One of the Saracens brought me a white belt that I tied over the blanket, after I had made a hole in it so that I could put it on. Another brought me a hood that I put over my head. And then, because I was afraid and unwell, I began to shake violently. I asked for something to drink and someone brought me a pot of water, but as soon as I had the water in my mouth to swallow it down, it gushed out through my nostrils. [324] Seeing this, I sent for my people and told them I was dying since I had an abscess in my throat. They asked me how I knew this and I showed them. As soon as they saw the water gush out through my nostrils they began to weep. When the Saracen knights there saw my people crying, they asked the Saracen who had saved us why they were weeping. He replied that he understood I had an abscess in my throat which meant I could not survive. Then one of the Saracen knights told the man who had protected us that he should reassure us, for he would give me something to drink by which I would be cured in two days. And so he did.

[325] My lord Ralph of Vanault, who was in my company, had had his hamstrings cut in the great Shrove Tuesday battle and could not stand on his feet. But know that an elderly Saracen knight who was on board the galley would carry him, hanging from his neck, to the latrines.

[326] The chief admiral of the galleys sent for me and asked me if I was the king's cousin. I said that I was not, and told him how and why the sailor had said that I was. And he said that I had acted wisely because otherwise we would all have been killed. He asked me whether I was in any way related to Emperor Frederick of Germany, who was still alive at that time, and I replied that I understood my lady my mother to be his first cousin.[2] He told me that he liked me the better for this. [327] While we were eating, he had a *bourgeois* from Paris brought before us. When this *bourgeois* arrived he said to me, 'My lord, what are you doing?' To which I replied 'Well, what

am I doing?' 'In God's name,' he said, 'You're eating meat on Friday!' When I heard this I thrust my plate aside. The admiral asked my Saracen why I had done this, and he told him. And the admiral responded that God would not hold this against me since I had not done it knowingly. [328] And know that the legate told me the same thing after we had left prison. But because of this I made sure that I fasted on bread and water every Friday in Lent from then on, as a result of which the legate was sorely angry with me since I was the only one of the great men who remained with the king.

[329] The following Sunday the admiral had me and all the other prisoners who had been captured on the water taken on to the bank of the river. My lord John, my good priest, fainted while they were bringing him out of the galley's hold. They killed him and threw him into the river. His clerk, who also fainted because he had the camp sickness, was struck on the head with a stone bowl. He too was killed and thrown into the river. [330] As they were bringing the other sick people out from the galleys where they had been held captive, there were Saracens ready, their swords drawn, to slay those who fell and to throw them all into the river. I told them, through my Saracen, that this struck me as a wicked thing to do since it was contrary to the teachings of Saladin, who said that one must not kill any man once one had given him one's bread and salt to eat.[3] In reply I was told that these men were worth nothing since their illnesses rendered them helpless.

[331] The admiral had all my sailors brought before me, and he told me that they had renounced their faith. I said that he should not have any confidence in them, for just as swiftly as they had abandoned us so would they abandon the Saracens, if they saw a time or place to do so. And the admiral replied that he agreed with me, for Saladin said that one never saw a bad Christian become a good Saracen, nor a bad Saracen become a good Christian.

[332] Afterwards he had me mounted on a palfrey and led me along beside him. We crossed a bridge of boats and went to Mansurah, where the king and his people were being held prisoner. We came to the entrance to a large pavilion where the

sultan's scribes were, and they wrote down my name. Then my
Saracen said to me, 'My lord, I will not follow you any further
because I cannot. But I beg you, my lord, to hold always this
boy you have with you by the hand, so that the Saracens do
not take him from you.' This child's name was Barthélemin and
he was the bastard son of the lord of Montfaucon. [333] When
my name had been written down, the admiral led me into the
pavilion where the barons were, together with more than
10,000 other people. When I entered there the barons all displayed such joy that you could not hear a thing and, praising
Our Lord, they said they thought they had lost me.

[334] We had hardly been there any time when one of the
most high-ranking men there made us all get up, and he led us
into another pavilion. The Saracens were holding many knights
and other people prisoner in a yard surrounded by an earthen
wall. These men were led out from the enclosure in which they
had been held, one by one, and the Saracens asked them, 'Do
you want to renounce your faith?' Those who refused to do so
were taken to one side and beheaded, while those who reneged
were taken to the other.

[335] At this point the sultan sent his councillors to talk to
us, and they asked to whom they should address the sultan's
message. We told them they should speak to the good Count
Peter of Brittany. There were people there called dragomans
who knew the Saracen language and French, and they translated
the Saracen into French for Count Peter. And these were their
words: 'My lord, the sultan has sent us to you to know if you
wish to be released.' The count replied, 'Yes.' [336] 'And what
will you give to the sultan in return for your release?' they
asked. 'Whatever is possible and bearable for us, within reason,'
said the count. 'Will you,' they asked, 'give any of the castles
in the possession of the barons of Outremer?' The count replied
that he did not have the power to do so, because the barons
held their castles from the emperor of Germany, who was still
alive at that time. They asked whether we would give any of
the castles of the Temple or Hospital in return for our release.
And the count responded that this was impossible, since when
the guardians of these castles were installed, they were made to

swear on relics that they would not hand over any of the castles in return for any man's freedom. They said it seemed to them that we had no desire to be released, and that they would leave and send men in who would indulge in some swordplay with us, as they had done with the others. And then they left.

[337] As soon as they left, a large body of men came into our pavilion: young Saracens with swords at their belts. They brought with them a man of great old age, completely white-haired, who had asked us whether it was true that we believed in a God who had been taken prisoner for us, was wounded and killed for us, and came back to life on the third day. And we replied, 'Yes.' Then he told us that we should not be disheartened if we had suffered these persecutions for him. 'Because,' he said, 'you have not yet died for him as he died for you. And if he had the power to bring himself back to life, you can be certain that he will free you when he pleases.' [338] Then he went away, and all the other young men after him. I was very glad about this because I had been quite convinced that they had come to cut off our heads. And it was not long after this that the sultan's men came who told us that the king had negotiated our release.

[339] After the departure of the old man who had reassured us, the sultan's councillors returned and told us that the king had negotiated our release, and that we should send four of our men to him to hear how this had been achieved. We sent my lord John of Vallery the *preudomme*, my lord Philip of Montfort, my lord Baldwin of Ibelin the seneschal of Cyprus and his brother my lord Guy of Ibelin. He was constable of Cyprus and one of the most distinguished knights I ever saw, and the man who most loved this country's people. These four men reported to us how the king had negotiated our release, which was as follows.

[340] The sultan's council tested the king as they had tested us, to see whether he would be willing to promise to surrender any of the Temple or Hospital's castles, or any of the castles of the barons of that land. And, as God willed it, the king responded to them exactly as we had done. They threatened him and told him that since he refused to do this they would

put him in the *barnacles*. [341] The *barnacles* is the most terrible
torture that can be inflicted on anybody. It is two pliable planks
with intersecting teeth at the ends, tied together with strong
straps of cowhide at the base. When they want to put people in
this contraption, they lie them down on their side and place
their legs inside, with the teeth on their ankles. Then they have
a man sit down on the planks, as a result of which not half a
foot of bone remains unbroken. And to make it as horrible as
possible, after three days, when the legs are swollen, they put
them back inside the *barnacles* and break all the bones again.
The king responded to this threat by saying that he was their
prisoner and they could do what they liked with him.

[342] When they saw that they could not prevail over the
good king with threats, they went back to him and asked him
how much money he was willing to give the sultan, surrendering
Damietta along with it. And the king replied to them that if the
sultan was willing to take a reasonable sum of money from him
for their release, he would advise the queen to pay it. They said,
'Why are you unwilling to commit to doing so?' And the king
replied that he did not know whether the queen, who was his
lady, would be prepared to do this. The council went back to
talk to the sultan and then reported to the king that if the
queen was willing to pay 1,000,000 gold bezants (equivalent
to 500,000 *livres*), the sultan would release the king. [343] The
king asked them, on oath, whether the sultan would release
them for this sum if the queen was willing to pay it. The
councillors went back to confer with the sultan, and on their
return they swore to the king that they would release him on
these terms. And as soon as they had sworn the king promised
the emirs that he would willingly pay the 500,000 *livres* for the
deliverance of his people, and he would return Damietta to
secure his own release, since a man of his rank should not buy
his freedom with money. When the sultan heard this he said,
'By my faith, this Frank is generous not to have bargained over
such a large sum of money. Go and tell him that I'm giving him
100,000 *livres* towards payment of the ransom.'

[344] The sultan then had the great men board four galleys
in order to take them to Damietta. On the galley into which I

was boarded were placed the good Count Peter of Brittany, Count William of Flanders, the good Count John of Soissons, my lord Humbert of Beaujeu constable of France, the good knight my lord Baldwin of Ibelin and my lord Guy, his brother.

[345] The men who had conducted us aboard the galley brought us to the bank in front of the lodgings the sultan had set up by the river, and you will now hear how they were arranged. In front of these lodgings there was a tower made of fir poles covered with dyed cloth. This was the gate to the lodgings. Inside the gate a pavilion had been set up in which the emirs left their swords and their armour when they went to speak to the sultan. Beyond this pavilion there was another gate like the first, and through this gate one entered a large pavilion that was the sultan's hall. Beyond the hall there was a tower, like the earlier ones, through which one entered the sultan's private chamber. [346] Beyond the sultan's chamber there was a garden, and in the middle of the garden there was a tower taller than all the others, where the sultan would go to survey the entire camp and all the surrounding land. A path led from the garden to the river, where the sultan had erected a pavilion in the water in which to bathe. The entire compound was surrounded by a wooden fence, the exterior of which was covered in blue cloth so that people outside could not see in, and all four of the towers were covered with cloth.

[347] We arrived at the place where this camp was set up on the Thursday before Ascension Day.[4] The four galleys in which we were being held prisoner were anchored in front of the sultan's lodgings, while the king was taken ashore to a pavilion close to the sultan's quarters. The sultan had made arrangements for Damietta to be surrendered to him on the Saturday before Ascension Day, when he would release the king.

[348] The emirs whom the sultan had dismissed from his council in order to replace them with his own men, whom he had brought back from foreign lands, conferred among themselves, and one shrewd Saracen said this: 'My lords, you can see the shame and dishonour that the sultan has inflicted on us, by removing us from the honourable positions in which his father had placed us. Because of this we should be certain

that should he find himself in the stronghold of Damietta, he will have us captured and killed in his prison, just as his father did to the emirs who captured the count of Bar and the count of Montfort. As a result it would be best, so it seems to me, for us to have him killed before he slips through our fingers.'

[349] The emirs went to the men of the *halqa* and asked them to kill the sultan immediately after the meal to which he had invited them. So it was that after they had eaten and the sultan was making his way to his chamber after having taken leave of his emirs, one of the knights of the *halqa*, the man who carried the sultan's sword, struck him with his own sword across the hand, between his four fingers, and split his hand open right up to his arm. [350] The sultan then returned to his emirs, who had ordered this to be done, and said to them, 'My lords, I appeal to you against the men of the *halqa* – they wish to kill me, as you can see.' The knights of the *halqa* responded to the sultan with one voice, saying, 'Since you say we wish to kill you, it would be better for us to do it than for you to kill us.'

[351] Then they had the kettledrums sounded, and all the army came to find out what the sultan wanted. In reply they were told that Damietta had been taken and that the sultan was on his way to the city having ordered that the army should go after him. They all armed themselves and spurred on towards Damietta. When we saw they were going in the direction of Damietta, we were very sad at heart, since we believed the city had been lost. The young and agile sultan fled, along with three of his bishops[5] who had dined with him, into the tower he had had built. This was the tower behind his chamber that you heard about earlier. [352] The members of the *halqa*, who were 500 men on horseback, tore down the sultan's pavilions and laid siege to him and the three bishops in that tower, from every side. They shouted to him that he should come down. He said that he would do so on condition that they guarantee his safety, but they replied that they would force him to come down; he was not yet in Damietta. They launched Greek fire at him, and the tower, made of fir poles and cotton cloth, was set alight quickly; I never saw a fire so fine and upright. When the sultan saw this he came down at great speed and made off in

flight towards the river along the path I told you about before.
[353] The men of the *halqa* had hacked through on to the path
with their swords, and as the sultan passed on his way to the
river one of them struck him a spear blow in his side. The sultan
fled for the river, trailing the spear behind him. His assailants
came down to the water and swam out to kill him in the river,
quite close to the galley where we were. One of the knights,
who was called Faracataye,[6] slit him open with his sword and
pulled the heart from his chest. Then he came to the king, his
hand all bloody, and said to him, 'What will you give me? For
I have killed your enemy for you, who would have put you to
death had he lived.' But the king gave no reply.

[354] At least thirty of them came on to our galley, drawn
swords in their hands and Danish axes hanging at their necks.
I asked my lord Baldwin of Ibelin, who knew the Saracen
language well, what these men were saying. He replied that
they said they had come to cut off our heads. Many people
were making confession to a brother of the Trinity[7] called John,
who was Count William of Flanders's priest. But for my part I
could not recall any sins I had committed. Instead I was thinking
that the more I tried to defend myself and the more I tried to
escape, the worse it would be for me. [355] And then I signed
myself with the cross and knelt at the feet of one of the Saracens,
who held a carpenter's Danish axe, and said, 'Thus died Saint
Agnes.'[8] My lord Guy of Ibelin, constable of Cyprus, knelt
down beside me and confessed himself to me. I said to him, 'I
absolve you by such power as God has granted me.' But when
I got up from that spot I could not remember anything that he
had said or told me.

[356] They made us get up from where we were and imprisoned us in the galley's hold; many of our people thought
they had done this because they did not want to attack us all
together, but rather to kill us one by one. We stayed there in a
miserable condition all that night; we were lying so close
together that my feet were touching the good Count Peter of
Brittany and his were right next to my face.

[357] Next morning the emirs had us brought out of where
we were being held, and their messengers told us that we were

to go and speak with them in order to renew the treaty the sultan had made with us. They told us that we should be sure that had the sultan lived he would have had the king's head cut off, and ours too. Those who were able to go there went; the count of Brittany, the constable and I, who were gravely ill, stayed behind. The count of Flanders went to speak to the emirs along with Count John of Soissons, the two Ibelin brothers, and the others who were in a fit state.

[358] They reached agreement with the emirs on condition that as soon as Damietta had been surrendered to them, they would release the king and the other great men who were there. The sultan had already sent the people of lower rank, except those he had killed, out of the city and in the direction of Cairo. He had done this against the terms of the agreement he had made with the king, which made it seem likely that he would have had us killed too as soon as he had possession of Damietta. [359] The king also had to swear to pay them 200,000 *livres* before leaving the river, and another 200,000 *livres* once he had reached Acre. According to the agreement they made with the king, the Saracens had to protect the sick people who were in Damietta, along with the crossbows, weapons and engines, and the salted meats, until such time as the king should send for them.

[360] The oaths that the emirs had to swear to the king were formulated thus: if they did not keep the agreement made with the king, they would be as dishonoured as he who, because of his sinfulness, goes on pilgrimage to Muhammad at Mecca with his head uncovered, and as dishonoured as those who leave their wives and then take them back afterwards. (In such cases, according to the law of Muhammad, no man can leave his wife and ever be able to take her back, unless he sees another man sleep with her before he does so.) [361] The third oath was this: that if they did not keep the agreement made with the king they would be as dishonoured as the Saracen who eats pig's flesh. The king willingly accepted from the emirs the oaths just described, because Master Nicholas of Acre, who knew the Saracen language, said that they could not swear a more powerful oath according to their law.

[362] When the emirs had sworn, they had the oath they wished the king to take written down. It was drawn up on the advice of priests who had converted to their faith. The text said this: that if the king did not keep the agreement he had made with the emirs, he would be as dishonoured as the Christian who denies God and his Mother, and is barred from the fellowship of his twelve companions and of all the saints. The king agreed readily to this. The last point of the oath said that if he did not keep terms with the emirs, he would be as dishonoured as the Christian who denies God and his law and who, scorning God, spits and tramples on the cross. [363] When the king heard this he said that, please God, he would never take this oath. The emirs sent Master Nicholas, who knew the Saracen language, to the king. He said to him, 'My lord, the emirs are deeply outraged that they swore an oath precisely as you asked, and yet you refuse to swear the oath they ask of you. You may be certain that if you do not swear it, they will behead you and all your people.' The king replied that they could do as they wished, for he would rather die a good Christian than live with the anger of God, his Mother and his saints.

[364] The patriarch of Jerusalem,[9] an old and venerable man aged eighty years, had obtained a safe conduct from the Saracens and had come to the king to help him negotiate his release. Now, the custom among Christians and Saracens is such that when the king or sultan dies, those who have come as envoys, whether to infidel or Christian lands, are captured and enslaved. Since the sultan who had granted him safe conduct was dead, the patriarch was held prisoner just as we were. When the king had given his response one of the emirs said that it was the patriarch who had advised him in drawing up the oath, and he said to the infidels, 'If you're willing to trust me I will make the king swear the oath, for I will send the patriarch's head flying into his lap.' [365] They did not want to follow his advice. Instead they seized the patriarch from the king's side and tied him to a tent pole with his hands behind his back, so tightly that his hands swelled up to the size of his head and blood spurted out across them. The patriarch called out to the king, 'My lord, swear the oath for God's sake; I will take the sin of

it upon my own soul, since you certainly intend to keep it.' I
do not know how the oath was finalized, only that the emirs
felt themselves satisfied by the oaths of the king and the other
great men who were there.

[366] After the sultan was killed, his musicians and instruments were brought before the king's tent, and the king was
told that the emirs had been in favour of making him sultan of
Egypt. He asked me whether I thought he would have taken
the kingdom of Egypt if it had been offered to him. I told him
that he would have been acting most foolishly had he done so
since these people had murdered their lord. But he told me that
in fact he would not have refused it. [367] And know that they
say the only reason this did not happen was because the Saracens said that the king was the most steadfast Christian one
could find. As proof of this they pointed out that each time the
king left his lodgings he prostrated himself on the ground in
the shape of the cross, and made the sign of the cross all over
his body. They said that if Muhammad had made them endure
so much hardship, they would never have continued to believe
in him, and that if their people were to make the king their
sultan, they would have to become Christians or all be killed.

[368] After the terms of the agreement had been confirmed
and sworn to by the king and the emirs, it was decided that
they would release us on the day following Ascension Day.[10]
As soon as Damietta was surrendered to the emirs, the king
himself and the great men who were with him would be set
free, as was outlined earlier. On the Thursday evening the men
in charge of our four galleys anchored them in the middle of
the river before the Damietta bridge. They put up a pavilion in
front of the bridge where the king went ashore.

[369] At sunrise my lord Geoffrey of Sergines went into
Damietta and surrendered the city to the emirs; the sultan's
banners were raised on the towers. The Saracen knights entered
the city and started to drink the wine. They were soon all drunk.
One of them came to our galley and drew his bloodied sword,
saying that for his part he had killed six of our people. [370]
Before Damietta was surrendered, the queen and all our people
inside the city, except those who were sick, were brought on

board our ships. The Saracens were under oath to protect the
sick, but they killed them all. The king's engines, which they
were also supposed to protect, were hacked to pieces, and they
did not keep the salted meats, which they were meant to look
after since they do not eat pork. Instead they made one pile of
salt pork and another of dead people and they set fire to both;
there was such a large blaze that it lasted throughout Friday,
Saturday and Sunday.

[371] The king and the rest of us whom the Saracens should
have released at sunrise were held until sunset. We did not
eat at all and neither did the emirs; they spent the whole day
arguing. One of the emirs spoke for those who shared his
opinion, 'My lords, if you listen to me and the others on my
side, we will kill the king and the great men here. That way we
would have nothing to fear for the next forty years since their
children are still small. We already have Damietta in our hands,
so we can do this with greater confidence.' [372] Another
Saracen, who was called Sebreci and was a Mauritanian by
birth, spoke against this view, saying, 'If we kill the king after
having killed the sultan, it will be said that the Egyptians are
the most wicked and most treacherous people in the world.'
The man who wished to have us killed spoke again and said,
'It is most true that we acted very wickedly in ridding ourselves
of the sultan by murdering him, since we went against Muhammad's commandment that instructs us to protect our lord as
the apple of our eye – see the commandment written down here
in this book. Now listen,' he said, 'to another commandment
of Muhammad that comes later.' [373] He turned over a page
of the book he was holding and showed them Muhammad's
other commandment, which was this: 'For the security of the
faith, kill the enemy of the law.'[11] 'So you can see that we have
acted against the commandments of Muhammad by having
killed our lord. We will do still worse if we do not kill the king,
no matter what assurances we may have given him, since he is
the strongest of the enemies the Saracen faith has.' [374] It was
as good as settled that we should die, and so it was that one of
the emirs who opposed us, believing we should all be killed,
came to the river and began to call out in the Saracen language

to those who were in charge of the galleys, lifting the turban from his head and signalling to them with it. They immediately weighed anchor and took us off at least a league in the direction of Cairo, and at that point we thought we were all lost, and many tears were shed.

[375] But, according to the will of God, who does not forget his own, it was agreed around sunset that we were to be released. So they took us back downstream and brought our four galleys to the bank. We asked to be allowed to go, and they said that they would not do so until we had eaten, 'For it would be shameful to the emirs for you to leave our prison fasting.' [376] We asked to be given food by someone, and then we would eat it. They told us that someone had gone to their camp to fetch it. The food they gave us consisted of pieces of cheese that had been baked in the sun to keep them free of maggots, and hard-boiled eggs that had been cooked four or five days earlier. In our honour they had painted the shells with different colours.

[377] They put us ashore and we went to join the king, whom they were bringing to the river from the pavilion in which he had been held. A good 20,000 Saracens came behind him on foot, swords at their sides. On the river in front of the king was a Genoese galley, on board which it appeared there was just one man. As soon as he saw the king on the riverbank he sounded a whistle, and on this signal eighty well-equipped crossbowmen leapt from the galley's hold, their crossbows drawn, and they immediately put bolts in the notches. As soon as the Saracens saw this they took flight like sheep; only two or three of them stayed with the king. [378] The men on board threw a plank on to the riverbank in order to bring the king aboard, along with his brother the count of Anjou, my lord Geoffrey of Sergines, my lord Philip of Nemours, the marshal of France who was known as 'du Mez', the master of the Order of the Trinity and me. The Saracens were keeping the count of Poitiers in prison until the king had given them the 200,000 *livres*' ransom he was obliged to pay them before he left the river.

[379] On the Saturday after Ascension Day, which was the day after our release, the count of Flanders, the count of

Soissons, and several other great men who had been held captive in the galleys came to take their leave of the king.[12] He told them that he thought they would do well to stay until his brother, the count of Poitiers, had been set free. They said they could not do so since their galleys were all ready to sail. They went aboard their galleys and set off for France, taking with them the good Count Peter of Brittany. He was so ill that he only survived another three weeks, and died at sea.

[380] We began to gather the ransom payment on that Saturday morning and continued to do so later on Saturday and all day Sunday until nightfall. We used scales to amass the payment, each measure being valued at 10,000 *livres*. At vespers on Sunday the king's men who were putting together the payment warned him there was a shortfall of at least 30,000 *livres*. The only men with the king were the king of Sicily, the marshal of France, the minister of the Trinity and me. Everyone else was preparing the payment.

[381] I said to the king that it would be sensible to send for the commander and the marshal of the Temple (the master being dead), so that he could ask them to lend him the 30,000 *livres* to ransom his brother. The king sent for them and told me I should speak to them. When I had done so Brother Stephen of Ostricourt, who was commander of the Temple, said to me, 'My lord of Joinville, the advice you have given the king is neither good nor reasonable, since you know that when we receive deposits we are bound by oath not to release them to anyone other than those who entrusted them to us.' A good number of hard and cruel words passed between us. [382] Then Brother Renaut of Vichiers, who was marshal of the Temple, said, 'My lord, do not concern yourself with this argument between the lord of Joinville and our commander for, as our commander said, we cannot give you anything without breaking our oath. As for what the seneschal has suggested – that since we cannot lend you what you need, you should take it – this is not such an outrageous thing to say, and you should act as you think best. And if you do take anything from us, we hold at least as much money of yours in Acre, so you can easily repay us.'

[383] I told the king that I would go if he so desired, and he

ordered me to do so. I went to one of the Temple's galleys, to their flagship in fact, and as I was about to go down into the ship's hold where the treasure was kept, I asked the commander of the Temple to come and observe what I took, but he would not deign to do so at all. The marshal said he would come and witness what violence I did him. [384] As soon as I was down where the treasure was kept, I asked the treasurer of the Temple, who was present, to give me the keys to a chest that was in front of me. He, seeing me thin and wizened by illness and in the same clothes I had worn in prison, said he would give me nothing. I saw a hatchet resting there, so I raised it and said I would use it as the king's key. When the marshal saw this he grasped my hand and said, 'My lord, we see clearly that you are using force against us. We will give you the keys.' He then ordered the treasurer to hand the keys to me, which he did. The treasurer was greatly taken aback when the marshal told him who I was.

[385] I discovered that the chest I had opened belonged to Nicholas of Choisy, one of the king's sergeants. I emptied it of what money I found inside and then went to the boat that had brought me there and sat in the bows. I fetched the marshal of France and left him with the treasure, while I stationed the minister of the Trinity on the deck of the galley. On board the galley the marshal passed the money to the minister, and the minister handed it to me where I was in the boat. When we approached the king's galley I began to call out to him, 'My lord, my lord, see how I am supplied!' And the saintly man was most pleased and happy to see me. We handed over what I had brought to those who were putting together the payment.

[386] The members of the king's council who had prepared the payment came to him when this was done and told him that the Saracens did not want to release his brother until they had the money in their hands. Some of those councillors advised the king against delivering the ransom to the Saracens until he had his brother back. The king replied that he would deliver it to them because he had an agreement with them, and the Saracens would keep their side of the agreement if they thought it was the right thing to do. Then my lord Philip of Nemours

told the king that they had cheated the Saracens by one measure of 10,000 *livres*. [387] The king was very angry and said he wanted us to return the 10,000 *livres* to the Saracens, because he had promised to pay them 200,000 *livres* before he left the river. Then I leant on my lord Philip's foot and told the king not to believe him, that what my lord Philip said was not true since the Saracens were the world's greatest cheats in such transactions. My lord Philip said I was in the right and that he had only spoken in jest. The king said that this was an ill-judged sort of joke. 'And I command you,' he said to my lord Philip, 'on the faith you owe me as my vassal, that if the 10,000 *livres* have not been paid, you should have them paid without fail.'

[388] Many people had advised the king to take himself aboard the ship that was waiting for him out at sea, in order to remove himself from the Saracens' hands. The king paid no attention to them, saying instead that he would not leave the river until he had paid the Saracens 200,000 *livres* as he had promised. As soon as the payment was made the king, without anybody urging him to do so, told us that he was now free of his oath and that we should leave that place and go to the ship out at sea.

[389] Our ship then set sail but we went at least one league before anyone talked to another. This was because we were troubled by the count of Poitiers's continuing captivity. At that point my lord Philip of Montfort arrived in a smaller vessel and called out to the king, 'My lord, my lord, speak with your brother the count of Poitiers, who is in this other boat.' Then the king cried, 'Bring a light! Bring a light!' And it was done. Our shared joy was as great as could be. The king went aboard the count's ship and we went with him. A poor fisherman went to tell the countess of Poitiers that he had seen the count of Poitiers set free, and she had him given twenty Parisian *livres*.

[390] I do not want to overlook certain things that happened in Egypt while we were there. First of all, I will tell you about my lord Walter of Châtillon. A knight named my lord John of Monson recounted to me that he had seen my lord of Châtillon on a road in the village where the king was captured. This road went straight through the village, so that you could see the

fields on one side and the other. My lord Walter of Châtillon was there in the road, his unsheathed sword in his hand. [391] When he saw the Turks were coming into the road, he charged at them with his sword in his hand and drove them from the village. As the Turks fled before him they showered him with arrows, since they could shoot things backwards just as well things forwards. Once he had driven them from the village, he got rid of the arrows that had landed on him, put his *surcote* back on, stood up in his stirrups, reached out his arms and brandished his sword, crying, 'Châtillon, knights! Where are my *preudommes*?' When he turned round and saw that the Turks were coming in from the other end of the village, he charged at them again, sword in hand, and chased them away. And he did this three times, in the way already described. [392] When the admiral of the Saracen galleys took me to join the people who had been captured on land, I enquired after my lord Walter of Châtillon from members of his entourage. I never found anyone who could tell me how he came to be captured, except that my lord John Fouinons, the good knight, told me that when he himself was taken off captive towards Mansurah, he came across a Turk mounted on my lord Walter of Châtillon's horse, with its crupper all bloody. He asked the Turk what he had done with the man whose horse it was, and the Turk replied that he had cut his throat right there on the horse. It seemed from the crupper that this was so; it was reddened with blood.

[393] There was a most valiant man in the army whose name was my lord James of Castel, bishop of Soissons. When he saw that our people were retreating towards Damietta, he, having a great desire to go to God, did not wish to return to the land where he was born. Instead he rushed to go to God, spurred on his horse and attacked the Turks all alone. They killed him with their swords and set him in God's company among the number of the martyrs.

[394] While the king was waiting for his people to make payment to the Turks for the release of his brother, the count of Poitiers, a very well dressed and very handsome Saracen came to the king and presented him with pots of milk and

flowers of several different kinds on behalf of the children of Nasac, the former sultan of Egypt.[13] He spoke in French when he presented these gifts. [395] The king asked him where he had learned French and he said that he had been a Christian. 'Be gone with you,' said the king, 'I'll not speak to you any more!' I took the man to one side and asked him about his situation. He told me that he had been born in Provins, that he had come to Egypt with King John[14] and that he had married there and was an important and wealthy man. And I said to him, 'Don't you understand that if you were to die in this condition you'd be damned and go to Hell?' [396] 'Yes,' he said, for he was sure that no faith was as good as that of the Christians. 'But I fear the poverty and reproach I would face if I were to go over to you. Every day people would say "Here comes the renegade!" So I prefer to live rich and at ease rather than put myself in the position I predict.' I told him that the reproach on Judgement Day, when every man will look on his own sin, would be much more severe than the reproach he was describing to me. I gave him plentiful and good advice, but to no effect. Thus he left me, and I never saw him again.

[397] You have already heard about the great ordeals that the king and the rest of us suffered. The queen did not escape these hardships, as you are about to hear. Three days before she gave birth reports reached her that the king had been taken prisoner; she was so alarmed by this news that whenever she was asleep in her bed she imagined her whole room was full of Saracens, and she cried out, 'Help! Help!' In order that the child she was carrying might not perish, she had an aged knight, who was eighty years old, sleep at the side of her bed and hold her by the hand. Every time she cried out he said, 'Don't be afraid, my lady – I am here.' [398] Before she gave birth she made everybody leave her chamber except that knight. She knelt before him and asked him to grant her one thing. The knight promised on oath that he would. She said to him, 'Should the Saracens take this city I call on you, by the faith you have given me, to cut off my head before they can capture me.' And the knight replied, 'Rest assured that I will do it readily, for I had already decided I would kill you before they took us.'

[399] The queen gave birth to a boy whose name was John.[15] He was given the second name Tristan on account of the great sadness into which he was born. On the very day she gave birth she was told that the people of Genoa, Pisa, and the other Italian cities wanted to flee Damietta. The next day she summoned them all to her bedside, and with the room completely full, she said to them, 'My lords, for the love of God do not leave this city, for you can see that if Damietta were lost my lord the king and all those who are captive would be lost too. And if that does not move you, may you take pity on this wretched woman lying here, and wait until I recover.' [400] They replied, 'My lady, how can we do so? We are dying of hunger in this city.' She told them that it would not be hunger that made them leave, 'For I will buy all the provisions in this city and from now on I will retain you all at the king's expense.' They talked among themselves, returned to her and confirmed that they would be willing to stay. The queen – may God absolve her – had all the food in the city purchased at a cost of over 360,000 *livres*. She had to leave her sick bed earlier than she ought to have, since the city had to be surrendered to the Saracens. The queen set off for Acre to wait for the king.

[401] While the king was waiting for the release of his brother, he sent Brother Ralph, the Dominican friar, to an emir called Faracataye who was one of the most trustworthy Saracens I ever encountered. The king informed him that he was greatly taken aback that he and the other emirs had allowed their treaty to be so wickedly broken, since the sick people that the Saracens were supposed to have been protecting had been killed and because they had made firewood of the engines and had burned the corpses of the sick people and the salted pork they should have been guarding too. [402] Faracataye replied to Brother Ralph, saying, 'Brother Ralph, tell the king that under my law I cannot put this right, and this pains me. And tell him from me that he should not make any show of his displeasure while he is in our hands, for he would be killed.' Faracataye advised the king to raise the issue again as soon as he arrived in Acre.

[403] When the king came aboard his ship he found that his

people had not prepared anything for him, no bed and no clothes. Until we reached Acre he had to sleep on the bedding the sultan had provided him, and he had to wear the clothes the sultan had ordered to be made for him and had presented to him. They were made of black samite, lined with vair and grey fur, with a great many solid gold buttons.

[404] I sat beside the king throughout the six days we were at sea, despite my sickness. He told me then how he had been captured and how, with God's aid, he had negotiated his ransom and ours. He had me tell him how I was captured on the river, and afterwards he told me I should be most grateful to Our Lord for having delivered me from such great dangers. He sorely lamented the death of the count of Artois, his brother, and said that this brother would not willingly have failed to come and visit him on board ship, unlike the count of Poitiers. [405] He also complained to me about the count of Anjou, who was on board the king's ship but did not keep him company at all. One day the king asked what the count of Anjou was doing, and he was told that he was playing backgammon with my lord Walter of Nemours. The king, who was trembling all over because his illness had weakened him, went and seized the dice and the board, and threw them into the sea. He berated his brother very strongly for having taken up playing dice games so soon. But my lord Walter fared much better; he tipped all the money on the table – of which there was a great deal – into his lap and carried it off.

CHAPTER 9

The Crusaders at Acre

(May 1250–March 1251)

[406] Hereafter you will hear of the many trials and tribulations I faced in Acre, from which God, in whom I trusted and in whom I trust still, delivered me. I am having these things written down so that those who hear them may have faith in God in the course of their trials and tribulations, and God will help them just as he did me.

[407] Let me say first of all that when the king arrived in Acre, all the city came down to the sea to greet him in a most joyful procession. Someone brought me a palfrey, but as soon as I had mounted it my heart gave out, and I told the man who had brought the horse to hold me so that I might not fall. With great difficulty I was brought up the stairs to the king's hall. I sat myself down at a window, with a child alongside me who was around ten years old and named Barthélemin; he was a bastard son of my lord Ami of Montbéliard, lord of Montfaucon. [408] While I was sitting there, with no one attending to me, a servant wearing a red *cote* with two yellow stripes came up to me. He greeted me and asked whether I recognized him. I said I did not, and he told me that he was from Oiselay, my uncle's castle. I asked him in whose service he was, and he told me he was not in anyone's service and that he would stay with me if I liked. I said that I would like it very much. He immediately went to fetch some white coifs and combed my hair very nicely. [409] The king then summoned me to eat with him, and I went wearing the garment that had been made for me out of scraps of my blanket when I was a prisoner. I left my blanket with the child Barthélemin, along with four lengths of camelin that had been given to me in prison for the love of

God. Guillemin, my new servant, came and carved for me, and he managed to get some food to the child while we were eating.

[410] My new servant told me he had arranged lodgings for me near to the baths, so that I could wash away the filth and sweat I had brought with me from prison. That evening, when I was in the bath, my heart gave out and I fainted; only with great effort was I lifted out of the bath and carried to my bed. The next day an elderly knight called my lord Peter of Bourbonne came to see me, and I retained him in my service. He stood pledge for me in the city for the clothes and equipment I needed. [411] When I was ready – a good four days after our arrival – I went to see the king. He scolded me and told me that I had been wrong to delay so long in seeing him. He ordered that, since I valued his love dearly, I should eat with him each morning and evening without fail, until such time as he had decided what we were to do, whether to return to France or to stay.

[412] I told the king that my lord Peter of Courtenay owed me 400 *livres* in wages, which he refused to pay. The king said he would have me paid out of the money he owed to the lord of Courtenay, and this is what he did. On the advice of my lord Peter of Bourbonne we kept forty *livres* for our expenses and placed the rest in safe keeping with the commander of the palace of the Temple.[1] Once I had spent the forty *livres*, I sent John Caym of Sainte-Menehould's father, whom I retained in my service while overseas, to fetch another forty *livres*. The commander told him that he did not have any of my money and that he did not know me. [413] I went to Brother Renaut of Vichiers, who had, with the king's help, become master of the Temple. (Brother Renaut had been helpful to the king while in prison, as I told you earlier.) I complained to him about the commander of the palace who refused to give me back the money I had entrusted to him. When he heard this Brother Renaut was greatly agitated and said to me, 'My lord of Join-ville, I have great affection for you. But rest assured that if you are not willing to withdraw this appeal, I will no longer hold you as a friend, for you wish people to believe that our brothers are thieves.' And I told him that, please God, I would not

withdraw it. [414] I spent four days feeling sick at heart, as would someone who has no more money to spend. After these four days the master came to me, all smiles, and told me he had found my money. They were able to trace these funds because it transpired that the former commander of the palace had been replaced. He had been sent to a village called Le Saffran, from where he returned my money.

[415] The bishop of Acre at that time, who was born in Provins, gave me the use of the priest's house in Saint Michael's parish. I had retained Caym of Saint-Menehould, who served me very well for two years, better than any man I ever had with me while in that country, and I had retained several other people too. It so happened that there was a small room by the head of my bed through which one entered the church. [416] A constant fever struck me, and I was bed-ridden by it, and the rest of my household too. All day, every day, I had no one to help me or to lift me up. I awaited nothing except death since I heard an ominous sound close by. There was not a single day when a good twenty corpses or more were not brought to the church and each time they came I heard from my bed the *Libera me, Domine*.[2] So I cried and gave thanks to God, and said to him, 'My Lord, may you be praised for this misery you are sending me, for I have been proud in my waking and in my sleeping, and I beg you, Lord, to help me and release me from this illness.' And he did this for me, and for all my people too.

[417] After these things had happened I asked my new servant, Guillemin, to show me his accounts, which he did. I found that he had cheated me out of a good ten *livres* or more (in the currency of Tours). When I asked him for the money he said he would repay me when he could. I dismissed him and told him I would give him what he owed me, since he had certainly earned it. Once the Burgundian knights had returned from prison I learned from them that they had brought Guillemin overseas in their company, and that he was the most obliging thief there ever was; whenever a knight was in need of a knife or a belt, gloves or spurs or anything else, Guillemin would go and steal it and then give it to him.

[418] While the king was in Acre his brothers resolved to

play dice. The count of Poitiers was such a courteous player that when he won he opened up the room and had all the gentlemen and gentlewomen summoned, if there were any about, and handed over fistfuls of money, his own as well as what he had won. When he lost money he guessed its value and bought it back from those he had been playing, whether the count of Anjou or others, and gave everything away, both his own money and the others'.

[419] One Sunday while we were at Acre the king sent for his brothers, the count of Flanders and the other great men, and said to them, 'My lords, my lady the queen, my mother, has informed me and begged me as earnestly as she can that I should go to France, because my kingdom is in great danger, since I have neither peace nor truce with the king of England. The men of this country to whom I have spoken have told me that if I were to go this land will be lost, since they would all go in my wake; no one would dare to stay here with so few people. I ask you,' he said, 'to think about this. And since the matter is a weighty one, I will give you a week's respite before you let me know what seems best to you.'

[420] During the week the legate came to me and said that he did not at all understand how the king would be able to stay, and urged me strongly to agree to return with him in his ship. I replied to him that I would not be able to do so since, as he knew, I had nothing; I had lost everything on the river when I was captured. [421] If I gave him this response it was not because I would not very gladly have gone with him, but because of a piece of advice that my cousin, my lord of Bourlé- mont – may God absolve him – had given me when I left to go overseas. 'You are going overseas,' he said. 'Take care of how you return, since no knight, whether rich or poor, can come back without shame if he leaves those of Our Lord's humbler people with whom he set out in Saracen hands.' The legate was irritated with me and told me I ought not to have refused him.

[422] The following Sunday we came before the king again. The king then asked his brothers, the count of Flanders and the other barons what advice they would give him as to whether he should stay or go. They all replied that they had appointed

my lord Guy Mauvoisin to pass on the advice they wanted to give the king. The king commanded him to speak in accordance with the barons' instructions. This is what he told the king: [423] 'My lord, your brothers and the great men here have considered your situation and have concluded that, for your own honour and that of your kingdom, you cannot remain in this country. Out of all the knights who came in your company – you brought 2,800 to Cyprus – not a hundred remain in this city. So they advise you, my lord, to go to France, and raise men and money with which you might speedily return to this country in order to avenge yourself on the enemies of God who held you in their prison.'

[424] The king did not wish to be bound by what my lord Guy Mauvoisin had said, so he asked the count of Anjou, the count of Poitiers, the count of Flanders, and several other great men who were sitting alongside them, and they all agreed with my lord Guy Mauvoisin. The legate asked Count John of Jaffa, who was next, what he made of things. The count of Jaffa begged the legate to withdraw his question. 'Since,' he said, 'my castles are on the frontier, and if I advise the king to stay, it might be thought that this was for my own benefit.' [425] The king then called on him, as earnestly as he could, to speak his mind. The count said that if the king could manage to stay in the field for a year, he would do himself great honour by remaining. Then the legate asked those who were sitting next to the count of Jaffa, all of whom agreed with my lord Guy Mauvoisin.

[426] I was the fourteenth person sitting opposite the legate. He asked me what I thought of this, and I replied that I agreed fully with the count of Jaffa. And the legate, who was very annoyed, asked me how the king could possibly sustain a campaign with so few men as he had. My reply to him was equally annoyed, since I had the impression he was trying to goad me. 'My lord, I will tell you, since it pleases you. [427] It is said, my lord – I do not know if it is true – that the king has not yet spent any of his money, but only the clergy's money.[3] So, the king should put his own money to use and send for knights from Morea and from overseas. When they hear that the king is offering sure and generous payment, knights will come to

him from all parts. In this way he could, please God, sustain the campaign for a year. If he were to stay the poor prisoners who were taken captive in God's service and his own might be released. They will never be set free if the king goes.' There was no one there who did not have close friends in prison, and so nobody spoke against me. Instead they all began to cry.

[428] After me the legate asked my lord William of Beaumont, who was then marshal of France, his opinion. He said that I had spoken very well, 'And I will tell you,' he said, 'the reason why.' His uncle, my lord John of Beaumont, the good knight, strongly desired to return to France. He shouted at his nephew most cruelly and said, 'You stinking piece of filth! What are you saying? Sit down and shut up!' [429] The king said to him, 'My lord John, you're in the wrong – let him speak.' But he replied, 'Indeed, my lord, I will not.' The marshal felt obliged to hold his tongue. No one else agreed with me after that besides the lord of Chacenay. Then the king said to us, 'My lords, I have listened to you carefully, and in a week's time I will let you know what choice I have made.'

[430] When we left his presence an assault on me began from all sides. 'My lord of Joinville, the king is a fool if he doesn't listen to *you* over the whole council of the kingdom of France!' When the tables had been laid, the king had me sit next to him to eat, in the place where he always had me sit when his brothers were not there. He did not say a word to me throughout the meal, which was not how he usually behaved; he was always attentive to me while we ate. I really thought he was angry with me because I had said that he had not yet spent any of his own money, and that he should be spending it freely.

[431] While the king was hearing grace I went to a barred window that was in an alcove near the head of the king's bed. I put my arms through the bars of the window and was thinking that if the king should return to France, I would go to the prince of Antioch[4] – who looked on me as a relative and had sent for me – until such time as another expedition came to the country which I could join and through which the prisoners might be released. This would accord with the advice the lord of Bourlémont had given me. [432] As I was there the king came

and leant on my shoulders, placing both his hands on my head.
I thought it was my lord Philip of Nemours, who had been
taunting me all day because of the advice I had given the king.
I said, 'Leave me in peace, my lord Philip!' By accident, as I
turned my head the king's hand fell across my face, and I knew
it was him by an emerald he was wearing on his finger. 'Keep
calm,' he said, 'I'd like to ask you how a young man like you
is so brave as to dare to recommend my staying against all
the great and wise men of France, who are urging me to go.'
[433] 'My lord,' I said, 'even if I had wickedness in my heart I
would not for any price have advised you to do so.' 'Do you
mean,' he said, 'that I would be doing wrong if I were to leave?'
'Yes, my lord, so help me God.' And he asked me, 'If I stay,
will you stay?' I told him, 'Yes, if I can, at either my own
expense or someone else's.' 'Then be completely at ease,' he
said, 'for I'm grateful to you for your advice. But don't tell
anyone that.' All that week [434] I was comforted by what he
had said and defended myself more vigorously against those
who attacked me. The inhabitants of that country are known
as 'colts'. My lord Peter of Avallon, who lived at Tyre, heard
that I was being called a colt because I had advised the king to
stay with the colts. He sent me word that I should stand up for
myself against the people who were calling me colt, and tell
them I would rather be a colt than a worn-out old nag like them.

[435] The next Sunday we all came before the king again.
And when the king saw that we were all present, he made the
sign of the cross on his mouth and called on the aid of the Holy
Spirit. (Or at least I think he did so – my lady my mother told
me that every time I wanted to say something I should call on
the aid of the Holy Spirit and make the sign of the cross on my
mouth.) Then he spoke to us. [436] This is what the king said:
'My lords, I am very grateful to those who advised me to go to
France, and I also offer thanks to those who urged me to stay.
In my opinion, there is no foreseeable danger that my kingdom
might be lost if I were to stay, since my lady the queen has
plenty of people with which to defend it. And I have also
considered what the barons of this land are saying: that if I
leave the kingdom of Jerusalem will be lost, since no one will

dare to stay after I have gone. [437] And so I have determined that I will not for any price leave the kingdom of Jerusalem to be lost, since I came to conquer and defend it. My decision is to stay for the time being. And so I say to you, the great men here, and to all the other knights who are willing to stay with me, that you should come and talk frankly to me; I will offer you enough money so that should you decide not to stay, it will not be my fault but your own.' Many of the people who heard this speech were downcast, and many of them wept.

[438] The king, so it is said, ordered his brothers to return to France. I do not know whether this was at their request or by his wish. The king's announcement that he would stay was made around the time of the feast of Saint John. It so happened that on the feast of Saint James (whose pilgrim I had been[5] and who had done many kind things for me) the king returned to his chamber after Mass and summoned the members of his council who remained with him. These were: my lord Peter the Chamberlain, who was the most loyal and upright man I ever came across in a king's household; my lord Geoffrey of Sergines, the good knight and *preudomme*; and my lord Giles le Brun, another good knight and *preudomme* whom the king had made constable of France after the death of the *preudomme* my lord Humbert of Beaujeu. [439] The king raised his voice as he spoke to them angrily: 'My lords, it is already a month since people found out I was going to stay, but I have not yet heard news that you have retained any knights in my service.' 'My lord,' they replied, 'we cannot do so. Because they want to go home each man has so high a price that we dare not give them what they ask.' 'Have you found anyone,' asked the king, 'who is less expensive?' 'Indeed, my lord,' they said, 'the seneschal of Champagne. But we dare not pay what he demands.'

[440] I was in the king's chamber and heard this exchange. Then the king said, 'Call the seneschal to me.' I went and knelt before him. He had me sit down and said to me, 'Seneschal, you know that I have a deep affection for you, but my people tell me that they find you unyielding. How can this be?' 'My lord,' I said, 'it cannot be otherwise. For you know that I was taken prisoner on the river and lost all I had; I have nothing at

all.' He asked me what I was demanding, and I said that I had asked for 2,000 *livres* for two-thirds of the year, until Easter. [441] 'Now tell me,' he said, 'have you secured the service of any knights?' And I said, 'Yes: my lord Peter of Pontmoulin and two men under his banner, at the cost of 400 *livres* each until Easter.' The king added up using his fingers. 'That makes,' he said, 'a cost of 1,200 *livres* for your new knights.' 'Consider, my lord,' I said, 'that I need at least 800 *livres* to provide myself with horses and equipment and to feed my knights, since you would not want us to eat with your household.' Then the king said to his men, 'I truly don't see anything excessive in this. I retain you,' he said, 'in my service.'

[442] After this the king's brothers and the other great men in Acre prepared their fleets. At his departure from the city the count of Poitiers borrowed jewels from those who were returning to France, and gave them freely and generously to those of us who were staying. Both the brothers entreated me earnestly to take care of the king, and they told me there was no one else staying in whom they had as much trust. Everyone was astonished at how sad the count of Anjou appeared when he saw he had to go aboard the ship. But he returned to France nonetheless.

[443] It was not long after the king's brothers had left Acre that messengers came from Emperor Frederick to the king with letters of credence. They told him that the emperor had sent them to secure our release. They showed the king the letters that the emperor had sent to the sultan who had died (the emperor had not known about that): the emperor ordered the sultan to have full confidence in what his messengers said with regard to the king's release. Many people said that it would not have benefited us if these messengers had arrived while we were in prison, because they thought the emperor had sent them to hinder rather than aid our release. The messengers found we had already been set free, and so they left.

[444] While the king was at Acre, the sultan of Damascus[6] sent messengers to him. He complained bitterly about the Egyptian emirs who had killed his cousin the sultan. He promised the king that if he decided to help him, he would deliver the

kingdom of Jerusalem to him, which was in his hands. The king decided that he would reply to the sultan of Damascus through his own envoys, and he sent them to the sultan. Along with the envoys to Damascus went Brother Yves le Breton, a friar of the Dominican order who knew the Saracen language. [445] While they were going from their lodgings to those of the sultan, Brother Yves saw an old woman crossing the street. In her right hand she was carrying a bowl full of fire, and in her left a flask full of water. Brother Yves asked her, 'What do you intend to do with those?' She replied that she wanted to burn Heaven with the fire and extinguish Hell with the water, so that neither would exist any more. And he asked, 'Why do you want to do that?' 'Because I wish no one to do good either for the reward of Heaven or from fear of Hell, but only to receive God's love, for he is so worthy of being honoured and can do all good things for us.'

[446] John the Armenian, who was the king's weapon-maker, went to Damascus to buy horn and glue for making crossbows. He saw a very ancient old man sitting in the market in Damascus. This old man called out to him and asked him if he was a Christian, and John said, 'Yes.' The old man said to him, 'You Christians must really hate each other, for I witnessed a time when King Baldwin of Jerusalem, who was a leper, defeated Saladin[7] even though he had only 300 armed men while Saladin had 3,000. Now your sins have reduced you to such a state that we round you up in the field like cattle.' [447] Then John the Armenian said that he had better keep quiet about the sins of the Christians because the sins of the Saracens were far greater. The Saracen replied that he had answered foolishly. John asked why, and the old man said that he would tell him, but that he had a question to ask first. He asked John whether he had any children. 'Yes,' he said, 'a son.' The old man asked which would be more aggravating, for him to receive a blow from the Saracen or from his son? John said that he would be more angry with his son than with the Saracen. [448] 'Now,' said the Saracen, 'I will give you the following response. You Christians are sons of God, called Christian after the name of Christ, and he has been so generous as to provide you with

teachers through whom you can learn when you are doing right
and when you are doing wrong. Because of this God is more
displeased with you when you commit a small sin than he is
with us when we commit a much bigger one, since we do not
realize it. We are so blind as to believe that we may be forgiven
our sins if we are able to wash in water before we die, for
Muhammad told us that at death we will be saved by water.'

[449] Once when I was going to Paris after my return from
overseas, John the Armenian was in my company. While we
were having a meal inside a tent a great crowd of poor people
were begging from us for the love of God, and were making a
great row. One of our number gave an order to a servant,
saying, 'Get up and chase these paupers away!' [450] 'Oh!' said
John the Armenian, 'that was a very bad thing to say. For if
the king of France now sent messengers bringing each of us
100 marks of silver, we would not drive them away. And yet
you chase off these envoys who are offering to give you the
greatest gift you could be given. They are asking you to give
them something for God's sake, which means that if you
give them something of yours, they will give you God. God said
with his own mouth that the poor have the power to give God
to us, and the saints say they can reconcile us to him. In the
same way that water extinguishes fire, charity extinguishes sin.
May you never,' said John, 'drive the poor away. Rather give
to them, and God will give to you.'

[451] Envoys from the Old Man of the Mountain[8] came to
the king while he was at Acre. The king had them come before
him when he returned from Mass. He had them seated before him so that there was an emir in front, finely clothed and
impressively equipped, and behind this emir was an impressively equipped young man who held three knives in his hand;
the blade of each knife fitted inside the handle of another. If
the king had rebuffed the emir the young man would have
presented these three knives to the king as a token of defiance.
Behind the man holding the knives was another who had a
length of linen wound round his arm; if he had refused the Old
Man of the Mountain's request, this too would have been
presented to the king, as a burial shroud.

[452] The king told the emir that he should speak as he wished. The emir handed him letters of credence and said, 'My lord sent me to ask you if you know him.' The king replied that he did not know him, since he had never met him, but he certainly had heard talk of him. And the emir said to the king, 'Since you have heard talk of my lord, I am greatly amazed that you haven't sent him sufficient of your wealth to secure his friendship. The emperor of Germany, the king of Hungary, the sultan of Egypt and the other rulers do so every year; they are well aware that they will not survive unless it is pleasing to my lord. [453] If you are not willing to do this, then have him acquitted of the tribute he owes to the Hospital and the Temple, and he will deem himself to have been paid by you.' At that time the Old Man of the Mountain made tribute payments to the Hospital and Temple because they had no fear of the Assassins. The Old Man could not gain anything by having the master of the Temple or the Hospital killed because he understood clearly that if he had one of them killed, another man, just as able, would immediately replace him. Because of this he was unwilling to lose any of the Assassins when he had nothing to gain by it. The king replied to the emir that he should return in the afternoon.

[454] When the emir returned he found the king seated with the master of the Hospital on one side of him and the master of the Temple on the other. The king then told him to repeat what he had said that morning, but the emir said he was not inclined to repeat himself in front of anyone except those who had been with the king earlier. The two masters told him, 'We order you to speak.' And he said that he would repeat himself, since they commanded it. Then the two masters had him told in the Saracen language to come and speak to them the following day in the Hospital, and so he did.

[455] The two masters told him that his lord was very bold to dare to send such harsh words to the king. They informed him that, were they not concerned about the honour of the king to whom the emir and his companions had come as envoys, they would have drowned them in Acre's filthy waters in defiance of his lord. 'We order you to return to your lord and to be back

here in two weeks, bringing such letters and jewels from him
that the king will deem himself satisfied and pleased with you.'

[456] Within two weeks the Old Man of the Mountain's
envoys came back to Acre. They brought the king the Old
Man's chemise and on their lord's behalf they told the king of
its significance: just as the chemise is closer to one's body than
any other piece of clothing, so the Old Man wanted to keep the
king closer in love than any other king. He sent the king his
ring, which was made of very fine gold and had his name
engraved on it; their lord informed them that with this ring he
formed a union with the king, wishing them to be as one from
this time forwards. [457] Among the other treasures he sent the
king was an elephant very finely made in crystal, an animal
called a giraffe also made in crystal, apples made from various
kinds of crystal, and backgammon and chess sets. All these
things were decorated with ambergris, which was fixed to the
crystal with fine gold settings. And know that their sweet smell
was such that as soon as the envoys opened the chests holding
these items the whole chamber seemed to be perfumed.

[458] The king sent his own envoys to the Old Man, along
with a great quantity of jewels, lengths of scarlet, gold cups and
silver bits for his horses. With these envoys he sent Brother
Yves le Breton, who knew the Saracen language. He discovered
that the Old Man of the Mountain did not believe in Muhammad. Instead he believed the law of Ali, who was Muhammad's
uncle. [459] Ali had enabled Muhammad to obtain his position
of authority, but once Muhammad became overlord of his
people he spurned his uncle and distanced himself from him.
When Ali saw this he drew as many people to him as he could
and taught them a different faith from the one taught by
Muhammad. Hence it is still the case that all those who follow
the law of Ali say that all those who follow the law of Muhammad are unbelievers, while all those who follow the law of
Muhammad say that all those who follow the law of Ali are
unbelievers.

[460] One of the points of the law of Ali is that when a man
is killed fulfilling his lord's command, his soul enters a happier
body than the one it dwelled in before. Because of this the

Assassins are unperturbed by facing death when their lord commands it, since they believe they will be happier once they have died than they had been previously.

[461] Another point is this: they believe no man can die before the day appointed for him.[9] But no one should believe this since God has the power to prolong our lives and to cut them short. The Bedouins hold the same belief and because of this they refuse to wear armour when they go into battle, since they think that to do so is to go against the commandment of their law. When they scold their children they say to them, 'Be accursed as the Frank who wears armour for fear of death.'

[462] Brother Yves found a book beside the head of the Old Man's bed in which were written several of Our Lord's sayings to Saint Peter during his time on Earth. And Brother Yves said, 'Ah, my lord – you should, for God's sake, read this book often, for these are very fine words.' The Old Man said that he did so, 'Because I hold my lord Saint Peter very dear, since at the beginning of the world when Abel was killed, his soul passed into Noah's body. When Noah was dead it passed into the body of Abraham, and from his body, when he died, it passed, at the time God came to Earth, into Saint Peter's body.' [463] When he heard this Brother Yves explained that this belief was not good, and he passed on much sound doctrine, but the Old Man did not want to believe it. Brother Yves related these things to the king when he returned to us. When the Old Man rode out he had a crier ride in front of him who carried a Danish axe that had a long handle covered with silver and with many blades embedded in it. He called out, 'Make way for the man who holds the death of kings in his hands.'

[464] I forgot to tell you what response the king gave to the sultan of Damascus. It was that the king was not inclined to join with him until such time as he knew whether the Egyptian emirs would restore the terms of the truce they had broken. He was sending envoys to them, and if they refused to restore the terms of the truce they had broken, he would willingly help the sultan avenge his cousin, the sultan of Egypt, whom the emirs had killed.

[465] While the king was in Acre he sent my lord John of

Valenciennes to Egypt. He demanded that the emirs make amends for the insults and injuries they had inflicted on the king. They said that they would do so willingly so long as the king would ally himself with them against the sultan of Damascus. My lord John of Valenciennes berated them strongly for the great outrages they had committed against the king, which I have already described, and advised them that it would be wise to release all the knights they were holding in prison, so as to soothe the king's heart towards them. This they did, and they also sent all the bones of Count Walter of Brienne[10] for burial in consecrated ground. [466] When my lord John of Valenciennes returned to Acre with 200 knights, not counting the other people he brought out of captivity, my lady of Sidon received the bones of Count Walter and had them buried at the Hospital in Acre. She was the cousin of Count Walter and the sister of my lord Walter, lord of Reynel, whose daughter John, lord of Joinville, took as his wife[11] after he returned from overseas. She arranged the service so that each knight offered a candle and a silver *denier*, and the king offered a candle and a gold bezant, all at her own expense. It was very surprising that the king went along with this, since we had never seen him offer anything other than his own money, but he did so this time as a courtesy.

[467] Among the knights my lord John of Valenciennes brought back with him, I discovered at least forty from the court of Champagne. I had *cotes* and green herigauts made for them and brought them before the king. I pleaded with him to be ready to do whatever was necessary to keep them in his service. The king listened to what they asked for and kept his peace. [468] A knight of his council said that I had been wrong to bring such a message to the king, who had spent 7,000 *livres* beyond his means. I told him that no good would come to him from saying things like this. Among those of us from Champagne we had lost at least thirty-five knights, all bannerets from the court of Champagne, and I told him, 'The king will not do well if he listens to you, seeing that he is so short of knights.' After saying this I began to weep heavily, and the king told me to be quiet; he would give the knights what I had asked.

The king took them into his service just as I wished and assigned them to my battalion.

[469] The king replied to the messengers from the Egyptian emirs that he would not make any truce with them unless they sent all the heads of Christians which had hung around the walls of Cairo since the time the count of Bar and the count of Montfort were taken, and unless they also returned all the children who had been captured while small and who had converted. They would also have to quit him of the 200,000 *livres* he still owed them. Along with these messengers to the Egyptian emirs the king sent John of Valenciennes, a distinguished and wise man.

CHAPTER 10

The Crusaders at Caesarea
(Reports Concerning the Tartars)

(March 1251–May 1252)

[470] At the start of Lent[1] the king readied himself and such men as he had to go to restore the fortifications at Caesarea, which had been torn down by the Saracens. Caesarea was twelve leagues from Acre in the direction of Jerusalem. My lord Ralph of Soissons,[2] who had stayed at Acre while he was ill, went with the king to refortify Caesarea. I don't know how it was, unless it was according to God's will, that the Saracens did us no harm during the course of that year. While the king was fortifying Caesarea the envoys returned to us from the Tartars, and I will tell you what news they brought.

[471] As I told you earlier, while the king was staying on Cyprus envoys came to him from the Tartars and gave him to understand that they would help him conquer the kingdom of Jerusalem from the Saracens. The king sent envoys back to them in turn, through whom he sent the Tartars a chapel made of scarlet. In order to draw them to our faith, he had the chapel embroidered to depict all the things in which we believe: the Annunciation of the angel, the Nativity, the baptism of God and the whole Passion, Ascension and coming of the Holy Spirit. He sent chalices, books, and everything needed to perform the Mass, along with two Dominican friars to sing Mass before them. [472] The king's envoys had arrived at the port of Antioch and from Antioch to the great king of the Tartars[3] it was a full year's journey, riding ten leagues a day. They discovered that all this land was subject to the Tartars, and they came across several cities they had destroyed, as well as great heaps of dead men's bones.

[473] The envoys asked how they had attained such power

as to be able to kill and overthrow so many people. This happened, the envoys reported to the king, because of their origins: they had come out of a vast sandy plain in which nothing good would grow. This desert plain began at a vast and wondrous rock face, which lies at the eastern end of the world. No man, according to the Tartars, ever went beyond these rocks, within which the people of Gog and Magog are enclosed, who will come at the end of the world, when Antichrist[4] arrives to destroy everything. [474] The Tartars lived in this plain and were subject to Prester John and the emperor of Persia,[5] whose land was beyond theirs, and to several other infidel kings, to whom they owed annual tribute payments and service in return for pasture for their animals, which were their only means of survival. Prester John, the emperor of Persia and the other kings held the Tartars in such disdain that when they brought their annual payments, the kings refused to receive them face to face, and instead turned their backs on them.

[475] Among the Tartars there was a wise man who scoured the plain and talked to all the worthy men of the deserts and villages, pointing out to them their servile condition and asking them all to give thought to how they could escape the servitude into which they were bound. He was able to gather them all at the edge of the desert, close to Prester John's lands, and explained things to them. Their response to him was that he should make a plan and they would follow it. He said they would not have the means to succeed if they did not have a king and lord over them; he explained to them how they might choose a king, and they were convinced. [476] This was the method: each of the fifty-two tribes should bring him an arrow marked with its name. By agreement of all the people, these fifty-two arrows would be placed in front of a five-year-old child, and the one the child picked up first would signal the tribe from which the king would come. When the child had picked up one of the arrows, the wise man had all the other tribes withdraw, while it was arranged that the tribe from which the king was to come should choose fifty-two of its wisest and best men. When they had been chosen, each man brought an arrow marked with his name. [477] It was then agreed that the

man whose arrow the child picked up would be made king. The child picked up one of them, and it so happened that this was the arrow of the wise man who had instructed them how to proceed. The people were so happy about this that everyone rejoiced. He told them to be quiet and said, 'My lords, if you wish me to be your king, swear to me, by him who made Heaven and Earth, that you will follow my commands.' And they swore to do so.

[478] The laws he gave them were intended to keep peace among the people. They were as follows: that no man should steal from another or strike another if he did not want to lose his hand, and nor should any man sleep with another man's wife or daughter if he did not want to lose his hand or his life. He gave them many other good laws in order to maintain peace.

[479] After he made these orders and arrangements he said to the people, 'My lords, the strongest enemy we have is Prester John, and I command you all to be ready to attack him tomorrow. But if it should so happen that he defeats us, which God forbid, then may each man do the best he can. If we get the better of him, I command that the fighting should last three days and three nights. And may no man be so bold as to turn his hands to looting rather than killing, for after we have victory I will share the booty among you so fairly and honestly that each man will feel satisfied.' Everyone agreed to this.

[480] The next day they attacked their enemies and, as God so willed, defeated them. They killed all those they found armed and able to defend themselves, while they spared those they found wearing religious garb: priests and other men of religion. The other peoples living in the lands of Prester John, who did not take part in the battle, placed themselves in subjection to the Tartars.

[481] One of the princes of the peoples just mentioned was lost for three months without anyone hearing any word of him.[6] When he returned he was neither hungry nor thirsty and believed he had only been away one night at the most. The story he told was that he had climbed a large hill on top of which he found a great number of people. They were the most beautiful people he had ever seen, the most elegantly dressed

and the most finely adorned. At the top of the hill he saw a
king, more beautiful than the others, more elegantly dressed
and more finely adorned, seated on a golden throne. [482] To
his right sat six crowned kings, finely adorned with precious
stones, and the same number to his left. Close by, to his right,
a queen was kneeling; she was speaking and pleading with him
to be mindful of her people. To his left was kneeling a very
handsome man with two wings as radiant as the sun, and
around the king were a great profusion of beautiful winged
people. [483] The king called to the prince and said to him,
'Have you come from the Tartar army?' He replied, 'Yes, indeed
I have.' 'Go to your king and tell him that you have seen me,
the lord of Heaven and Earth, and tell him to offer thanks to
me for the victory I gave him over Prester John and his people.
And tell him from me that I grant him power to subdue the
whole Earth.' 'My lord,' said the prince, 'how will he believe
me?' [484] 'Tell him to believe you by these signs: you are going
to do battle with the emperor of Persia with 300 men, and no
more. So that your great king may believe I have power to do
all things, I will grant victory to overthrow the emperor of
Persia, who will fight you with 3,000 men-at-arms and more.
Before you go into battle with him, ask your king to give you
the priests and other men of religion that he took in the battle
with Prester John. You and all your people must firmly believe
what they teach you.'

[485] 'My lord,' said the prince, 'I will not know the way to
go back unless you give me a guide.' And the king turned
towards a large group of knights, so finely armed that it was a
wonder to behold, called one of them and said, 'George, come
here!' The knight came and knelt, and the king said to him,
'Arise, and take this man safely to his lodgings.' And he did so
in an instant. [486] The moment his men and the rest of the
army saw him they were so overjoyed that no one could describe
it. He asked the great king for the priests and he gave them
to him. This prince and all his people received the priests'
instruction so welcomingly that they were all baptized. After
this he took 300 men-at-arms, had them confess and arm themselves, and set out to attack the emperor of Persia. They

overcame him and drove him from his kingdom, and he fled to the kingdom of Jerusalem. It was this emperor who defeated our people and captured Count Walter of Brienne,[7] as you will hear later.

[487] This Christian prince's people were so numerous that the king's envoys told us that the army had 800 chapels mounted on wagons. The Tartars' lifestyle was such that they did not eat bread at all, and lived off meat and milk. The best meat they have is horsemeat, which they steep in a marinade before drying it, until it can be sliced like black bread. The best drink they have, and the strongest, is mare's milk infused with herbs. The great king of the Tartars was presented with a horse bearing flour, brought from three months' journey away, and he gave it to King Louis's envoys.

[488] The Tartars have many Christian people in their lands who follow the Greek religion;[8] the people ruled over by the Christian prince I have been talking about among others. When the Tartars want to make war on the Saracens, these Christian people are sent to fight them, while they send Saracens against Christians when they are in conflict with them. All manner of childless women go into battle with them; they pay women to fight just as they do the men, according to their vigour. The king's envoys said that the male and female soldiers eat together in the lodgings of the great men they serve. The men dare not touch the women in any way, on account of the law their first king had given them. [489] They eat the flesh of any and every kind of animal that dies in their camp. The women with children take care of and attend to the horses, as well as preparing provisions for the people who are going into battle. The soldiers place raw meat between their saddles and saddle-blankets; when all the blood has been pressed out, they eat it, still completely raw. What they cannot eat they toss into a leather bag, and when they are hungry they open the bag, always eating the oldest piece first. I once encountered a Khwarizmian, one of the emperor of Persia's men who was guarding us in prison, and when he opened his bag we had to hold our noses since we could not stand the stench that came from it.

[490] Now let me return to my subject, and say that when

the great king of the Tartars had received the king's envoys and gifts, he sent for several kings who were not yet subject to him, assuring them safe conduct. He erected the chapel for them and said to them, 'My lords, the king of France has come under our sway: see here the tribute he has sent us. If you do not submit to us, we will send for him to come and overthrow you.' There were a good number of them who, out of fear of the king of France, placed themselves at the mercy of this king.

[491] The king's envoys returned with those of the Tartars, who brought letters from their great king to the king of France. They said, 'Peace is a good thing, for in a peaceful land those who go on four feet eat the grass undisturbed while those who go on two feet work the ground, from which good things come, in tranquillity. [492] We point this out to warn you that you cannot have peace unless you are at peace with us. Prester John rose against us, and other such kings,' – they named a great many – 'and we have put them all to the sword. So we advise you to send us enough gold and silver each year for us to keep thinking of you as friends. If you do not do this we will destroy you and your people as we did those others we mentioned before.' And you may know that the king greatly regretted having sent his envoys to the great king of the Tartars.

[493] Now let me return to my subject, and say that while the king was refortifying Caesarea, my lord Elnart of Seninghem arrived in the camp. He told us that he had hired his ship in the kingdom of Norway, which is at the western edge of the world, and in coming to the king he skirted all of Spain and had to pass through the Straits of Morocco.[9] He came through great danger before reaching us. The king retained him in his service along with his nine other knights. He told us that in the land of Norway the nights were so short in the summer that each night you would see the light of the passing day at sunset at the same time as the light of dawn. [494] He and his men took up hunting lions and caught a number of them at great risk to themselves. They would shoot at the lions as they were spurring their horses on as hard as they could. After they had fired their arrows the lion would pounce at them and would have caught them and eaten them had they not dropped an old piece

of clothing, which the lion leapt upon, tore to shreds and devoured, thinking he had trapped a man. While he was tearing this apart someone else came back to shoot at the lion, which then left the rags to charge at him. But as soon as the man dropped another a piece of cloth, the lion pounced on it. And by doing this the men killed the lions with their arrows.

[495] While the king was refortifying Caesarea, my lord Narjot of Toucy came to him. The king said that Narjot was his cousin, since he was a descendant of one of King Philip's sisters, whom the emperor himself had married.[10] The king retained him and the nine knights with him for a year, and they then returned to Constantinople, from where they had come. He told the king that the emperor of Constantinople and the other great men in the empire were at that time allied with a people called the Cumans, in order to have their help against Vatatzes, who was then emperor of the Greeks.[11] [496] To confirm that each side would aid the other loyally, the emperor and the great men who were at Constantinople with him were required to cut themselves and put their blood into a large silver cup. The king of the Cumans and the other great men who were with him did the same, mixing their blood with our men's and diluting it with wine and water. They drank from it and so did our men. Then they said they were blood brothers. They also made a dog run among our men and theirs; they hacked the dog to bits with their swords and our men did the same. And they said that if one side were to let the other down, they would be torn to pieces in the same way.

[497] My lord of Toucy told us about another highly remark-able thing he saw while he was in the Cumans' camp. A rich knight had died and they had made a deep and wide grave for him in the ground. He was seated in it, nobly attired on a chair. His best horse and his best sergeant were lowered in with him, still alive. Before being placed in the trench with his lord, the sergeant took leave of the king of the Cumans and the other great lords. As he took leave of them they filled his purse with a great quantity of gold and silver and said to him, 'Return what I am giving you to me when I arrive in the other world.' And he said, 'I will do so most willingly.' [498] The great king

of the Cumans gave him a letter addressed to their first king, informing him that this *preudomme* had lived a very good life and performed excellent service and should be rewarded for it. When this was done the sergeant was placed in the grave with his lord and with the horse, still alive, and then they threw planks over the grave and nailed them down firmly, and before they went to bed, everyone in the army ran to bring stones and earth; they made a great mound on top of the men they had buried, in remembrance of them.

[499] While the king was refortifying Caesarea I went to see him in his lodgings. As soon as he saw me come into his chamber, where he was talking to the legate, he got up, took me to one side and said, 'You know that I have only retained you until Easter; will you please tell me what I have to give you in order to keep you with me for a year from then?' I told him I did not want him to give me any more money than he had done already, but that I wanted to make a different bargain with him. [500] 'Since you get angry when you are asked for something,' I said, 'I want you to agree that if I ask for something from you during this year, you will not get angry. And, should you refuse my request, I will not get angry.' Hearing this he began to laugh out loud and said that he would retain me on these terms. He took me by the hand and led me over to the legate and his council and told them about the bargain we had struck. They were very happy about this because I was the richest man in the army.

[501] Hereafter I will tell you how I ordered and arranged my affairs during the four years I stayed in that land after the departure of the king's brothers. I had two chaplains with me who said my hours to me; one of them sung Mass for me as soon as the day's dawn appeared, while the other waited until my knights and the knights attached to my battalion had got up. Once I had heard my Mass I went out with the king. When the king wanted to go out riding, I kept him company, but on a number of occasions messengers came to him and we had to work all morning.

[502] My bed was placed in my pavilion in such a way that no one could enter without seeing me lying on it. I did this to

remove any suspicion with regard to women. When the feast of Saint Rémy[12] approached, I had pigs bought for my pigsty, sheep for my sheepfold, and flour and wine to provide for the household all winter. I did this because supplies became more expensive in winter due to the sea, which is more treacherous in winter than in summer. [503] I bought at least a hundred barrels of wine, and I always had the best one drunk first. I diluted the valets' wine with water and that of the squires with less water. At my own table my knights were provided with a large flask of wine and a large flask of water, and they diluted the wine as they pleased.

[504] The king had placed fifty knights in my battalion. Each time I ate I had ten of these knights at my table along with my own ten. They sat on mats on the ground and ate facing one another, as was customary in that country. Every time someone called us to arms I sent five knights, known as *diseniers*, since this was one man for every ten in the battalion. Every time we rode out in arms, all fifty knights ate in my lodgings on our return. On every feast day of the year I invited all the great men in the army, which meant it was necessary on some occasions for the king to borrow some of my guests.

[505] Hereafter you will hear about the sentences and judgements I saw passed at Caesarea while the king was staying there. First I will tell you about a knight who was caught in a brothel. In accordance with the custom of the country he was offered a choice, which was this: either the prostitute would lead him through the camp by a cord tied round his genitals while he was wearing just his chemise, or he would lose his horse and his armour and be expelled from the camp. The knight surrendered his horse and armour to the king and left the camp. [506] I went to beg the king to give me that horse for a poor gentleman in the army. The king told me this request was not reasonable since the horse was worth at least eighty *livres*. And I replied to him, 'Why have you broken our agreement by getting angry about the request I made of you?' He said to me, laughing, 'Say whatever you like, I am not getting angry.' I did not get the horse for the poor gentleman, however.

[507] The second sentence was this: the knights of our battalion were chasing a wild animal called a gazelle, which is very similar to a deer. The brothers of the Hospital charged at them, drove them off and chased them away. I complained to the master of the Hospital, who replied to me that he would make amends to me in accordance with the custom of the Holy Land, which was such that he would make the brothers who had committed this offence eat sitting on their cloaks until the victims should allow them to get up. [508] The master kept his promise; when we saw that they had been eating while sitting on their cloaks for some time, I went to the master and found him eating his own meal. I asked him to have the brothers who were eating sitting on their cloaks in front of him get up. The knights against whom the offence had been committed also asked him to do so too. He replied to me that he would not do any such thing, since he did not want the brothers to abuse those people who came to the Holy Land on pilgrimage. When I heard this I sat down with the brothers and began to eat with them, and told the master that I would not get up until the brothers did. He told me I was forcing his hand but agreed to my request. He had me and those of my knights who were with me eat with him, while the brothers went to eat with the others at a table.

[509] The third judgement I saw delivered at Caesarea was this: one of the king's sergeants, who was known as the Glutton, laid hands on a knight from my battalion. I went to complain about this to the king. He told me that I could easily overlook this, or so it seemed to him, since the sergeant had only pushed the knight. And I told him that I certainly would not overlook it and that if he did not make amends to me, I would leave his service, since his sergeants pushed knights around. [510] He had amends made to me. And the amends were such, in accordance with the custom of the country, that the sergeant came to my lodgings barefoot, wearing his chemise and breeches and nothing else, and with a naked sword in his hand. He knelt before the knight, took the sword by its point and offered the pommel to the knight, and said, 'My lord, I make amends to you for laying hands on you, and have brought you this sword

so that, if you wish, you can cut off my hand.' I urged the knight to pardon the man's ill temper, and he did so willingly.

[511] The fourth punishment was this: Brother Hugh of Jouy, who was marshal of the Temple, was sent to the sultan of Damascus on behalf of the master of the Temple. He went to negotiate an agreement with the sultan regarding a large area of land formerly held by the Temple. Under their agreement the sultan would hold one half of that land and the Templars the other. Terms were agreed subject to the king's approval. Brother Hugh came back with an emir who was an envoy of the sultan of Damascus, and he brought a written document attesting the agreement. [512] The master of the Temple told the king about this and he was greatly taken aback. He said that the master had been overly bold to have made any agreement or to have held any talks with the sultan without consulting him. The king wanted redress from the master. And this was how redress was given. The king had the side panels of three of his pavilions lifted. Inside were all the people of the army who wished to be present. The master of the Temple and all the brothers came there barefoot right through the camp, because their quarters were outside it. The king made the master sit down in front of him with the sultan's envoy, and addressed the master at the top of his voice: [513] 'Master, you will tell the sultan's envoy that you regret having made any pact with him without speaking to me. And, since you did not consult me, you release him from whatever agreement you made, and return the written record of it to him.' The master took the document, handed it to the emir and then said, 'I return to you this agreement that I made in error, which I regret having done.' The king then told the master to rise and to have all his brothers do likewise, and he did so. 'Now you will kneel,' said the king, 'and make amends to me for having gone against my will.' [514] The master knelt and held out the hem of his mantle to the king, and offered up all that the Temple possessed to be taken as reparation, in whatever way the king should deem fit. 'I command first of all,' said the king, 'that Brother Hugh, who negotiated this agreement, will be banished from the entire kingdom of Jerusalem.' Neither the master, who as godfather

to the count of Alençon (who was born at Château Pèlerin)[13] was very close to the king, nor the queen nor anyone else could help Brother Hugh, and he had to leave the Holy Land and the kingdom of Jerusalem.

CHAPTER II

The Crusaders at Jaffa

(May 1252–June 1253)

[515] While the king was refortifying the city of Caesarea the Egyptian envoys returned to him bringing a treaty, the terms of which had been laid down by the king and were described earlier. The terms agreed between the king and the Egyptians stated that the king had to go on a certain day to Jaffa, while the Egyptian emirs had to swear to be at Gaza on the same day in order to restore the kingdom of Jerusalem to the king. The king and the great men of the army swore to uphold the treaty brought by the envoys, and we were bound on oath to aid them against the sultan of Damascus.

[516] When the sultan of Damascus found out we were allied with the Egyptians, he sent at least 4,000 well-armed Turks to Gaza, where the Egyptians were due to arrive, since he well knew that if they were to join forces with us it might lead to his downfall. Despite this the king did not abandon the march to Jaffa. When the count of Jaffa saw that the king was coming, he readied his castle so that it certainly gave the impression of being a defensible city. On each battlement – of which there were a good 500 – there was a shield bearing his arms and a pennon. This was a fine thing to see, since his arms were of *or* with a cross *patée gules*. [517] We set up camp in the fields around the castle, which was situated on the sea, and we surrounded it from shore to shore. Straightaway the king undertook to fortify a new settlement built around the old castle and extending to the sea on both sides. On numerous occasions I saw the king himself carrying a load of earth to the trenches so that he might receive the indulgence.

[518] The Egyptian emirs broke the terms they had promised

us, since they did not dare go to Gaza because of the forces the sultan of Damascus had there. But they did uphold the agreement in so far as they sent to the king all the heads of Christians they had hung from the walls of the castle at Cairo since the capture of the counts of Bar and Montfort. The king had these buried in consecrated ground. The Egyptians also sent the king the children who had been captured at the same time as him; they were loath to do so because the children had already abjured their faith. Along with them they sent the king an elephant, which he sent on to France.

[519] While we were staying at Jaffa an emir from the sultan of Damascus's forces came to cut down the corn in a village three leagues from our camp. It was decided that we would attack him. When he realized we were coming he took flight. As he was making off, a young man of noble birth gave chase and brought two of his knights to the ground without breaking his lance. But he struck the emir in such a way that his lance snapped off in the man's body.

[520] The envoys of the Egyptian emirs said that if the king would set a day when they could join him, they would come without fail. The king decided he should not refuse them and told them a day; they promised him on oath that they would be at Gaza on that date.

[521] While we waited for the date given by the king to the Egyptian emirs, the count of Eu, who was still a squire at that time, arrived in the camp bringing with him my lord Arnold of Guines, the good knight, and his two brothers. The count had nine men with him in all. He remained in the king's service, and the king made him a knight.

[522] At that time the prince of Antioch[1] returned to the camp with his mother, the princess. The king showed him great honour and knighted him most nobly. He was no more than sixteen years old, but I never encountered a young man so level-headed. He asked the king to give him an audience in his mother's presence, and the king consented. This is what he said to the king, with his mother there to hear it: [523] 'My lord, it is quite true that my mother should continue to act as regent for another four years, but it is not right that she should allow

my land to be run down or abandoned. I am saying this, my lord, because in her hands the city of Antioch is being lost. I beg you, my lord, to ask her to provide me with money and men with which I might go to the aid of my people at Antioch and support them. She certainly should do this, my lord, because great expense would be incurred if I were to stay with her in the city of Tripoli, yet this great expenditure would achieve nothing.' [524] The king listened very willingly, and used all his powers of persuasion with the prince's mother so that she would provide as much as the king could extract from her. As soon as the prince left the king he went to Antioch, where he fulfilled his responsibilities very well. Since he had made the prince a knight, the king gave him permission to quarter his arms, which are *gules*, with those of France.[2]

[525] With the prince came three minstrels from Greater Armenia; they were brothers going on pilgrimage to Jerusalem. They had three horns which made a sound that seemed to come right out of their faces. If you had heard them as they started to play, you would have said that these were the calls of swans taking flight from a lake – they made such sweet and graceful melodies that it was marvellous to hear. [526] They performed three amazing acrobatic feats: a cloth was placed under their feet and, from a standing start, they turned a somersault, landing upright with their feet on the cloth. Two of them did this backwards, and the oldest of them did so too, but when he did it facing forwards he signed himself with the cross, because he was afraid of breaking his neck as he turned.

[527] Because it is a good thing that the memory of the count of Brienne, who was count of Jaffa[3], is not forgotten, I will tell you about him hereafter. He held Jaffa for several years and defended it for a long time through his own vigour. He lived in large part off what he won from the Saracens and enemies of the faith. On one occasion he overcame a great number of Saracens who were carrying cloths of gold and silk; he seized all of it and when he had brought it back to Jaffa, he shared everything among his knights so that there was none left for himself. It was his habit, once he had parted from his knights, to shut himself in his chapel and spend a long time in prayer

before going to lie down with his wife for the night. She was a very virtuous and very wise woman and was the sister of the king of Cyprus.

[528] The emperor of Persia, whose name was Barbaquan and had, as I mentioned earlier, been defeated by one of the Tartar princes, came with his whole army into the kingdom of Jerusalem and captured the castle of Tiberias. It had been fortified by my lord Odo of Montbéliard, the constable, who was lord of Tiberias on behalf of his wife. This did great harm to our people, for the emperor ravaged everything he came across outside Château Pèlerin, Acre, Safad and Jaffa too. And having done this damage he made for Gaza to meet the sultan of Egypt, who had come there to torment and plunder our people.

[529] The barons of the kingdom and the patriarch decided that they should go and attack the emperor before the sultan of Egypt arrived. They sent for the sultan of Hims[4] to help them. He was one of the best knights in all the infidel lands, and they greeted him with such honour in Acre that cloth of gold and silk was laid on the ground everywhere he went. Our people and the sultan went together to Jaffa. [530] The patriarch had excommunicated Count Walter because he refused to return a tower at Jaffa called the Tower of the Patriarch to him. Our men pleaded with Count Walter to go with them to fight the emperor of Persia, and he said he would do so willingly if the patriarch would absolve him until they returned. The patriarch refused to do so, but the count set off and went with them nonetheless. Our men were in three battalions, one of which was Count Walter's, another the sultan of Hims', while the last was that of the patriarch and the barons of that land. The Hospitallers were in the count of Brienne's battalion.

[531] They rode out until their enemy came into sight. As soon as our people saw them they stopped, and the enemy did likewise. They also formed three battalions. While the Khwarizmians organized their forces, Count Walter came to our men and cried out to them, 'My lords, for God's sake, let's go at them – we're giving them time by stopping!' But they all refused to take any notice of him. [532] Seeing this, Count Walter went to the patriarch and requested absolution from him as I have

already described, but the patriarch refused to do so. The count of Brienne had with him a valiant clergyman who was the bishop of Ramla and had performed many fine knightly deeds alongside the count, and he said to him, 'My lord, don't let it trouble your conscience that the patriarch does not absolve you, since he's in the wrong and you're in the right. I absolve you in the name of the Father, and of the Son, and of the Holy Spirit. Now let's get at them!' [533] They spurred on and attacked the emperor of Persia's battalion, which was in the rearguard. A very great number of people on both sides were killed there and Count Walter was captured. This happened because all our men fled shamefully; some of them were so desperate in their flight that they were drowned in the sea. This despair came upon them when one of the emperor of Persia's battalions faced the sultan of Hims; the sultan defended himself vigorously but of the 2,000 Turks he had taken there, only 280 remained when he left the field.

[534] The emperor decided to go and lay siege to the sultan in the castle of Hims, since it seemed that the sultan would not be able to hold out for long after having lost so many men. When the sultan realized what was happening he came to his people and told them he was going to go to fight the emperor's army, for if he allowed them to lay a siege he would be lost. He arranged things so that all his poorly armed men were sent into a hidden valley from where, as soon as they heard the sultan's drums sounded, they attacked the emperor's camp from the rear and began to kill the women and children. [535] The emperor had gone out into open country to fight the sultan and had him in sight, but no sooner did he hear the cries of his people than he returned to his camp to rescue the women and children. The sultan and his men then attacked them, and to good effect; of the 25,000 of them there was left neither man nor woman. They were all put to the sword and killed.

[536] Before the emperor of Persia approached Hims, he had brought Count Walter outside Jaffa and hung him by his arms from a gibbet. They told him that they would not cut him down until they were in possession of the castle of Jaffa. As he was hanging there by his arms Count Walter cried out to the people

in the castle that they should not surrender the town no matter what harm the Persians did to him, and that if they did surrender it he himself would kill them.

[537] When the emperor saw this, he sent Count Walter to Cairo as a gift to the sultan, along with the master of the Hospital and several other prisoners he had taken. At least 300 of the emperor's men escorted the count to Cairo and therefore were not killed when the emperor died outside Hims. These Khwarizmians lined up against us on the Friday,[5] coming to attack us while we were on foot. Their banners were red with a jagged edge right back to the lance, and they had heads made out of hair on their lances that looked like the heads of devils.

[538] A number of the merchants of Cairo appealed to the sultan to impose justice on Count Walter for the great harm he had done to them. The sultan gave them leave to go and take vengeance on him, and they went to torment and kill him in the prison. We may believe that because of this he is among the number of the martyrs in Heaven.

[539] The sultan of Damascus took his forces that were at Gaza and went into Egypt. The emirs came to fight him. The sultan's battalion defeated the emirs they faced, while the other battalion of the Egyptian emirs overcame the sultan of Damascus's rearguard. The sultan, who was wounded in the head and the hand, retreated to Gaza. Before he left Gaza the Egyptian emirs sent envoys to the sultan and made peace with him. They broke all their agreements with us and from that time onwards, we had neither peace nor truce with the rulers of Damascus or of Egypt. And know that even when we had our greatest number of men-at-arms there were never more than 1,400 of them.

[540] While the king encamped outside Jaffa, the master of Saint Lazarus[6] spotted cattle and other things he thought might be seized as bountiful plunder at a location near Ramla, three leagues away. Since he had no formal position within the army, he did whatever he liked without talking to the king, and so off he went. When he had gathered his booty the Saracens attacked him, and overcame him so thoroughly that of all the men with him in his battalion only four escaped. [541] As soon as he got

back to the camp he raised a call to arms. I went to arm myself and asked the king to allow me to go; he gave me permission and told me I should take the Templars and Hospitallers with me. When we arrived, we found that the valley where the master of Saint Lazarus had been defeated had been invaded by a different group of Saracens. While these Saracens were examining the corpses, the master of the king's crossbowmen attacked them, and before we could get there our men had overcome them, killing several of them.

[542] One of the king's sergeants and one of the Saracens had brought each other to the ground with lance blows. Another of the king's sergeants, seeing this, seized the two men's horses and started to lead them away to steal them. He hid inside the city walls of Ramla so that no one would see him, but as he was leading them away, an old cistern he was passing over collapsed underneath him. Someone told me that he and the three horses had fallen to the bottom. I went to take a look and saw that the cistern was still collapsing around them; they narrowly escaped being completely buried. But we returned without any losses besides those of the master of Saint Lazarus.

[543] As soon as the sultan of Damascus had made peace with the Egyptians, he ordered those of his men who were at Gaza to return to him. As they did so they passed within less than two leagues of our camp. They never dared to attack us, even though they were 20,000 Saracens and 10,000 Bedouins. Before they came close to our camp, the king's master of crossbowmen and his battalion had kept watch over them for three days and three nights, so that they might not make a surprise attack on our army.

[544] On Saint John's Day, after Easter,[7] the king was listening to his sermon. While it was being delivered one of the master of crossbowmen's sergeants came into the king's chapel, fully armed, and told him that the Saracens had surrounded the master. I asked the king to allow me to go and he gave me permission, saying that I should take with me as many as 400 or 500 men-at-arms. He named those he wished me to take. As soon as we left the camp the Saracens who had cut the master of crossbowmen off from the camp went to join an emir who,

along with at least 1,000 men-at-arms, was in position on a knoll in front of the master of crossbowmen. [545] Fighting began between the Saracens and the master of crossbowmen's sergeants, of whom there were around 280. Each time the emir saw that his men were being hard pressed, he sent so many men as reinforcements that our sergeants were forced back on to the master's battalion. When the master saw that his men were under pressure, he sent them 100 or 120 men-at-arms who, in turn, forced the Saracens back on to the emir's battalion.

[546] While we were there the legate and the barons of that land, who had stayed with the king, told him he had been very foolish when he had put me in harm's way. On their advice the king sent to recall me and the master of crossbowmen too. The Turks took themselves off, and we returned to the camp. Many people were amazed that they did not come and attack us, and some said that they would not have held back were it not for the fact that they and their horses had all been short of food at Gaza, where they had stayed for nearly a year.

[547] When these Saracens had moved on from the region outside Jaffa, they arrived before Acre and told the lord of Arsuf, who was constable of the kingdom of Jerusalem, that they would destroy the city's gardens if he did not send them 50,000 bezants. He informed them that he would not send them anything. Then the Saracens drew up their battalions all along the sands of Acre, so close to the city that you could have fired at them with a frame-mounted crossbow. The lord of Arsuf came out of the city to defend the gardens and took up position on Saint John's Mount, where the cemetery of Saint Nicholas is located. Our unmounted sergeants came out of Acre and started to harass the Saracens using bows and crossbows.

[548] The lord of Arsuf called for a Genoese knight whose name was my lord John le Grand and ordered him to go to retrieve the members of the rank and file who had left Acre, so that they might not put themselves in danger. While he was bringing them back, a Saracen began to call out to him in the Saracen language that he would joust with him if he wished, and John said that he would do so gladly. As my lord John made off towards the Saracen to joust, he looked over to his

left and saw a small troop of Turks, at least eight of them, who
had stopped to watch the encounter. [549] He abandoned his
joust with the Saracen who had challenged him and made for
this group of Turks, who were standing still to watch the joust.
He struck one of them right through his body, throwing him
down dead. When the others saw this they charged at my lord
John. As he was coming back in the direction of our people,
one of them struck him a great mace blow on his iron cap. As
the man passed, my lord John's sword caught the cloth wrapped
round his head, sending the turban flying into the fields. (They
wore these turbans when they fought because they can withstand heavy sword blows.) [550] Another of the Turks spurred
at him, aiming to strike him between the shoulders with his
lance. My lord John, seeing the lance coming, swerved out of
the way, and as the Saracen passed he gave a back-handed blow
with his sword against the man's arm which sent the lance flying
into the fields. Thus John returned, leading his foot soldiers. He
struck these three fine blows in front of the lord of Arsuf and
the great men who were at Acre, and in front of all the women
who were on the walls of the city to observe the Saracens.

[551] This large force of Saracens outside Acre dared not
fight us (as you heard earlier) or the people of Acre. But when
they heard it said, and it was true, that the king had undertaken
to have the town of Sidon fortified, and with just a few good
men-at-arms, they set out in that direction. When lord Simon
of Montceliard, master of the king's crossbowmen and commander of the king's men at Sidon, found out that this force
was on its way, he retreated to the city's castle, which is very
strong and surrounded by the sea on all sides. He did so because
he knew well that he did not have the means to resist them. He
sheltered as many people with him as he could, but this was
only a few since the castle was very small. [552] The Saracens
launched themselves on the town, encountering no resistance
because it was only partially enclosed by walls. They killed
more than 2,000 of our people and made off for Damascus
with the plunder they had seized. When the king heard this
news he was furious – if only he could have made up for the
loss! This worked out well for the barons of the kingdom of

Jerusalem, since the king had wanted to go and fortify a hill where once, in the time of the Maccabees, there had been an ancient fortress.[8] This castle was located on the road from Jaffa to Jerusalem. [553] The barons of Outremer disagreed with the plan to refortify this castle. It was five leagues from the sea which meant that no provisions could reach us from the coast; they would be seized by the Saracens, who were stronger than we were. When the news reached the camp from Sidon that the town had been destroyed, the barons of the land came to the king and told him that it would do him more honour if he were to refortify Sidon, which the Saracens had destroyed, than to build a new fortress. The king agreed with them.

[554] While the king was at Jaffa he was told that the sultan of Damascus would allow him to go to Jerusalem under a safe conduct. The king held lengthy deliberations to discuss the offer. In the end no one advised him to go, since he would have to leave Jerusalem in the hands of the Saracens.

[555] The king was presented with an example. When the great King Philip departed from before Acre to go to France, he left all his people behind in the camp with Duke Hugh of Burgundy (the grandfather of the duke who died recently).[9] While the duke remained at Acre with King Richard of England, news reached them that they could take Jerusalem the following day if they so wished; all the sultan of Damascus's knights had gone to join him in a war he was waging against another sultan. They readied their armies: the king of England's was the first battalion and the duke of Burgundy came after with the king of France's men. [556] Once they saw that they were in a position to take the city, the king was informed by the duke's forces that he should not go any further; the duke was withdrawing, for the sole reason that it might not be said that the English had taken Jerusalem. While they were having this discussion, one of the king's knights called out to him, 'My lord, my lord, come here and I will show you Jerusalem!' And when he heard this the king threw his *surcote* over his eyes as he wept, and said to Our Lord, 'Dear Lord God, I beg you not to let me see your holy city, since I cannot deliver it from the hands of your enemies.'

[557] This example was presented to the king because if he, the greatest Christian king, were to make his pilgrimage without delivering the city from the enemies of God, all the other kings and all the other pilgrims who came after him would think it was acceptable to make their pilgrimage just as the king of France had done, and would be unconcerned about the deliverance of Jerusalem.

[558] King Richard performed so many feats of arms in his time overseas that when the Saracens' horses took fright at a bush, their masters would say to them, 'Do you think it's King Richard of England?' And when the Saracen women's children cried, they would be told, 'Be quiet! Be quiet! Or I'll go and find King Richard, who'll kill you.'

[559] The duke of Burgundy about whom I have told you was a physically very able knight, but he was never thought of as wise in matters pertaining to either God or the world, as was demonstrated by the incident mentioned before. The great King Philip alluded to this when he was told that Count John of Chalon had a son who was named Hugh after the duke of Burgundy. The king asked that God might make him 'as brave a man' as the duke from whom he took the name Hugh. [560] King Philip was asked why he had not said 'as much a *preudomme*'. 'Because,' said the king, 'there is a great difference between a "brave man" and a "*preudomme*".[10] For there are many brave knights in the land of the Christians and the Saracens who have never believed in God or his Mother. And because of this I tell you,' he said, 'that God gives a great gift and great grace to the Christian knight whom he allows to be valiant in body and whom he permits to be in his service, by protecting him from mortal sin. He who conducts himself thus should be called "*preudomme*", since this prowess comes as a gift from God. Those of whom I spoke before can be called "brave men", since they are brave in body but fear neither God nor sin.'

[561] It is impossible to speak of the great quantities of money the king spent in fortifying Jaffa since they were beyond measure. He built a wall with twenty-four towers round the town, from the sea on one side of it to the sea on the other,

while the trenches inside and outside the walls were cleared of mud. There were three gates, one of which was built by the legate, along with a section of the wall. [562] To demonstrate to you the great expense to which the king went, I will tell you that I asked the legate how much that gate and section of wall had cost him. He asked me how much I thought it had cost, and I guessed that the gate he had had built cost him at least 500 *livres*, and the section of wall 300 *livres*. He told me – may God help him – that the gate and section of wall had cost him a good 30,000 *livres*.

CHAPTER 12

The Crusaders at Sidon

(June 1253–April 1254)

[563] When the king had finished the fortification of the town of Jaffa, he decided he would go and restore the fortifications at the city of Sidon, which the Saracens had torn down. He set off to go there on the feast of the apostles Saint Peter and Saint Paul,[1] and the king and his army camped outside the castle of Arsuf, which was a very strong one. That evening the king summoned his men and told them that, if they would agree to it, he would go and capture one of the Saracens' cities, which was called Nablus. This city is called Samaria in ancient scripture.[2] [564] The Templars, Hospitallers and the barons of the land were agreed in their response: it would be good to try to take that city but they would never consent to the king's going there in person, since if anything were to happen to him the whole land would be lost. The king said that he would not let them go at all if he was not going with them. Because of this the plan went no further, since the lords of that land refused to agree to his going.

[565] After several days on the march we arrived at the sands of Acre, where the king and his army set up camp. While we were there a large group of people from Greater Armenia approached me. They were going on pilgrimage to Jerusalem, having paid a large fee to the Saracens who were escorting them there. Through an interpreter who knew their language and ours they begged that I might show them the saintly king. [566] I went to where the king was sitting in a tent, leaning against the tent pole; he was sitting on the sand without a carpet or anything else beneath him. I said to him, 'My lord, there's a large crowd of people from Greater Armenia outside who are

going to Jerusalem. They have asked me, my lord, to show them the saintly king, but I've no desire to kiss your bones just yet!' He laughed out loud and told me that I should go and fetch them, and so I did. And when they had seen the king they commended him to God, and he them.

[567] Next day the army rested at a place called Colt's Crossing, where there are many fine springs which are used to water the plants that produce sugar. As we were encamped there one of my knights said to me, 'My lord, I've set up your tents for you in a nicer spot than the one you had yesterday.' Another knight, who had chosen the previous site for me jumped up, enraged, and shouted at him at the top of his voice, 'How dare you talk about what I've done like that!' And he leapt at the other knight, seizing him by the hair. I shot to my feet and struck the second knight between the shoulders with my fist. He let his colleague go, and I said to him, 'Now get out of my quarters for, so help me God, you'll never be in my service again!' [568] The knight took himself off, looking utterly dejected, but he came back to me with my lord Giles le Brun, constable of France. Because my lord Giles saw that the knight was very sorry for his foolish behaviour, he pleaded with me as earnestly as he could to take him back into my household. I replied that I would not do so unless the legate absolved me of my oath. They went to the legate and told him how things stood. He told them that he was not able to absolve me since the oath was a reasonable one – the knight had certainly deserved it. I am telling you about this to put you on your guard against making an ill-advised oath. For, as the wise man says, 'He who swears readily will readily be forsworn.'

[569] The following day the king went and set up camp before the city of Sur, which is called Tyre in the Bible. There the king called the great men of the army to him and asked their advice as to whether it would be good for him to go and capture the town of Banyas before going to Sidon. We all thought that it would be good for the king to send some of his men, but no one was in favour of his going there in person. It was only with great difficulty that he was dissuaded from doing so. It was thus agreed that the count of Eu would go with

my lord Philip of Montfort the lord of Tyre, my lord Giles le Brun the constable of France, my lord Peter the Chamberlain, the master of the Temple and the members of his order, and the master of the Hospital and the brothers of his order too.

[570] We armed ourselves at nightfall and arrived a little after the break of day in a plain before the town called Banyas, which is called Caesarea Philippi in ancient scripture. A spring called Jor issues forth in the city while another, very fine spring, called Dan issues forth on the plains outside it. When the streams from these two springs meet, they are called the River Jordan, in which God was baptized.

[571] By the agreement of the Templars and of the count of Eu, of the Hospital and of those barons of that land who were present, it was decided that the king's battalion should advance between the castle and the town. I was in this battalion at that time (since the king had retained the forty knights of my own battalion) along with the *preudomme* my lord Geoffrey of Sergines. The men from that land would enter the city from the left-hand side and the Hospitallers from the right, while the Templars would enter the town straight ahead along the road by which we had arrived.

[572] We kept moving until we came near to Banyas and found that the Saracens there had overwhelmed the king's sergeants and driven them from the town. Seeing this, I went to the *preudommes* who were with the count of Eu and said to them, 'My lords, if you don't come to where we were directed, between the town and the castle, the Saracens will kill those of our men who have entered the town.' The going was very treacherous since the place we needed to reach was so perilously situated; there were three pairs of dry walls to pass, the bank was so steep that a horse could barely keep its footing, and the small hill we had to reach was guarded by a great number of Turks on horseback. [573] While I was speaking to these men I saw that our unmounted sergeants were breaking down the walls. When I saw this, I told my companions that it had been commanded that the king's battalion should go to where that body of Turks was, and since we were under orders, I would go. I and my two knights set off in the direction of the men

who were breaching the walls; I saw one mounted sergeant who thought he could cross the wall, but his horse fell on top of him. When I saw this I got down on foot and took my horse by the bridle. When the Turks saw us coming, as God so willed it, they abandoned the position we had been instructed to reach. From that spot where the Turks had been a sheer rock face dropped down into the city.

[574] Once we were there, the Turks having left, the Saracens inside the town gave up all hope and abandoned the town to our people without a fight. While I was there the marshal of the Temple heard that I was in danger and so he climbed up towards me. As I was high up on that hill, the Germans who were in the count of Eu's battalion came up after me, and when they saw the mounted Turks fleeing towards the castle, they set off to go after them. I told them, 'My lords, what you're doing is wrong – we're in the place we were commanded to take and you're going beyond your orders.'

[575] The castle that sits above the town is named Subayba, and is set a good half a league up into the mountains of Lebanon. The hill that rises up to the castle is scattered with rocks as large as great chests. When the Germans realized they were foolish to be giving chase, they turned back. Seeing this the Saracens attacked them on foot, striking great mace blows at them, from on top of the rocks, and tearing off their horses' caparisons. [576] Realizing our unfortunate situation the sergeants who were with us began to get scared. I told them that if they ran away I would have them thrown out of the king's service for good. And they said to me, 'My lord, we're not playing by the same rules: you're on horseback if you should choose to flee, but we're on foot and the Saracens will kill us.' I said to them, 'My lords, I assure you I am not going to flee, for I will stay with you, on foot.' I dismounted and sent my horse over to the Templars, who were the length of a good crossbow-shot behind us. [577] As the Germans retreated the Saracens hit one of my knights, whose name was my lord John of Bussy, in the throat with a crossbow bolt, and he fell down dead right in front of me. His uncle, my lord Hugh of Ecot, who had shown his great worth in the Holy Land, said to me,

'My lord, come and help us bring my nephew down from there.'
'I wish bad luck,' I said, 'on whoever does help you. You went
up there without my command. If any harm has come to you
it was well deserved. You take him down to the rubbish heap,
but I'm not moving from here until someone sends for me.'

[578] When my lord John of Valenciennes heard what danger
we were in, he went to my lord Oliver of Termes and the other
leading men of the Languedoc and said to them, 'My lords, I
urge and command you on behalf of the king to help me fetch
the seneschal.' While my lord John was securing assistance my
lord William of Beaumont came to him and said, 'There's no
point bothering with that, for the seneschal is dead.' John of
Valenciennes replied to him, 'Whether dead or alive, I will take
news of him to the king.' Then he set off and came in our direction, to where we'd climbed up on the mountain. As soon as he
reached us, he asked me to come to speak to him, and so I did.

[579] Then my lord Oliver of Termes told me that we were
in great peril in that place. It would not be possible for us to
go back down the way we had come up without great danger,
since the bank was so treacherous and the Saracens would bear
down on us. 'But if you are willing to trust me I will get you
away from here without loss.' And I told him that he should
make whatever plan he wanted, and I would go along with it.
[580] 'I'll tell you,' he said, 'how we're going to escape. We'll
follow the whole length of this slope – just as if we were going
towards Damascus – and the Saracens over there will think we
want to attack them from the rear. Once we're on the plain
we'll spur on round the city, crossing the stream before they
can catch up with us. And we'll do great harm to them too,
because we'll set fire to the threshed corn in those fields.'
[581] We did just as he told us; he had us take canes (the kind
from which flutes are made), put coals inside them and set them
among the threshed corn. In this way God brought us back to
safety through the quick thinking of Oliver of Termes. And
know that when we arrived at the camp where our people were,
we discovered that none of them was armed since no one was
concerned about our situation. The next day we returned to
Sidon, where the king was.

[582] We discovered that the king himself had undertaken to have the bodies of the Christians that the Saracens had killed (as was described earlier) buried. He had personally carried the bodies, all rotting and stinking, to place them in trenches in the ground, and he never once covered his nose, although others did so. He had workers come from all around and he set about refortifying the city with high walls and large towers. And when we arrived in the camp we found that he himself had marked out for us the places where we should set up our tents. He assigned me a place alongside that of the count of Eu since he knew that the count enjoyed my company.

[583] I will tell you some of the pranks the count of Eu played on us. I had set up my quarters so that I ate with my knights in the light of a doorway. The door faced the count of Eu's lodgings and he, being very inventive, made a little catapult that he used to throw things at us. He kept a lookout until we sat down to eat and positioned his catapult within range of our table. Then he had it fired, breaking our pots and glasses. I am not sure who had given the count a young bear, but once, after I had acquired a number of hens and capons, he let it loose among them; it had killed a dozen of them before anyone arrived. The woman who looked after the birds beat the bear off with her stick.

[584] While the king was fortifying Sidon, merchants arrived in the camp who told us that the king of the Tartars had captured the city of Baghdad and the Saracens' pope, the lord of that town, who was called the caliph of Baghdad.[3] The merchants related to us the manner in which they had taken the city of Baghdad and its caliph, which was this: when the king of the Tartars had laid siege to the caliph's city, he informed the caliph that he would be willing to arrange a marriage between the caliph's children and his own. The caliph's advisers urged him to agree to the marriage. [585] The king of the Tartars instructed the caliph to send up to forty of his councillors and most eminent men to swear to the marriage, and he did so. Again the king of the Tartars ordered him to send forty of the richest and best men he had, and the caliph did so. A third time the king commanded the caliph to send forty of the best men

he had and the caliph did so. Seeing that he had all the leading men of Baghdad the king of the Tartars concluded that the lower-ranking people of the city would not be able to defend themselves without leadership. He had all 120 great men beheaded and then attacked the town, capturing it and the caliph too.

[586] To hide his treachery and to throw blame on to the caliph for the capture of the city, the king of the Tartars had the caliph taken and put into an iron cage, denying him food for as long as it is possible to do so without killing a man. The king then asked him if he was hungry, and the caliph said yes, which was no wonder. At that point the king of the Tartars had a great golden platter loaded with jewellery, studded with precious stones, brought before the caliph and he said to him, 'Do you recognize these jewels?' And the caliph replied yes, 'They were mine.' The king asked if he loved them very much, and the caliph replied that he did. [587] 'Since you love them so much,' said the king of the Tartars, 'take as many as you want, and eat.' The caliph replied that he could not, since this was not food that could be eaten. Then the king said, 'Now you can see how you might have defended yourself. If you had given your treasure – which is no longer of any use to you – to fighting men, spending your riches would have meant you were well defended against us. But now they have let you down in the greatest need you have ever known.'

[588] While the king was fortifying Sidon, I went to hear the Mass performed for him at daybreak. He told me I should wait for him because he wanted to go out riding, and I did so. Once we were out in the fields we came across a little church and saw, while still on horseback, that a priest was singing the Mass. The king told me this church had been built in honour of the miracle that God performed in casting out the Devil from the body of the widow's daughter.[4] He said that if I was willing he would go inside to listen to the Mass begun by the priest. I told him I thought this would be a good thing to do. [589] When the time came to give the kiss of peace, I noticed that the clerk who was assisting in singing the Mass was large, dark, thin and hairy. I was worried that if he brought the pax,

it might turn out that he was one of those wicked Assassins, and he would be able to kill the king. I went to take the pax from the clerk and carried it to the king. When the Mass had been sung and we had mounted our horses, we encountered the legate in the fields. The king went up to him and called me over, and said to the legate, 'I wish to complain to you about the seneschal; he brought the pax to me and refused to let the poor clerk there offer it to me.' [590] I told the legate the reason why I had done so, and he said I had acted very properly. The king replied, 'Most certainly not.' There was a heated discussion between them during which I kept quiet. I have related this incident to you so that you might see the king's great humility. The Evangelist speaks of the miracle that God performed for the widow's daughter, saying that God was, when this happened, *in parte Tyri et Sidonis*, because at that time the city of Sur that I have mentioned was called Tyre, while the city of Sayette that I have mentioned was called Sidon.

[591] While the king was fortifying Sidon, envoys came to him from a great lord from distant Greece, who styled himself the Grand Comnenus, lord of Trebizond.[5] They brought a variety of jewels as a gift to the king. Among other things they brought bows made of horn, with nocks to hold the string screwed into the bow.[6] When the bows were drawn these nocks showed themselves to be very precisely cut and well made. [592] They asked the king to send their lord a young woman from his household so that he might marry her. The king replied that he had not brought any such women with him from over-seas and suggested they might go to the emperor at Constantinople, the king's cousin, and ask him to provide them with a wife for their lord who would be of both the emperor's and the king's line. He did this because the emperor had an alliance with this great and wealthy man against Vatatzes, who was at that time emperor of the Greeks.

[593] Queen Margaret, who had recently recovered from the birth of my lady Blanche, who was born at Jaffa,[7] arrived at Sidon by sea. When I got word that she had arrived I got up from the king's presence and went to meet her and escort her to the castle. [594] When I returned to the king, who was in his

chapel, he asked whether the queen and the children were well, and I told him they were. He said to me, 'When you got up from my presence I was sure you were going to meet the queen and because of that I delayed the sermon for you.' I am telling you these things because I had already spent five years with him, and never yet had I heard him speak about the queen or the children to me or anyone else. And it seems to me that this conduct was not becoming, to be so distant from his wife and his children.

[595] On All Saints' Day[8] I invited all the great men of the army to my lodgings, which were by the sea. A poor knight came there in a boat along with his wife and four sons. I had them come and eat in my lodgings. When we had eaten, I called the rich men together and told them, 'Let's do a really good deed and remove the burden of his children from this man. If each of you will take one, so will I.' Each of the great men chose one of the children, and they were fighting with each other over them. When the poor knight saw this he and his wife began to weep with joy. [596] It so happened that when the count of Eu returned from eating at the king's lodgings, he came to see the great men who were in my quarters and took my child, who was twelve years old, away from me. That boy served the count so well and so loyally that when we returned to France, the count arranged a marriage for him and made him a knight. And every time the count and I happened to be in the same place, the young man could barely tear himself away from me. He said to me, 'My lord, may God reward you, for it was you who placed me in this honourable position.' I do not know what became of the three other brothers.

[597] I asked the king to permit me to go on pilgrimage to Our Lady of Tortosa.[9] This was a very popular place of pilgrimage because it was the first altar ever to be built on Earth in honour of the Mother of God. And Our Lady performed great miracles there. Among other miracles there was once a man who was out of his mind, who had the Devil in his body. As his friends who had brought him to the shrine were praying to the Mother of God to give him health, the enemy within him replied to them, 'Our Lady is not here. She is in Egypt to help

the king of France and the Christians, who will today arrive in that country on foot to face the mounted infidels.' [598] The miracle was recorded in writing that very day and was reported to the legate, who told me about it with his own mouth. And you may be certain that she did help us and would have helped us more if we had not angered her and her Son, as I mentioned to you before.

[599] The king gave me permission to go there and told me in great confidence that I should buy a hundred lengths of camelin in various colours to give to the Franciscans when we arrived in France. This set my heart at ease, for I was sure he would not stay much longer overseas. When we arrived at Tripoli my knights asked me what I intended to do with the lengths of camelin, and begged me to tell them. 'Perhaps,' I said, 'I've stolen them to make some money.'

[600] The prince[10] – may God absolve him – gave us the warmest welcome and showed us as much honour as he could, and would have given lavish gifts to me and my knights, if we had been willing to take them. But we refused to take anything besides some of his relics, which I took to the king with the lengths of camelin I had purchased for him.

[601] I also sent four lengths of camelin to my lady the queen. The knight who took them to her carried them wrapped in a white cloth. When the queen saw him come into her chamber, she knelt before him, and the knight in turn knelt down before her. The queen said to him, 'Get up, lord knight, you do not have to kneel when you are carrying relics.' But the knight said, 'My lady, these are not relics, rather pieces of camelin that my lord is sending to you.' When the queen and her ladies-in-waiting heard this, they began to laugh and the queen said to my knight, 'Tell your lord that this will be a sorry day for him, seeing as he made me kneel before his camelin.'

[602] While the king was at Sidon someone brought him a stone that split into fragments. It was the most marvellous stone in the world because when you lifted off a fragment, you found the form of a sea-fish between the two pieces. The fish was made of stone but its form lacked nothing – not eyes, not bones, not colour or anything else. It was just the same as if it were

alive. The king gave me a stone and I found a tench inside, brown in colour and made just as a tench should be.

[603] At Sidon news reached the king that his mother was dead.[11] He displayed such profound grief that for two days no one could speak to him. After that he sent one of his chamber valets to fetch me. Once he saw that I had come into his presence in his chamber, where he was all alone, he reached out his arms and said to me, 'Ah! Seneschal, I have lost my mother!' [604] 'My lord, that doesn't surprise me,' I said, 'since she had to die. But I am surprised that you, a man of good sense, have demonstrated such great sadness. For you know that the wise man says that a man should not allow whatever distress he has in his heart to appear on his face, because he who does so makes his enemies happy and his friends upset.' He had many splendid services held overseas, and afterwards he sent a pack-horse to France, loaded with letters to churches asking that they might pray for his mother.

[605] My lady Marie of Vertus – a very virtuous lady and a very pious woman – came to tell me that the queen appeared to be in the depths of grief and asked me to go and comfort her. When I got there I found she was crying, and I told her that the man who said you should not depend on a woman spoke the truth, 'For it is the woman whom you most hated who is dead, and yet you show such grief.' She told me that she was not crying for the queen but for the king, who was overwrought by his displays of grief, and for her daughter (later the queen of Navarre)[12] who was left in the guardianship of men.

[606] The harshness of Queen Blanche towards Queen Margaret was such that Queen Blanche had used all her powers to prevent her son being in his wife's company except in the evening when he went to bed with her. The residence that both the king and Queen Margaret most liked to stay at was at Pontoise, because there the king's chamber was on an upper floor, with the queen's chamber directly below. [607] They had arranged things so that they would hold their conversations in a spiral staircase that led from one chamber to the other, and they had organized it so that when the ushers saw Queen Blanche coming to her son the king's chamber, they would

knock on the door with their staffs, and the king would run to his chamber to ensure that his mother would find him there. The ushers outside Queen Margaret's chamber did the same thing when Queen Blanche was approaching, so that she would find Queen Margaret there.

[608] On one occasion the king was at the side of the queen his wife, who was in great danger of dying because she had been injured during childbirth. Queen Blanche came and took her son by the hand and said to him: 'Come away, you've no business here.' When Queen Margaret saw that his mother was leading the king away, she called out, 'Alas! You won't let me see my lord whether I live or die!' And then she passed out and people thought she was dead. The king, thinking she was dying, came back, and with great difficulty she was brought round.

[609] At the point when the city of Sidon was nearly completely fortified, the king had several processions performed inside the camp. At the end of the processions the legate had people pray that God might direct the king's affairs according to his will, so that the king might do what was most pleasing to God, whether to return to France or to stay overseas.

[610] One day, after these processions had been held, the king called me into a garden from where I had been sitting with the great men of that land, and he made me turn my back on them. Then the legate said to me, 'Seneschal, the king is very pleased with your service, and would very gladly ensure your profit and honour. And to set your mind at rest he told me that I should let you know he has set his affairs in order to return to France this coming Easter.' And I replied to him, 'May God let him do his will in this way!'

[611] The legate then got up and said that I should accompany him to his lodgings, which I did. There he shut himself away – just him and me, nobody else – in the place where he kept his robes. He took both my hands in his and began to weep most heavily. Once he was able to speak he said to me, 'Seneschal, I am very happy and give thanks to God that the king, you and the other pilgrims may escape from the great peril you have faced in this land. But I am very uneasy in my heart that I must leave your godly company and go to the court

of Rome, among the unfaithful people there. [612] However, I'll tell you what I'm proposing to do. I'm thinking of arranging matters so that I can stay behind for a year after you, in the hopes of spending all my funds on fortifying the suburbs of Acre. That way I can quite clearly show the people at Rome that I'm not bringing back any money, and they won't come running after me looking for handouts.'

[613] I once reported to the legate two sins about which one of my priests had informed me. And he replied to me in this way: 'No one knows as much as I do how shameful the sins committed here in Acre are. Because of this it is fitting that God should take vengeance on them in such a way that the city of Acre be washed with the blood of its people, and that other people should come to live there.' The *preudomme*'s prophecy was fulfilled, at least in part, for the city was certainly washed in the blood of its inhabitants.[13] But those people who should live there have not yet arrived. May God send good people, such as will be to his liking!

[614] After this the king sent for me and ordered me to go and arm myself, and my knights too. I asked him why, and he said this was in order to take the queen and his children as far as Tyre, seven leagues away. I did not raise any objection, even though this was a most dangerous undertaking seeing as we had neither truce nor peace with the people of either Egypt or Damascus. We arrived in peace by nightfall without any problem – God be thanked – although we twice had to get down from our horses in enemy territory to make a fire and cook food in order to feed and nurse the children.

[615] When the king left the city of Sidon, which he had fortified with high walls and large towers and with wide, clear ditches inside and out, the patriarch and the barons of the land came to him and spoke to him thus: [616] 'My lord, you have fortified the city of Sidon, that of Caesarea, and the suburbs of Jaffa, which is of great benefit to the Holy Land. You have also greatly strengthened the city of Acre with the walls and towers you have built there. In spite of this, my lord, having considered matters among ourselves we do not see that your staying longer would benefit the kingdom of Jerusalem. Because of this we

advise and urge you to go to Acre during this coming Lent and to prepare for your voyage so that you might return to France after Easter.' In accordance with the advice of the patriarch and the barons, the king left Sidon and went to Tyre, where the queen was, and from there we went to Acre at the beginning of Lent.

CHAPTER 13

The Journey Home

(April–July 1254)

[617] Throughout Lent the king had his ships – of which there were thirteen, both *nefs* and galleys – readied for the return to France. The *nefs* and galleys were prepared in time for the king and queen to go aboard their *nef* on the eve of the feast of Saint Mark,[1] after Easter. The wind was favourable as we set sail. On Saint Mark's Day the king told me that he had been born on that day, and I said that he might well say that he had also been reborn on that day, for he was indeed reborn when he escaped from that perilous land.

[618] On the Saturday we came in sight of Cyprus and a mountain on the island which is called the Mountain of the Cross. That Saturday a fog rose over the island and came down from the land on to the sea. Because of this our sailors, who saw the mountain above the fog, thought we were further away from the island than we were. This meant that they sailed on confidently, with the result that our ship struck a sandbank in the sea. It so happened that if we had not found and hit this stretch of sand, we would have struck a hidden expanse of rocks that would have shattered our ship completely and shipwrecked and drowned us all.

[619] The moment our ship struck, a great cry went up on board. Everyone was shouting, 'Alas!' The sailors and others pounded their hands together, each of them afraid he would drown. When I heard this I got up from the bed, in which I was lying, and went to the ship's castle with the sailors. After I arrived there Brother Raymond, who was a Templar and was in charge of the sailors, said to one of his valets, 'Throw down your lead', and he did so. And as soon as he had thrown it, the

valet cried out and said, 'Alas! We're aground!' When he heard this Brother Raymond ripped his clothes down to his belt and began to tear at his beard, crying, 'Woe is me! Woe is me!' [620] At that moment one of my knights, whose name was lord John of Monson (he was the father of Abbot William of Saint-Michel), did me a great kindness; without saying a word he brought me one of my fur-lined *surcotes* and threw it over my shoulders because I was wearing nothing besides my *cote*. I shouted at him, saying, 'What use to me is this *surcote* you've brought, when we're drowning?' And he said to me, 'By my soul, my lord, I would rather we were all drowned than that you should die having been taken ill from the cold!'

[621] The sailors cried out, 'Ahoy there, galley! Take the king aboard!' But none of the king's four galleys that were nearby would come close. They were very wise in this, for there were at least 800 people in the ship who would all have leapt into the galleys to save themselves, sinking them all as a result.

[622] The man with the lead threw it down a second time and came back to Brother Raymond to tell him that the ship was no longer aground. Then Brother Raymond went to tell this to the king, who was lying face down on the ship's bridge with his arms stretched out in the shape of a cross, barefoot, wearing just a *cote* and completely dishevelled. He was prostrate before the body of Our Lord[2] which was kept on the ship, as a man would be who was convinced he was going to drown. As soon as daybreak came, we saw in front of us the rocks on which we would have struck if the ship had not hit the sandbank.

[623] The following day the king sent for the ships' master mariners, who sent four divers down to the bottom of the sea. Into the sea they dived and when they came back, the king and the master mariners listened to them one after the other, so that each diver did not know what the others had said. They found out from the four divers that as our ship scraped against the sandbank, eighteen feet of the keel on which the ship was built had been torn away.

[624] The king then summoned the master mariners before us and asked what advice they would give him about the damage

his ship had suffered. They discussed this with each other and urged the king to get off his ship and to go aboard another. [625] 'We advise you to do this,' they said, 'because we're convinced that all the timbers of your ship have been dislodged, which makes us worried that when your ship reaches the high seas, it won't be able to withstand the pummelling of the waves without breaking up. The same thing happened when you were coming from France: a ship ran aground then too, and when it reached the high seas, it could not withstand the force of the waves. Because of this it broke apart and everyone on board was killed except one woman and her child, who found safety on a piece of the ship's debris.' And I can bear witness that what they said was true, for I saw that woman and her child in the count of Joigny's lodgings in the city of Paphos; the count was providing for them for the love of God.

[626] Then the king asked my lord Peter the Chamberlain, my lord Giles le Brun, constable of France, my lord Gervase of Escrennes, the king's master cook, the archbishop of Nicosia, who was his seal bearer and later became a cardinal, and me what our advice to him would be on this matter. And we replied to him that in all earthly matters one should put faith in those who know most about them: 'Because of which we advise you, for our part, to do whatever the mariners recommend to you.'

[627] Then the king said to the mariners, 'I ask you, on your honour, if the ship was yours and it was loaded with your merchandise, would you leave it?' And they all replied as one that they would not; for they would rather put themselves at risk of drowning than buy a ship that would cost them 4,000 *livres* and more. 'Then why are you advising me to disembark?' said the king. 'Because,' they said, 'the stakes aren't equal; no gold or silver can be worth as much as your person or those of your wife and children who are on board. And because of this we cannot advise you to put either yourself or them in danger.'

[628] Then the king said, 'My lords, I have listened to your opinion and the opinion of my men. Now I will tell you my own, which is that if I leave the ship, there are more than 500 people on board who will stay on the island of Cyprus out of fear of physical danger – for there is not one among them who

does not love his life as much as I do mine – and who perhaps
might never return to their homeland. Because of this I would
rather place my own person, my wife and my children at risk
in God's hands than that I should do such harm to so great a
number of people as there are on board.'

[629] The great harm the king would have done to the people
on his ship can be seen by the case of Oliver of Termes, who
was on board the king's ship. He was one of the bravest men I
ever saw and had conducted himself better than anyone else in
the Holy Land. He did not dare remain with us for fear of
drowning. Instead he stayed on Cyprus and encountered such
difficulties that it was a year and a half before he returned to
the king, even though he was a powerful and wealthy man who
could easily have paid for his passage. So consider what the
humbler people would have done who had no means with
which to pay, when a man like him had such great problems.

[630] We passed from this danger, from which God had
saved us, into another. The wind that had cast us on to Cyprus,
where we should have been drowned, got up with such strength
and fury that it threw us back on to the island by force. The
sailors threw out their anchors against the wind, but the ship
could not be stopped until they had thrown out five of them.
It was necessary to take down the sides of the king's cabin on
the deck, although no one dared stay in it since they feared the
wind would carry them into the sea. The constable of France,
my lord Giles le Brun, and I had been sleeping in the king's
cabin below deck when, all of a sudden, the queen opened the
door, thinking she would find the king there. [631] I asked her
what she was looking for, and she told me that she had come
to speak to the king, so that he might make a promise to God
or his saints to go on some pilgrimage, by which God might
deliver us from the peril in which we found ourselves; the
sailors had told her we were in danger of drowning. I said to
her, 'My lady, promise to make a pilgrimage to my lord Saint
Nicholas of Varangéville, and I will stand pledge for him that
God will bring you, the king and your children back to France.'
'Seneschal,' she said, 'I would do so most willingly, but the king
is so contrary that if he knew I had made this promise without

him, he would never let me go on the pilgrimage.' [632] 'There
is at least one thing you can do,' I said. 'If God brings you back
to France, you can promise him a silver ship of five marks for
the king, yourself and your three children. And I will stand
pledge that God will bring you back to France, for I've sworn
to Saint Nicholas that if he should rescue us from the danger
we've been in tonight, I will go from Joinville on foot and
shoeless in order to pray to him.' And she said that she would
promise the silver ship of five marks to Saint Nicholas and told
me that I was her pledge for it. I told her I would be so most
willingly. She left there and was gone only a short while, before
she returned to us and told me, 'Saint Nicholas has saved us
from this peril, for the wind has dropped.'

[633] When the queen – may God absolve her – returned to
France, she had the silver ship made in Paris; in it were the
king, queen and the three children, all made of silver, along
with the sailors, mast, rudder and rigging, all made of silver,
and the sails likewise. The queen told me the work had cost
100 *livres*. When the ship was completed the queen sent it to
me at Joinville so I could have it taken to Saint Nicholas, and I
did so. I saw it once more at Saint Nicholas, when we were
taking the king's sister to join the king of Germany[3] at
Haguenau.

[634] Now let me return to our subject and say that after we
had escaped these two perils, the king sat down on the ship's
bench and had me sit at his feet. He said to me, 'Seneschal, God
has certainly demonstrated his great power, for one of his lesser
winds – not one of the four great winds – nearly drowned the
king of France, his wife and children, and all his company. So
we must be grateful to him and offer him thanks for the danger
from which he delivered us.

[635] 'Seneschal,' said the king, 'the saints tell us that when
people are struck by such tribulations, or by illness or other
persecutions, these are warnings from Our Lord. For just as
God says to those who are saved from serious illness, "Now
you see clearly that I might well have killed you if I had so
wished", so he can say to us, "You can see clearly that I might
have drowned you all if I had so wished." [636] So we must,'

said the king, 'look into ourselves for anything that might be
displeasing him and because of which he wanted to frighten us.
And if we find anything displeasing to him, we should purge
ourselves of it, for if we do otherwise after such a warning as
he has given us, he will come down upon us with death or some
other great suffering that would hurt our bodies and souls.'

[637] The king went on, 'Seneschal, the saint says, "Lord
God, why are you warning us? For if you had lost us all, you
would not have been any worse off because of it, and if you
saved us all, you would not have been any richer as a result.
And we can see from this," says the saint, "that these warnings
God gives us are not made in order to further his benefit or to
prevent his harm. It is only because of the great love he has for
us that he prompts us through these warnings to see our own
failings clearly and to rid ourselves of that which displeases
him." Now let us do so,' said the king, 'and we will be acting
wisely.'

[638] We left the island of Cyprus once we had taken on
board fresh water and other things we needed. We came to an
island called Lampedusa where we caught a great many rabbits.
We also found an old hermitage among the rocks, along with
the gardens made by the hermits who had lived there in the
past. There were olive trees, fig trees, vine stocks and other
trees there; the stream from a spring ran through the garden.
We went with the king to the far end of the garden and found
an oratory. The first chamber was whitewashed and had a cross
of red earth. [639] We entered the second chamber and found
two bodies of dead men, from which all the flesh had rotted
away. Their ribs still held together and the bones of their hands
were on their chests; they were laid out facing the East in the
same way bodies are buried in the ground. When we went back
on board our ship we were missing one of our sailors, whom
the ship's master thought had stayed behind in order to become
a hermit. Because of this Nicholas of Soisy, the master of the
king's sergeants, left three sacks of biscuit on the shore so that
the man might find them and live off the biscuit.

[640] When we left Lampedusa we came in sight of a large
island in the sea that was called Pantelleria and was inhabited

by Saracens who were subject to the king of Sicily and the king of Tunis. The queen asked the king to send three galleys to fetch fruit for her children. The king agreed and ordered the master of the galleys so that once the king's *nef* had passed in front of the island, his galleys should be ready to return to him. The galleys reached the island via one of its ports, but it so happened that when the king's *nef* passed in front of the port we received no word from them.

[641] The sailors then began to murmur among themselves. The king had them summoned and asked them what they made of the situation, and the sailors told him it seemed likely to them that the Saracens had captured his men and the galleys. 'But we advise and urge you, my lord, not to wait for them because you are between the kingdom of Sicily and the kingdom of Tunis, neither of which has any love for you. If you let us sail on you will have been saved from danger once again tonight, for we will bring you through these straits.' [642] 'Truly,' said the king, 'I will not follow your advice that I should leave my people in the hands of the Saracens without at least doing what I can to free them. I order you to turn your sails – we're going to attack them.' When the queen heard this she began to show signs of deep distress and said, 'Alas! This is all my doing!'

[643] While the sails were being turned on the king's *nef* and on the others, we saw the galleys leaving the island. When they reached the king he asked the sailors why they had done this. They replied that they had no choice; it was the fault of certain sons of Parisian *bourgeois*. Six of them had been eating fruit in the gardens and the sailors could not find them but did not want to leave them behind. The king ordered that these six be put in the boat trailing behind his ship, at which they began to cry and wail, 'My lord, for God's sake, fine us as much as we can pay, but don't put us in the place where thieves and murderers are put, because it will always be a reproach to us.' [644] The queen and all the rest of us did what we could to dissuade the king, but he refused to listen to anyone. Therefore, the young men were put in the ship's boat and stayed there until we reached land. They were in great danger there because when the sea was rough, the waves were as high as their heads, and

they had to huddle down so that the wind would not carry them off into the sea. And this served them right since their greed ended up setting us back significantly: we were delayed for a whole week because the king made the ships change course.

[645] We had another adventure at sea before the end of our voyage. As she was helping the queen to bed, one of her *béguines*, who was not taking proper care, threw the cloth that had been wrapped round her head into the bottom of the iron pot in which the queen's candle was burning. And when the *béguine* had gone to bed in the cabin below the queen's, where the other women slept, the candle burned down far enough to set the cloth alight, and from there the fire spread to the sheets that were covering the queen's clothes. [646] When the queen woke up she saw the whole cabin engulfed in flames. She leapt up, quite naked, snatched the cloth and threw it, still burning, into the sea and then seized the sheets to put out that fire. The young men in the boat trailing behind the ship could be faintly heard calling out, 'Fire! Fire!' I lifted my head and saw the cloth still burning brightly on the sea, which was very calm. I put on my *cote* as quickly as I could and went to sit with the sailors.

[647] While I was sitting there my squire, who slept at the foot of my bed, came to me and told me that the king was awake and had asked where I was. 'And I told him that you had gone to the latrines but the king said, "You're lying!"' While we were talking there, along came Master Geoffrey, the queen's clerk, who said to me, 'Don't be worried, because it's clear what did happen.' And I said to him, 'Master Geoffrey, go and tell the queen that the king is awake and that she should go to him to reassure him.'

[648] Next day the constable of France, my lord Peter the Chamberlain, and my lord Gervase the baker said to the king, 'What happened last night? We've heard talk of a fire.' I did not say a word. And then the king said, 'Unfortunately it seems the seneschal is more reticent than I am, so I will tell you what it was that meant we might all have burned last night.' [649] He told them what happened and said to me, 'Seneschal, I command you that from now on you should not to go to

bed before you have put out all fires on board, apart from the large fire in the ship's hold. And know that I will not go to bed until you have reported back to me.' And I did this for as long as we were at sea; once I had reported back to him the king went to bed.

[650] We had another adventure while at sea. My lord Dragonet, a great man from Provence, was sleeping one morning on board his ship, which was a full league ahead of ours. He called one of his squires and said to him, 'Go and cover that porthole – the sun's shining in my face.' The squire saw that he would not be able to cover the porthole except by going over the side of the ship. So he climbed out, and while he was covering the porthole, he lost his footing and fell into the water. There was no boat trailing behind this ship, for it was only small, and he was immediately left behind by it. Those of us in the king's ship saw him but thought he was a bundle or a small barrel, because the man who had fallen into the water made no effort to save himself. [651] One of the king's galleys took him aboard and brought him to our ship, where he recounted to us how this had happened. I asked him why he had made no effort to save himself either by swimming or in another way. He replied to me that there had been no need and no point in trying to save himself, because as soon as he had started to fall, he commended himself to Our Lady of Vauvert, and she had held him up by the shoulders from the time he fell until the king's galley picked him up. To honour this miracle I had this scene depicted in my chapel at Joinville, and in the windows at Blécourt.

[652] After we had been at sea for ten weeks we arrived at a port two leagues from the castle of Hyères which belonged to the count of Provence,[4] who later became king of Sicily. The queen and all the king's council agreed that he should land there, since this was his brother's territory. The king replied to us that he would not disembark until he had arrived at Aigues Mortes, which was in his own territory. He held fast to this view all that Wednesday and Thursday, no one could convince him otherwise.

[653] In these Marseilles-built ships there are two rudders, each of which is connected to a tiller so ingeniously that you

can turn the ship to right or left in the same time it takes to turn a horse. On the Friday the king was sitting on one of these tillers. He called me and said, 'Seneschal, what do you think of this business?' And I told him, 'My lord, it would serve you right if what happened to my lady of Bourbon were to happen to you. She refused to disembark at this port but went back out to sea in order to go to Aigues Mortes, and remained at sea for seven weeks.' [654] The king then summoned his council and told them what I had said, and asked them what they advised him to do. They all advised him to disembark since it would not be wise, having already come through the perils of the sea, to endanger himself, his wife and his children further. The king agreed with the advice we gave him, which made the queen very happy.

[655] The king left the sea at the castle of Hyères with the queen and his children. During the king's stay at Hyères, while horses were being procured for the journey to France, the abbot of Cluny, who later became the bishop of Olena,[5] gave him two palfreys – one for the king and the other for the queen – that would be worth at least 500 *livres* today. When he had presented them the abbot said to the king, 'My lord, I have some business that I will come to talk to you about tomorrow.' When the next day came the abbot returned. The king listened to him most attentively and at great length. Once the abbot had gone, I came to the king and said to him, 'I'd like to ask you, if I may, whether you listened to the abbot more graciously because he gave you those two palfreys yesterday?' [656] The king thought for a while and said, 'In truth, I did.' 'My lord,' I said, 'do you know why I asked you this?' 'Why was it?' he asked. 'So that, my lord, I might advise and urge you that once you have returned to France you should forbid all your sworn councillors to receive gifts from people who have business to settle with you. Because you may be certain that if they do receive gifts, your councillors will listen more readily and attentively to those people who have given them things, just as you did to the abbot of Cluny.' The king then summoned his entire council and straightaway told them what I had said to him, and they said that I had given him sound advice.

[657] The king heard talk of a Franciscan friar called Brother Hugh[6] who was greatly renowned. Because of this the king sent for this Franciscan in order to meet him and to hear him speak. On the day Brother Hugh came to Hyères we looked out along the road by which he was approaching and saw that a great crowd of people was following him on foot, both men and women. The king had him deliver a sermon. The first part of the sermon concerned men of religion, and he said, 'My lords, I see too many men of religion at the king's court and in his company . . .', and he added, 'there's me, for a start.' He said that such men of religion were not in a position to achieve salvation (unless Holy Scripture lies to us, which is impossible). [658] 'For Holy Scripture tells us that a monk cannot live outside his cloister without mortal sin, just as a fish cannot live out of water. And if these religious who are with the king say they are cloistered, I say that it is the largest cloister I have ever seen, for it stretches from this side of the sea to the other. If they say that a man can lead a harsh life in order to save his soul in this cloister, I do not believe them. Rather I tell you that in their company I have eaten a great quantity and variety of meats, and drunk fine wines, strong and clear ones. Because of this I am sure that if they had been in their cloister they would not have been as comfortable as they are with the king.'

[659] In his sermon he instructed the king that he should conduct himself in accordance with the wishes of his people. At the end of his sermon he said that he had read the Bible and the books that may be read alongside it, but never – in either the books of the faithful or of unbelievers – had he read of any kingdom or lordship that had been lost or had changed hands from one king or lord to another for any reason other than a lack of justice. 'So the king should take care, now that he is going to France,' he said, 'to offer such justice to his people that he will retain God's love, so that God will not take the kingdom of France from him during his lifetime.'

[660] I told the king that he should not let Brother Hugh leave his company. And he told me that he had already pleaded with him as strongly as he could, but the friar refused to do anything for him. Then the king took me by the hand and said,

'Let's go and ask him once more.' We went to him and I said, 'My lord, do what the king asks of you – stay with him while he remains in Provence.' And he replied to me, greatly irritated, 'Certainly, my lord, I will not. I will go instead to a place where God will love me better than he would if I were in the king's company.' He stayed with us for one day and left the next. Since then I have heard that his body lies in the city of Marseilles, where he performs many beautiful miracles.

[661] On the day of the king's departure from Hyères, he left the castle on foot because the hill was very steep. He went so far on foot that, since his own palfrey had not come, it was necessary for him to get up on to mine. When his own palfrey did arrive he launched an assault of angry words against his squire Ponce. Once he had roundly scolded Ponce I said to him, 'My lord, you should be more patient with squire Ponce, for he has served your grandfather and father as well as you.' [662] 'Seneschal,' he said, 'he has not served us. Rather we have served him by putting up with him in our household despite his bad habits. King Philip, my grandfather, told me that you should reward the members of your household in accordance with the quality of service they give – one more, another less. He also said that no man can be a good governor of lands unless he knows how to withhold just as firmly as he knows how to give. And I tell you these things,' said the king, 'since this world is so grasping that there are few people who consider the salvation of their souls or the honour of their persons if they have the chance to seize other people's property either justly or unjustly.'

[663] The king travelled across the county of Provence as far as a city called Aix-en-Provence. It was said that the body of the Magdalene lay there, and we went into a cave high up in the cliffs where she was believed to have spent seventeen years as a hermit.[7] When the king reached Beaucaire and I had seen him into his own lands and authority, I took my leave of him and made my own way via the lands of my niece the dauphine of the Viennois, of my uncle the count of Chalon and of his son the count of Burgundy.

CHAPTER 14

King Louis's Personal and Governmental Reforms

(1254–67)

[664] After I had spent some time at Joinville and attended to my affairs, I went to join the king, whom I found at Soissons. He was so overjoyed to see me that everyone there was astonished. Among them were Count John of Brittany and his wife, the daughter of King Thibaut,[1] who offered homage to the king for the rights she claimed in Champagne. The king referred her claim and that of King Thibaut II of Navarre, who was also present, to the Paris *parlement* so that it might hear and do justice to both parties.

[665] The king of Navarre and his council came to the *parlement*, and the count of Brittany did so too. At the *parlement* King Thibaut asked whether he might have my lady Isabella, the king's daughter, as his wife. And although the Champenois contingent were talking behind my back about the deep affection for me the king had displayed at Soissons, I did not let this stand in the way of my going to the French king to talk about the proposed marriage. The king said, 'Go and make peace with the count of Brittany and then we will make our marriage.' I told him that he should not reject the marriage because of this dispute, but he replied to me that he would on no account proceed with it until peace was made, so that it might not be said that in marrying his children he disinherited his barons.

[666] I reported this exchange to Queen Margaret of Navarre and to the king, her son, and their council. Hearing this they hastened to make peace. After the peace was achieved the king of France gave his daughter to King Thibaut and a splendid and solemn wedding took place at Melun. King Thibaut took

Isabella from there to Provins, where they were greeted by a multitude of barons and by lavish celebrations.

[667] After the king's return from overseas his conduct was so devout that never again did he wear vair or grey fur or scarlet, nor golden stirrups and spurs. His clothes were made of camelin or dark-blue wool, his blankets and clothes were trimmed with deerskin or lambskin or with fur from the legs of hares. He was so restrained in his eating habits that he never ordered any dish other than what the cooks prepared for him; he ate whatever was put in front of him. He mixed his wine in a glass goblet, adding an appropriate amount of water according to the strength of the wine; he held the goblet in his hand while the wine was being blended behind his table. Every day he fed his poor people and had money given to them after the meal.

[668] When the great men's minstrels came into the hall with their viols at the end of the meal, he waited until the minstrel had finished his performance to hear grace. He then stood up and the priests in front of him said grace for him. When we were in his chamber in private, he would sit at the foot of his bed and whenever the Dominican and Franciscan friars present mentioned a book he might like to have read to him he would say, 'You'll not read me anything, for there's no after-dinner book as good as a *quodlibet*, that is a discussion in which every man says what he likes.' Whenever great men from abroad dined with him, he was pleasant company for them.

[669] I will tell you about his sound judgement. People sometimes asserted that there was no one in his council as wise as he was himself. This was apparent because when someone discussed a matter with him, he did not simply say, 'I will take advice on this.' Rather, when he saw the right way to proceed quite clearly and straightforwardly, he responded immediately, completely independently of his council. I heard he made such a response to a request made of him by all the bishops in the kingdom of France, which was as follows. [670] Bishop Guy of Auxerre, speaking on behalf of all the bishops, said to him, 'My lord, these archbishops and bishops here present have charged me to inform you that the Christian community is crumbling

to pieces in your hands and will disintegrate further if you do
not attend to the matter, since no one today fears excommunication. We recommend, my lord, that you command your *baillis*
and sergeants to force those who have been under sentence of
excommunication for a year and a day to give satisfaction to
the Church.' The king replied to them, without taking any
advice, that he would willingly order his *baillis* and sergeants
to compel excommunicates as the bishop requested, but that he
should be given evidence whether the sentence was justified or
not. [671] The bishops deliberated among themselves and
replied to the king that they would not allow him to pass
judgement in matters pertaining to religious authority. And in
response the king told them that in matters pertaining to him
he would never give them such authority, and nor would he
order his officials to force excommunicates to have themselves
absolved, whether their sentence was just or unjust, 'For if I
were to do so I would act against God and against justice. I will
give you an example. The bishops of Brittany kept the count of
Brittany excommunicate for a full seven years before his sentence was overturned by the papal court. If I had compelled
him to reconcile himself after the first year, I would have done
so wrongly.'

[672] It so happened that after our return from overseas the
monks of Saint-Urbain[2] elected two abbots. Bishop Peter of
Châlons – may God absolve him – rejected them both and
blessed as abbot my lord John of Mymeri, giving him the
crozier. I did not wish to accept him as abbot since he had
wronged Abbot Geoffrey, who had appealed against John and
taken his case to Rome. I kept the abbey under my own control
until the said Geoffrey managed to obtain the crozier, thus
depriving the man to whom the bishop had given it. While
this dispute continued the bishop excommunicated me, which
prompted very angry exchanges at a Paris *parlement* between
me and Bishop Peter of Châlons, and between Countess Margaret of Flanders and the archbishop of Rheims, whom she
accused of lying. [673] At the next *parlement* all the prelates
begged the king to come and speak with them in private. When
he returned from this meeting he came to those of us in the

room where pleas were heard. He laughed as he told us of the heated discussion he had had with the bishops. The archbishop of Rheims had begun by saying to the king, 'My lord, what are you going to do about the guardianship of the abbey of Saint-Rémy at Rheims, of which you deprived me? For I swear by the relics here present I would not for all the kingdom of France wish to be burdened by such a sin as you bear.' 'By those same relics here present,' said the king, 'I swear that your personal greed means you would do so for Compiègne alone, so one of us is forsworn.' [674] 'The bishop of Chartres asked me,' said the king, 'to return those possessions of his I was holding. And I told him that I would not do so until such time as I had been paid what was due to me, and said that although he had performed homage to me as my vassal, he did not conduct himself well and loyally towards me when he sought to deprive me of what was mine by right.' [675] The bishop of Châlons then said, "My lord, what are you going to do for me about the lord of Joinville, who is withholding the abbey of Saint-Urbain from this poor monk?"' 'My lord bishop,' said the king, 'you have agreed among yourselves that no excommunicate should be allowed to give evidence in a secular court, and I have seen letters sealed with thirty-two seals that say that you have been excommunicated. Therefore, I will not hear you until you have been absolved.' I am telling you these things so that you might see clearly how he dealt with matters that concerned him on his own, through his sound judgement.

[676] After I had settled matters in his favour, Abbot Geoffrey of Saint-Urbain answered the goodwill I had shown him with bad, and appealed against me. He gave our saintly king to understand that the abbey was in the king's guardianship. I asked the king to find out the truth of the matter, whether the guardianship was his or mine. 'My lord,' said the abbot, 'you should do no such thing, please God, but rather conduct a formal trial involving the abbey and the lord of Joinville, for we would prefer our abbey to be under your protection than under the protection of the person who owns its lands.' Then the king said to me, 'Is he right that the guardianship of the abbey is mine?' 'Certainly not, my lord,' I said, 'it is mine.'

[677] Then the king said, 'It may well be that you are lord of the abbey's lands, but that does not mean you have the right to the guardianship of the abbey. But, may it please you, lord abbot, according to what you have said and what the seneschal has said, the guardianship must pertain either to him or to me. I would not, despite what you have said, do anything other than find out the truth of the matter for myself. For I would be doing a great wrong to my own vassal if I were to bring him before the court, presenting his claim for formal judgement, when he has offered to tell me the truth of the matter straightforwardly.' The king was informed as to the truth and, the truth being known, he delivered the guardianship of the abbey to me and provided me with documents to this effect.

[678] As a result of the saintly king's negotiations the king of England and his wife and children came to France to conclude a peace between the two kingdoms.[3] The king's councillors were very much opposed to this peace agreement, and they said to him, 'Sir, we are very surprised that you want to give the king of England such a large part of the lands taken from him by yourself and your ancestors through your conquests and his forfeit. It seems to us that if you think you hold this land wrongfully, you are not being fair to the king of England because you are not returning to him all the conquests made by yourself and your ancestors, while if you think you hold it rightfully, it seems to us that you are simply abandoning whatever land you return to him.' [679] The saintly king responded in this way: 'My lords, I am sure that the king of England's ancestors were justly deprived of the territories I hold; the lands I am handing over to him are not being given because I have any obligation to him or to his heirs, but in order to foster love between his children and mine, who are first cousins. And it seems to me that I am putting the land I give to good use, since before this he was not my vassal, but now he will do homage to me.'

[680] He worked harder than any other man in the world to build peace among his subjects, and especially among great men who held neighbouring lands and among the kingdom's princes, as he did between the count of Chalon (the lord of

Joinville's uncle) and his son the count of Burgundy, who were warring fiercely when we returned from overseas. To achieve peace between father and son he sent some of his councillors to Burgundy at his own expense, and through his efforts the two generations made peace.

[681] Later there was a major conflict between King Thibaut II of Champagne[4] on one side and Count John of Chalon and his son, the count of Burgundy, on the other over the abbey of Luxeuil. To bring an end to this war my lord the king sent my lord Gervase of Escrennes, who was master cook of France at that time, and through his negotiations they came to peace.

[682] After this war had been brought to an end by the king, another great conflict arose between Count Thibaut of Bar and Count Henry of Luxembourg, who had married the count of Bar's sister. It so happened when they were doing battle with each other outside Prény that Count Thibaut of Bar captured Count Henry of Luxembourg along with the castle of Ligny, which belonged to the count of Luxembourg by right of his wife. To bring the war to a peaceful end the king sent, at his own expense, my lord Peter the Chamberlain, the man whom he trusted above all others in the world. The king's efforts were enough to bring the two sides to peace.

[683] As for the foreigners whom the king brought to peace, certain of his councillors said that he did wrong not to leave them to their wars; if he had allowed them to impoverish themselves they would not have been able to attack him as easily as they would if they were plentifully rich. The king answered these councillors and said they were wrong, 'For if neighbouring princes see me leaving them to their wars, they might discuss this together and say, "The king, in his malice, allows us to keep fighting." If their hatred for me on this account should lead them to attack me, I might very well lose, not to mention the fact that I would have won the hatred of God, who says, "Blessed are the peacemakers." '[5] [684] As a result the Burgundians and Lorrainers, whom the king had reconciled, loved him so much and were so obedient to him that I saw them come to the royal court in Rheims, Paris and Orléans seeking judgement from him on disputes that had arisen between them.

[685] The king so loved God and his sweet Mother[6] that he severely punished all those he could ascertain had spoken basely of them or had sworn blasphemous oaths. I saw that he had a goldsmith put in the stocks at Caesarea. He was wearing his breeches and chemise and had the guts and innards of a pig piled round his neck – there was such a quantity that it came right up to his nose. I heard it said that after my return from overseas he had the nose and lips of one Parisian *bourgeois* branded, although I did not see this myself. And the saintly king said that he would willingly be branded with a hot iron if it would mean his kingdom was rid of all foul oaths.

[686] I spent at least twenty-two years as a member of his entourage and never heard him swear by God, or by his Mother or his saints. When he wanted to emphasize a point he said, 'Truly it was so', or 'Truly it is so.' [687] I never heard him say the name of the Devil, unless it appeared in a book where there was reason to use it, or unless it was mentioned in the saint's life recounted in the book. And it is a great shame to the kingdom of France and to the king[7] that he tolerates talk of the Devil, to the extent that people can barely speak at all without saying, 'In the name of the Devil!' And it is a great abuse of speech when one sends to the Devil a man or woman who has been destined for God since the time of their baptism. In the house at Joinville anyone who say these things earns himself a slap on the face or the hand – such bad language has nearly been stamped out there.

[688] The king asked me whether I washed the feet of the poor on Maundy Thursday, and I replied I did not, since it did not strike me as a seemly thing to do. He told me that I should not despise doing this, for God had done so, 'And you would be particularly reluctant to do what king of England does; he washes and kisses the feet of lepers.'

[689] Before he went to bed he had his children come before him and recounted to them the deeds of good kings and emperors and told them that they should follow the good example of these men. He also told them of the wicked deeds of powerful men who through their debauchery, plunder and greed had lost their kingdoms. 'I remind you of these things,'

he said, 'so that you may take care to avoid them and so that God is not angered by you.' He had them learn the hours of Our Lady and made them recite the hours of each day in front of him to accustom them to listening to Divine Office when they would be governors of their own lands.

[690] The king was so generous in his charity that wherever he went in his kingdom, he made gifts to impoverished churches, to leper-houses, to almshouses, to hospitals and to poor gentlemen and gentlewomen. Every day he gave food to a great number of the poor, not to mention those who ate in his own hall; on many occasions I saw him cut their bread and pour their drink himself.

[691] Numerous abbeys were built in his time: Royaumont, the abbey of Saint-Antoine near Paris, the abbey of Lys and the abbey of Maubuisson, as well as several other convents of Dominicans and Franciscans. He built the almshouses at Pontoise and at Vernon, the hospital for the blind at Paris and the convent for Franciscan nuns at Saint-Cloud that his sister, Lady Isabella, founded with his permission.

[692] Whenever a benefice of the Holy Church reverted to the Crown, the king would seek advice from good men of religion and from others before granting it. Once he had taken advice he granted these benefices of the Holy Church in good faith, fairly and according to God's will. He refused to give any benefice to a cleric if he would not give up any other Church benefices he held. In every town in his kingdom he had not visited before he went to the convents of Dominicans and Franciscans, if there were any, to ask for their prayers.

[693] How the king reformed his *baillis*, his *prévôts* and his mayors, how he put new ordinances in place, and how Stephen Boileau was *prévôt* of Paris.[8]

After King Louis returned to France from overseas he conducted himself with great devotion towards Our Lord and with great justice towards his subjects. He deliberated and concluded that it would be a very fine and good thing to reform the kingdom of France. He began by setting down a general ordinance for all his subjects throughout the kingdom of France, which was as follows:

[694] We, Louis, by God's grace king of France, ordain that all our *baillis*, viscounts, *prévôts*, mayors and all others, in whatever matter it may concern and in whatever office they may hold, must swear that, for as long as they hold an office or the status of *bailli*, they will deal fairly with all people without exception – the poor as well as the rich, strangers as well as friends – and that they will maintain the usages and customs that are good and proven. [695] And if it should happen that these *baillis* or viscounts or others (including sergeants and foresters) should be convicted of acting in contravention of their oath, it is our will that they be punished in their possessions, and in their persons if the crime warrants it. The *baillis* will be punished by ourselves, and the others by the *baillis*.

[696] Moreover, the other *prévôts, baillis* and sergeants will swear to maintain faithfully our revenue and our rights, not suffering our rights to be suppressed, usurped or diminished. In addition to this they will swear not to take or receive, either in person or through others, any gold or silver, any indirect benefit or anything else unless it be fruit, bread or wine or another gift worth up to ten *sous*, which sum must not be exceeded. [697] With this they will swear not to take, or cause to be taken, any gift of whatever kind made to their wives or children, or to their brothers and sisters, or to any person however close to them. And as soon as they discover that such gifts have been received, they will return them as soon as possible. Also, they will swear not to receive any gift of whatever kind from a person under their jurisdiction nor from any other person who may have reason to bring a case or give evidence before them.

[698] Moreover, they will swear not to give or send any gift to any member of our council, nor to their wives, children or friends, nor to those who will receive their accounts on our behalf, nor to any *enquêteur* sent by us to their *bailliage* or *prévôté* to make enquiry about them. With this they will swear to have no part in any sale of our revenues, rights or coinage, or anything else pertaining to us.

[699] And they will swear and promise that if they know of

any official, sergeant or *prévôt* under them who is disloyal, rapacious, usurious or consumed by any other vice for which they should be removed from our service, they will not protect them on account of any gift or promise or personal affection or anything else. Rather they will in good faith judge and punish them.

[700] Moreover, our *prévôts*, viscounts, mayors, foresters and other sergeants, mounted or on foot, will swear not to give any gift to their superiors, or to their wives or to children in their ward.

[701] And because we desire that these oaths be made on a sound basis, we require them to be taken in open session, in front of everyone, clerics and laymen, knights and sergeants, notwithstanding that they may already have taken the oath in our presence. In this way they should fear the sin of abandoning their oaths not only out of fear of God and ourselves, but because of the fear of public shame.

[702] We will and ordain that all our *prévôts* and *baillis* should abstain from blasphemous swearing against God and Our Lady and any of the saints, and they should avoid games of dice and taverns. We desire the manufacture of dice to be banned throughout our kingdom, and for prostitutes to be put out of their houses; whoever rents a house to a prostitute will surrender one year's rent for the house to the *prévôt* or *bailli*.

[703] Further, we expressly forbid our *baillis* to buy, in person or through an agent, property or land within their own *bailliage* or in another, without our permission for as long as they are in our service. And if such purchases are made, it is our will that the property be forfeited and should remain in our hands.

[704] We forbid our *baillis* for as long as they are in our service to marry their sons or daughters or other people in their ward to any person from their *bailliage* without our specific consent, nor may they place them in a religious house in their *bailliage* or obtain for them a benefice of the Holy Church or any property. Further, they may not demand provisions or lodgings at any religious house or in its vicinity at the expense of the community of religious. As we have stated, it is not our

will that these prohibitions on marriage and the acquisition of
property should extend to *prévôts* or mayors or to others of
lesser office.

[705] We order that neither *baillis* nor *prévôts* nor others
should employ too great a number of sergeants or beadles so
that the people might not be burdened by them, and it is our
will that the beadles be nominated in open court, otherwise
their office will not be recognized. It is our will that when our
officers are sent to a distant location or to any foreign country,
they should not be given credence without letters from their
superiors.

[706] We order that no *bailli* or *prévôt* in our service should
oppress good people with sentences that exceed what is just,
and neither should any of our subjects be imprisoned for an
unpaid debt, unless it is owed to us.

[707] We ordain that no *bailli* of ours should impose a fine
on any of our subjects for debts owed by them or for any
offence, unless it is determined in open court where it may be
considered and assessed on the advice of trustworthy men, even
if payment has already been made to the *bailli*. [708] If it should
happen that the accused does not wish to wait for the court to
offer judgement on his fine, he may offer a certain sum of
deniers as determined by usual practice. We desire that the
court accept that sum if it is reasonable and fitting, and if it is
not it is our will that the fine be determined as laid out above,
the accused submitting himself to the will of the court. We
forbid the *bailli* or the mayor or the *prévôt* to use threats,
menaces or any wiles to compel our subjects to pay a fine,
whether openly or clandestinely, or to make accusations against
them without reasonable cause.

[709] We ordain that those who hold *prévôtés*, viscounties
or other offices may not sell them to anyone without our permission. And if a group of people should purchase one of the
aforementioned offices, we desire that one of these purchasers
should perform its duties on behalf of all the others and enjoy
the customary privileges relating to long-distance travel, taxes
and other charges. [710] We forbid them to sell the said offices
to brothers, nephews or cousins after having purchased them

from us. Nor may they use their status to recall debts owed to them, unless they be debts pertaining to their office; their personal debts should be called in under the authority of the *bailli*, just as if they were not in our service.

[711] We forbid *baillis* and *prévôts* to inconvenience our subjects involved in cases brought before them by moving from place to place. Rather they should hear these cases in the customary locations, so that our subjects do not abandon pursuit of their rights because of the effort or expense involved.

[712] Moreover, we order that they should not deprive any man of his possessions without full consideration of the cause or without our express command, and nor may they burden our people with new exactions in the form of new taxes or fees. Nor may they summon men to military service in order to raise money from them, for we desire that no one who owes military service should be summoned to the army without good cause, while those who wish to fulfil their military service in person should not be compelled to redeem the service they owe with a money payment.

[713] Further, we forbid *baillis* and *prévôts* to prevent grain or wine or other produce being taken out of our kingdom without good reason. When it is fitting that such a prohibition be made, we desire that it be made in committee with the advice of *preudommes*, free from suspicion of fraud or deceit.

[714] Likewise it is our will that all former *baillis*, viscounts, *prévôts* and mayors shall, once they have left their offices, stay in the region where they held that office for forty days, either in person or by proxy, in order to respond to the new *baillis* concerning their misconduct towards anyone who might wish to file a complaint against them.

[719] In all these measures we have ordained for the benefit of our subjects and of our kingdom, we reserve to our majesty the power to clarify, amend, add and retract as seems fit to us.[9]

Through this ordinance the condition of the kingdom of France was greatly improved, as many wise and aged people attest.

[715] At that time the office of *prévôt* of Paris used to be sold to the *bourgeois* of the city, or to one among them. And so it

was that any of these men, having purchased the office, would tolerate the scandalous behaviour of his children and nephews; these youths could rely on the protection of their parents and friends who held the *prévôté*. The humbler people were sorely oppressed as a result and could not assert their rights against the rich men because of the lavish presents and gifts the wealthy gave to the *prévôt*. [716] During that time anyone who told the truth to the *prévôt*, or who wanted to uphold an oath so as not to be forsworn in the matter of a debt or anything else he was obliged to answer for, was fined and punished by the *prévôt*. Because of the great injustices and the great robberies committed by the *prévôts*, the humbler people did not dare stay in the king's lands; instead they went to live in other *prévôtés* and in other lordships. The king's districts were so empty that when the *prévôt* held his court no more than ten or twelve people came.

[717] Besides, there were so many criminals and thieves in Paris and beyond that the whole country was full of them. The king, who was very mindful of how the humbler people were being looked after, saw the whole truth. And so he refused to allow the position of *prévôt* of Paris to be sold any more. He gave a generous and substantial salary to those who were to hold the post thereafter and abolished all the bad customs by which the people could be burdened. He made enquiries throughout the region and the kingdom as to where he might find a man who would do good and firm justice, and who would not spare the rich man any more than the poor. [718] He was told about Stephen Boileau,[10] who upheld and protected the office of *prévôt* so effectively that no criminal, thief or murderer dared remain in Paris; if he did he would be swiftly hanged or executed and no parent or relative or gold or silver could save him. The king's territories began to improve, and people came to them because of the sound justice done there. There was such population growth and regeneration that the king's revenues from land sales, legal proceedings, trade and other sources doubled in value compared with earlier times.

[720] From his childhood the king had compassion for the poor and needy. It was the custom that wherever the king went

120 poor people each day would, without fail, be provided with bread and wine and meat or fish; during Lent and Advent the number of poor people fed rose. On many occasions it happened that the king himself served them, set food before them and carved the meat, and when they left he gave them money with his own hand. [721] Moreover on the eve of solemn feasts he would serve the poor with these things before he ate or drank himself. As well as all this, every day he had elderly and infirm men eat lunch and dinner in his company, giving them the same food he ate himself. After having eaten they left with a sum of money. [722] Besides all this, the king gave such large and generous alms each day to needy men and women of religion, to impoverished hospitals, poor sick people and other needy communities, as well as to poor gentlemen, gentlewomen, unmarried girls, prostitutes, widows, pregnant women, and to poor labourers who because of old age or illness could not work or keep up their craft or trade, that one could hardly calculate their value. Because of this we might well say that he was happier than the Roman Emperor Titus, whom ancient writings record was greatly saddened and distressed on any day when he had not performed an act of kindness.[11]

[723] From the time he began to rule his kingdom on his own behalf and could give attention to such matters, he started to build churches and numerous religious houses, among which the abbey of Royaumont holds the highest and most honoured place. He built several almshouses – those at Paris, Pontoise, Compiègne and Vernon – and provided them with substantial revenues. He founded the abbey of Saint-Matthieu at Rouen, where he housed Dominican nuns, and the abbey of Longchamp, where he installed Franciscan nuns, and endowed them with large revenues for the nuns to live off. [724] He gave his mother permission to found the abbey of Lys near Melun-sur-Seine, and that of Maubuisson outside Pontoise, and then granted them substantial revenues and properties. He founded the hospital for the blind outside Paris to house poor blind people from the city and had a chapel built for them so that they could hear Divine Office. He established the Carthusian house of Vauvert outside Paris and assigned the monks who

served Our Lord there a sufficient income. [725] Soon afterwards he had another house built outside Paris, on the road to
Saint-Denis; it was called the House of the Daughters of God.
He placed a great many women in that house who through
poverty had given themselves up to sins of lust, and provided
them with an income of 400 *livres* to support themselves. He
also built houses for *béguines* in several places in his kingdom
and gave them revenues to maintain themselves, ordering that
women who wanted to make a commitment to live chastely
should be received into them.

[726] Some of those close to him grumbled that he gave so
much charity that the cost was excessive. And he said to them,
'I prefer it that my extravagant expenditure be incurred through
giving charity for the love of God than through worldly pride
or vainglory.' And the king's great expenditure on charity never
meant that he failed to spend generously within his own household from day to day. The king gave freely and abundantly at
parlements and at assemblies of barons and knights, and the
hospitality he extended at his court was very courteous and
generous, more so than had been the case at the courts of his
ancestors for many years before.

[727] The king loved all men and women who gave themselves to the service of God and wore the religious habit; none
of them ever came to him without receiving something to support their way of life. He provided for the Carmelite friars and
bought them a property by the Seine near Charenton, where he
had a house built for them. He bought them vestments, chalices,
and those things necessary to perform the service of Our Lord.
Afterwards he provided for the Augustinian friars and bought
a farmstead for them from a Parisian *bourgeois* along with all
the possessions associated with it, and had a church built for
them outside the Montmartre gate. [728] He provided for the
Friars of the Sacks,[12] giving them a site on the Seine near to
Saint-Germain-des-Prés where they installed themselves,
although they did not stay there very long since the order was
soon suppressed. After the Friars of the Sacks had been housed
another sort of friars appeared, called the Order of the White
Mantles, and they asked the king to help them establish them-

selves at Paris.[13] In order to accommodate them the king bought them a house and some old buildings in its vicinity near the old Temple gate at Paris, quite close to the weavers' district. This order was suppressed at the Council of Lyons held by Gregory X.[14] [729] Later another sort of friars came who called themselves the Friars of the Holy Cross[15] and wore crosses on their chests. They asked the king for his help and he gave it willingly, housing them in a street called the Temple Crossroads, which is called Holy Cross Street today. In this way the good king installed men of religion all round the city of Paris.

[730] One Lent, following the events just described, it so happened that the king summoned all his barons to Paris. I excused myself to him on account of a quartan fever I was suffering at the time, and asked that he might do without me. He let me know that he most certainly did want me to come, since he had good physicians at Paris who knew well how to cure a quartan fever. [731] And so I went to Paris. When I arrived there, late on the eve of the feast of Our Lady observed in March,[1] I could find no one – neither the queen nor anyone else – who was able to tell me why the king had summoned me. It so happened – as God willed it – that I fell asleep during matins. As I slept I thought I saw the king kneeling in front of an altar, and I thought I saw several prelates in their vestments dressing him in a chasuble made of red Rheims serge. [732] After having this vision I called my lord William, my priest, who was very learned, and related what I had seen to him. And he said to me, 'My lord, you will see the king take the cross tomorrow.' I asked him why he thought so, and he told me that it was on account of the dream I had experienced. 'For the chasuble of red serge signified the cross, which was reddened with the blood God poured out on it from his side and from his hands and feet, and the chasuble being made of Rheims serge signified that this crusade will achieve little, as you will also see if God grants you a long enough life.'

[733] When I had heard the Mass at the church of the Magdalene in Paris, I went to the king's chapel and found him there. He had gone up on to the reliquary platform and was having the relic of the True Cross fetched down. As the king came

down again, two knights from his council began to talk to one another. One of them said: 'Never believe me again if the king doesn't take the cross now.' And the other replied that, 'If the king does take the cross, this will be one of the saddest days there has ever been in France. For if we don't take the cross we'll lose the king, and if we do take the cross we'll lose God, since we would not be taking the cross for him, but out of fear of the king.'

[734] As it happened, the king took the cross the following day along with his three sons, and, in accordance with my priest's prediction, it turned out that this crusade achieved little. I came under heavy pressure from the king of France and the king of Navarre to take the cross myself. [735] I replied to them that while I had been overseas in the service of God and the king, and in the aftermath of my return, the officials of the kings of France and Navarre had oppressed and impoverished my people to such an extent that there would never be a time when they and I would be in a worse position. I told them that if I wanted to act in accordance with God's will I would stay here in order to help and protect my people. For if I were to expose my life to the dangers of the pilgrimage of the cross when I could quite clearly see that this would be to the harm and detriment of my people, I would incur the anger of God, who offered up his life in order to save his people.

[736] I deemed all those who advised the king to go to have committed a mortal sin, for during the time he was in France the whole kingdom was at peace both within itself and with its neighbours, and since his departure the condition of the kingdom has done nothing but decline. [737] Those who advised the king to go committed a great sin because of his very weak physical condition; he could not bear to travel either in a carriage or on horseback. His frailty was such that he allowed me to carry him in my arms from the count of Auxerre's residence, where I took my leave of him, to the house of the Franciscans. But even in this feeble state, if he had stayed in France he might have lived a while longer and done much good.

[738] I do not want to say or relate anything concerning his expedition to Tunis, since I was not there – thank God – and I

do not want to say or include in my book anything of which I am not certain. My subject is our saintly king, nothing else, and therefore, I will simply say that after his arrival at Tunis, before the castle at Carthage, he was seized by a diarrhoea sickness while his oldest son, Philip, fell ill with a quartan fever and the same diarrhoea that afflicted the king. The king took to his bed, feeling sure that he would soon pass from this world to the other. [739] He called for my lord Philip, his son, and commanded him to uphold, just as if he were making out his will, all the teachings he was leaving him. These teachings[2] are written out here in French and were, so it is said, written down by the king's own saintly hand.

[740] 'Dear son, the first thing I admonish you is to apply your heart to the love of God, for without doing so no man can be saved. Keep yourself from doing anything displeasing to God, by which I mean any mortal sin; you should rather endure all manner of torments than commit a mortal sin.

[741] 'If God sends you hardship, you should accept it patiently, give thanks to Our Lord for it and know that you have deserved it and that he will direct events for your own good. If he gives you good fortune, give humble thanks to him for it, so that a blessing that should make you more worthy does not lead you into pride or any other fault by which you will be diminished. For we should not make war on God with his own gifts.

[742] 'Make confession often, and choose as your confessor a *preudomme* who knows how to instruct you as to what you should do and what you should beware of. You should conduct yourself in such a way that your confessor and your friends are not afraid to make you aware of your faults. Listen devotedly to the services of the Holy Church without mocking or making light of them. Pray with both your heart and tongue, especially when the consecration is performed during the Mass. Your heart should be tender and compassionate towards the poor, the wretched and the suffering; comfort and help them as much as you can.

[743] 'Uphold the good customs of your kingdom and abolish the bad. Do not be covetous of your people; do not burden

your conscience by imposing taxes or charges unless you have an urgent need to do so.

[744] 'If anything weighs heavy on your heart, immediately tell your confessor or another *preudomme* who is not full of frivolous talk, and then you will be able to cope with it more easily.

[745] 'Make sure that you have faithful *preudommes* in your company who are not full of greed, both laymen and men of religion, and talk to them often. Shun and remove yourself from the company of wicked men. Listen willingly to the word of God, keep it in your heart, and secure for yourself prayers and indulgences. Love that which is beneficial to you and your virtue, and loathe all wickedness wherever it may be.

[746] 'Let no one be so bold as to say anything in your presence which might attract or incite men to sin, or to defame and slander others behind their backs. Nor should you permit anything denigrating to God or his saints to be said in your presence. Give frequent thanks to God for all the blessings he has given you, so that you might be worthy of receiving more.

[747] 'To uphold justice and be fair to your subjects, you should be trustworthy and firm, not turning to right or left; follow the straight path and support the side of the poor until such time as the truth is revealed. And if anyone brings a case against you, do not draw any conclusion until you know the truth of the matter; in this way your councillors will make their judgement more assuredly in accordance with the truth, whether for you or against you.

[748] 'If you are in possession of anything that belongs to someone else, whether by your own doing or that of your ancestors, you should return it immediately if the fault is certain. And if the situation is unclear, have it investigated speedily and diligently by men of sound judgement.

[749] 'You should take care to ensure that your people and your subjects live under you in peace and in accordance with the law. Likewise you should keep the good towns and communes of your kingdom in the condition and freedom in which your ancestors maintained them. If there is anything that requires reform, do what is needed and set matters straight,

keeping these communities in your favour and love. For the strength and wealth of these large towns will give rise to a fear of wronging you among foreigners and your own people, especially your peers and barons.

[750] 'Honour and love all representatives of the Holy Church, and make sure that no one may diminish or deprive them of the gifts and alms offered to them by your ancestors. They say that King Philip, my grandfather, was once told by one of his councillors that the men and women of the Holy Church were doing him great harm by usurping his rights and encroaching on his justice, and that it was a great wonder that he allowed this to go on. The good king replied that he knew what the councillor had said to be true but, in view of the blessings and honours granted to him by God, he would rather let some of his rights be lost than engage in a dispute with the men and women of the Holy Church.

[751] 'Honour and respect your father and mother and follow their commands. Give benefices of the Holy Church to good men of pure life, and do so with advice from *preudommes* and virtuous people.

[752] 'Beware of embarking on a war against a Christian without long deliberation. If it is necessary to do so, then protect the Holy Church and those who have done no wrong. If wars or disputes arise among your subjects, bring them to peace as quickly as possible.

[753] 'Take special care to have good *prévôts* and good *baillis*, and enquire often of them and of those in your household concerning their conduct and whether they are guilty of excessive greed, dishonesty or trickery. Work to rid your lands of all base sins; in particular you should combat the swearing of blasphemous oaths and heresy with all your power. Make sure that your household expenditure is reasonable and measured.

[754] 'And finally, most sweet son, have Masses sung and prayers said for my soul throughout your kingdom, and dedicate a full and special share of all your good deeds to me. My sweet, dear son, I offer you all the blessings a kind father can give to his son. May the blessed Trinity and all the saints keep

you and defend you from all ills, and may God grant you grace always to do his will, so that he may be honoured by you and so that you and we may be together with him after this mortal life and praise him without end. Amen.'

[755] When the good king had given his instructions to his son my lord Philip, his sickness began to worsen grievously. He asked for the sacraments of the Holy Church and was seen to receive them in sound mind and with the proper understanding, for when he was anointed and the seven psalms were said, he spoke the verses in response. [756] I have heard my lord the count of Alençon, the king's son, recall that when he was approaching death he called on the saints to help and comfort him. He called on my lord Saint James in particular as he said his prayer which begins 'Esto, Domine', 'O God be the sanctifier and protector of your people.' He then called on my lord Saint Denis of France to aid him when he said his prayer which has this meaning: 'Lord God, grant that we may despise the riches of this world so that we may fear no adversity.' [757] And I heard from my lord of Alençon – may God absolve him – that his father then called out to my lady Saint Genevieve. After this the king had himself laid in a bed covered with ashes and placed his hands on his chest; as he looked towards Heaven he returned his spirit to our creator, at the same hour at which the Son of God died on the cross[3] for the salvation of the world.

[758] It is a pious and fitting thing to weep for the passing of this saintly prince, who maintained his kingdom in so saintly and honest a manner and who gave such generous alms and instituted so many fine ordinances there. Just as the scribe who has made a book illuminates it with gold and azure, this king illuminated his kingdom with the beautiful abbeys he built there, and the great number of hospitals and houses of Dominicans and Franciscans and other religious that have already been mentioned.

[759] Good King Louis passed from this world on the day following the feast of Saint Bartholomew the apostle[4] in the year of Our Lord's incarnation, the year of grace 1270. His bones were kept in a casket and brought back for burial at Saint-Denis in France; he was buried there where he had chosen

to have his tomb[5] and where God has since, through his merits, performed many fine miracles for him.

[760] Afterwards, through the efforts of the king of France and at the command of the pope,[6] the archbishop of Rouen and Brother John of Samois (who later became a bishop) came to Saint-Denis in France and stayed there for a long while in order to enquire into the life, works and miracles of the holy king. I was summoned to go to them, and they kept me for two days. After having heard testimony from me and from others, their findings were taken to the papal court at Rome. The pope and the cardinals examined this evidence carefully, and on the basis of what they saw, they did the king justice and placed him among the number of the confessors.[7] [761] This was a cause, as it should still be, of great joy throughout the kingdom of France and great honour to all those of his heirs who wish to emulate him in conducting themselves virtuously, as well as to those of his lineage who wish to follow him in their good works. It should bring great shame to those of his heirs who seek to do wrong, for fingers will be pointed at them and they will be told that the saintly king from whom they issue would have spurned such wicked behaviour.

[762] After this good news arrived from Rome the king appointed the day following the feast of Saint Bartholomew[8] for the translation of the saintly body. When the saintly remains had been exhumed, they were carried out to the platform that had been prepared for them. The then archbishop of Rheims – may God absolve him – and my nephew my lord Henry of Villars, who was archbishop of Lyons at that time, were at the head of the party that bore them, with several other archbishops and bishops whose names I do not know behind them.

[763] Brother John of Samois delivered the sermon there, and among the other great deeds performed by our saintly king he mentioned one that I had given sworn testimony of, and which I had seen for myself. He said, [764] 'So that you might understand that he was the most trustworthy man of his age, I want to tell you that he was so honest that in his dealings with the Saracens he wished to be bound by an agreement he had made with them on a purely verbal basis. If he had not upheld

it he would have profited by 10,000 *livres* and more.' Brother
John then recounted all the details as they are written down
above. And when he had reported what had happened he said,
'Don't think I am misleading you, for I can see the man here
who gave evidence of this to me under oath.'

[765] Once the sermon had ended, the king and his brothers,
with help from other members of their family, carried into the
church the saintly body to which they should offer due rever-
ence, for a great honour has been done to them and resides
only in them, as I said to you before. Let us pray that the saintly
king might plead with God to give us that which we need for
the good of our bodies and souls. Amen.

[766] In what follows I would like to describe certain things
concerning our saintly king that I saw in my sleep and which
will be to his honour. In my dream I had the impression that I
saw him outside my chapel at Joinville; he was, so it seemed to
me, wonderfully happy and at ease in his heart. I too was very
glad to see him in my castle, and I said to him, 'My lord, when
you leave this place I will put you up at one of my houses in
my town called Chevillon.' Laughing, he replied to me, 'My
lord of Joinville, by the faith I owe you, I do not wish to leave
here so soon.'

[767] When I woke up I reflected on this, and it struck me
that it would be pleasing to God and to the saintly king if I
were to offer him a resting place in my chapel. And I did just
that, for I established an altar dedicated to God and to him,
and endowed it with an income in perpetuity to enable Masses
to be sung there in his honour forever. I have brought these
things to the attention of my lord King Louis, who has inherited
his name, since it appears to me that he would do God's will
and our saintly King Louis's, if he would seek out relics of the
true body of that saint and send them to the said chapel of Saint
Lawrence at Joinville, so that those who visit his altar might
increase their devotion to him.

[768] I hereby inform everyone that I have set down here a
great number of the deeds of our saintly king that I saw and
heard myself, as well as a good number of his deeds that I found
in a book in the French language[9] and which I have had written

down in this work. I am bringing these things to your attention so that those who hear this book might believe firmly what it says about those things I did truly see and hear myself. I cannot state whether the other things written down here are true since I neither saw nor heard them. [769] This was written in the year of grace 1309, in the month of October.

Appendix I

TWO 'CRUSADE SONGS'

The lyrics to these two Old French songs have been chosen primarily because they were composed in the context of the crusade campaigns narrated by Geoffrey of Villehardouin and John of Joinville. Their lyricists may serve as representatives of the literary milieu in which these crusader–authors existed, and Joinville might have written the second song himself.

Both were included in a collection of twenty-nine published in 1909 by Joseph Bédier and Pierre Aubry under the title *Les Chansons de Croisade*.[1] Although the term 'crusade song' has proved a convenient one for historians and literary scholars interested in the relationship between the crusades and contemporary literature, it is not a label that would have been recognized by people in the Middle Ages as marking out a distinct genre. Rather, crusading themes appeared in songs of a range of different types: exhortation or propaganda, celebrating or lamenting specific crusading events, and love. A further reason for including these songs is that they demonstrate the contrasting contexts in which crusading themes were explored by thirteenth-century lyricists; the first is a love song, the second a complaint about particular crusading circumstances.

The English translations are my own.

'S'onques nus hom pour dure departie'

The lyrics were most probably written by Hugh V of Berzé, a knightly poet from Burgundy (in the east of the French-speaking lands) who took part in the Fourth Crusade.[2] Hugh's cross-taking, in which he was joined by his father, was reported by Villehardouin (Conquest, § 45). Born between 1165 and 1170, Hugh of Berzé composed the lyrics to at least five surviving songs. Towards the end of his life (he probably died in 1220 or shortly thereafter) he composed an extended work in verse known as his Bible, *which is work of moral and social critique and reflection. In this song, the combination of the themes of love and crusading enabled the lyricist to explore the 'separation motif' – the suffering endured by a crusader who desires to stay near his beloved but is duty- and honour-bound to leave. The specific circumstances of the Fourth Crusade barely intrude on the lyrics, although an allusion to the crusader–lover's presence in Lombardy in the* envoi, *or brief concluding verse, evokes the journey made by the campaign's French participants to their mustering point at Venice.*

I

S'onques nus hom pour dure departie
Doit estre saus, jel serai par raison,
C'onques torte ki pert son compaignon
Ne fu un jor de moi plus esbahie.
Chascuns pleure sa terre et son païs,
Quant il se part de ses coreus amis;
Mais il n'est nus congiés, quoi ke nus die,
Si dolerex com d'ami at d'amie.

II

Li reveoirs m'a mis en la folie
10   Dont m'estoie gardés mainte saison.
D'aler a li or ai quis l'ocoison
Dont je morrai, et, se je vif, ma vie
Vaura bien mort, car chil qui est apris
D'estre envoisiés et chantans et jolis
A pis assés, quant sa joie est faillie,
Que s'il morust tot a une foïe.

III

Mout a croisiés amorous a contendre
D'aler a Dieu ou de remanoir chi,
Car nesuns hom, puis k'Amors l'a saisi,
20   Ne devroit ja tel afaire entreprendre.
On ne puet pas server a tant signor.
Pruec ke fins cuers ki bee a haute honor

Ne porroit pas remanoir sans mesprendre,
Pour ce, dame, ne me devés reprendre.

IV

Se jou seüsse autretant a l'emprendre
Ke li congiés me tormentast ensi,
Je laissasse m'ame en vostre merchi,
S'alasse a Dieu grasses et merchis rendre
De ce que ainc soffristes a nul jor
Ke je fuisse baans a vostre amor;   30
Mais je me tieng a paiet de l'atendre,
Puis que chascuns vos aime ensi sans prendre.

V

Un confort voi en nostre dessevrance
Que Dieus n'avra en moi que reprochier;
Mais, quant pour lui me convient vos laissier,
Je ne sai rien de greignor reprovance;
Car cil que Dieus fait partir et sevrer
De tel amor que n'en puet retorner,
A assés plus et d'ire et de pesance
Que n'avroit ja li rois, s'il perdoit France.   40

VI

Ahi! dame, tot est fors de balance.
Partir m'estuet de vos sans recovrier.
Tant en ai fait que je nel puis laissier;
Et s'il ne fust de remanoir viltance
Et reprochiers, j'alaisse demander
A fine Amor congié de demorer;
Mais vos estes de si trés grant vaillance
Que vostre amis ne doit faire faillance.

Mout par est fous ki s'en vait outre mer
Et prent congié a sa dame a l'aler;   50
Mais mandast li de Lombardie en France,
Que li congiés doble la desirance.

Translation:

I

If ever a man, for having undergone a cruel separation, deserved to be saved it would be me, and with good reason. For no turtle dove that lost its mate was ever more distraught than me. Every man weeps for his lands and his country when he takes leave of the friends closest to his heart, but there is no farewell – whatever they say – as sorrowful as that between lover and beloved.

II

Seeing her again has plunged me into a madness from which I had shielded myself for many a year. In going to her I flirted with death, and though I am yet alive my life will be as good as death, since a man who is used to being light-hearted, singing and joyful, comes to a much worse end when his joy has run out than if he were killed in an instant.

III

An amorous crusader faces a great dilemma as to whether he should go to God or remain here; and so no man, once he has been seized by Love, should commit himself to such an undertaking. It is impossible to serve so many masters. But because a noble heart that yearns for the highest honour cannot stay here without transgressing, you should not, my lady, reprove me.

IV

If I had fully understood when I embarked on this endeavour that taking my leave would torment me so, I would have left my soul in your mercy and gone to offer grateful thanks to God that you ever allowed me to aspire to your love. But I deem myself sufficiently rewarded by the hope of it, since each man loves you in this way: without return.

V

I find one comfort in our separation, which is that God will have nothing to reproach me for. But since it is on his account that I must leave you, I can think of no greater cause for complaint. For the man who is made to leave by God and who is severed from a love he could not deny, is much more angered and distressed than the king would be if he lost France.

VI

Ah! My lady, there can no longer be any doubt. I am compelled to leave you and have no recourse. I have come so far that I cannot turn back, yet if there were not shame and reproach in staying, I would go and ask noble Love for permission to remain here. But you are of such very great worth that your lover must not fail to do his duty.

The man who sets off overseas, taking leave of his lady on his departure, is quite mad; might he rather have sent word from Lombardy to her in France, since parting doubles desire.[3]

'Nus ne porroit de mauvese reson'

In contrast to the previous song, the lyrics to 'Nus ne porroit de mauvese reson' are very much concerned with the crusading events that accompanied its composition. This song was written at Acre in 1250, during the period in which King Louis IX was deciding whether to stay in the East or return home to France. Among the composer's concerns are the plight of those crusaders who were either killed or remained captive in the wake of Louis IX's failed campaign in Egypt (verses II and III) and the shame that would be incurred if they were not aided and avenged (V). In order to salvage the situation, the lyricist calls on the king to employ the large quantities of money he has not yet spent (IV).

These specific complaints, concerns and recommendations were among those presented by Joinville in the passages of The Life of Saint Louis *that deal with the decision as to whether to stay in Syria in 1250 (§§ 419–37). This, together with the lyricist's apparent connection with Champagne (verse V), has fuelled conjecture that Joinville may himself be the writer. Factors arguing against this theory include the fact that he did not mention having composed such a song in* Life, *and the strength of the lyricist's criticism of Louis IX.[4] Ralph of Soissons, a well-known Champenois lyricist and participant in three crusades, including both of those led by Louis IX (see § 470 of* Life *for his presence in Syria in the wake of Louis's first crusade campaign), has also been proposed as the lyricist of this song.*[5]

I

Nus ne porroit de mauvese reson
Bonne chançon ne fere ne chanter;
Pour ce n'i vueill mettre m'entencion,
Que j'è assez autre chose a penser;
Et non pour quant la terre d'outre mer
    Voi en si trés grant balance
Qu'en chantant vueil proier le roy de France
Qu'il ne croie couart ne losengier
De sa honte ne de la Dieu vengier.

II

10   Hé! gentilz roys, quant Diex vous fist croisier,
Toute Egypte doutoit vostre renon.
Or perdez tout, s'ainsi voulez lessier
Jherusalem en tel chetivoison;
Car quant Diex fist de vous election
    Et seigneur de sa venjance,
Bien deüssiez mostrer vostre puissance
De revengier les morts et les chetis
Qui pour Dieu sont et pour vous mort et pris.

III

Rois, vous savez que Diex a po d'amis
20   Ne onques mès n'en ot si grant mestier;
Car par vous est ses pueples mors et pris,
Ne nus fors vous ne leur porroit aidier,
Ke povrer sont cil autre chevalier,
    Si criement la demorance,
Et s'en tel point leur feïssiez faillance,
Saint et martir, apostre et innocent
Se plaindroient de vous au jugement.

IV

> Rois, vous avez tresor d'or et d'argent
> Plus que nus rois n'ot onques, ce m'est vis,
> Si en devez doner plus largement
> Et demorer pour garder cest païs,
> Car vous avez plus perdu que conquis,
>   Si seroit trop grant vitance
> De retorner atout la mescheance;
> Mais demorez, si ferez grant vigor,
> Tant que France ait recovree s'onor.

30

V

> Rois, s'en tel point vous metez au retor,
> France diroit, Champaigne et tote gent
> Que vostre los avez mis en trestor
> Et gaaignié avez mains que nïent;
> Et des prisons qui vivent a torment
>   Deüssiez avoir pesance;
> Bien deüssiez querre leur delivrance:
> Quant pour vous sont et pour Jhesu martir,
> C'est granz pechiez ses i laissiez morir.

40

Translation:

I

No one can compose or sing a pleasing song on an unsavoury theme, and because of this I would rather not address this topic, since I have plenty of other things to think about. And yet I see the land of Outremer in such very great peril that I wish, through song, to entreat the king of France that he should not heed cowards and flatterers when his shame and God's vengeance are at stake.

II

Alas! Noble king, when God had you take the cross all Egypt was in fear of your renown. Yet now you will lose everything if you are thus willing to leave Jerusalem in such captivity; for since God chose you for your role and as master of his vengeance you should certainly make your power felt in order to avenge the dead and the prisoners,[6] who for God and for you were killed and taken captive.

III

O king, you know that God has few friends, although he has never had greater need of them; it was on your account that his people were killed and taken captive and no one but you is able to help them, for these other knights are poor and are frightened to stay. And if you let them down in this matter, the saints and martyrs, apostles and innocents, will speak out against you at the judgement.[7]

IV

O king, you have stores of gold and of silver greater than any king ever had, or so it seems to me. You should give of them more generously and stay to defend this land, for you have lost more than you have won and it would be too great an outrage to return with such misfortune. Stay instead, and exert great effort, sufficient that France might recover its honour.

V

O king, if you set out to return at this time, those in France and Champagne, and everyone else, will say that you have abandoned your good name and won less than nothing. You should be mindful of those prisoners who are living in torment and you should certainly strive for their deliverance: it is a great sin to leave them here to die since it is for you and for Jesus that they are martyrs.

NOTES

1. *Les Chansons de Croisade*, ed. Joseph Bédier and Pierre Aubry (Paris: Champion, 1909), pp. 121–31, pp. 259–67. Bédier edited the lyrics, Aubrey the melodies.
2. A case may be made for attributing this song to Guy, the castellan of Coucy, another participant in the Fourth Crusade (see Ville-hardouin's *Conquest*, §§ 7, 114, 124), but Hugh of Berzé is deemed the more likely lyricist by both Joseph Bédier and the most recent editor of Hugh's lyric oeuvre (Bédier and Aubry

(eds.), *Les Chansons de Croisade*, pp. 122–3; Luca Barbieri (ed.),
Le Liriche di Hugues de Berzé (Milan: Edizioni C.U.S.L., 2001),
pp. 246–7).

3. *might he rather have sent word from Lombardy to her in France,
    since parting doubles desire*: The sense of these lines is hard to
    grasp. Bédier suggests that the songwriter wants to encourage
    crusaders to avoid a face-to-face farewell with their lovers, since
    this will only intensify the pain of their desire. Barbieri says that
    the songwriter, who is already on his way to Venice and is in
    Lombardy as he writes, wishes to instruct the singer to take
    greetings to his lady back in France that will express his absence-
    fuelled fondness. (*Le Liriche di Hugues de Berzé*, pp. 255, 257).

4. Gaston Paris, 'La chanson composée à Acre en Juin 1250',
    Romania, 23 (1894), pp. 508–24.

5. Ineke Hardy, '"Nus ne poroit de mauvaise raison" (R1887): A
    case for Raoul de Soissons', *Mediem Aevum*, 70 (2001), pp. 95–
    111; Cathrynke Dijkstra, 'Raoul de Soissons: A postscript',
    Medium Aevum, 72 (2003), pp. 108–12.

6. *the dead and the prisoners*: Those killed during Louis IX's cru-
    sade campaign in Egypt, and those who had been taken prisoner
    with him in 1250 but who had not yet been released. These
    people were rank and file members of the crusade army, of lower
    social status and no wealth.

7. *at the judgement*: On Judgement Day.

Appendix II

EPITAPH FOR GEOFFREY III OF JOINVILLE

In 1311 an epitaph composed in Old French by John of Joinville to honour the memory of his great-great-grandfather, Geoffrey III of Joinville (d. 1188), was inscribed and placed at Geoffrey's tomb at the Cistercian abbey of Clairvaux. As well as noting Geoffrey III's praiseworthy conduct as a Christian and as a knight, it provides an outline genealogy of the Joinville family from the mid-twelfth century into John of Joinville's own lifetime. With the exception of John's uncle, William, who had a distinguished career in the Church, all the individuals mentioned took part in crusades and their achievements in the East feature prominently among those actions deemed worthy of note. The inscription placed at Clairvaux is unfortunately no longer extant; the translation presented here is made from the 'restored' version of Natalis de Wailly, which was prepared using two transcriptions of the epitaph made in the seventeenth and eighteenth centuries.[1] (The translation is mine.)

Lord God almighty, I pray to you that you may have tender mercy on Geoffrey, lord of Joinville, who lies here, and to whom you showed such grace in this world that he founded and built in his lifetime numerous churches for you: first, the abbey of Ecurey, of the Order of Cîteaux; also the abbey of Jovilliers of the Order of Prémontré; likewise the house at Mathons of the Order of Grandmont; also the priory of Val d'Osne of Molesmes and the church of Saint Lawrence at the castle of Joinville. Wherefore all those who have issued from him should have hope in God and trust that God has set him among his company, since the saints bear witness that the man who builds God's house on earth prepares his own house in Heaven. He was the best knight of his age, as is apparent from the great deeds he performed on this side of the sea and on the other;[2] it was because of this that the seneschalcy of Champagne was awarded to him and to his heirs, who have held it ever since. From him issued Geoffrey, who was lord of Joinville and who lies at Acre.[3] This Geoffrey was the father of William, who lies in the lead-covered tomb and was bishop of Langres and then archbishop of Rheims. This William was the full brother of Simon, who was lord of Joinville and seneschal of Champagne; he too was among the number of the good knights on account of the great prizes he won as a warrior on this side of the sea and on the other – he was with King John of Acre at the capture of Damietta.[4] This Simon was the father of John, lord of Joinville and seneschal of Champagne, who is still alive and who had this inscription made in the year 1311 – may God grant him what he knows to be needful to his soul and body. The aforementioned Simon was also the brother of Geoffrey Trouillart,[5] who too was the lord of Joinville and seneschal of Champagne and who, because of the great deeds he performed on this side of the sea and on the other, was also among the number of the good knights. Since he died in the Holy Land without any direct heirs, and in order that his renown should not fade, John (the lord still living) brought his shield back from there after having stayed overseas in the service of our saintly King Louis for a period of six years. And this king did many kind things for the said lord. This lord of Joinville placed the shield in the church of Saint Lawrence so that people might pray for him, the aforementioned Geoffrey's prowess being illustrated on his shield since King Richard of England did him the honour of quartering Geoffrey's arms with his own. This Geoffrey passed over from this world in August of the year of grace 1192.[6] May he rest in peace.

NOTES

1.   *Histoire de Saint Louis, Credo et lettre à Louis X*, ed. Natalis de Wailly (Paris: Librairie Firmin Didot, 1874), pp. 544–7.
2.   *on this side of the sea and on the other*: Geoffrey III of Joinville participated in the Second Crusade.
3.   *Geoffrey . . . lies at Acre*: Geoffrey IV of Joinville died at Acre in 1190, during the course of the Third Crusade.
4.   *Simon . . . the capture of Damietta*: Simon of Joinville (d. 1233) took part in the capture of Damietta by the forces of the Fifth Crusade in 1219 (see § 165 of Joinville's *Life of Saint Louis*).

5.   *Geoffrey Trouillart*: Geoffrey V of Joinville, who died in around
     1204 at Krak des Chevaliers in Syria, was among the group who
     had taken the cross for the Fourth Crusade but chose to sail to
     the Near East rather than join the main army of the Fourth
     Crusade that went on to capture Constantinople; these men were
     roundly and repeatedly condemned by Geoffrey of Villehardouin
     in *The Conquest of Constantinople* (see, for example, §§ 96,
     229).

6.   *This Geoffrey passed over from this world in August of the year
     of grace 1192*: The date is erroneous; none of the Geoffreys
     mentioned in the epitaph died in 1192. It seems most likely
     that the author meant to direct the reader's thoughts back to
     Geoffrey III, the principal subject of the epitaph and the man
     whose tomb it marked.

Notes

THE CONQUEST OF CONSTANTINOPLE

CHAPTER I

PREPARATIONS FOR THE FOURTH CRUSADE

1. *the Roman Pope Innocent ... Fulk of Neuilly*: Pope Innocent III
    (r. 1198–1216), King Philip II of France (known as Philip Augus-
    tus, r. 1180–1223) and King Richard I of England (r. 1189–99).
    Fulk of Neuilly (d. 1202), a charismatic preacher whose sermons
    (many of which focused on the moral failings of late-twelfth-
    century society) had attracted attention and aroused enthusiasm
    in the regions around Paris before he became involved in the
    preaching of the Fourth Crusade.
2. *in France*: In this instance indicates the area around Paris known
    as the Ile-de-France.
3. *Thibaut ... Chartres*: Count Thibaut III of Champagne (d. 1201)
    and Count Louis I of Blois and Chartres (d. 1205).
4. *the start of Advent*: 28 November 1199.
5. *nephews and first cousins of the king of France and nephews
    of the king of England*. Thibaut's and Louis's mothers were
    half-sisters of both Philip II of France and Richard I of England,
    hence they were nephews of both kings. Their fathers were both
    brothers of Philip II's mother, making them first cousins of the
    French king as well.
6. *Simon of Montfort*: Count Simon of Montfort (d. 1218), most
    famous now for his leadership of the Albigensian Crusade, which
    began in 1208 and was fought against Cathar heretics and their
    supporters in south-west France. The identities and careers of
    the French crusaders here are the subject of a detailed study by
    the historian Jean Longnon, *Les compagnons de Villehardouin:*

Recherches sur les croisés de la quatrième croisade (Geneva: Droz, 1978). Unless the conventionally used form is different, the names and toponyms used here generally follow those proposed by Longnon. A toponym is a second name derived from a place name with which an individual (or their ancestors) claimed a connection, often of lordship.

7. *Geoffrey of Joinville . . . his brother Robert*: Geoffrey V of Joinville (d. *c.* 1204) and his brother Robert (d. 1205) were uncles of John of Joinville, author of *The Life of Saint Louis* (hereafter *Life*).

8. *Guy the castellan of Coucy*: Guy (d. 1203) was one of the famed songwriters to take part in the Fourth Crusade. It is possible that he wrote the lyrics to 'S'onques nus hom pour dure departie' (see Appendix I), although it is more often attributed to Hugh of Berzé. See also § 124.

9. *Ash Wednesday, Count Baldwin of Flanders and Hainaut*: 23 February 1200; Count Baldwin IX of Flanders and Hainaut (d. 1205) was the future emperor of Constantinople.

10. *Conon of Béthune*: Conon of Béthune (d. 1219 or 1220) was a loyal servant of the counts of Flanders and Hainaut, future emperors of Constantinople. He stayed in the Latin empire after the fall of Constantinople and in 1219 was appointed its regent. Conon of Béthune was also a poet of renown; the lyrics of ten of his songs have survived; most are love songs, though the crusades also feature as an important theme.

11. *the first week of Lent*: Lent began on 7 February 1201.

12. *Enrico Dandolo*: Enrico Dandolo (d. 1205) had ruled Venice as doge since 1192. Unlike most other European rulers at this time, this position was by election rather than inheritance; Dandolo's appointment followed an already lengthy career, much of it spent in service to the Venetian government at home and overseas. The date most often proposed for his birth is 1107, which would have made him at least 93 in 1201.

13. *for nine months*: The treaty itself says that the Venetians would provide provisions for one year. This is a rare example of an apparent conflict between Villehardouin's account and documentary evidence.

14. *94,000 marks*: This is the sum given in the manuscripts representing the earliest surviving tradition of Villehardouin's work (other manuscripts have 85,000 marks, which was that stated in the documents that later confirmed this arrangement). It is not clear whether the discrepancy here is a result of Villehardouin

having misremembered the details (this would be surprising), due to scribal error, or whether the initial sum quoted was later revised. The last is favoured by Queller and Madden, who propose that the total charge of 94,000 marks was reduced to 85,000, the fee for knights having been renegotiated down from 4 marks to 2 marks (Donald Queller and Thomas Madden, *The Fourth Crusade: The Conquest of Constantinople*, 2nd edn (Philadelphia: University of Pennsylvania Press, 1997), p. 11).

15. *the feast of Saint John*: 24 June, for Saint John the Baptist.

16. *he did most willingly*: Other sources suggest that Innocent III was less than wholehearted in his support for the arrangement, or at least that he issued caveats concerning the implementation of the treaty (Queller and Madden, *The Fourth Crusade*, pp. 18–20).

17. *the Mont Cenis pass ... King Tancred*: The pass was a route through the Alps connecting France and Italy. Count Walter III of Brienne (d. 1205) married Elvira, daughter of King Tancred of Sicily (r. 1189–94).

18. *Thus the count died*: On 25 May 1201.

19. *his father*: Count Henry I 'the Liberal' of Champagne (d. 1181), for more on whom see §§ 76 and 89–92 of Joinville's *Life*.

20. *She ... was pregnant with a son*: Count Thibaut IV of Champagne (b. 30 May 1201–1253), who would become king of Navarre in 1234.

21. *at the end of the month*: In late June 1201.

22. *Marquis Boniface of Montferrat*: Boniface (d. 1207) held Montferrat, in northern Italy, as a fief from the king of Germany, Philip of Swabia (r. 1198–1208). Although it cannot be proven, Villehardouin's confidence about Marquis Boniface's enthusiasm for the crusade is probably an indication that the two men had met and talked when Villehardouin passed through Montferrat during his return journey from Venice in the spring of 1201.

23. *the feast of the Holy Cross in September*: The feast of the Exaltation of the Holy Cross, 14 September 1201.

24. *Hugh of Berzé ... son of that name*): The younger Hugh of Berzé (d. 1220 or soon after) was one of the small group of accomplished poets and songwriters who set out on the Fourth Crusade. A crusade-related song generally attributed to him, 'S'onques nus hom pour dure departie', is given in Appendix I.

25. *The pilgrims would gladly ... so willed it*: See § 79.

352   NOTES

CHAPTER 2
THE CRUSADE ARMY AT VENICE

1. *After Easter, as Pentecost approached*: In the period between 14 April and 2 June 1202.
2. *an island . . . Saint Nicholas*: The Lido.
3. *the Straits of Morocco*: The Straits of Gibraltar.
4. *The king of Hungary has captured Zara in Slavonia*: Zara (modern-day Zadar, Croatia) was a port town on the Dalmatian coast which had been captured from the Venetians by King Bela III of Hungary (r. 1173–96) in 1186, now ruled by his successor, King Emeric of Hungary (r. 1196–1204).
5. *a great feast was being celebrated*: It is not entirely clear which feast is referred to, though the Nativity of the Virgin (8 September 1202) is most likely.
6. *lost his eyesight after sustaining a head wound*: Dandolo's blindness and its cause have been of great interest to both contemporary and recent commentators on the Fourth Crusade. Around 1202 there were rumours that Dandolo had been blinded as a result of an assault made on him at the imperial court during a trip to Constantinople in 1172 (on which trip see § 130 and ch. 4, note 8), and this fuelled the belief that he sought revenge on the Byzantines through the Fourth Crusade, but the story is now dismissed as baseless. (Thomas Madden, *Enrico Dandolo and the Rise of Venice* (Baltimore: Johns Hopkins University Press, 2003), pp. 63–8).
7. *Isaac . . . Alexius*: Isaac II Angelus (r. 1183–95 and 1203–4); Alexius III Angelus (r. 1195–1203).
8. *King Philip of Germany, who had married his sister*: Philip of Swabia, king of Germany (r. 1198–1208), was married to Irene Angelus (d. 1208).
9. *he chose his messengers and sent them to Marquis Boniface of Montferrat*: Although this was probably the first time that most of the crusade's leading men had heard about Alexius's situation, Marquis Boniface had met him the previous year and must have discussed the upcoming crusade and the possibility that it might promote Alexius's cause.

CHAPTER 3

THE CONQUEST OF ZARA

1. *the feast of Saint Rémy*: 1 October.
2. *On the eve of the feast of Saint Martin*: The feast is on 11 November, so 10 November 1202.
3. *breaking the chain*: Traffic in and out of ports was often controlled using a chain strung across the opening of the harbour that could be moved to allow vessels to pass.
4. *the March passage to Syria*: Most voyages from western Europe to the Near East were made during two key periods of the year: spring (March and April) and late summer (August and September).
5. *The abbot of Vaux*: Guy, abbot of the Cistercian monastery of Les-Vaux-de-Cernay, in northern France. The counts of Montfort, including Count Simon (see § 4), were closely associated with Vaux, and Abbot Guy and Count Simon were allies both in their opposition to the diversion of the Fourth Crusade to Constantinople and, later, in prosecuting the Albigensian Crusade.
6. *The abbot of Loos*: Simon, abbot of the monastery of Loos in Flanders, was an associate of the Flemish Count Baldwin, who would come out in favour of the diversion to Constantinople (see § 98).
7. *the French party*: Here 'French' covers the crusaders in general, most of whom came from French-speaking lands.
8. *the Flemish fleet you heard about earlier*: See §§ 48–9.
9. *The pope told . . . his sons*: It is clear from his letters that Innocent III was not as understanding and accommodating as Villehardouin suggests. His response to events at Zara was one of disappointment and anger, although he did make arrangements to absolve the crusaders from their excommunication. The situation regarding the Venetians was less straightforward since they had not requested absolution, believing they had done no wrong. Innocent III's letters to the crusade army on this matter are translated in Alfred Andrea, *Contemporary Sources for the Fourth Crusade* (Leiden and Boston: Brill, 2000), pp. 39–48.

CHAPTER 4

FROM ZARA TO CONSTANTINOPLE

1.   *at Easter*: 6 April 1203.
2.   *the feast of Saint Michael*: 29 September 1203.
3.   *the eve of Pentecost*: 24 May.
4.   *Cape Malea and the straits in the sea*: A peninsula on the southerly cost of mainland Greece, it lies at the end of the body of water that separates the Greek mainland from the island of Cythera.
5.   *Negroponte*: The island of Euboea.
6.   *the Abydos channel, where the Straits of Saint George enter the open sea*: We know the Abydos channel as the Dardanelles. The 'Straits of Saint George' was the medieval name for the body of water stretching east from the point where the Dardanelles meet the Aegean, via the Sea of Marmara to the Bosporus.
7.   *never was such a great project undertaken by as many men*: It is suggested that Villehardouin intended to emphasize how few men (rather than how large a number) were involved in this major undertaking, and that key words may have been omitted from the manuscripts (*La conquête de Constantinople*, ed. Edmond Faral, 2 vols., Les classiques de l'histoire de France au moyen âge 18–19 (Paris: Société d'édition 'Les belles lettres', 1938–9, 2nd edn, 1961), Vol. I, p. 131, n. 3.
8.   *I have been here before*: Dandolo had visited Constantinople on an abortive mission to Emperor Manuel I Commenus (r. 1143–80) in 1172, following the mass arrest of Venetians in the Byzantine empire and confiscation of their property in 1171. He went to Constantinople again in 1183, following the release of Venetians from prison.
9.   *the feast . . . June*: 24 June 1203.
10. *the emperor of Constantinople's lord admiral*: Michael Stryphnos, lord admiral of the Byzantine navy and brother-in-law of Alexius III's wife Euphrosyne.
11. *Not a single person . . . fear and dread of Emperor Alexius*: It is apparent from a letter sent by the leaders of the crusade army that not only did the people of Constantinople fail to show support for the young prince Alexius, but that they made a noisy and boisterous display of their disdain for him and his Latin allies (see Andrea, *Contemporary Sources*, pp. 79–85). But this was not fear of Alexius III, rather young Alexius simply did not enjoy any meaningful support in the city: see §§ 194–5.

CHAPTER 5

THE FIRST SIEGE OF CONSTANTINOPLE

1. *the fifth*: I.e. the fifth day, 10 July 1203.
2. *Bohemond's castle, which was an abbey*: The monastery of Saints Cosmos and Damian, called 'Bohemond's castle' by Villehardouin and his colleagues because Bohemond of Taranto, the first Latin prince of Antioch (d. 1111), had made his base there when the First Crusade passed through Constantinople in 1096–7.
3. *Constantine Lascaris*: A member of one of Byzantium's foremost families. For his brother Theodore, see § 313 and Ch. 9, note 6.
4. *one Thursday morning*: 17 July 1203.
5. *English and Danish men*: Members of the Varangian guard, an elite mercenary force that had been employed by the Byzantine emperors since the ninth century; originally made up of Scandinavians, although following the upheavals of the Norman Conquest in the second half of the eleventh century displaced Englishmen also joined, and the force continued to draw recruits from both regions. See also § 185.
6. *The empress . . . sister of the king of Hungary*: Margaret (d. after 1223), the sister of King Emeric of Hungary (r. 1196–1204).
7. *many people from the army went to look at Constantinople*: While Villehardouin does not linger to describe Constantinople and its wonderful sights, Robert of Clari provides a lengthy account of what he saw after the city fell to the crusaders in April 1204 (*The Conquest of Constantinople*, trans. Edgar Holmes McNeal (New York: Columbia University Press, 1936, reprinted 2005), pp. 102–13).
8. *the new emperor . . . beginning of August*: Alexius was crowned on 1 August 1203, becoming Emperor Alexius IV Angelus (r. 1203–4).

CHAPTER 6

ALLIANCES RENEWED AND ABANDONED

1. *the feast of Saint Michael*: 29 September 1203.
2. *Johanitsa, the king of Vlachia and Bulgaria*: Kalojan (d. 1207), known as Johanitsa, was the ruler of territory north of the Byzantine empire's lands in Thrace (on the western side of the Straits of

Saint George). The Vlachs and Bulgars were peoples who had been a significant presence in the Balkans and on the western fringes of the empire for several centuries, but the Byzantines had managed to contain them and keep them as subject peoples. In 1186 two brothers, Peter and Asen, led the Vlacho-Bulgars in a revolt, and they formed what is sometimes referred to as the second Bulgarian empire. Kalojan, their younger brother, sought recognition of the independence of his people and his territory. Before the arrival of the Fourth Crusade he had courted the support of Pope Innocent III, and, while he had not received coronation as an emperor as he had hoped, his approaches had nonetheless been favourably received, and he would be crowned as a king by a representative of the papacy in late 1204. In the meantime the leaders of the crusade army dismissed Kalojan's friendly overtures, and he would prove a dangerous challenger when the Latins set about establishing themselves as the rulers of Romania.

3. *the feast of Saint Martin*: 11 November 1203.
4. *This Greek was called Mourtzouphlus*: Alexius Ducas (d. 1204; Alexius V Ducas, r. 1204) had been involved in Constantinople's complex political intrigues before 1203 and had been appointed by Alexius IV as *protovestarius* (chamberlain). His nickname refers to his bushy eyebrows.
5. *the scarlet boots*: High office was often signalled by shoe-colour in Byzantium. Scarlet (or purple) boots were part of the emperor's regalia.
6. *you who die here ... the pope has granted you*: This statement effectively made the crusaders' war against Mourtzouphlus a crusade in its own right, although receipt of an indulgence in most other cases did not require the beneficiaries' death.
7. *the Russian Sea*: The Black Sea. Philia lay on the coast north-west of Constantinople.
8. *around Candlemas*: 2 February 1204.
9. *Bohemond ... King Leon, the ruler of the Armenians*: Prince Bohemond IV of Antioch (d. 1233); King Leon I of Armenia (r. 1198–1219).

CHAPTER 7

THE SECOND SIEGE OF CONSTANTINOPLE

1. *the Thursday after mid-Lent*: 8 April 1204.
2. *they fired with petraries and mangonels one against the other*:

Villehardouin's meaning here is uncertain; in his edition Faral suggested that shots fired at the city's defences by engines on the ships that had retreated struck those still close to the walls (*La conquête de Constantinople*, II, p. 41, n. 2).

3. *a wind known as Boreas*: The north wind.
4. *the Monday before Palm Sunday*: 12 April 1204.
5. *the sister of the king of France, the former empress, and the sister of the king of Hungary, another former empress*: Agnes of France (d. 1220), the sister of King Philip II, had been married first to Emperor Alexius II Comnenus (r. 1180–83) and on his death to his successor, Andronicus I Comnenus (r. 1183–5). She would subsequently marry Theodore Branas (d. after 1206) (see § 403). The other former empress is Margaret of Hungary (§ 185).
6. *Palm Sunday and the following Easter Sunday*: 18 and 25 April 1204.

CHAPTER 8

THE ELECTION OF AN EMPEROR AND ITS AFTERMATH

1. *The count of Saint-Gilles was so jealous ... lost that land*: In the aftermath of the fall of Jerusalem to the forces of the First Crusade in 1099, Raymond IV of Saint-Gilles, count of Toulouse (d. 1105), had hoped to become the first ruler of Jerusalem, but Godfrey of Bouillon was elected (he humbly refused the title of king, and ruled only 1099–1100). Jealous anger prompted Count Raymond to abandon Jerusalem; he and his forces only relented and returned to aid their colleagues when the threat of an attack by the Egyptians arose.
2. *all the land on the other side of the Straits of Saint George, towards the land of the Turks, along with the island of Greece*: The lands claimed by the empire in Asia Minor and Morea (the Peloponnese peninsula, sometimes also referred to as Achaea).
3. *at the hour of God's birth*: At midnight.
4. *three weeks after Easter*: 16 May 1204.
5. *the marquis of Montferrat asked ... the kingdom of Salonika*: The appeal to Marquis Boniface of Salonika (Thessalonika) was doubtless in part due to its proximity to Hungary, but may also have arisen from a belief that it belonged to the Montferrat family by right: in 1180 Boniface's younger brother, Renier of Montferrat, had married a Byzantine princess and had, so some

sources assert, been granted the kingdom of Salonika. It is likely
that it was granted as a fief of some sort, but Renier did not
obtain the power and status of a king. He had little chance to
enjoy these possessions, however; he and his wife were killed in
1183 by their political opponent Emperor Andronicus I.

6. *the empress who was the first wife of Emperor Alexius (who had
    previously fled the city)*: Euphrosyne, the wife of Emperor Alexius
    III, who had fled in the wake of the first siege of Constantinople
    by the crusaders and Venetians (§ 182).

7. *a high-ranking Greek man called Sgouros*: Leon Sgouros (d.
    c. 1208), archon of Corinth and the Argolid, was one of a number
    of the Byzantine aristocracy who was able to seize significant
    lands and power for themselves in more far-flung regions of the
    empire (in his case in Greece, in the regions around the towns of
    Corinth, Nauplia and Thebes).

8. *Another Greek, called Michael*: Michael Ducas (d. c. 1214), the
    illegitimate son of a member of the Byzantine aristocracy and a
    cousin of Emperors Isaac II and Alexius III, seems initially to
    have seen alliance with the Latins as his best hope for personal
    advancement after their conquest of Constantinople. New oppor-
    tunities soon presented themselves; after his break with Boniface
    in 1204, Michael Ducas would go on to establish himself as the
    ruler of Epirus in western Greece.

CHAPTER 9

THE LATINS TAKE POSSESSION OF THEIR
LANDS AND THE GREEKS RESIST

1. *the feast of All Saints*: 1 November 1204.

2. *a column in the centre of the city of Constantinople*: Situated
    in the Forum of Theodosius, one of the city's principal public
    spaces.

3. *Alexius's scarlet boots and imperial robes*: The imperial regalia
    consisted of scarlet (or purple) boots and a floor-length purple
    cloak (*chlamys*), which would have been lavishly bejewelled and
    embroidered.

4. *He later sent Emperor Alexius to prison in Montferrat*: Alexius
    was held in northern Italy for several years, until he was ransomed
    by Michael Ducas. He returned to the eastern Mediterranean by
    1210 and sought to supplant his son-in-law Theodore Lascaris
    (see § 313) as the Greek ruler of western Asia Minor, but

was captured in 1211 and imprisoned at the monastery of Hyacinthos, where he died later.

5. *On the following feast of Saint Martin*: 11 November 1204.
6. *Theodore Lascaris*: Theodore Lascaris (d. 1221), the husband of Emperor Alexius III's daughter, Anna, crossed the Straits of Saint George in 1203 and established a base in Asia Minor. In 1205 he had himself proclaimed as emperor of a Byzantine successor state based at the city of Nicaea.
7. *the feast of our lord Saint Nicholas*: 6 December 1204.
8. *the Saturday before mid-Lent*: 19 March 1205.
9. *Michael*: Michael Ducas (see § 301).

CHAPTER 10

JOHANITSA'S FIRST CAMPAIGNS AGAINST THE LATIN EMPIRE

1. *the Tuesday before Palm Sunday*: 29 March 1205.
2. *Palm Sunday*: 3 April 1205.
3. *Easter*: 10 April 1205.
4. *Peter of Bracieux ... Count Louis's men*: They had returned from their campaign of conquest in the region of Espigal (§ 305).
5. *the day after ... reached the city*: 17 April 1205.

CHAPTER 11

THE REGENCY OF HENRY OF HAINAUT

1. *Makri ... Bera*: These lands were close to the Aegean coast; Anseau had been sent to take possession of them on Geoffrey's behalf.
2. *Pentecost*: 29 May 1205.
3. *Paulician heretics*: Paulicianism and its development are the subject of scholarly disagreement; there is consensus that this religious sect had its roots in Armenia, with the Armenian sources dating its emergence to the fifth century (or earlier) and the Greek sources to the seventh century. A belief in dualism (the existence of two divine powers, one good and one evil, with power in the spiritual and materials worlds respectively) is suggested by some of the later Greek material. It has therefore been proposed that Paulicianism was a descendant of early Manichaeism, although a direct link is unproven. Scholars agree that the Paulicians

rejected the orthodoxy of the Greek Church and, more specifically, that they were iconoclasts.

4. *Theodore Branas ... married the king of France's sister*: See
    § 249 and Ch. 7, note 5.

5. *the fourth day before the feast of Saint Mary at Candlemas*:
    30 January 1206. Villehardouin includes the day of the feast
    itself (2 February) as one of the four: see § 410.

6. *The cardinal who was the Roman pope's legate*: Cardinal-priest
    Benedict of Saint Susanna had been sent by Innocent III in the
    early summer of 1206 as his representative in Romania.

7. *the eve of the feast ... in June*: 23 June 1206.

8. *a castle called Rodestuic*: It is uncertain exactly what place Ville-
    hardouin refers to, but this castle and the others mentioned
    in the episode were probably strongholds dotted along the
    valley of the River Arda, north of Demotika and west of
    Adrianople.

CHAPTER 12

WAR ON TWO FRONTS IN EMPEROR
HENRY'S EARLY REIGN

1. *the Sunday after the feast of Our Lady Saint Mary in August*:
    20 August 1206 (the feast of the Assumption is on the 15th).

2. *Eustace, Emperor Henry of Constantinople's brother*: Henry's
    youngest brother must have come from Europe after the empire
    fell into his family's hands. He would become a leading figure in
    the Latin empire, where he remained until his death after 1217.

3. *the feast of All Saints*: 1 November 1206.

4. *the Sunday following the feast of Our Lady Saint Mary at
    Candlemas*: 4 February 1207.

5. *for Lent to have arrived*: Lent began on 7 March in 1207.

6. *the Saturday of mid-Lent*: 31 March 1207.

7. *Stirione, who was the admiral of Theodore Lascaris's fleet*:
    Stirione was a mercenary mariner (or pirate) who had joined
    Lascaris's service.

8. *the feast of Saint John in June*: 24 June 1207.

THE LIFE OF SAINT LOUIS

PROLOGUE

1. *Louis ... Champagne and Brie*: Louis was the son of King Philip IV of France (r. 1285–1314) and reigned as King Louis X of France, 1314–16. He inherited the kingdom of Navarre and the counties of Champagne and Brie in 1305 from his mother Queen Joan of Navarre (r. 1274–1305), countess of Champagne.

2. *'Attend first ... for you'*: Luke 12:31.

3. *they failed to set him among ... the martyrs*: When Louis IX (r. 1226–70) was canonized in 1297 as Saint Louis, he was designated a confessor, an individual whose life bears special witness to his or her faith, rather than the circumstances of his or her death as would be the case for a martyr. Cf. § 760.

4. *the sickness that had struck the camp*: On the nature of this sickness, see § 291.

5. *his brothers*: Louis IX was the oldest of the four sons of King Louis VIII of France (r. 1223–6) to survive to adulthood. His brothers were Count Robert of Artois (d. 1250), Count Alphonse of Poitiers (d. 1271) and Count Charles of Anjou (d. 1285), crowned king of Sicily in 1266 and often referred to by this title by Joinville.

6. *Acre ... thirty when it was lost*: Acre was captured by the Mamluks in May 1291.

PART I

LOUIS'S SANCTITY IN WORD

CHAPTER I

KING LOUIS'S HOLY WORDS AND PIOUS TEACHINGS

1. *he would not even lie to the Saracens regarding an agreement*: See §§ 386–7 and §§ 763–4.

2. *the father of the current king*: King Philip III of France (r. 1270–85), father of Philip IV.

3. *Master Robert of Sorbon*: Robert of Sorbon (d. 1274), theologian and founder of the Sorbonne school in Paris.

4. *'restore' grates one's throat because of its 'r'-sounds*: The word Joinville uses is *rendre*, with two rolled 'r's.

5. *King Thibaut*: King Thibaut II of Navarre, who was Count Thibaut V of Champagne (r. 1253–70).

6. *garbino*: The south-west wind in the Mediterranean.

7. *the body of Our Lord*: The consecrated host, placed in the ship before departure.

8. *Saint Anselm*: Saint Anselm (d. 1109) was a scholar and monk, who became abbot of the Benedictine monastery of Bec in Normandy then archbishop of Canterbury. His writings include prayers, meditations and several famous theological treatises, but Monfrin could not find a source for the teaching cited here in any of Anselm's surviving works (John of Joinville, *Vie de Saint Louis*, ed. Jacques Monfrin (Paris: Dunod, 1995), p. 405, n. to § 40).

9. *the articles of faith … the Credo*: The articles of faith are the points laid out in the Credo, or Christian Creed (profession of faith). Joinville composed a text that expounded and explained the articles as set forth in the Creed, intended as source of comfort and spiritual strength to the dying. See *Text and Iconography for Joinville's Credo*, ed. Lionel J. Friedman (Cambridge, MA: Mediaeval Academy of America, 1958). Latin Christians in the thirteenth century used the version known as the Nicene Creed.

10. *the king of France … La Rochelle in Poitou*: In the late twelfth century the ruling house of England, the Plantagenets, possessed extensive territories on both sides of the Channel, and while they were technically vassals of the French Crown for much of their continental lands, they often set themselves in opposition to the king of France. The long-running tension between the Capetians and Plantagenets came to a head when King John of England (r. 1199–1216) refused to attend the court of peers of France in 1202 to answer for an alleged offence; this provided the pretext for Louis IX's grandfather, Philip II, to confiscate the Plantagenets' continental fiefs, and John was not strong enough to resist the seizure of extensive lands. His heir, Henry III of England (r. 1216–72), made a concerted effort to regain these losses, using Gascony (in the south-west of modern France, the only continental lands on which the Plantagenets had retained a firm hold) as his base. Poitou, to the north of Gascony, became a focus of the struggle: La Rochelle (on Poitou's Atlantic coast) had long been loyal to England but was captured from Henry in 1224. Two years later, when Louis IX came to the throne in

France, the first of a series of fragile truces was made, but conflict between the kings of England and France continued to resurge intermittently.

11. *the count of Montfort . . . defending the Albigensian lands*: Count Amaury of Montfort commanded forces defending conquests made for the French Crown in south-west France in the course of the Albigensian Crusade (1208–29), which had targeted Cathar heretics and their protectors. Amaury died in captivity after being taken prisoner while on crusade in 1239, and his fate had an important place in the memory of Joinville and his contemporaries (see §§ 286–8, 348, 469, 518).

12. *a Franciscan friar*: Hugh of Digne (d. *c.* 1285, also known as Hugh of Barjols): see § 657.

13. *The peace agreement he sealed with the king of England*: The Treaty of Paris (1258) agreed by Louis IX and King Henry III of England (r. 1216–72) surrendered extensive territories in France to the English, but required Henry to do homage to Louis as his vassal for all his possessions on the continent.

14. *we are married to two sisters*: Louis's wife, Margaret of Provence (d. 1295), and Henry's wife, Eleanor of Provence (d. 1291), were daughters of Count Raymond Berengar of Provence (d. 1245; he was the IV or V of that name, depending on what numbering you choose to follow).

15. *the case of my lord Renaut of Trie*: Joinville misremembered: it was not Renaut of Trie but his son, Matthew.

PART II

LOUIS'S SANCTITY IN DEED

CHAPTER 2

KING LOUIS CONFRONTS
REBELLIOUS BARONS

1. *the feast of Saint Mark the Evangelist*: 25 April 1214.
2. *the first Sunday of Advent*: 29 November 1226.
3. *'Ad te levavi animam meam'*: Psalm 24:1–2 (Vulgate).
4. *Saint James . . . Saint Genevieve*: Saint James the Great (d. 44), the first of Christ's apostles to be martyred. His was among the most popular saints' cults of the later Middle Ages: the site of

his supposed burial at Santiago de Compostela in Spain was the most highly prized pilgrimage destination after Jerusalem and Rome (see § 438). Saint Genevieve (d. *c.* 500) lived most of her life and died in Paris; her cult has focused on her personal piety and role as protectress of the French capital.

5.   *his mother*: Blanche (d. 1252), daughter of the king of Castile.

6.   *the count of Boulogne, his uncle*: Philip Hurepel (d. 1234), half-brother of King Louis VIII.

7.   *Count Peter of Brittany*: Peter of Dreux, known as Peter Mauclerc (d. 1250) was count of Brittany by right of his wife. Although he was no longer count of Brittany after 1237, when his son reached his majority, Joinville refers to him by this title throughout the *Life*.

8.   *Count Thibaut of Champagne, who later became king of Navarre*: Count Thibaut IV of Champagne (d. 1253), king of Navarre from 1234.

9.   *Count Henry the Liberal had two sons by Countess Marie, who was sister of the king of France and of King Richard of England*: Count Henry I 'the Liberal' of Champagne (d. 1181) married Marie of France (d. 1198), the daughter of King Louis VII of France (r. 1137–80) and Eleanor of Aquitaine (d. 1204). After her parents' marriage was annulled, Marie became half-sister to Philip II of France (born of Louis's subsequent marriage to Adela of Champagne (d. 1206)), and to Richard I of England (r. 1189–99; born of Eleanor's subsequent marriage to King Henry II of England (r. 1154–89)). The 'two sons' were Henry II of Champagne (d. 1197) who ruled the county from 1187 to 1190, before leaving it in his mother's hands when he left to join the Third Crusade. He was succeeded by his brother, Thibaut III (d. 1201), who would have led the Fourth Crusade had he not died unexpectedly (see *Conquest*, §§ 35–7).

10. *laid siege to and captured Acre*: The Third Crusade, 1189–92, when Acre was surrendered to the French and English kings in 1191.

11. *'The Book of the Holy Land'*: It is not clear what text Joinville is referring to, but it may be one of the Old French continuations of William Archbishop of Tyre's *Historia rerum in partibus transmarinis gestarum*, a famous twelfth-century history of events in the Latin East.

12. *Henry of Champagne*: Henry II of Champagne gave up the county to his brother following his marriage to Isabella, daughter of King Amaury I of Jerusalem (r. 1162–74).

13. *queen of Cyprus*: Alice (d. 1247), older daughter of Henry and

Isabella of Jerusalem, married King Hugh I of Cyprus (r. 1205–18).

14. *the king only held these fiefs in pledge*: Louis may have taken possession of the lands as surety for a loan rather than purchasing them outright.

15. *her daughter married the great Count Walter of Brienne*: Queen Alice's daughter was named Marie. For her husband, Count Walter IV of Brienne, see §§ 527–38 and ch. 9, note 10.

16. *Count Thibaut the Great*: Count Thibaut II of Champagne, who was also Count Thibaut IV of Blois (d. 1152), father of Henry the Liberal (see note 9).

17. *the count of Poitiers ... feast of Saint John*: Louis's younger brother, Alphonse, knighted on 24 June 1241.

18. *the great King Henry of England*: King Henry II.

19. *the count of Boulogne ... Saint Elizabeth of Thuringia*: Alphonse, younger son of King Alphonse I of Portugal (r. 1211–23) was count of Boulogne on behalf of his wife; ruled Portugal as King Alphonse III (r. 1245–79). Saint Elizabeth (d. 1231) was the daughter of King Andrew II of Hungary (r. 1205–35) and was married to Landgrave Ludwig IV of Thuringia (d. 1227). She is sometimes referred to as Saint Elizabeth of Hungary. She had one son, Hermann. Some sources date his death to January 1241, others to January 1242; the Saumur festivities were held on 24 June 1241, so if Joinville did indeed see Hermann there he cannot have died before that date.

20. *the count of La Marche ... the queen of England*: Isabella (d. 1246), widow of King John of England, married as her second husband Hugh of Lusignan, count of La Marche (d. 1249).

21. *the king of England ... the king of France*: This episode was part of a long-running conflict between Henry III of England and the kings of France (see ch. 1, n.10). The county of Poitou had been a particular focus of this conflict, and Louis's decision in 1241 to grant it to his brother Alphonse was unpopular with Count Hugh of La Marche, whose leading role in the region was challenged as a result. Count Hugh's resistance of Capetian overlordship was supported by Henry III.

22. *I had not yet put on a hauberk*: Putting on a hauberk (the most important element of a knight's armour) symbolized the start of a fully-fledged military career; Joinville was probably seventeen when these events took place in 1242, and had not yet seen real combat.

CHAPTER 3

KING LOUIS'S CRUSADE VOW AND
THE VOYAGE TO CYPRUS

1. *taken seriously ill at Paris*: Louis was actually at Pontoise, north-west of Paris.

2. *the eve of Easter*: 18 April 1248.

3. *I had not 1,000 livres-worth of lands ... my mother was still alive*: The income from Joinville's lands was less than 1,000 *livres* per year. While his mother, Beatrice, was alive she continued to receive the profits of the land she had brought to the Joinville family as her dowry; they passed to her son after her death in 1261.

4. *John, lord of Apremont, count of Sarrebrück*: Joinville made an error; the count of Sarrebrück was Geoffrey.

5. *I was not his man*: Joinville was not a vassal of the king in 1248, but became one in 1252, during the crusade, when the king granted him an annual income in recognition of his good service.

6. *three of his sergeants from the Châtelet*: The *Châtelet* was Paris's foremost law court, run by the *prévôt*, and in this instance 'sergeants' means law-enforcement officers attached to the court.

7. *our own country*: Champagne.

8. *the white order*: The Cistercians (see Glossary).

9. *my staff and purse*: Traditionally given to departing pilgrims to signal their special purpose and status.

10. *Veni creator spiritus*: 'Come, Holy Spirit, creator' (Latin), a hymn often sung to call for God's blessing on a new endeavour, marking the solemnity of the occasion.

11. *the Barbary coast*: The northern coast of Africa, west of Egypt.

12. *the great king of the Tartars*: Joinville refers to the Mongols as Tartars; the 'king' is Eljigidei (d. 1251/2), a Mongol general in Persia and appointee of the qaghan (great khan) Güyüg (r. 1246–8). The title 'king of the Tartars' refers to several people: see §§ 143, 472, 584.

13. *two Dominican friars who knew the Saracen language*: One was Andrew of Longjumeau, who already had some experience in dealing with the Mongols; he had been among a number of mendicant friars dispatched to Mongol rulers in different regions by Pope Innocent IV (r. 1243–54) in 1245.

14. *the empress of Constantinople*: Marie of Brienne (d. 1275), the wife of Emperor Baldwin II of Constantinople (r. 1228–61, d. 1273).

15. *the legate*: Odo of Châteauroux (d. 1273).
16. *the sultan of Iconium*: Iconium was the former name of Konya, and at this time it was the chief city of the Seljuq sultans of Rum in Asia Minor. The sultan of Rum was Kaya'us II (r. 1246–61).
17. *the king of Armenia*: King Hethoum of Armenia (r. 1226–69).
18. *The king of Armenia ... the king of the Tartars*: The events presented here do not fit neatly with the historical record. King Hethoum did send an embassy to Güyüg in 1247 and the Armenians submitted to Mongol authority, but the Mongols' great victory over the sultan of Rum had taken place several years earlier, in 1243.
19. *The sultan of Egypt ... the sultan of Hama*: Joinville names the second sultan as 'le soudanc de Hamant', 'Hamant' being the name by which French speakers knew the city of Hama, but this episode in fact concerned the city and ruler of Hims. As-Salih Ayyub, sultan of Egypt (r. 1240–49, also sultan of Damascus, 1245–9) laid siege to an-Nasir Yusuf, sultan of Aleppo (r. 1236–60) after the latter seized Hims in 1248. There is no truth in the story of poisoning: as-Salih Ayyub was already ill before he came to Hims.

CHAPTER 4

THE FALL AND OCCUPATION OF DAMIETTA

1. *the Friday before Pentecost*: 21 May 1249, but Joinville's dating of the crusaders' embarkation conflicts with that of most other sources: 13 May. Jacques Monfrin suggests that Joinville provided the wrong date (and of the landing at Damietta – see § 150) because he made an error when checking his dates in a calendar, starting his calculations by looking at an entry for 1250, rather than 1249 ('Joinville et la prise de Damiette (1249)', *Académie des Inscriptions et Belles-Lettres, comptes rendus des séances* (1976), pp. 268–85).
2. *the prince of Morea*: William of Villehardouin (d. 1278); his father, Geoffrey (d. 1228), the first of the Villehardouin dynasty to hold the title of prince of Morea, was the nephew of Geoffrey of Villehardouin, author of *The Conquest of Constantinople*. On Geoffrey's involvement in the establishment of Latin rule in Morea, see *Conquest*, §§ 327–30.
3. *the Friday before Trinity Sunday*: 28 May 1249, but most other sources give the landing as 5 June (see note 1).

4. *my lady of Beirut ... and of mine)*: Eschiva of Montbéliard was the widow of Balian of Ibelin, lord of Beirut (d. 1247). The Joinville and Montbéliard families had been connected by the marriage of Count Richard III of Montbéliard (d. 1227), Eschiva's paternal uncle, to Agnes of Auxonne (d. 1223), John of Joinville's maternal aunt.

5. *the standard of Saint-Denis*: This banner, known as the Oriflamme, came from the abbey of Saint-Denis near Paris with which the kings of France had a particularly close relationship; it served as a sacralizing symbol of French royal power and a rallying point for the French in battle.

6. *a large battalion of Turks*: The crusaders' opponents are called either 'Saracens' or 'Turks' by Joinville. Turks is often used, as here, to refer to members of the Ayyubid and Mamluk sultans' mounted forces, many of whom were of Turkish origin, but Joinville often seems to use the names interchangeably (for example, §§ 216–17, 220).

7. *the count of Jaffa ... the Joinville lineage*: John of Ibelin, count of Jaffa (d. 1266); Joinville could claim the count as a relative as a result of the same marriage that linked him to Eschiva, lady of Beirut (see note 4). Count John's mother was a sister of Count Richard III of Montbéliard, John of Joinville's uncle by marriage.

8. *his arms, which are or with a cross patée gules*: The count's arms displayed a red (*gules*) cross with flared arms (wider at each end than at the centre) on a gold (*or*) background.

9. *Te Deum Laudamus*: 'We praise you, O God' (Latin), a hymn of praise, often sung in thanksgiving and celebration and now usually referred to simply as the *Te Deum*.

10. *the Petit Pont in Paris*: One of the principal bridges over the Seine, on which many shops and workshops were built.

11. *it was by starvation that King John took it in our fathers' time*: John of Brienne (r. 1210–25, on behalf of his wife and daughter) was king of Jerusalem at the time of the Fifth Crusade and led its forces, including Joinville's father, during the lengthy siege that ended in their capture of Damietta in 1219.

12. *Et pro nihilo habuerant terram desiderabilem*: 'They despised the pleasant land' (Latin), Psalm 105:24 (Vulgate).

13. *The patriarch*: The patriarch of Jerusalem, Robert of Nantes (d. 1254).

14. *the feast of Saint Rémy*: 1 October 1249.

CHAPTER 5

THE CRUSADERS VENTURE ALONG
THE RIVER NILE

1. *the beginning of Advent*: The first Sunday of Advent 1249 was 28 November.
2. *Saint Nicholas's Day*: 6 December 1249.
3. *the feast of Saint Rémy*: 1 October.
4. *this country*: Champagne and the French-speaking lands, where Joinville was dictating his work and expected it to be read.
5. *It was to this Rexi branch*: It was in fact the Tanis branch, also known as the Ashmun–Tannah branch or the Bahr as-Saghir, which broke off from the Damietta branch of the Nile not far downstream from Mansurah, and flowed north-east towards the site of the ancient city of Tanis and into Lake Manzalah.
6. *Scecedin . . . Emperor Frederick had knighted him*: Fakhr ad-Din ibn al-Shaykh (d. 1250) was a prominent power broker in the Near East in the preceding decades. He had helped secure the sultanate of Egypt for as-Salih Ayyub and was appointed temporary commander-in-chief of the Egyptian forces until such time as the late sultan's son, Turanshah (see ch. 7, note 7), would arrive in Egypt from Syria. Frederick II, king of Sicily (r. 1198–1250), king of Germany (r. 1212–50), western emperor (r. 1220–50).
7. *the feast of Saint Sebastian*: 20 January.

CHAPTER 6

THE BATTLE OF MANSURAH

1. *Shrove Tuesday*: 8 February 1250.
2. *a banner vivré*: A banner bearing zig-zag markings.

CHAPTER 7

FROM VICTORY TO CAPTIVITY

1. *the law of Ali, who was Muhammad's uncle*: Ali (d. 661) was in fact the Prophet Muhammad's cousin and son-in-law, and became the fourth leader (caliph) of the Islamic community after Muhammad's death, and as such he is honoured by all Muslims.

Shi'ite Muslims believe that Ali and his descendants were and are the only rightful successors (imams) of Muhammad and they reject the caliphs chosen before and after Ali, whose supporters would come to be known as Sunni Muslims. Although mainstream Shi'ism did not reject Muhammad as Prophet, sects within Shi'ism emerged that were known as the *ghulat* ('extremists', or 'those who exaggerate [in the faith]'). Among the range of ideas attributed to the *ghulat* were ones that emphasized Ali's role over that of Muhammad in various ways, although it is difficult to know how accurately these reports reflect actual belief among these marginal groups. See also §§ 458–9.

2. *when a man dies . . . happier body than before*: A belief in the transmigration of the soul (metempsychosis) was associated with a number of marginal groups within Islam, and was ascribed to the Nizari Isma'ilites (the Assassins), although it is hard to know how accurate these reports were. On a source from which metempsychosis might have entered the doctrine of the Nizari in Syria, see Farhad Daftary, *The Isma'ilis: Their History and Doctrines*, 2nd edn (Cambridge: Cambridge University Press, 2007), p. 372. See § 460.

3. *the first day of Lent*: 9 February 1250.

4. *a valiant Saracen . . . commander in place of Scecedin*: Probably the Mamluk general called Baybars (see § 286).

5. *on Friday*: 11 February 1250.

6. *captured the count of Montfort . . . king of Armenia*: Counts Amaury of Montfort and Henry of Bar, leading participants in the Barons' Crusade, did not return from what became a notorious rout of crusader forces at Gaza in 1239. Count Amaury was captured, and perhaps Count Henry too, although he may have died on the battlefield. Baybars (d. 1277) was a Mamluk general of great ability and ruthlessness who became sultan of Egypt and Syria in 1260. The Mamluks overran Armenia in 1266.

7. *the sultan who had died had a son*: Turanshah (d. 1250), the last Ayyubid sultan of Egypt.

8. *the camp sickness*: Probably scurvy.

9. *Easter*: 27 March 1250.

10. *Tuesday evening after the octave of Easter*: 5 April 1250. Octave signifies the seventh day after a feast or a festival (the eighth including the day of the feast itself).

CHAPTER 8

THE CRUSADERS IN CAPTIVITY

1. *a Saracen, who came from the emperor's lands*: A Muslim man from the lands of Frederick II, the western emperor. He ruled the kingdom of Sicily and other territories with a significant Muslim population.

2. *related to Emperor Frederick of Germany, . . . my mother to be his first cousin*: Joinville overstated the closeness of the relationship: one of his maternal great aunts had married Frederick I (r. 1152–90), who was Frederick II's grandfather.

3. *teachings of Saladin . . . salt to eat*: The notion that people who had received hospitality should be protected by their host was commonplace in both Muslim and Christian societies. While there is no known reference to Saladin, the sultan of Egypt and Syria (r. 1174–93), making a specific pronouncement on this point, its importance is alluded to in Ibn al-Athir's account of his encounter with Reynald of Châtillon (d. 1187). As lord of the Transjordan Reynald had pursued a very aggressive campaign against the Islamic neighbours of the Latin kingdom of Jerusalem, but he was captured by Saladin's forces at the battle of Hattin in 1187. Saladin reportedly denied Reynald permission to drink, since it would not have been fitting to kill his prisoner (which he did) after having granted this hospitality (*Arab Historians of the Crusades*, trans. Francesco Gabrieli and E. J. Costello (Berkeley: University of California Press, 1969), p. 124).

4. *the Thursday before Ascension Day*: 28 April 1250.

5. *his bishops*: His imams. In this instance imam refers to a prayer leader, although imam is also the term by which Shi'ites refer to the descendants of the Prophet whom they believe to be their rightful leader (see ch. 7, note 1).

6. *Faracataye*: Faras ad-Din Aktay (d. 1254), a Mamluk general. See also §§ 401–2.

7. *a brother of the Trinity*: A member of the Order of the Holy Trinity, founded in 1198 with the primary purpose of ransoming Christians held captive by the Muslims.

8. *Thus died Saint Agnes*: Reputedly a victim of the persecutions of Christians by the Roman authorities in the early fourth century, killed by the sword.

9. *The partiarch of Jerusalem*: See ch. 4, note 13.

10. *the day following Ascension Day*: 6 May 1250.

11. *we went against Muhammad's commandment . . . kill the enemy
of the law*: It cannot be known whether this conversation has
any basis in fact, or how Joinville might have learned of it if
it did. Any suggestion as to what 'commandments' or text are
referred to here is therefore speculative, and it may be that these
and other elements in this episode are partly or wholly imaginary.
Bearing this in mind, it is possible that these 'commandments'
were *hadiths* written down in a book that cannot be identified
(*hadiths* are teachings that in theory emanated from Muhammad
and his companions, although over the centuries ideas and prin-
ciples from many sources came to be presented as *hadiths*, so
that there were a vast number in circulation). If this is the case,
the first of these *hadiths*, presented as an injunction from
Muhammad to protect one's lord, may reflect a belief that established governments should not be undermined. A scriptural basis
for this principle is found in the Koran *sura* 4, verse 59: '. . . obey
God and obey the Apostle and those in authority among you'
The Koran, trans. N. J. Dawood, rev. edn (Harmondsworth,
Penguin Classics, 2006). The second possible *hadith*, presented
as an injunction from the Prophet that enemies of Islam should
be killed, relates to the doctrine of *jihad*, which has a complex
development and scriptural foundation, with Joinville's wording
reminiscent of *sura* 9, verse 5 of the Koran: '. . . slay the idolaters
wherever you find them'. It is also possible that Joinville misunderstood the injunctions given in the Koran as those of
Muhammad (rather than of God, as Muslims believe) and that
the 'commandments' he meant to refer to were the scriptural
verses themselves, and the 'book' the Koran.

12. *the count of Flanders . . . came to take their leave of the king*: This
statement is contradicted by the count of Flanders's apparent
presence in Acre in the following months (see §§ 419 and 424).

13. *Nasac, the former sultan of Egypt*: It has been suggested that this
might be either al-Mu'azzam, sultan of Damascus (r. 1218–27),
or his son, an-Nasir Daud (r. Damascus, 1227–9, subsequently
ruler of Transjordania; d. 1259); both of them engaged in power
struggles with the sultans of Egypt and had looked on the Christians as potential allies (Joinville, *Vie de Saint Louis*, ed. Monfrin,
p. 421, note to § 394).

14. *he had come to Egypt with King John*: With the forces of the
Fifth Crusade, which were in Egypt 1217–21 and were led by
John of Brienne (see ch. 4, note 11).

15. *John*: John of France (d. 1270), known as John Tristan. The

sixth child to be born to Louis and Margaret (and the second to bear the name John).

CHAPTER 9

THE CRUSADERS AT ACRE

1. *the palace of the Temple*: The Templar community in Acre. For Brother Renaut, see §§ 382–4.
2. *Libera me, Domine*: 'Deliver me, O Lord' (Latin), a responsory anthem sung as part of the Office for the Dead.
3. *the clergy's money*: Money raised from taxes on the Church.
4. *the prince of Antioch*: Bohemond V of Antioch (d. 1252). If there was a relationship between Joinville and Bohemond by blood or marriage, it has not been identified.
5. *the feast of Saint John . . . Saint James . . . pilgrim I had been*: 24 June and 25 July 1250. Joinville may have undertaken a pilgrimage to the shrine of Saint James at Compostela in north-west Spain.
6. *the sultan of Damascus*: An-Nasir-Yusuf (r. 1250–60).
7. *King Baldwin of Jerusalem . . . defeated Saladin*: King Baldwin IV of Jerusalem (r. 1174–85) defeated the numerically superior forces of Saladin at Montgisard in 1177.
8. *the Old Man of the Mountain*: The name given to the leader or master of the Assassins, an Isma'ili sect (Isma'ilism is a branch of Shi'ism) with radical social and political aims as well as religious views deemed heretical by other Muslims. Assassination was their favoured tactic against their opponents, both Muslim and Christian.
9. *they believe no man . . . the day appointed for him*: A scriptural basis for this belief may be found in the Koran, *sura* 3, verse 145: 'No one dies unless God wills. The term of every life is fixed.'
10. *Count Walter of Brienne*: Count Walter IV of Brienne, count of Jaffa, died at an uncertain date after being taken captive in 1244: see §§ 527–38.
11. *took as his wife*: Joinville married Alice of Reynel, his second wife, in 1260 or 1261.

CHAPTER 10

THE CRUSADERS AT CAESAREA (REPORTS CONCERNING THE TARTARS)

1. *At the start of Lent*: The first day of Lent was 1 March 1251.
2. *My lord Ralph of Soissons*: A songwriter and serial crusader, Ralph of Soissons took part in the Barons' Crusade of 1239 and in Louis IX's two campaigns, of 1248–54 and 1270. He may have written the lyrics to 'Nus ne porroit de mauvese reson' in Appendix I.
3. *from Antioch to the great king of the Tartars*: Louis IX's envoys probably went via Persia, from where they were sent further east by the Mongol general Eljigidei (see § 133 and ch. 3, note 12), to the court of Oghul Qaimish, who was regent of behalf of her late husband, the qaghan Güyüg. She was holding court near Emil, in the central Asian steppe.
4. *the people of Gog and Magog ... Antichrist*: The historically unidentifiable King Gog and the people of his kingdom, Magog, were enemies of Israel (see, for example, Ezekiel 38:2–3). The prophecy of their role in the Apocalypse appears in Revelation 20:7. The Antichrist is foretold in Scripture (named in 1 John 2, 18 and 22, 1 John 4, 3, and 2 John 7) and was understood in the Middle Ages to be an incarnation of evil who would appear on earth in the last days of time and reign in Jerusalem before being defeated at Christ's second coming.
5. *Prester John and the emperor of Persia*: Prester John was the name given to a mythical Christian king who was rumoured to rule somewhere far to the east of the Latin settlements in Syria. The emperor was the ruler of the Khwarizmian empire in central and eastern Persia.
6. *One of the princes ... any word of him*: The story that follows has been seen by some as a fantasy of Joinville, but variations on it may be found in the works of authors writing in both East and West. See Lionel J. Friedman, 'Joinville's Tartar Visionary', *Medium Aevum*, 27 (1958), pp. 1–7.
7. *attack the emperor of Persia ... captured Count Walter of Brienne*: The Mongols invaded and overran the Khwarizmian empire in the 1220s, prompting the last surviving member of the imperial dynasty, Jalal ad-Din (d. 1231), to flee westwards. It was one of the men who succeeded him as commander of the

itinerant Khwarizmian Turks, Berke Khan, who inflicted defeat
on the Christians and took Count Walter captive (see § 528).

8.   *Christian people ... who follow the Greek religion*: Monfrin
     clarifies that adherents of Greek (Orthodox) Christianity were
     not numerous in the Mongol lands: the people referred to were
     more likely to have been Nestorian Christians (Joinville, *Vie de
     Saint Louis*, ed. Monfrin, p. 426, n. to § 488).

9.   *the Straits of Morocco*: The Straits of Gibraltar.

10. *Narjot of Toucy ... emperor himself had married*: Joinville is
     mistaken: it was not Narjot of Toucy (d. 1241), but his son Philip
     (d. 1277) who came to Acre in 1251. Philip's grandmother was
     King Philip II of France's sister Agnes (d. 1220), who had been
     married to two Byzantine emperors (see *Conquest* § 249). Philip
     of Toucy held lands in the Latin empire of Constantinople.

11. *Vatatzes ... emperor of the Greeks*: John III Ducas Vatatzes
     (r. 1221–54), emperor at Nicaea.

12. *the feast of Saint Rémy*: 1 October.

13. *the master ... Château Pèlerin*: Renaut of Vichiers, who had
     been appointed master of the Temple in the course of Louis's
     crusade (see § 413), was chosen as godfather to his son Peter,
     count of Alençon (d. 1284), who was born at the Templar strong-
     hold of Château Pèlerin (Atlit) in 1251.

CHAPTER 11

THE CRUSADERS AT JAFFA

1.   *the prince of Antioch*: Prince Bohemond VI of Antioch, count of
     Tripoli (r. Antioch 1252–68; Tripoli 1252–75).

2.   *to quarter his arms, which are gules, with those of France*: The
     prince displayed the French king's insignia (a golden fleur-de-lys
     on a blue background) in the upper left and lower right quarters
     of his own red shield.

3.   *the count of Brienne, who was count of Jaffa*: Count Walter IV
     of Brienne, count of Jaffa. He died at an uncertain date after
     being taken captive in 1244. The events Joinville reports took
     place in that year.

4.   *the sultan of Hims*: Al-Mansur Ibrahim, ruler of Hims (d. 1246),
     was a leading figure in the resistance to the Khwarizmians, and
     in 1246 he inflicted the defeat on them that would lead to the
     break-up of their forces.

5. *These Khwarizmians lined up against us on the Friday*: The battle at Mansurah on 11 February 1250.

6. *Saint Lazarus*: The Order of Saint Lazarus, a military order some of whose members were lepers.

7. *Saint John's Day, after Easter*: 6 May 1253, the feast of Saint John before the Latin Gate.

8. *the Maccabees . . . fortress*: Members of a Jewish family (descendants of Mattathias) who violently resisted pagan rule and oppression in the second century BC; their struggles are recounted in the two books of the Old Testament that bear their name (deemed canonical by the Roman Catholic Church, apocryphal in the Protestant tradition). Joshua Prawer has suggested that the fortress site may have been either Yalu (also known as Castellum Arnaldi) or Suba (*Histoire du Royaume Latin de Jérusalem*, 2 vols. (Paris: Editions du Centre Nationale de la Recherche Scientifique, 1969–70), vol. 2, p. 355); for more on these sites and their exact locations, see Denys Pringle, *Secular Buildings in the Crusader Kingdom of Jerusalem: An Archaeological Gazetteer* (Cambridge: Cambridge University Press, 1997), pp. 96, 106–7.

9. *King Philip departed from before Acre . . . Duke Hugh of Burgundy (the grandfather of the duke who died recently)*: In 1191 King Philip II of France left the Third Crusade at Acre and placed the French forces there under the command of Duke Hugh III of Burgundy (d. 1192). The word translated here as 'grandfather' ('aieul' in Old French) is an important and difficult one as regards the dating of *The Life of Saint Louis*. If Joinville used 'aieul' with the specific meaning 'grandfather', then this would refer to Hugh III's grandson, Hugh IV, who died in 1272, and we may therefore place the composition of *Life* not long after that date. But 'aieul' can also be used more generally about an ancestor of any kind, in which case Joinville's reference might be to Robert II of Burgundy, who died in 1306.

10. *a great difference between a 'brave man' and a 'preudomme'*: The contrast is lost in translation: in the original Old French 'brave man' is *'preu homme'*.

CHAPTER 12

THE CRUSADERS AT SIDON

1. *the feast of the apostles Saint Peter and Saint Paul*: 29 June 1253.
2. *This city is called Samaria in ancient scripture*: Joinville was mistaken: in Scripture it is called Shechem.
3. *While the king was fortifying . . . the caliph of Baghdad*: Joinville seems to have been confused about the timing and when and how reports arrived further west: Baghdad was sacked by the Mongols in 1258, when Hülegü, the Ilkhan of Persia (d. 1265), led an attack on the city following which Caliph al-Mustas'im was put to death.
4. *the miracle . . . the widow's daughter*: Matthew 15:21–8; Mark 7:24–30.
5. *from distant Greece . . . Grand Comnenus, lord of Trebizond*: Manuel I Comnenus, emperor of Trebizond (r. 1238–63), ruler of one of the Byzantine successor states founded after Constantinople fell to the Latins in 1204. Trebizond lies on the Black Sea coast of Asia Minor, and although it was in Greek hands it was not located in or near the lands we would identify as Greece.
6. *bows made of horn . . . screwed into the bow*: The staves would have been a composite of wood and horn, with horn nocks (the notched tips attached at both ends of the stave to hold the bowstring in place).
7. *my lady Blanche, who was born at Jaffa*: Blanche (d. 1323) was Louis and Margaret's third daughter (the first, who had died, had the same name), and the third of their children to be born during Louis's first crusade.
8. *All Saints' Day*: 1 November 1253.
9. *Our Lady of Tortosa*: Although it is not certain that Tortosa was the site of the first shrine to the Virgin as Joinville says, it was one of the earliest: a chapel dedicated to her was built there before the fourth century (consecrated by Saint Peter (d. *c.* 64), according to one legend). The extant cathedral church of Our Lady of Tortosa was constructed in the twelfth and thirteenth centuries.
10. *The prince*: Prince Bohemond. See § 522 and ch. 11, note 1.
11. *his mother was dead*: Blanche of Castile died in late November 1252, and the report that Louis did not get this important news until he was in Sidon (July 1253 at the earliest) is striking. Monfrin points out that Joinville may have misremembered the

length of the delay: other sources say Louis heard this news at Jaffa, in May or June (Joinville, *Vie de Saint Louis*, ed. Monfrin, p. 432, n. to § 603).

12. *her daughter (later the queen of Navarre)*: Isabella (d. 1271), who in 1255 married Thibaut V of Champagne, king of Navarre.

13. *The preudomme's prophecy was fulfilled . . . blood of its inhabitants*: This is usually assumed to be a reference to the fall of Acre to the Mamluks in 1291, although Joinville might have been referring to the War of Saint Sabas, a bloody conflict fought between the Genoese and Venetian contingents in Acre, 1256–61.

CHAPTER 13

THE JOURNEY HOME

1. *the eve of the feast of Saint Mark*: 24 April 1254.
2. *the body of Our Lord*: The consecrated host.
3. *the king's sister to join the king of Germany*: In 1300 Joinville escorted Blanche, King Philip IV of France's sister, who was going to marry Rudolph (d. 1307), the son of Holy Roman Emperor Albert I (r. 1298–1308).
4. *the count of Provence*: Louis's brother Charles, who is usually identified as the count of Anjou or king of Sicily, but who also held the county of Provence on behalf of his wife.
5. *the abbot of Cluny, who later became the bishop of Olena*: Abbot William of Pontoise, who in 1258 became bishop of Olena in Morea.
6. *a Franciscan friar called Brother Hugh*: Hugh of Digne (d. c. 1285), also known as Hugh of Barjols. Additional evidence of this man's widespread popularity and reputation as an impressive intellect and speaker comes from Salimbene of Adam, a fellow Franciscan: 'one of the greatest scholars in the world and a fine preacher, pleasing to the learned and the unlearned alike' who was not afraid to confront those in authority (*The Chronicle of Salimbene de Adam*, trans. Joseph L. Baird (Binghamton, NY: Center for Medieval and Early Renaissance Studies, 1986), pp. 216–17).
7. *a cave . . . as a hermit*: Mary Magdalene (d. first century) was a witness to Christ's resurrection. The legend of her later travels to Provence, where she achieved many conversions before retiring to the mountains to live a number of years as a hermit, is first

attested in the eleventh century. The supposed site of her hermitage, the Sainte-Baume (Holy Cave), situated in the Massif de
la Sainte-Baume, about 25 miles (40 kilometres) south-east of
Aix-en-Provence, is still a pilgrimage destination.

CHAPTER 14

KING LOUIS'S PERSONAL AND
GOVERNMENTAL REFORMS

1. *his wife, the daughter of King Thibaut*: Blanche, the daughter of
   King Thibaut I of Navarre (Count Thibaut IV of Champagne),
   claimed she was the rightful heir to Champagne, which had
   passed to her younger half-brother, Count Thibaut V of Champagne (King Thibaut II of Navarre).

2. *Saint-Urbain*: Joinville's ancestors are known to have been guardians of the Benedictine abbey of Saint-Urbain from at least the
   early eleventh century. Such monks hoped for patronage and protection from their guardians, but these relationships were rarely
   straightforward. For example, there had been tension between the
   monks of Saint-Urbain and the lords of Joinville for generations,
   the monks accusing their guardians on a number of occasions of
   exploiting their resources or undermining their interests.

3. *a peace between the two kingdoms*: The Treaty of Paris (1258).
   See § 65 and ch. 1, note 13.

4. *King Thibaut II of Champagne*: King Thibaut II of Navarre,
   count of Champagne. Joinville has conflated his two titles.

5. *"Blessed are the peacemakers"*: Matthew 5:9.

6. *The king so loved God and his sweet Mother*: Joinville drew
   heavily on a version of the *Grandes Chroniques de France* for
   much of the text that follows. The production of the *Grandes
   Chroniques* – a translation into Old French of texts relating to
   the history of France, originally written in Latin – had been
   undertaken at the abbey of Saint-Denis at Louis IX's request.
   The sections concerning his reign were translated from a life of
   the king written by William of Nangis. Joinville borrowed heavily
   from the *Grandes Chroniques*'s description of the king's personal
   qualities or piety while adding his own take on them (see, for
   example, his comments on blasphemy, §§ 685–7). The *Grandes
   Chroniques* were also Joinville's source for the great ordinance
   of 1254 (§§ 693–714 and 719) and Louis's teachings to his son,
   Philip (§§ 740–54).

7. *the king*: Philip IV of France.

8. *How the king reformed ... of Paris*: This is the only place in Joinville's work where the text provides a heading for what follows. On §§ 693–714, 719, see note 6.

9. *In all these measures ... to us*: This section is out of numerical order: in surviving manuscripts it appears after § 718, but this is almost certainly an error by an early copyist. For the sake of clarity it has been moved to follow § 714, and as a result a sentence from the end of that section has been omitted to avoid an awkward repetition ('Through this ordinance the kingdom of France was greatly improved').

10. *Stephen Boileau*: Stephen (d. 1270) had been *prévot* of Orléans before Louis brought him to Paris in 1261.

11. *the Roman Emperor Titus ... act of kindness*: This image of Emperor Titus (r. AD 79–81) was familiar to medieval audiences and was drawn from the account of his life written in the second century by the Roman historian Suetonius (*The Twelve Caesars*, trans. Robert Graves, rev. with an introduction by Michael Grant (Harmondsworth: Penguin, 2000), p. 256, § 8).

12. *the Friars of the Sacks*: Officially called the Order of Penance of Jesus Christ; first established a religious community at Hyères, in Provence, probably shortly before the middle of the thirteenth century and granted approval by the papacy in 1251 (but see note 14).

13. *the Order of the White Mantles ... at Paris*: The Williamite Friars (or the Order of Saint William), but in fact the order to which Louis IX made the donation described here was the Order of Blessed Mary Mother of Christ (see note 14). The confusion probably stems from the fact that their site was subsequently given to the Williamites.

14. *the Council of Lyons held by Gregory X*: Pope Gregory X (r. 1271–6) summoned and presided over a general council of the Church held at Lyons in 1274; among the issues discussed and ruled on was the growing number of small and often poorly organized religious groups that had emerged since the foundation of the first mendicant orders (orders characterized by a reliance on alms as their means of support rather than the possession of property) in the early thirteenth century. The Church ruled in 1274 that there should be only four mendicant orders – the Franciscans, Dominicans, Augustinians and Carmelites – and the others were suppressed.

15. *the Friars of the Holy Cross*: The Order of the Holy Cross, a

mendicant order founded around the middle of the thirteenth century; it abandoned mendicancy rather than face suppression.

CHAPTER 15

KING LOUIS'S SECOND CRUSADE, DEATH AND CANONIZATION

1. *the eve of the feast of Our Lady observed in March*: 24 March 1267.

2. *These teachings*: The text that follows (§§ 740–54) was taken by Joinville from a manuscript of the Old French *Grandes Chroniques de France*. The original transcript (also in the vernacular) of Louis's instructions has been lost, and it cannot be verified whether he did write it in his own hand. The surviving manuscript sources attest at least two traditions of the teachings (there are long and short versions); for an account of the complex development of these traditions and a critical edition, see *The Teachings of Saint Louis: A Critical Text*, ed. David O'Connell, University of North Carolina Studies in the Romance Languages and Literatures 116 (Chapel Hill: University of North Carolina Press, 1972).

3. *at the same hour at which the Son of God died on the cross*: At three o'clock in the afternoon.

4. *the day following the feast of Saint Bartholomew the apostle*: 25 August 1270.

5. *His bones ... his tomb*: As Joinville suggests, Louis's body was not buried in its entirety at the abbey of Saint-Denis. Immediately after his death his innards had been removed and the flesh boiled from his bones; the bones (the most precious of the king's remains) were buried at Saint-Denis and probably also his heart, but his entrails and flesh were taken by his brother Charles to his kingdom of Sicily, to the cathedral of Monreale.

6. *the king of France and at the command of the pope*: King Philip III called for the canonization process and a number of popes played a part in promoting this cause; it was Martin IV (r. 1281–5) who eventually oversaw the public enquiry in which Joinville and others took part.

7. *they did the king justice and placed him among the number of the confessors*: Pope Boniface VIII (r. 1294–1303) issued the official declaration of Louis's canonization as a confessor in 1297. Joinville's comment on the justness of this decision would

seem to conflict with his complaint that Louis should have been canonized as a martyr (see § 5).

8.   *the day following the feast of Saint Bartholomew*: 25 August 1298.

9.   *a book in the French language*: A version of the *Grandes Chroniques de France* (see ch. 14, note 6).

Glossary

Assassins, The The Nizaris, members of an Isma'ili sect (Isma'ilism is a branch of Shi'ite Islam) were known as *Hasishiyya* (Arabic), or 'Assassins' to Latin Christians. They had radical social and political aims as well as religious views deemed heretical by other Muslims. Murder was a favoured tactic against their opponents, both Muslim and Christian, and it is from them that the term 'assassin' entered western languages. Their leader was a mysterious figure known as the Old Man of the Mountain.

bahariz Young male slaves bought by the Ayyubid sultans of Egypt and trained for membership of their elite bodyguard, the *halqa*. The name probably comes from the location of their base on an island in the Nile called Bahr an-Nil.

bailli The primary representative of the French king in a region, or *bailliage*, a *bailli* was appointed by the Crown and reported directly to the royal administration on its judicial and financial affairs; his responsibilities included oversight of the *prévôt* and other officials.

banneret A knight who had enough wealth and status to lead a small band of knights; his leadership was signalled by his banner.

barbican A high-sided defensive structure built to create a passage across a bridge or to lead to a gate; usually designed to confine attacking forces (see *Conquest*, § 171), but the barbican described by Joinville was intended as a defensive shield (*Life*, §§ 294-6).

Bedouins Nomadic pastoralists of the Near East and Arabia, set apart from other Muslims by Joinville because of their way of life and religious beliefs (see *Life* §§ 249-52).

béguin/béguine A member of a religious community devoted to a life of prayer and good works but not bound by formal vows.

bezant A name used in the West for the Egyptian gold dinar coin; Joinville gives an exchange rate of two bezants to one *livre* in § 342 of the *Life*.

bourgeois/bourgeoise An individual formally recognized as the citizen of a particular town or city.

burbots Eel-like freshwater fish.

camelin Woollen fabric of middling quality, sometimes made of camel hair.

camlet A high-quality, soft woollen cloth, perhaps made of angora wool.

caparison The cloth covering for a horse saddle or harness that could serve as both protection and decoration.

Carthusians Members of an austere religious order that takes its name from its first community, La Grande Chartreuse, founded in the late eleventh century. Carthusians devote themselves to silent prayer and contemplation.

castellan Lord of a castle and its dependent lands.

cendal Silk fabric of light weight, relatively modest in cost.

chamberlain An official with responsibility for valuable property and finances in a royal or noble household.

chancellor An official who oversaw the production, distribution and preservation of written correspondence and documentation within a royal or noble household or an institution; often closely involved in the wide range of business conducted by the individual or institution.

chemise An undergarment for the upper body, usually made of linen and worn by both men and women.

Cistercians Members of the Order of Cîteaux (named after the site of their first house, established at the end of the eleventh century), whose emphasis on simplicity and poverty in religious life proved popular with monastic recruits and lay patrons. Sometimes referred to as the white order, or white monks, because of the simple white robes they wore.

coif A close-fitting cap tied under the chin; in everyday use normally made of white linen or cotton, while a coif made of mail would be worn under a combatant's helmet.

compline See **hours**.

constable A leading official within a royal or noble household; although the specific responsibilities would vary over time and between households, the role was primarily military, in which matters the constable usually received assistance from a **marshal**.

cote The basic clothing worn by both men and women in the thirteenth century; a loose-fitting tunic with long sleeves, usually ankle- or calf-length, and often worn with a belt. A *surcote* or **mantle** (or both) might be worn over the *cote*.

cross, to take the To take a vow to join a crusade campaign. This act could be marked by the attaching of a cross to the crusader's clothes as a symbol of his or her commitment (see *Conquest* § 68).

Cumans A nomadic Turkish people whose origins were in the Eurasian steppe; by the start of the thirteenth century their migrations had created a concentration of Cuman population in the steppe north and west of the Black Sea, and they were forced further west by the Mongol invasions that first had an impact on eastern Europe in the 1220s; the Cumans constituted both a potentially dangerous presence and a source of military manpower and alliances for the rulers along the eastern fringes of Europe.

denier The smallest unit of currency used in most regions of western Europe during the central and later Middle Ages, the *denier* related to the *sou* and *livre* as the penny did to the shilling and pound in the British pre-decimal system: twelve *deniers* to one *sou*, twenty *sou* (240 *deniers*) to one *livre*. The *denier* and *livre* were minted as silver coins, while the *sou* had only a notional value: no *sou* coins were in circulation. Coinage of different appearance and value was minted in different regions; under Louis IX the money of Tours was dominant in France, although that of Paris was also in regular use (100 Tours *deniers* were worth approximately 80 Paris *deniers*).

Divine Office See **hours.**

doge Title given to the man elected as the chief representative of the city of Venice.

Dominicans Members of a religious order, the Order of Friars Preachers, founded by Saint Dominic (d. 1221) in the early thirteenth century. Like the **Franciscans,** Dominican friars rejected the cloistered lifestyle of monks and the affluence of many monastic orders. Instead they lived within the wider Christian community, supporting themselves by begging for alms and ministering to the people through preaching (hence the Dominicans' official name).

dragoman An interpreter; a native Arabic speaker who had learned French.

emir A military commander in the Muslim lands, sometimes exercising local rulership.

enquêteur An investigator appointed by the king of France to hear and rule on complaints lodged against royal officials.

falchion A sword with a broad and curved blade.

fief Possessions (property, rights or revenues) granted by a lord to a vassal.

Franciscans Members of the Order of Friars Minor, which had its origins in the life and teachings of Saint Francis of Assissi (d. 1226).

He had emphasized the spiritual value of humility and poverty (both personal and institutional) and of ministry to the neediest people in society. Like the **Dominicans**, Franciscans sought to live a religious life in the world rather than removed from it.

Franks Originally the name given to the members of a confederation of tribes first attested in the lower Rhine region in the third century. One of their descendants, Clovis (r. *c.* 481–511) achieved the conquest of the former Roman province of Gaul, much of which was comprised of lands that would later become modern France. France takes its name from the term 'Frank', and both 'Franks' and 'French' were used in the thirteenth century to describe people from the kingdom of France and from the French-speaking lands. In addition, 'Franks' was sometimes used to refer to Latin Christians more generally, often to distinguish them from other groups of people, such as Greek Christians or Muslims.

galley A long ship equipped with oars for easy manoeuvring and power when the seas were calm, and with sails to catch the winds on the open seas.

gambeson A padded tunic worn by combatants under their armour to prevent its metal chafing.

Greek fire A highly combustible liquid first produced for the Byzantine army and used as an incendiary weapon; although the recipes were kept secret, the main ingredient was almost certainly petroleum.

Greeks Adherents of Greek (Orthodox) Christianity. This term was used by westerners to describe the Orthodox population of the lands ruled over by the emperor of Constantinople.

hairshirt A simple garment made from rough animal hair and worn as an act of penitential humility.

halqa Elite bodyguard of the Ayyubid sultans of Egypt, made up of mamluks (highly trained slave soldiers, in particular those trained in the *bahariz*). The name means 'circle', suggesting the close and supposedly protective relationship of the *halqa* with the sultans. Members of the *halqa* assassinated the last of the Ayyubid rulers of Egypt in 1250, and the regime they established is known as the Mamluk sultanate.

hauberk A mail tunic worn to protect a combatant's body from neck to thigh, often with sleeves to protect the arms.

herigaut An outer garment with wide sleeves that were slit so that the wearer could take his arms out of them without removing the rest of the garment.

homage A symbolic act through which a **vassal** publicly acknowledged his or her obligation to his or her lord.

Hospitallers Members of the Order of the Hospital of Saint John of Jerusalem, a military religious order that required a commitment to a life of prayer and warfare for the protection of Christian populations and for the defence and extension of Christian-ruled lands. Their role was similar to that of the **Templars**, although the Order of the Hospital had originated as an institution intended to care for the sick and poor, and it maintained these charitable functions throughout the crusading period and beyond.

hours The celebration of psalms and prayers at eight times during the day; together the hours constitute the Divine Office:
lauds (in the early morning)
prime (around 6 a.m.)
sext (around 9 a.m.)
terce (around 12 noon)
none (around 3 p.m.)
vespers (towards evening; after the day's end but before the sun has set)
compline (after sunset)
matins (late at night, around 2 a.m.)

indulgence A promise of a release from the penance (penalty) due for sins committed and confessed; a plenary indulgence released the recipient from the obligation to do penance for all sins committed and confessed up to that point.

Khwarizmians Formidable nomadic Turkish warriors who had their origins in central Asia but were forced west by Mongol invasions in the third decade of the thirteenth century; as allies of Ayyubid Egypt they inflicted the final loss of Jerusalem on the Christians in 1244.

Latins Adherents of Latin (Catholic) Christianity. This term is used to describe the Catholic population of western Europe collectively.

league A measurement of distance not standardized in the Middle Ages, with many regional variations.

legate A representative of the pope, appointed by him to speak and act on his behalf in matters concerning a specific community within Christendom, such as a crusade army.

liege lord A **vassal**'s primary lord, to whom he owed direct loyalty.

liegeman A **vassal** who owed direct loyalty to a lord.

livre See *denier*.

man-at-arms A skilled warrior trained to assist members of the knightly class in battle; would fight on horse or on foot. Some were identified as **squires** or **sergeants**.

mangonel A missile-throwing engine. Although often used interchangeably with **petrary**, mangonel might refer more specifically to a type of engine that used torsion through twisted ropes to pull back and then release missiles placed in a cup at the end of a wooden arm.

mantle A cloak or loose outer garment worn over a *cote* and *surcote*.

mark A measurement of weight used for large quantities of silver and gold: one mark was 8 ounces (238.5 grams).

marshal A high-ranking official within a royal or noble household or a military order; while the range of duties performed varied, they generally exercised an authority in military matters that was second only to that of the **constable**.

matins See **hours**.

nef A round ship (shorter, broader and higher than a **galley**); often had a **ship's castle** at either end of the deck, and would have been the type of ship that carried most thirteenth-century travellers across the Mediterranean.

none See **hours**.

Old Man of the Mountain See **Assassins**.

Outremer 'The land overseas' (*la terre d'outre mer* in Old French); often used by Villehardouin, Joinville and their contemporaries for the lands in which the Christian holy places associated with Christ's life were located and which they sought to capture or defend through their crusades.

palfrey A good-quality riding horse.

parlement A gathering of the royal court (the king and his councillors); over the late thirteenth and early fourteenth century, the meaning narrowed to signify France's royal court of justice.

pax A small stone tablet or metal plate bearing an image (sometimes of the Virgin Mary or one of the saints, but most often of the crucifixion) that would be kissed by the celebrant of Mass and by his congregation as a means of sharing the kiss of peace.

petrary A stone-throwing engine. See also **mangonel**.

plenary indulgence See **indulgence**.

preudomme A man who embodied an ideal blend of personal qualities in both his internal disposition and outward conduct. In the definition cited by Joinville (*Life*, §§ 559–60), dependent on God-fearing piety as well as physical bravery.

Premonstratensians Members of the Order of Canons Regular of Prémontré, founded in the twelfth century. Canons regular lived in settled communities and according to a rule (the Premonstratensians followed the Augustinian Rule), but unlike their monastic counterparts they served the wider Christian community as priests, performing the liturgy, preaching and providing pastoral care.

prévôt An administrator of French royal justice and finances within a specific region known as a *prévôté*; in the second rank of the royal administration and overseen by the *baillis*. Their role in Paris was somewhat different, and under Louis IX evolved to have the same responsibilities and status as a *bailli*.

provost Within the military orders, the man second-in-command to the master.

quartan fever A fever that becomes intense every fourth day (by medieval reckoning; we would say every third day).

quodlibet A free-ranging debate.

relics Objects closely associated with a departed saint (such as body parts or items they came into intimate contact with) that were venerated by subsequent generations. 'Relics' is the usual translation of the old French word *sainz* or *sains*, although it is possible that in instances when oaths were sworn *sur sains* this may refer to the Holy Gospels (see, for example, *Conquest*, § 31).

Romania The name by which Villehardouin and his contemporaries referred to the territories ruled by the emperors of Constantinople.

rouncy A horse of modest value that might be used as a riding horse or in battle as a mount for non-knightly combatants.

samite A rich silk fabric of great expense, sometimes interwoven with gold or silver thread.

scarlet Woollen fabric of the highest quality, often but not always red in colour; the name for the colour was taken from the cloth (rather than the other way round).

seneschal A leading official in a royal or noble household. Even more than was the case for other such officials, his particular duties varied over time and between households; in earlier times seneschals had often enjoyed a position in the forefront of political, administrative and military affairs, but by the thirteenth century (as with Joinville as seneschal of Champagne) the military role had receded while the political influence and prestige remained.

sergeant Usually refers to a skilled warrior, trained to fight alongside knights and to act as an assistant to them; together with **squires** sergeants are called **men-at-arms**. Also a name given to representatives of the law courts (as in *Life*, § 116).

ship's castle A tower-like structure raised from the deck of a ship, in which high-ranking passengers would be housed and on top of which would be a platform protected by crenellations.

sou See *denier*.

squire A knight's assistant, trained to fight alongside them; young men who planned or hoped to become knights might be called squires. Together with **sergeants** squires are called **men-at-arms**.

surcote A long over-tunic, often but not always sleeveless, worn over a *cote* in everyday dress or a *hauberk* in battle; often slit front and back to allow freedom of movement, especially when the wearer was on horseback.

Tartars Used by Joinville and his contemporaries to refer to the Mongols, members of a confederation of nomadic peoples from the inner Asian steppe who came together under the leadership of Chingiz (or Genghis) Khan in the late twelfth century. Over the course of the thirteenth century they conquered an empire stretching from the Carpathian mountains in the west to China and the Pacific in the east.

Templars Members of the Order of the Knights of the Temple of Solomon (or Order of the Temple), a military religious order that required them to both pray and fight in order to protect Christian people and to defend and extend Christian-ruled territories (see also **Hospitallers**). For their headquarters they were granted the al-Aqsa mosque in Jerusalem, which they believed to be the site of the Temple of Solomon, hence their name.

terce See **hours**.

tertian fever A fever that becomes intense every third day (by medieval reckoning; we would say every second day).

tiretaine Woollen fabric of relatively low quality and sometimes made of a mix of wool and fibres such as linen or cotton.

turcopole A mercenary soldier recruited from the native populations of the Near East.

vair Squirrel fur, grey and white in colour.

vassal A person who owes service (often including military service) and loyalty to a lord who has granted him or her a **fief**.

vespers See **hours**.

vidame A person who held lands from a bishop or abbot, and was required to represent his ecclesiastical lord and protect his interests in secular affairs.

Indexes

The two indexes provided for the works list the names of people and places (villages, towns, cities and regions) by the numbered paragraphs or sections. **People's names are listed alphabetically by their first name,** with those sharing a first name arranged according to their toponym, or according to their last name if they have no toponym.

THE CONQUEST OF CONSTANTINOPLE

Abydos, 125, 127, 305, 310, 321

Achard of Verly, 345

Acre, 317

Adramyttion, 321-3, 340, 380

Adrianople, 269, 272-4, 281-7, 289, 311, 335-7, 344, 349-53, 362, 365, 367-9, 371, 375, 380-82, 384, 391, 395-7, 404, 422-9, 432, 441-4, 446, 448-9, 451-2, 461, 463, 472-6, 478-80, 482, 485, 488, 490-92, 494, 496-7

Agnes of France, empress of Constantinople, 249, 403, 413, 423

Agnes of Montferrat, empress of Constantinople, 450, 457-8, 496

Aimery of Villeray, 10, 302

Aimon of Pesmes, 45, 114, 152

Akilo, 451

Alard Maquereau, 12, 32

Alexander of Villers, 74

Alexius III Angelus, emperor of Constantinople, 70, 134, 136-7, 141, 143-4, 146, 156, 158, 171, 176-7, 179-82, 202, 266, 270-74, 309, 313

Alexius IV Angelus, emperor of Constantinople, 70-72, 91-3, 111-12, 116, 123, 144-6, 182-3, 187-91, 193-6, 199, 201-3, 207-10, 212-15, 220-23, 306

Alexius V Ducas ('Mourtzouphlus'), emperor of Constantinople, 221-3, 227-8, 241, 243, 245-6, 266-7, 270-72, 306-8

Ancona, 70

Andrew Dureboise, 242, 407,
  409
Andrew Valera, 436
Andros, 123
Anseau of Cayeux, 9, 149, 322,
  403, 421, 430, 436, 453, 462,
  478, 493
Anseau of Courcelles, 382
Anseau of Remy, 484–5
Antioch, 230
Apollonia, 320
Apros, 390–91, 403, 413–15
Apulia, 33, 54, 79
Arcadiopolis, 337–9, 344, 390,
  403, 413
Arta, 301
Athyra, 420

Baldwin of Aubigny, 376
Baldwin of Beauvoir, 8, 148,
  177, 226, 322, 430, 434
Baldwin IX, count of Flanders
  and Hainaut (emperor of
  Constantinople), 8, 12, 40,
  48–9, 51, 54, 61, 98–9, 103,
  105, 115, 121, 123, 147, 158,
  170, 177, 194, 201, 245, 256,
  258, 260–61, 263–5, 267,
  269–70, 272–83, 285–6,
  288–90, 292–6, 299–300,
  302, 304, 306, 309, 311–12,
  314–18, 336–7, 339–40,
  342–4, 347–51, 354, 356,
  358, 360, 364, 370, 380–84,
  387, 389, 398–9, 439, 496
Baldwin of Neuville, 361
Beauvais, 413
Bègues of Fransures, 292–3,
  413–14
Benedict of Saint-Susanna,
  cardinal, 427
Bernard of Moreuil, 7, 50, 231

Bernard of Somergem, 8
Beröe, 444, 451
Berthold, count of
  Katzenellenbogen, 74, 279
Bizöe, 390, 403, 421, 428, 430,
  432
Blanche of Navarre, countess of
  Champagne, 37
Blisme, 445
Bohemond IV, prince of Antioch
  and count of Tripoli, 230
Boniface, marquis of
  Montferrat, 41–5, 61, 72, 79,
  91, 98–9, 111–12, 115, 123,
  138, 141, 145, 153, 170, 183,
  201, 207, 209, 245, 247,
  249–50, 252, 256, 258,
  261–5, 275–9, 281–9, 293,
  295–301, 309, 324, 326–7,
  331, 389, 392, 398, 450,
  456–7, 495–500
Brindisi, 113
Bruges, 8
Bulgarophygon, 344

Cairo, 30
Cariopolis, 373–4
Chalcedon, 134–6
Champagne, 3, 5, 35, 42
Charax, 460, 481
Charles of Fraisne, 408–9
Christopolis, 280
Clarembaut of Chappes, 5, 114,
  151
Compiègne, 11
Conon of Béthune, 8, 12, 144,
  211, 213, 268, 286, 368, 377,
  430, 436, 466, 478, 496
Conrad, bishop of Halberstadt,
  74
Constantine Lascaris, 167,
  322–3

Constantinople, 70, 127–8, 131,
    133–4, 136–7, 144, 146,
    158–60, 162, 164, 190, 192,
    196, 201, 203, 205, 207, 227,
    229, 232–3, 244–5, 247, 255,
    266–9, 272, 282–5, 288, 295,
    297–8, 301, 302, 305–14,
    317–18, 324–5, 334, 339,
    343, 345, 347, 349, 367–9,
    375–8, 386–90, 393, 400,
    403, 407, 411, 419–23,
    426–7, 441–3, 452, 457–62,
    465–6, 470, 477–9, 482, 485,
    490, 497
Corfu, 110, 112–13, 119, 197
Corinth, 301, 324, 331
Coron, 330
Cortacopolis, 381, 383
Cyzicus, 454–5, 462–3, 476,
    479, 481, 487, 489

Daonum, 418
Demotika, 279, 282, 287, 289,
    297, 299, 335, 391, 397, 404,
    422–6, 428–9, 431–2, 442,
    444, 446, 449
Dietrich of Diest, 74
Dietrich of Looz, 74, 306, 322,
    402, 407, 430, 436, 455, 478,
    480–84, 486, 489
Drama, 456
Dreux of Beaurain, 8, 434
Dreux of Cressonsacq, 7, 109
Dreux of Etroeungt, 332
Durazzo, 111–12

Ecry-sur-Aisne, 3
Egypt, 30, 93, 96, 198
Emeric, king of Hungary, 63,
    100, 109, 264
Enguerrand of Boves, 7, 109
Enos, 457

Enrico Dandolo, doge of Venice,
    15–26, 28–32, 61–3, 65–9,
    80–84, 86, 90, 103, 111,
    129–31, 144–6, 172–3, 175,
    179, 184, 194, 210–11, 213,
    224, 239, 252, 259–60,
    267–8, 282–3, 286, 288,
    293, 295–6, 298, 340, 351,
    364–6, 369, 375, 379, 384,
    386, 388
Espigal, 305, 319, 341, 387, 453
Estanor, 159, 191
Eului, 491
Euphrosyne, empress of
    Constantinople, 266, 309
Eustace, brother of Emperor
    Henry of Constantinople,
    446, 453, 462, 478, 493
Eustace of Canteleux, 9, 149,
    302
Eustace of Conflans, 5, 33
Eustace of Heumont, 361
Eustace of Le Marchais, 168
Eustace of Salperwick, 8, 273,
    281–2
Evrard of Montigny, 5

Flanders, 48, 273, 317, 388, 415
Fraïm, 433
France, 1–2, 4, 7, 18, 27, 32,
    42, 200, 247, 388, 415
François of Colemi, 8
Frederick of Yerres, 7, 361
Fulk of Neuilly, 1–3, 44–5, 73

Garnier, bishop of Troyes, 5
Genoa, 32
Geoffrey of Beaumont, 10, 102
Geoffrey of Cormeray, 6
Geoffrey V of Joinville,
    seneschal of Champagne, 5,
    38–9

Geoffrey, count of Perche, 10,
    40, 46
Geoffrey of Villehardouin,
    marshal of Champagne
    (marshal of Romania), 5, 12,
    27, 32–5, 38, 41, 53, 120,
    151, 174, 184, 186–8, 211,
    218, 250, 268, 283–7, 296–7,
    299, 325, 343–4, 348–9, 354,
    356, 362–6, 369, 371–5,
    378–9, 382, 384, 386, 430,
    436–8, 457, 460, 466, 468,
    478, 496
Geoffrey of Villehardouin,
    nephew of the marshal of
    Champagne (prince of
    Morea), 5, 325–30
Gerard, a count from
    Lombardy, 138, 367
Gerard of Mauchicourt, 8,
    291
Germany, 72, 91, 101
Gervase of Châteauneuf, 6, 296,
    352
Giles, nephew of Milon le
    Bréban, 464
Giles of Aunoi, 291
Giles of Landas, 90
Giles of Trazegnies, 54, 231
Giles of Trit, 345
Godfrey of Bouillon, ruler of
    Jerusalem, 257
Guy of Chappes, 5, 114, 151
Guy of Conflans, 45, 114, 152,
    409
Guy, castellan of Coucy, 7, 114,
    124
Guy, count of Forez, 45, 50
Guy of Houdain, 9
Guy, abbot of Les-Vaux-de-
    Cernay, 83, 95, 97, 109
Guy of Montfort, 109

Guy of Pesmes, 45, 114, 152
Guy of Plessis, 5

Henry of Airaines, 50
Henry of Arzillières, 5, 54
Henry I, count of Champagne, 37
Henry of Hainaut (emperor of
    Constantinople), 8, 48, 148,
    168, 170, 177, 201, 226–7,
    245, 250, 269, 272, 310,
    321–3, 340, 347, 380–81,
    383, 385–7, 390–91, 395,
    397–8, 402–403, 411,
    419–21, 423, 426–30, 432,
    434–5, 440–53, 455, 457–63,
    465–72, 476–8, 480–82,
    485–97, 500
Henry of Longchamp, 54
Henry of Montreuil, 6
Henry of Saint-Denis, 7
Henry of Ulm, 74
Heraclea, 417–18
Hervé of Beauvoir, 6
Hervé of Châteauneuf, 6,
    102
Hugh of Beaumetz, 8, 430,
    434
Hugh of Berzé (the elder), 45
Hugh of Berzé (the younger),
    45
Hugh of Boves, 109
Hugh of Bracieux, 6
Hugh of Chaumont, 50
Hugh of Coligny, 45, 201, 279,
    284, 392–3
Hugh of Cormeray, 6
Hugh of Saint-Denis, 50
Hugh, count of Saint-Pol, 9, 40,
    53, 61, 98–9, 115, 149, 170,
    201, 255, 291, 314, 334–5
Hugh of Tiberias, 316
Hungary, 393–4

Innocent III, pope, 1–2, 31, 83, 105–7, 254, 368, 377, 388
Ipsala, 495–6
Isaac II Angelus, emperor of Constantinople, 70, 111, 144–6, 182–3, 185–91, 202, 212, 223, 262, 306, 309

James of Avesnes, 8, 114, 160, 201, 226, 279, 284, 324, 331–2
James of Bondues, 345
Jerusalem, 18, 27, 257
Johanitsa, see Kalojan
John Bliaut, 388, 493
John of Choisy, 407, 409
John Foisnon, 5, 151
John of Friaize, 6, 12, 105, 359, 361
John of Frouville, 102
John of Heumont, 361
John of Nesle, castellan of Bruges, 8, 48, 103
John of Noyon, 105–7, 290
John of Pomponne, 409
John of Vierzon, 6, 376, 379
John of Villers, 50, 231
John of Yerres, 7, 361

Kalamata, 330
Kalojan, ruler of the Vlacho-Bulgars (King Johanitsa), 202, 273, 276, 311, 333, 335, 339, 345, 350, 352, 354–6, 371, 374, 386–7, 389, 392–4, 398–401, 404, 412–14, 416–20, 422, 424–5, 428–9, 431–3, 439, 442–4, 446–7, 451, 456, 459, 461, 472–5, 488, 491, 497, 499
Kibotos, 460, 463–8, 471

Lagny-sur-Marne, 1
Leon I, king of Armenia, 230
Leon Sgouros, 301, 324, 331
Leopadeion, 320, 341
Lombardy, 32, 47, 53, 70, 138, 141, 367, 450
Louis I, count of Blois and Chartres, 3, 6, 12, 40, 52–3, 56, 61, 98–9, 102, 115, 150, 170, 201, 245, 263, 268, 282–3, 286, 288, 292–3, 295–6, 298, 304–5, 314–15, 336, 340–41, 348, 351–3, 358–60, 364, 369–70, 376, 379, 381
Lyons, 153

Macaire of Sainte-Menehould, 5, 151, 312, 342, 347, 411, 421, 430, 436, 446, 460, 464, 478, 481
Makri, 382
Manassiers of l'Isle, 5, 138, 151, 268, 283, 287, 343–4, 354, 356, 362
Margaret of Hungary, empress of Constantinople, 185–6, 212, 249, 262, 264, 275, 279, 287, 297, 300
Marie, countess of Flanders and Hainaut, 8, 317–18
Marmara, 476
Marseilles, 50, 103, 121, 229, 317
Matthew of Montmorency, 7, 38, 79, 91, 151, 170, 184, 200
Matthew of Walincourt, 8, 148, 169, 177, 312, 342, 347, 361
Michael Ducas, 301, 328–9
Michael Stryphnos, 139

Milon le Bréban, 5, 12, 151,
    211, 268, 368, 377, 430, 436,
    457, 464, 466, 468, 478
Modon, 103, 325, 328–9
Moniac, 435, 440
Morea, 327–8, 330
Mosynopolis, 266, 270, 273–5,
    495–8
Mourtzouphlus, see Alexius V
    Ducas

Nauplia, 301, 324, 326, 331, 389
Negroponte, 123
Neuilly, 1
Nicaea, 304, 455, 481, 486
Nicholas of Jenlain, 160
Nicholas of Mailly, 9, 48, 103,
    322, 388
Nicholas Rosso, 141–4
Nicomedia, 312, 342, 347, 455,
    460, 480–83, 485–7, 489
Nikitza, 344, 349
Nivelon, bishop of Soissons, 7,
    44, 105–7, 260, 388

Odo III, duke of Burgundy,
    38–9, 41
Odo the Champenois of
    Champlitte, 45, 114, 138,
    152, 226, 262
Odo of Dampierre, 45, 114, 152
Odo of Ham, 8, 367
Ogier of Saint-Chéron, 5, 114,
    138, 151
Oliver of Rochefort, 6
Orry of l'Isle, 6, 409
Othon of la Roche, 152, 284, 450

Pamphilon, 369–70, 397–8, 402
Panedon, 417
Panormos, 319
Paris, 1

Pavia, 53
Payen of Orléans, 6, 305, 319,
    341, 369, 420, 430, 436, 453,
    476–7, 479
Peter of Amiens, 9, 114, 149, 291
Peter, bishop of Bethlehem, 361
Peter of Bracieux, 6, 91, 169,
    305, 319, 341, 369–70, 396,
    430, 436, 453–4, 462, 476–7,
    479, 489
Peter Bremond, 45, 50
Peter Capuano, papal legate 2,
    368, 377
Peter Coiseau, 114
Peter of Frouville, 6, 102, 379
Peter of Nesle, 9
Peter of Radinghem, 452, 461
Peutaces, 353
Philadelphia, 316
Philia, 226
Philip of Alsace, count of
    Flanders, 8, 48, 103
Philip II, king of France, 1, 3,
    42, 249, 423
Philip of Swabia, king of
    Germany, 70, 72, 91–3,
    111–12, 188
Philippopolis, 304, 311, 345–6,
    382, 399–402
Piacenza, 32, 54
Pisa, 32
Poemanenos, 319–20, 322
Provence, 45

Ralph of Tiberias, 316
Raymond IV of Saint-Gilles,
    count of Toulouse, 257
Renaut of Dampierre, 5, 54, 231
Renaut of Montmirail, 4, 102,
    315, 352, 361
Renier of Mons, 8, 289, 300
Renier of Trit (the elder), 8, 296,

304, 311, 345–7, 382, 399–400, 402, 435, 437–40
Renier of Trit (the younger), 8, 345
Richard of Dampierre, 45, 114, 152
Richard I, king of England, 1, 3
Robert of Boves, 7, 81, 105–6
Robert of Frouville, 6
Robert of Joinville, 5, 33
Robert of Le Quartier, 6
Robert Mauvoisin, 7, 109
Robert of Ronsoy, 7, 151, 312, 342, 347, 361
Rodestuic, 433
Rodosto, 366, 374–5, 377–8, 381, 383–7, 397, 410, 415–17
Roger of Marcke, 8
Roger of Suitre, 74
Romania (Byzantium, the Latin empire of Constantinople), 93, 103, 110, 188, 282, 304, 322, 404, 409, 412, 416, 422, 424–5, 461, 500
Rotrou of Montfort, 10, 79
Roussion, 402, 405–10

Salonika, 264–5, 276–81, 289–90, 299–300, 302, 309, 324, 389, 393, 398, 450, 456
Scutari, 136–7, 141
Selymbria, 387, 411, 421, 426–7, 490
Serres, 280, 290, 392–4, 398–9, 456, 495–6
Simon, abbot of Loos, 97, 206
Simon of Montfort, 4, 38, 109
Simon of Neauphle, 109
Soissons, 11, 40, 43
Stenimaka, 346, 400, 402, 435–7, 440
Stephen of Perche, 10, 46, 79, 315–16, 352, 361

Stirione (admiral of Theodore Lascaris's fleet), 476, 479
Syria, 79, 95–7, 102–3, 106, 117, 121, 197–8, 229, 315–16, 318, 325

Tancred, king of Sicily, 33
Tchorlu, 267, 337, 339, 343, 390, 418
Theodore Branas, 403, 413, 422–3, 426, 441–2
Theodore Lascaris, 313, 319, 322–3, 387, 453–5, 459, 463, 472, 476, 479–82, 486–9
Thermae, 451–2
Thibaut I, count of Bar-le-Duc, 39, 41
Thibaut III, count of Champagne and Brie, 3, 5, 8, 12, 35–8, 40, 43
Thierry of Flanders, 8, 48, 103, 493
Thierry of Termonde, 316, 322, 402, 405–6, 408–9
Trajanopolis, 382
Troyes, 35, 37

Venice, 14–15, 20, 22, 30, 32, 34, 36, 44, 47–53, 55–7, 71, 76, 79, 174, 193, 229, 231
Vermandois, 367
Verona, 70
Villain of Looz, 407, 409
Villain of Nully, 5, 54, 231
Vlachia, 394, 414, 416–17, 420, 461

Walter, bishop of Autun, 45, 50
Walter of Bousies, 8
Walter III, count of Brienne, 5, 33, 113
Walter of Escornais, 430, 493
Walter of Fuligny, 5

Walter of Godonville, 6, 12

Walter of Montbéliard, 5, 33

Walter of Nesle, 9

Walter of Neuilly, 167, 361

Walter of Saint-Denis, 7, 50

Walter of Stombe, 8

Walter of Vignory, 5

Werner of Borlanden, 74, 101

Wierich of Daun, 74

William of Arles, 392

William of Aulnay, 7, 114

William, advocate of Béthune, 8, 376

William of Blanvel, 337, 343

William of Champlitte, 45, 138, 152, 167, 201, 226, 262, 279, 284, 327–30

William, vidame of Chartres, 102

William of Gommegnies, 8, 434

William of Gy, 169

William of Nully, 5, 231

William of Perchay, 436, 478, 481–3, 485

William of Sains, 6, 460, 463

Yves of La Jaille, 10, 79

Zara, 63, 77–81, 100, 105–6, 111

THE LIFE OF SAINT LOUIS

Abel (Old Testament), 462

Abraham (Old Testament), 462

Acre, 11–12, 76–7, 135, 137, 147, 359, 382, 400, 402–403, 406–7, 418–19, 442–4, 451, 455–6, 465–6, 470, 528–9, 547–8, 550–51, 555, 565, 612–13, 616

Adam, abbot of Saint-Urbain, 123

Agnes, Saint, 355

Agnes of France, empress of Constantinople, 495

Aigues Mortes, 652–3

Aix-en-Provence, 663

Albert I, Holy Roman Emperor, 633

Albi, 50

Alexandria, 183, 191

Ali (relative of the Prophet Muhammad), 249, 458–60

Alice of Champagne, queen of Cyprus, 78–9, 82, 85–6, 88

Alice of Grandpré (John of Joinville's first wife), 110, 238

Alice of Reynel (John of Joinville's second wife), 466

Alphonse, count of Boulogne and king of Portugal, 96

Alphonse, count of Poitiers, 93–4, 98–9, 108, 179–80, 182–3, 200, 202, 232, 274–5, 302, 378–9, 386, 389, 394, 404, 418, 424, 442

Amaury, count of Montfort, 50, 286, 288, 348, 469, 518

Ami of Montbéliard, lord of Montfaucon, 332, 407

Anselm, Saint, 40

Antioch, 472, 523–4

Apremont, lord of (identity uncertain), 273

Archambaut of Bourbon, 94

Arles, 119, 124

Armenia, 143, 525, 565–6

Arnold of Guines, 521
Arsuf, 563
Artaud of Nogent, 89–91
Aubert of Narcy, 176
Auxonne, 119, 123

Baghdad, 584–5
Baldwin II, emperor of
    Constantinople, 139, 495, 592
Baldwin of Ibelin, seneschal of
    Cyprus, 268, 339, 344, 354,
    357
Baldwin IV, king of Jerusalem, 446
Baldwin of Rheims, 157
Banyas, 569–72
Barbaquan, see Berke Khan
Barthélemin, illegitimate son of
    Ami of Montbéliard, 332,
    407, 409
Baybars, 261, 286
Beatrice of Auxonne (John of
    Joinville's mother), 45, 112,
    323, 326, 435
Beatrice of Savoie, dauphine of
    the Viennois, 663
Beaucaire, 663
Berke Khan, commander of
    Khwarizmian Turks
    ('Barbaquan'), 528–30, 533–7
Blanche of Castile, queen of
    France, 71–4, 95–7, 105,
    107, 419, 436, 603–8, 724
Blanche of Champagne (wife of
    John I, count of Brittany), 664
Blanche of France (daughter of
    King Louis IX), 593
Blanche of France (sister of King
    Philip IV), 633
Blécourt, 122, 651
Bohemond V, prince of Antioch
    and count of Tripoli, 431
Bohemond VI, prince of Antioch

and count of Tripoli, 522–5,
    600
Boniface VIII, pope, 760
Brittany, count of (identity
    uncertain), 64, 671
Burgundy, 680, duke of (identity
    uncertain), 555

Caesarea, 135, 470, 493, 495,
    499, 505, 509, 515, 616, 685
Cairo, 183–4, 358, 374, 469,
    518, 537–8
Carthage, 69, 738
Caym of Sainte-Menehould,
    412, 415
Champagne, 78, 82, 85, 89, 92,
    200, 467–8, 664
Chaource, 86
Charenton, 727
Charles, count of Anjou, king of
    Sicily, 108, 200–201, 209–10,
    212, 226–7, 266–8, 296, 302,
    378, 380, 405, 418, 424, 442,
    652
Chartres, bishop of, 674
Château Pèlerin, 514, 528
Château Thierry, 80–81
Cheminon, abbot of, 120–22
Chevillon, 766
Compiègne, 673, 723
Constantinople, 139, 495, 592
Corbeil, 35, 72, 74
Cyprus, 13, 15–16, 23, 39,
    129–30, 133, 136–7, 141,
    143, 180, 423, 471, 618,
    628–30, 638

Damascus, 444–6, 552, 614
Damietta, 7, 9, 148–9, 163–5,
    167–70, 172, 179, 181–2,
    184, 191, 292, 294, 301–2,
    304–5, 314–15, 342–4,

Damietta – *contd.*
  347–8, 351–2, 358–9,
  368–71, 399–400
Denis, Saint, 756
Doulevant, 319
Dragonet of Montaubon, 650

Egypt, 8, 69, 131–2, 140,
  146–7, 183, 187, 189–91,
  252, 275, 280, 287, 366, 390,
  395, 465, 539, 597, 614
Eleanor of Provence, queen of
  England (wife of Henry III,
  king of England), 65, 678
Elizabeth of Thuringia (or
  Hungary), Saint, 96
Eljigidei (Mongol general),
  133–4
Elnart of Seninghem, 493–4
Enguerrand of Coucy, 94
Epernay, 83
Erart of Brienne (the older), 78
Erart of Brienne (the younger),
  137, 150–51, 153
Erart of Chacenay, 429
Erart of Sivry, 223–7
Erart of Vallery, 295
Eschiva of Montbéliard, 151

Fakhr ad-Din ibn al-Shaykh
  ('Scecedin'), 196, 198–9,
  261
Faracataye, *see* Faras ad-Din
  Aktay
Faras ad-Din Aktay
  ('Faracataye'), 353, 401–402
Fontainebleau, 21
Fontaine l'Archevêque, 123
Fourcaut of Merle, 218
France, 30, 48, 55, 61, 69, 72,
  77, 78, 81, 102, 135, 140,
  379, 411, 419, 423, 428,
  430–32, 436, 438, 442, 518,
  524, 555, 596, 599, 604,
  609–10, 616, 617, 625,
  631–3, 655–6, 659, 669, 673,
  678, 687, 693, 719, 733,
  736–7, 756, 759–61
Frederick II, western emperor,
  196, 198, 321, 326, 336, 443,
  452
Frederick of Louppy, 224–5

Gascony, 100, 102
Gaza, 515–16, 518, 520, 528,
  539, 543, 546
Genevieve, Saint, 70, 757
Genoa, 399
Geoffrey of Bourlémont, 421,
  431
Geoffrey of Joinville, lord of
  Vaucouleurs, 110
Geoffrey of La Chapelle, 81
Geoffrey of Meysembourg,
  296
Geoffrey of Rancogne, 104
Geoffrey, abbot of Saint-Urbain,
  672, 676
Geoffrey, count of Sarrebrück,
  109, 113 (wrongly identified
  as John), 119
Geoffrey of Sergines, 173, 302,
  308–9, 369, 378, 438, 571
Geoffrey of Villette, 59
Gervase of Escrennes, 626, 681
Giles le Brun, constable of
  France, 30, 438, 568–9, 626,
  630, 648
Gobert of Apremont, 109
Gregory X, pope, 728
Guy of Dampierre, count of
  Flanders, 108
Guy V, count of Forez and
  Nevers, 86

Guy VI, count of Forez, 201
Guy of Ibelin, constable of
    Cyprus, 268, 339, 344, 355,
    357
Guy Mauvoisin, 247, 271–2,
    422–5
Guy of Mello, bishop of
    Auxerre, 61, 670

Haguenau, 633
Hama, see Hims
Henry II, count of Bar, 286,
    288, 348, 469, 518
Henry of Brancion, 275
Henry I, count of Champagne,
    76, 79, 89–92
Henry II, count of Champagne,
    76, 78–9
Henry of Cône, 276
Henry I, king of Cyprus, 527
Henry II, king of England, 95
Henry III, king of England, 48,
    65, 100, 102, 105, 419,
    678–9, 688
Henry, count of Grandpré, 110
Henry, count of Luxembourg,
    682
Henry of Ronnay, provost of the
    Hospital, 244
Henry of Villars, archbishop of
    Lyons, 762
Hethoum, king of Armenia,
    142–3, 286
Hims, 534, 536–7; (wrongly
    identified as Hama), 144, 196
Hugh X le Brun, count of La
    Marche, 93, 98–100, 102–4,
    109
Hugh XI le Brun, count of La
    Marche, 109
Hugh III, duke of Burgundy,
    555–6, 559

Hugh IV, duke of Burgundy,
    82–4, 108, 148, 216, 230,
    235, 265, 276, 294
Hugh of Chalon, count of
    Burgundy, 559, 663, 680–81
Hugh of Châtillon, count of
    Saint-Pol, 96, 108
Hugh of Digne, 55–6, 657–60
Hugh of Ecot, 224–5, 577
Hugh of Jouy, marshal of the
    Temple, 511, 514
Hugh of Landricourt, 297–8
Hugh of Til-Châtel, lord of
    Coublanc, 222
Hugh of Vaucouleurs, 154
Hülegü, Ilkhan of Persia, 584–7
Humbert of Beaujeu, constable
    of France, 94, 173, 175, 215,
    233–4, 236, 238, 243, 247,
    344, 357, 438
Hyères, 55, 652, 655, 657, 661

Isabella of Angoulême (wife of
    King John of England, and of
    Hugh X le Brun, count of La
    Marche), 99, 103–4
Isabella of France (sister of
    Louis IX, king of France), 691
Isabella of France, queen of
    Navarre, 605, 665–6
Isabella of Jerusalem (wife of
    count Henry II of
    Champagne), 78
Isle-Aumont, 84, 86

Jaffa, 515–16, 519, 527–30,
    536, 540, 547, 552, 554, 561,
    563, 593, 616
James, Saint, 70, 225, 438, 756
James of Castel, 393
Jerusalem (the city of), 133,
    470, 525, 552, 554–7, 565–6

Jerusalem (the kingdom of),
   252, 301, 436–7, 444, 471,
   486, 514, 515, 528, 552, 616
Joan, countess of Champagne
   and queen of Navarre (wife of
   King Philip IV of France), 2, 18
Joan of Châteaudun, countess of
   Montfort, 140
Joan of Toulouse, wife of
   Alphonse of Poitiers, 389
Jocelin of Cornant, 193, 304
John of Acre, 140
John the Armenian, 446–7,
   449–50
John of Beaumont, 150–51,
   172, 428–9
John of Brienne, king of
   Jerusalem and emperor of
   Constantinople, 165, 169, 395
John II of Brienne, count of Eu,
   140, 521, 569, 571–2, 574,
   582–3, 596
John I, count of Brittany, 35,
   664–5
John II, duke of Brittany, 35
John of Bussy, 577
John Caym of Sainte-
   Menehould, 412
John, count of Chalon, 277,
   559, 663, 680–81
John of Chalon, count of
   Auxerre, 737
John Clément, lord of Mez,
   marshal of France, 378, 380,
   385
John, count of Dreux, 93
John III Ducas Vatatzes, Greek
   emperor at Nicaea, 495, 592
John, king of England, 65
John Fouinons, 392
John of France (son of Louis IX),
   399

John of Gamaches, 240
John II of Ibelin, count of Jaffa,
   158–60, 424–6, 516
John III of Ibelin, lord of Arsuf,
   constable of the kingdom of
   Jerusalem, 547–8, 550
John II, count of Joigny, 88
John of Joinville (the older),
   seneschal of Champagne,
   passim, named at 1, 19, 84,
   109, 260, 381–2, 413, 430,
   466, 675–6, 680, 766
John of Joinville (the younger), 110
John Le Grand, 548–50
John of Monson, 390, 620
John of Mymeri, 672
John II of Nesle, count of
   Soissons, 57, 94, 237–9, 242,
   344, 357, 379
John of Orléans, 217
John of Samois, 760, 763–4
John Sarrasin, 67
John, count of Sarrebrück, see
   Geoffrey, count of Sarrebrück
John of Seignelay, 236
John of Valenciennes, 465–7,
   469, 578
John of Vallery (the older),
   168–9, 230–32, 243, 339
John of Vallery (the younger), 295
John of Voisey, 258–60
Joinville, 84, 110, 120, 122, 241,
   632–3, 651, 664, 687, 766–7
Josserand of Brancion, 275–8
Josserand of Nanton, 275
Jully, 86

Kaya'us II, sultan of Rum
   (Iconium), 141–3

Lagny, 89
Laignes, 86

Lampedusa, 638–40
Lazarus, master of the Order of Saint, 540–42
Ligny, 682
Limassol, 137
Louis, count of Champagne and king of Navarre (King Louis X of France), 1–2, 18, 767
Louis VIII, king of France, 105, 661
Louis IX, king of France (Saint Louis), *passim*
Louis of France (son of King Louis IX), 21
Lucienne of Segni (mother of Bohemond VI, prince of Antioch), 522–3
Lusignan, 98–9
Lyons, 123–4, 728

Manuel I Comnenus, Greek emperor at Trebizond, 591
Mansurah, 9, 219, 233, 237, 247, 289, 332, 392
al-Mansur Ibrahim, ruler of Hims, 529–30, 533–5
Margaret of Bar (wife of Henry, count of Luxembourg), 682
Margaret of Bourbon, queen of Navarre (wife of Thibaut IV, count of Champagne, king of Navarre), 666
Margaret, countess of Flanders, 672
Margaret of Provence, queen of France (wife of Louis IX, king of France), 65, 137, 146, 342–3, 370, 397–400, 514, 593–4, 601, 605–8, 614, 616, 617, 627–8, 630–34, 640, 642, 644, 645–7, 652, 654–5, 731

Margaret of Reynel, lady of Sidon, 466
Marie of Brienne, empress of Constantinople, 137–40
Marie of Cyprus (wife of Walter IV, count of Brienne and of Jaffa), 88, 527
Marie of France, countess of Champagne, 76
Marie of Vertus, 605
Marseilles, 56, 113, 125, 653, 660
Martin IV, pope, 760
Mary Magdelene, Saint, 663
Mathilda, lady of Bourbon, 653
Matthew II, duke of Lorraine, 85
Matthew of Marly, 173
Matthew of Trie (wrongly identified as Renaut of Trie), 66–7
Maud, countess of Boulogne, 66
Maurupt, dean of, 129, 180
Mecca, 360
Melun, 666, 724
Metz, 112
Montlhéry, 48–9, 73
Morea, 148, 154, 427
Muhammad the Prophet, 249, 360, 367, 372–3, 448, 458–9
al-Mustas'im, caliph of Baghdad, 584–7

Nablus, 563–4
Narjot of Toucy, *see* Philip of Toucy
an-Nasir Yusuf, sultan of Aleppo and of Damascus, 144, 444, 464–5, 511–13, 515–16, 518–19, 539, 543, 554

Nicholas, Saint, 256, 632
Nicholas of Acre, 361, 363
Nicholas of Choisy, 385
Nicholas of Soisy, 639
Nicosia, 136
Noah (Old Testament), 462
Nogent l'Artaud, 90
Norway, 493

Odo of Châteauroux, papal
    legate, 139, 162–3, 167–8,
    180–81, 328, 420–21,
    424–8, 499–500, 546,
    561–2, 568, 589–90, 598,
    609–13
Odo of Montbéliard, constable
    of the kingdom of Jerusalem,
    528
Oghul Qaimish (widow of the
    Mongol quaghan Güyüg),
    472, 487, 490
Oiselay, 408
Old Man of the Mountain
    (leader of the Assassins), 249,
    451–3, 455–8, 462–3
Oliver of Termes, 16, 578–81,
    629
Orléans, 684

Pantelleria, 640, 643
Paphos, 137, 625
Paris, 60–61, 73, 98, 106,
    114–15, 164, 310, 327, 449,
    633, 664, 672, 684, 691,
    715–18, 723–5, 728–9,
    730–31, 733
Peter, Saint, 462
Peter of Auberive, 227
Peter of Avallon, 196–7,
    434
Peter Barbet, archbishop of
    Rheims, 762

Peter of Bourbonne, 410, 412
Peter of Courtenay, 177, 208,
    236, 412
Peter of Dreux, count of
    Brittany, 74–5, 79–82, 93,
    183, 237, 247, 335–6, 344,
    356–7, 379
Peter of Fontaine, 59
Peter of France, count of
    Alençon, 4, 514, 756–7
Peter of Hans, bishop of
    Châlons, 672, 675
Peter of Noville, 237, 239
Peter of Pontmoulin, 441
Peter of Vieille Bride, master of
    the Hospital, 537
Peter of Villebéon, called Peter
    the Chamberlain, 438, 569,
    626, 648, 682
Philip II, king of France, 76–7,
    105, 555, 559–60, 661–2,
    750
Philip III, king of France, 25, 37,
    738–9, 755, 760
Philip IV, king of France, 25, 37,
    42, 687, 762, 765
Philip Hurepel, count of
    Boulogne, 72
Philip of Montfort, 310–12,
    339, 389, 569
Philip of Nanteuil, 138, 173
Philip of Nemours, 378, 386–7,
    432
Philip of Toucy (wrongly
    identified as Narjot), 495
Pisa, 399
Poitiers, 98–100, 104
Poitou, 48
Pontoise, 606, 691, 723–4
Prény, 682
Prester John, 474–5, 479–80,
    483–4, 492

Provence, 650, 660, 663
Provins, 34, 395, 415, 666

Ramla, 540, 542, bishop of,
    532
Ralph of Coucy, 219
Ralph Grosparmi, archbishop of
    Nicosia, 626
Ralph of Soissons, 470
Ralph of Vanault, 222, 225,
    227, 325
Renaut of Menoncourt, 224
Renaut of Trie, see Matthew of
    Trie
Renaut of Vichiers, marshal
    (later master of the Temple),
    185-6, 381-4, 413-14,
    454-5, 511-14, 569
Rexi, 191, 264
Rheims, 673, 684, 731-2
Richard I, king of England,
    76-8, 555-6, 558
Robert, count of Artois, 94,
    108, 183-4, 200, 218-19,
    233, 244, 261, 290, 404
Robert III, count of Dreux, 82
Robert of Nantes, patriarch of
    Jerusalem, 167, 364-5,
    529-30, 532, 615-16
Robert of Sorbon, 31-2, 35-6,
    38
Roche-de-Glun, La, 124
Rochelle, La, 48
Rome, 611-12, 672, 760, 762
Rouen, 723

Safad, 528
Saffran, Le, 414
Saintes, 101-2
Saladin, sultan of Egypt and
    Damascus 330-31, 446,
    555

as-Salih Ayyub, sultan of Egypt,
    144-5, 148, 163, 172, 177,
    184, 191, 196, 198, 264,
    287-8, 348, 528-9, 537-8
Saumur, 93, 95
Scecedin, see Fakhr ad-Din ibn
    al-Shaykh
Scotland, 21
Sebreci, a Mauritanian, 372
Sézanne, 83
Sharamsah, 196
Sicily, 641
Sidon, 551, 553, 563, 569, 581,
    584, 588, 590-91, 593,
    602-3, 609, 615-16
Simon of Joinville, seneschal of
    Champagne, 45, 84
Simon of Montceliard, 551
Simon of Nesle, 57
Soissons, 664-5
Spain, 72, 493
Stephen Boileau, 693, 718
Stephen of Ostricourt,
    commander of the Temple,
    381-3
Stephen, count of Sancerre, 89,
    92
Syria, 132

Taillebourg, 100-101
Tanis, 191
Thibaut II, count of Bar, 682
Thibaut V, count of Blois, 89,
    92
Thibaut II, count of
    Champagne, 89
Thibaut III, count of
    Champagne, 76, 79
Thibaut IV, count of
    Champagne, king of Navarre,
    75, 79-83, 85-9, 92-3,
    664

Thibaut V, count of
    Champagne, king of Navarre,
    34, 37, 664–6, 681, 734–5
Thierry III, count of
    Montbéliard, 151, 158
Thomas of Beaumetz,
    archbishop of Rheims, 672–3
Tiberias, 528
Titus, Roman emperor, 722
Tortosa, 597
Tripoli, 523, 599
Troyes, 82, 84, 89–90
Tunis, 5, 641, 738
Turanshah, sultan of Egypt,
    287–8, 292, 301, 335–6,
    339–40, 342–53, 357–8, 364,
    366, 369, 372–3, 403, 443–4,
    464
Tyre, 434, 569, 590, 614, 616

Val, lord of, 197
Vernon, 691, 723
Vertus, 83
Villain of Versy, 154
Vincennes, 59–60

Walter, bishop of Acre, 415
Walter of Autrèches, 174–6
Walter IV, count of Brienne and
    Jaffa, 88, 465–6, 486, 527,
    530–33, 536–8
Walter V, count of Brienne, 88
Walter of Châtillon, 108, 243,
    256–7, 268–9, 295, 308,
    390–92

Walter of Curel, 203–4
Walter of la Horgne, 273
Walter of Nemours, 405
Walter of Reynel, 466
William of Auvergne, bishop of
    Paris, 46–9
William of Beaumont, marshal
    of France, 428–9, 578
William of Boon, 240
William of Châteauneuf, master
    of the Hospital, 454–5,
    507–8, 569
William of Dammartin, 154
William of Dampierre, count of
    Flanders, 108, 232, 272–4,
    292, 344, 354, 357, 379, 419,
    422, 424
William of Flavacourt,
    archbishop of Rouen, 760
William, count of Joigny, 14,
    625
William of Mello, 61
William of Monson, abbot of
    Saint-Michel, 620
William of Pontoise, abbot of
    Cluny (bishop of Olena),
    655–6
William of Sonnac, master of the
    Temple, 219, 245, 269–70
William of Villehardouin, prince
    of Morea, 148

Yves le Breton, Dominican friar,
    444–5, 458, 462–3

THE STORY OF PENGUIN CLASSICS

Before 1946 ... 'Classics' are mainly the domain of academics and students; readable editions for everyone else are almost unheard of. This all changes when a little-known classicist, E. V. Rieu, presents Penguin founder Allen Lane with the translation of Homer's *Odyssey* that he has been working on in his spare time.

1946 Penguin Classics debuts with *The Odyssey*, which promptly sells three million copies. Suddenly, classics are no longer for the privileged few.

1950s Rieu, now series editor, turns to professional writers for the best modern, readable translations, including Dorothy L. Sayers's *Inferno* and Robert Graves's unexpurgated *Twelve Caesars*.

1960s The Classics are given the distinctive black covers that have remained a constant throughout the life of the series. Rieu retires in 1964, hailing the Penguin Classics list as 'the greatest educative force of the twentieth century.'

1970s A new generation of translators swells the Penguin Classics ranks, introducing readers of English to classics of world literature from more than twenty languages. The list grows to encompass more history, philosophy, science, religion and politics.

1980s The Penguin American Library launches with titles such as *Uncle Tom's Cabin*, and joins forces with Penguin Classics to provide the most comprehensive library of world literature available from any paperback publisher.

1990s The launch of Penguin Audiobooks brings the classics to a listening audience for the first time, and in 1999 the worldwide launch of the Penguin Classics website extends their reach to the global online community.

The 21st Century Penguin Classics are completely redesigned for the first time in nearly twenty years. This world-famous series now consists of more than 1300 titles, making the widest range of the best books ever written available to millions – and constantly redefining what makes a 'classic'.

The Odyssey continues ...

The best books ever written

PENGUIN 🐧 CLASSICS

SINCE 1946

Find out more at www.penguinclassics.com